DESTINY

PART ONE

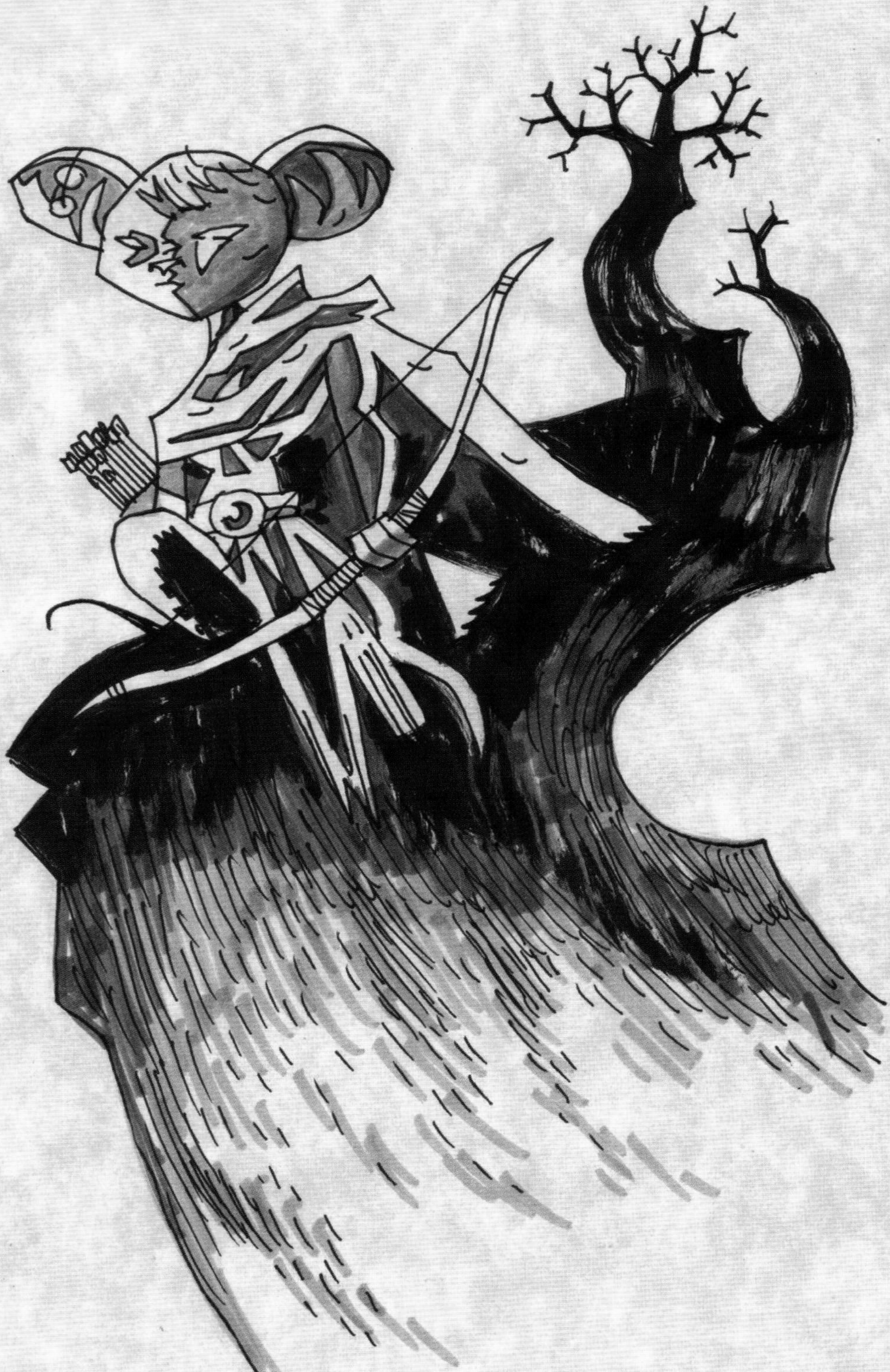

VOLUME TWO

DESTINY
PART ONE

CREATED BY
BRYAN J.L. GLASS &
MICHAEL AVON OEMING

STORY BY
Glass & Oeming
WRITTEN BY
Bryan J.L. Glass
ART BY
Michael Avon Oeming
& Victor Santos
COLORS BY
Veronica Gandini
LETTERING BY
James H. Glass

EDITING BY
Judy Glass
INTERIOR PRODUCTION BY
Harry Lee
BOOK DESIGN BY
James H. Glass
PHOTOSHOP FX BY
James H. Glass
COVER PAINTED BY
Michael Avon Oeming
LOGO BY
Oeming, Kristyn Ferretti,
Tim Daniel & James H. Glass

IMAGE COMICS, INC.

ROBERT KIRKMAN - CHIEF OPERATING OFFICER • ERIK LARSEN - CHIEF FINANCIAL OFFICER • TODD McFARLANE - PRESIDENT
MARC SILVESTRI - CHIEF EXECUTIVE OFFICER • JIM VALENTINO - VICE PRESIDENT

ERIC STEPHENSON- PUBLISHER • RON RICHARDS - DIRECTOR OF BUSINESS DEVELOPMENT • JENNIFER DEGUZMAN - PR & MARKETING DIRECTOR • BRANWYN BIGGLESTONE - ACCOUNTS MANAGER
EMILY MILLER - ACCOUNTING ASSISTANT • JAMIE PARRENO - MARKETING ASSISTANT • EMILIO BAUTISTA - SALES ASSISTANT • JAEMIE DUDAS - ADMINISTRATIVE ASSISTANT
KEVIN YUEN - DIGITAL RIGHTS COORDINATOR TYLER SHAINLINE - EVENTS COORDINATOR • DAVID BROTHERS - CONTENT MANAGER • JONATHON CHAN - PRODUCTION MANAGER
DREW GILL - ART DIRECTOR • JANA COOK - PRINT MANAGER • MONICA GARCIA - SENIOR PRODUCTION ARTIST
VINCENT KUKUA - PRODUCTION ARTIST • JENNA SAVAGE - PRODUCTION ARTIST • ADDISON DUKE - PRODUCTION ARTIST

FOR INTERNATIONAL RIGHTS, CONTACT: FOREIGNLICENSING@IMAGECOMICS.COM

THE MICE TEMPLAR, VOL. 2: DESTINY PART ONE
ISBN: 978-1-60706-257-8
SECOND PRINTING

For Harry
—Bryan & Jim

For Aunt Carol and Uncle Larry
Thank you for all the support that allowed
me to make my dreams as an artist come true!
—Mike

For Silvia
The mice true fan.
For my family
Who read and listen to my own adventures.
—Victor

For Leo Freites
My true inspiration, art companion and love.
For my parents
Who are always there for me.
—Veronica

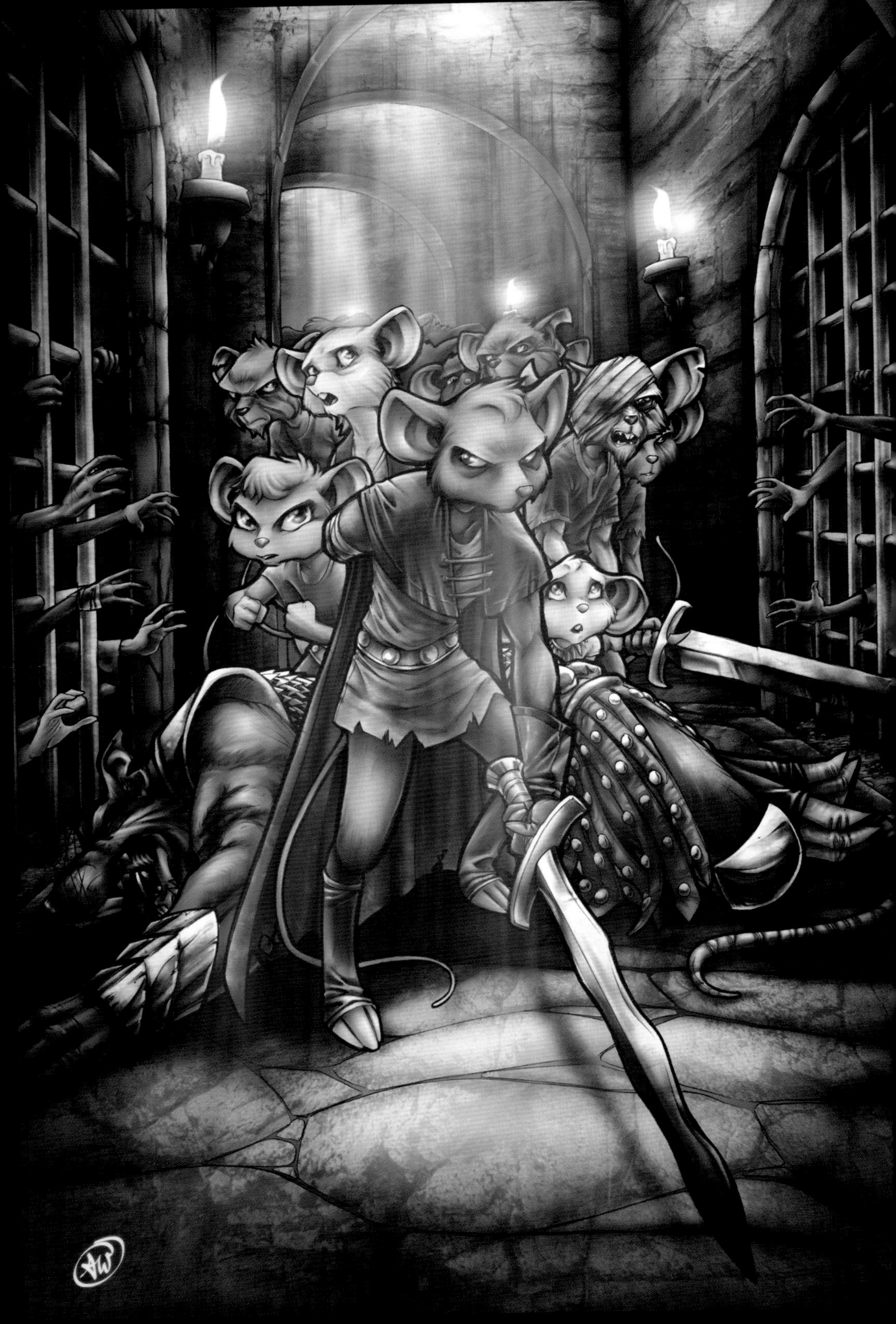

Illustration by Adam Withers

Foreword by Gail Simone

...Fantasy is Impossible

No one seems to be sure exactly from whose deathbed it was uttered, but there's a famous and multiply-attributed theatrical quote that I always thought didn't quite go far enough.

I think it should be, "Dying is easy, comedy is hard. And fantasy is IMPOSSIBLE."

Those who choose the fantasy genre as their canvas have to be either insane or fearless. Like the other field which shares a common (and committed) audience, that of science fiction, there's always the danger of that Wile E. Coyote moment, when the principals are running on thin air, until the very moment they look down. That terrible moment when you realize you can't walk on a platform of dreams and wisps of smoke, and the ground is waiting to swallow you up at terminal velocity. That moment when you suddenly stop thinking about the story and realize pointy ears really aren't all that evocative of alien-ness, or when you can't help laughing at the goofy faux-Nordic names you've given your characters' gods, or the ridiculous battle bikini you've given your leading lady, or that — damn, damn, *damn* — your horrifying hellspawn looks like a bad CGI joke.

Every writer of the fantastic has had that moment, I suspect, when you suddenly realize you've just produced something that can only be shown to and understood by the already converted. A random episode of any recent *Star Trek* series might well be both incomprehensible and hilarious to those who didn't grow up with Spock or Data. *The Lord of the Rings* films must have utterly baffled many filmgoers who hadn't read the books. And I've seen more than one superhero film reduce the audience to fits of uncomfortable giggles.

It's not like horror. Everyone's been afraid and everyone knows, secretly, that there really is a boogeyman. Nor is it like romance: everyone's been in love, or even better, in lust. But Science Fiction and Fantasy create something from nothing; they build their edifices purely out of spun ether and the goodwill of the audience. And the proof of what a difficult chore that really is can be defined more by the ever-increasing pile of carcasses of Those Who Failed, rather than the few meager successes.

The audience hasn't ever ridden a dragon, you see. They haven't had tea with badgers. They haven't defeated wintry despot queens for the soul of a loved one. There's no shared experience, no sensory memory to draw from.

Belief in the work isn't enough. Commitment to the work isn't enough. We've all seen sincere efforts hit the credibility wall and collapse in upon themselves.

And talent alone isn't enough. Beautiful but empty films and novels and comics are a dime a dozen.

I think what's needed is all those things, plus something else. A window into the human soul. Forget the walking trees and the talking cats. It's the human soul that is so essential to caring what happens in these never-were lands. When a gifted writer and a brilliant artist show you daring, or heartbreak, or loyalty — when they portray it just so, just exactly in the way that most moves us — it's the understanding and empathy of our humanity that makes that connection possible, even if the character is a rabbit protecting its warren from an evil enemy rabbit general.

Tolkien infused his work with this...I often think that his surroundings ended up in the various races in his books: the wizards might represent the wise-but-absent-minded professors of his academic days, the hobbits and dwarfs the good natured and Earthly pleasure-loving working classes, and so on. Tolkien despised the idea of his works being allegorical, but it's hard not to see post-war England all throughout his novels.

It's proven time and again: a great creator can show you something you know damn well is impossible, and twist and turn your heart like a fish on a line. In short, they not only make you gasp and weep, but they make you a collaborator in your own emotional turmoil. Congratulations: you forgot you were reading about rodents. You were the coyote, you looked down, and you're still floating high above the desert below. They showed you Narnia, Metropolis, Oz. They showed you something you know isn't there, but somehow, you find yourself dreading the end, because you don't want to leave.

This is where I think *The Mice Templar* is most remarkable. I can't recall the last fantasy-based graphic novel I read that was so literate, so charming, so thrilling and so ridiculously wonderful that it nearly defies description.

It's full of life, characters who are complex and fun, heroes to root for and care about, and darkly hideous things in the shadows. Everyone has a story and every story is told deftly and enviably emotively by Bryan Glass. He's chosen not to do amateur dives from poolside, but instead to do the writing equivalent of Olympic aqua-gymnastics from the high board. I haven't read anything else by him at this point, but I will give him perhaps the highest compliment I can give a writer...

That boy is a world-builder.

The art in this book — man, the art. I have the first collection in hardback. If I dared part with it (and if I had any friends), this would be the book I would give to friends who didn't "get" what comics and graphic novels could be like. It's stunning. There are pages that knock the wind out of me on my fifth and sixth

readings. I wouldn't have thought that anyone could keep up with the art of the series' original artist and co-creator, Michael Oeming.

I have no idea where they found just the people to do that. Victor Santos, with color artist Veronica Gandini, are every bit the high-wire artists that the series' creators are. Thumb through this book, and you see gorgeously scary scenes of isolation and fear, followed immediately by airy and ethereal water-color imagery from dazzling perspectives. It's a bravura performance, and in lesser hands, well, let's just say the coyote would have met the ground in a manner most unpleasant. Add in ridiculously beautiful and evocative double-page spreads, and wrap it in museum-worthy covers by Oeming himself — it's a little sinful, really. It's so pretty, it feels like it should be bad for your health.

Finally, *Mice Templar* has a delightfully Earthy, lusty, and sometimes bloody quality that differentiates it quite nicely from other anthropomorphic tales, and gives it an emotional heft that socks you in the gut and leaves you gasping with surprising consistency. There's a lot of courage in these pages, and speaking as a fellow comics creator who knows a tough gig when she sees it, there's a lot of courage BEHIND the pages, too.

Lunatics or daredevils, thanks for making *Mice Templar*, guys. It is the good, good stuff.

Gail Simone
January 2010

Gail Simone is the acclaimed writer of *Birds of Prey*, *Secret Six*, *Welcome to Tranquility* and *Wonder Woman*, published by Wildstorm and DC Comics.

Adam Withers is one half of the noted husband/wife team that created and produces *The Uniques* and the upcoming *Rainbow In the Dark*.

CONTENTS

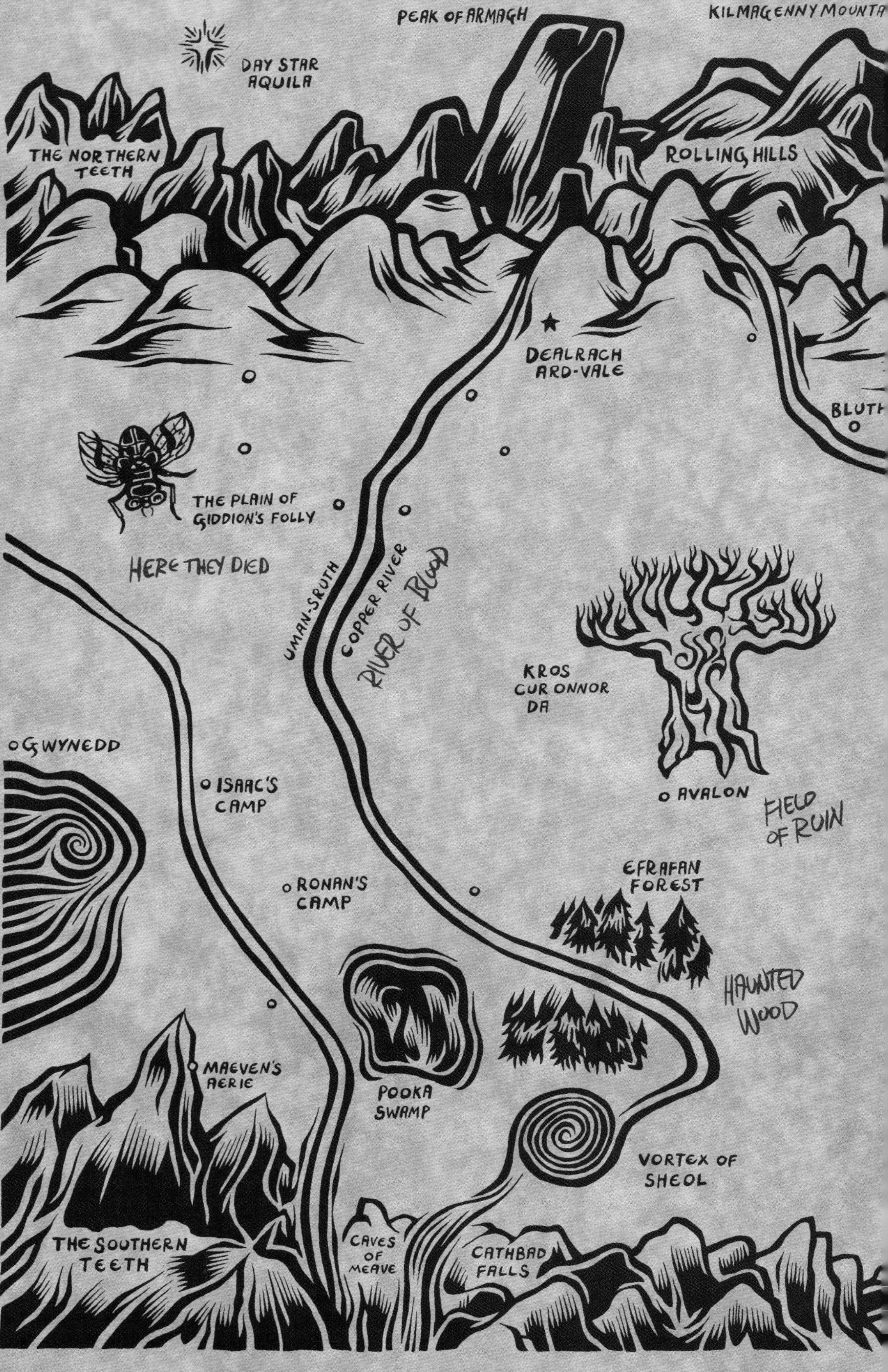
PEAK OF ARMAGH
KILMAGENNY MOUNTA
DAY STAR
AQUILA
THE NORTHERN
TEETH
ROLLING HILLS
DEALRACH
ARD-VALE
BLUTH
THE PLAIN OF
GIDDION'S FOLLY
HERE THEY DIED
UMAN-SRUTH
COPPER RIVER
RIVER OF BLOOD
KROS
CUR ONNOR
DA
GWYNEDD
ISAAC'S
CAMP
AVALON
FIELD
OF RUIN
RONAN'S
CAMP
EFRAFAN
FOREST
HAUNTED
WOOD
MAEVEN'S
AERIE
POOKA
SWAMP
VORTEX OF
SHEOL
THE SOUTHERN
TEETH
CAVES
OF
MEAVE
CATHBAD
FALLS

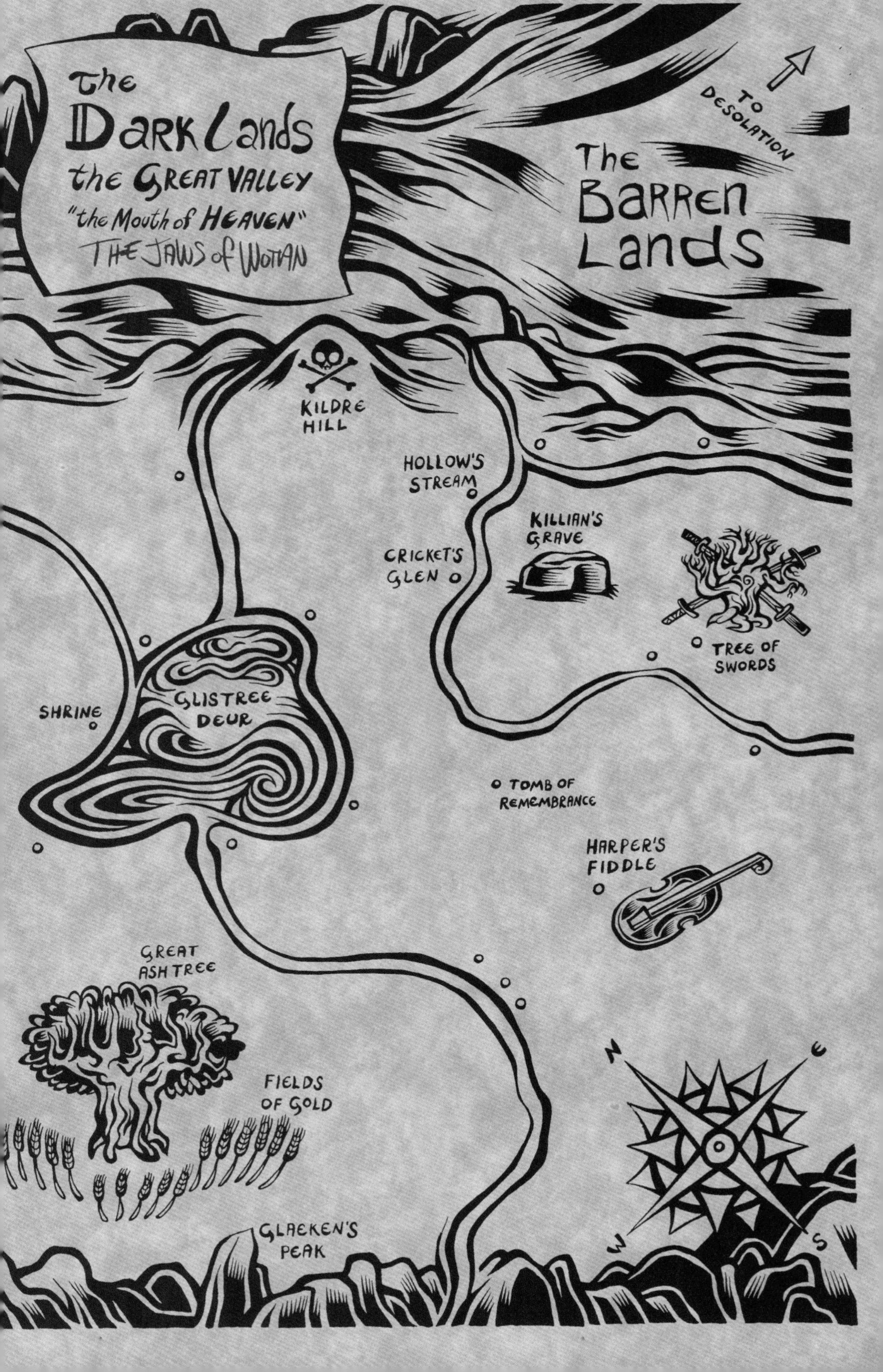
The Dark Lands
the Great Valley
"the Mouth of Heaven"
The Jaws of Wotan
To Desolation
The Barren Lands
Kildre Hill
Hollow's Stream
Killian's Grave
Cricket's Glen
Tree of Swords
Glistree Deur
Shrine
Tomb of Remembrance
Harper's Fiddle
Great Ash Tree
Fields of Gold
Glaeken's Peak
N
E
W
S

PROLOGUE

CHRONICLES OF THE TEMPLAR

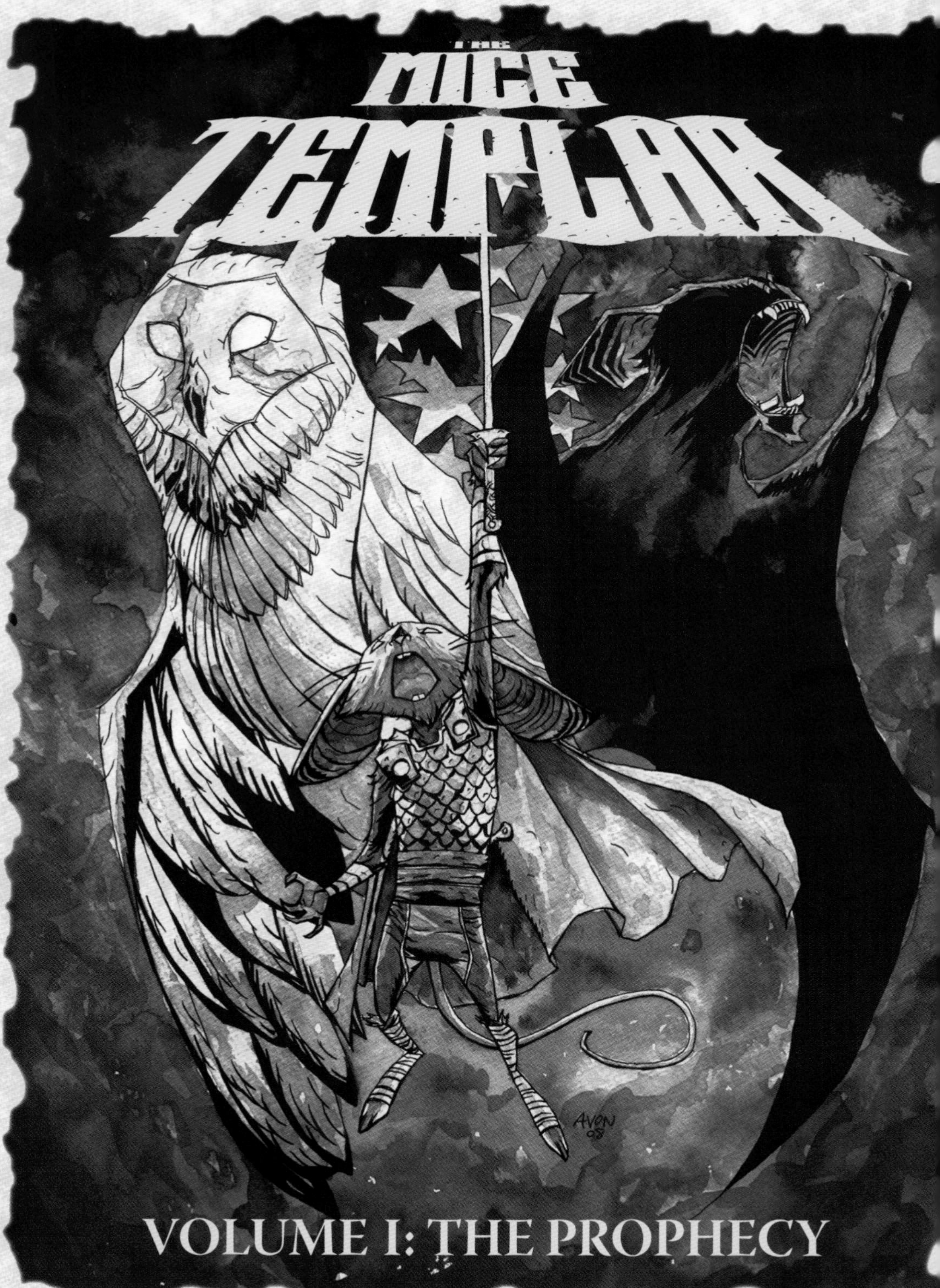
THE
MICE
TEMPLAR
VOLUME I: THE PROPHECY

THE TEMPLAR HAVE FALLEN...

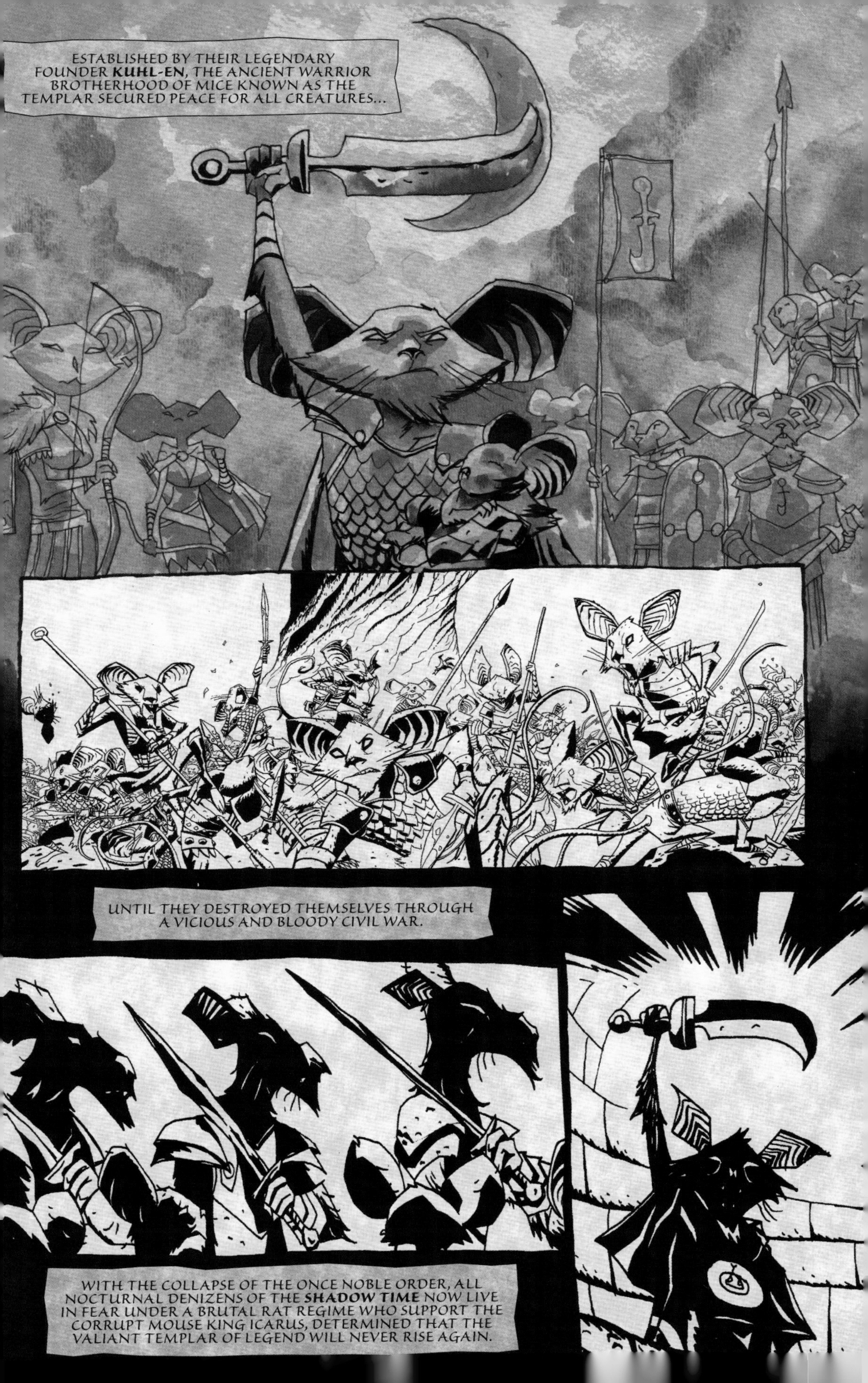
ESTABLISHED BY THEIR LEGENDARY FOUNDER KUHL-EN, THE ANCIENT WARRIOR BROTHERHOOD OF MICE KNOWN AS THE TEMPLAR SECURED PEACE FOR ALL CREATURES...
UNTIL THEY DESTROYED THEMSELVES THROUGH A VICIOUS AND BLOODY CIVIL WAR.
WITH THE COLLAPSE OF THE ONCE NOBLE ORDER, ALL NOCTURNAL DENIZENS OF THE SHADOW TIME NOW LIVE IN FEAR UNDER A BRUTAL RAT REGIME WHO SUPPORT THE CORRUPT MOUSE KING ICARUS, DETERMINED THAT THE VALIANT TEMPLAR OF LEGEND WILL NEVER RISE AGAIN.

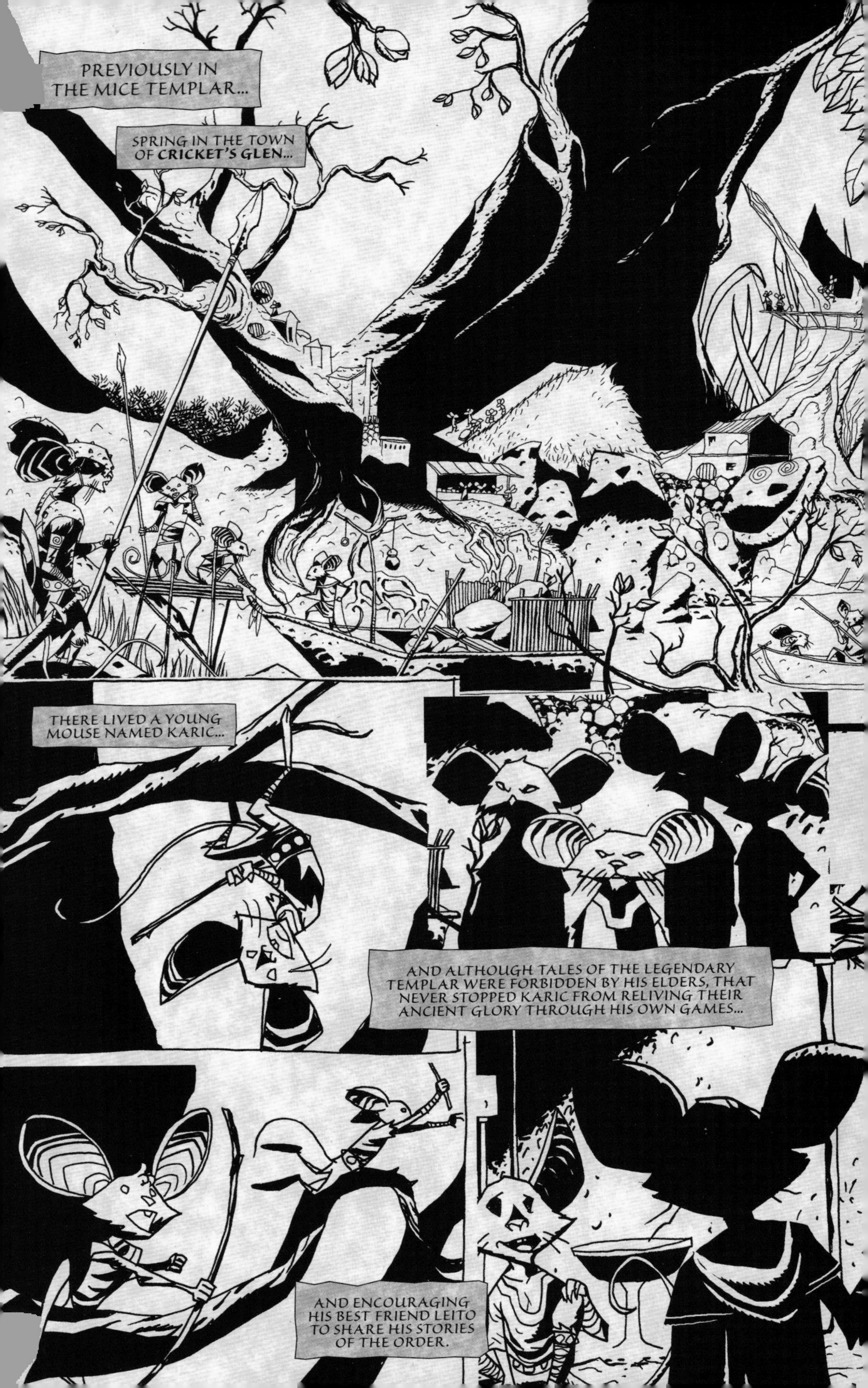
PREVIOUSLY IN THE MICE TEMPLAR...
SPRING IN THE TOWN OF CRICKET'S GLEN...
THERE LIVED A YOUNG MOUSE NAMED KARIC...
AND ALTHOUGH TALES OF THE LEGENDARY TEMPLAR WERE FORBIDDEN BY HIS ELDERS, THAT NEVER STOPPED KARIC FROM RELIVING THEIR ANCIENT GLORY THROUGH HIS OWN GAMES...
AND ENCOURAGING HIS BEST FRIEND LEITO TO SHARE HIS STORIES OF THE ORDER.

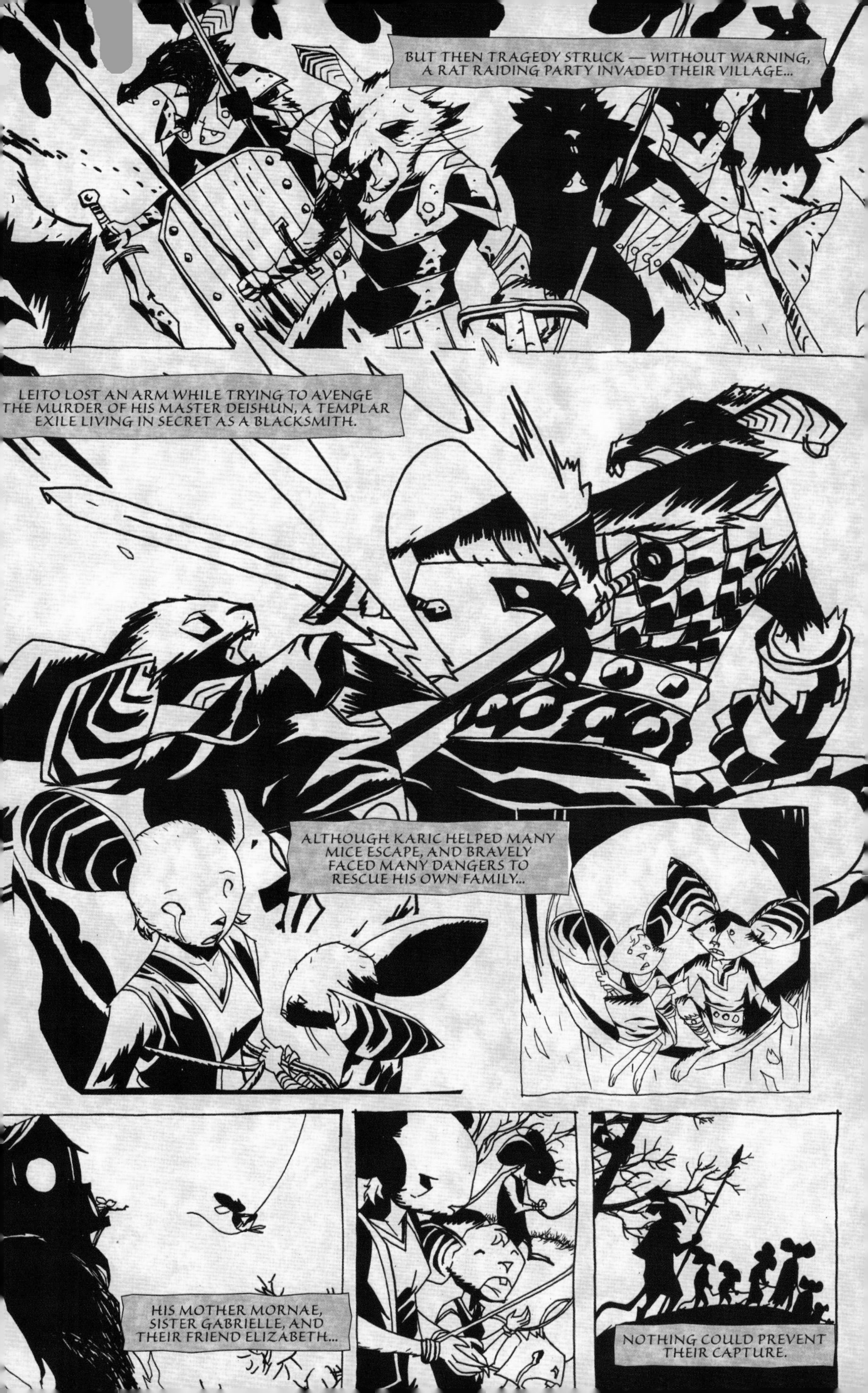
BUT THEN TRAGEDY STRUCK — WITHOUT WARNING, A RAT RAIDING PARTY INVADED THEIR VILLAGE...
LEITO LOST AN ARM WHILE TRYING TO AVENGE THE MURDER OF HIS MASTER DEISHUN, A TEMPLAR EXILE LIVING IN SECRET AS A BLACKSMITH.
ALTHOUGH KARIC HELPED MANY MICE ESCAPE, AND BRAVELY FACED MANY DANGERS TO RESCUE HIS OWN FAMILY...
HIS MOTHER MORNAE, SISTER GABRIELLE, AND THEIR FRIEND ELIZABETH...
NOTHING COULD PREVENT THEIR CAPTURE.

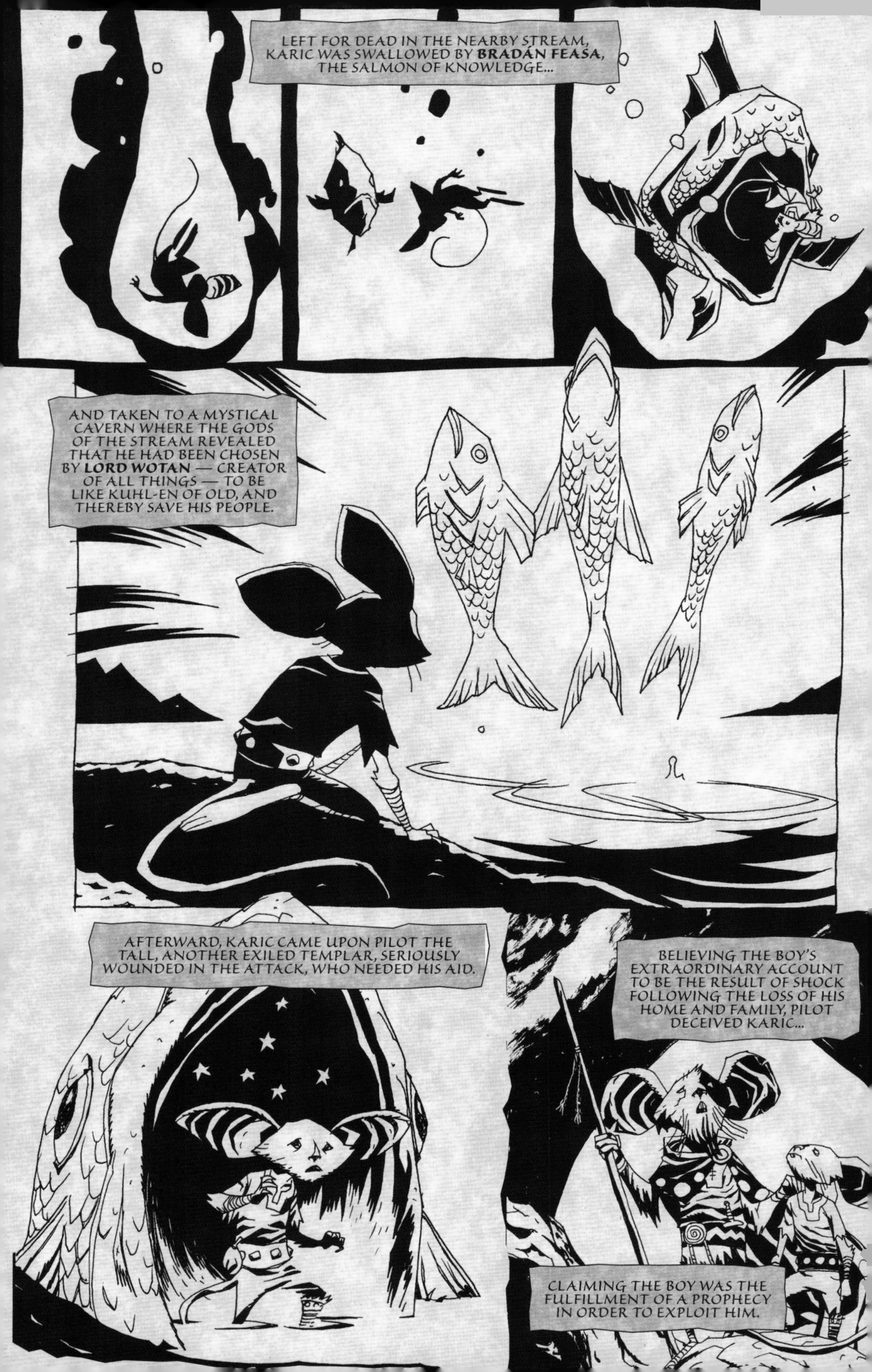
LEFT FOR DEAD IN THE NEARBY STREAM, KARIC WAS SWALLOWED BY **BRADÁN FEASA**, THE SALMON OF KNOWLEDGE...
AND TAKEN TO A MYSTICAL CAVERN WHERE THE GODS OF THE STREAM REVEALED THAT HE HAD BEEN CHOSEN BY **LORD WOTAN** — CREATOR OF ALL THINGS — TO BE LIKE KUHL-EN OF OLD, AND THEREBY SAVE HIS PEOPLE.
AFTERWARD, KARIC CAME UPON PILOT THE TALL, ANOTHER EXILED TEMPLAR, SERIOUSLY WOUNDED IN THE ATTACK, WHO NEEDED HIS AID.
BELIEVING THE BOY'S EXTRAORDINARY ACCOUNT TO BE THE RESULT OF SHOCK FOLLOWING THE LOSS OF HIS HOME AND FAMILY, PILOT DECEIVED KARIC...
CLAIMING THE BOY WAS THE FULFILLMENT OF A PROPHECY IN ORDER TO EXPLOIT HIM.

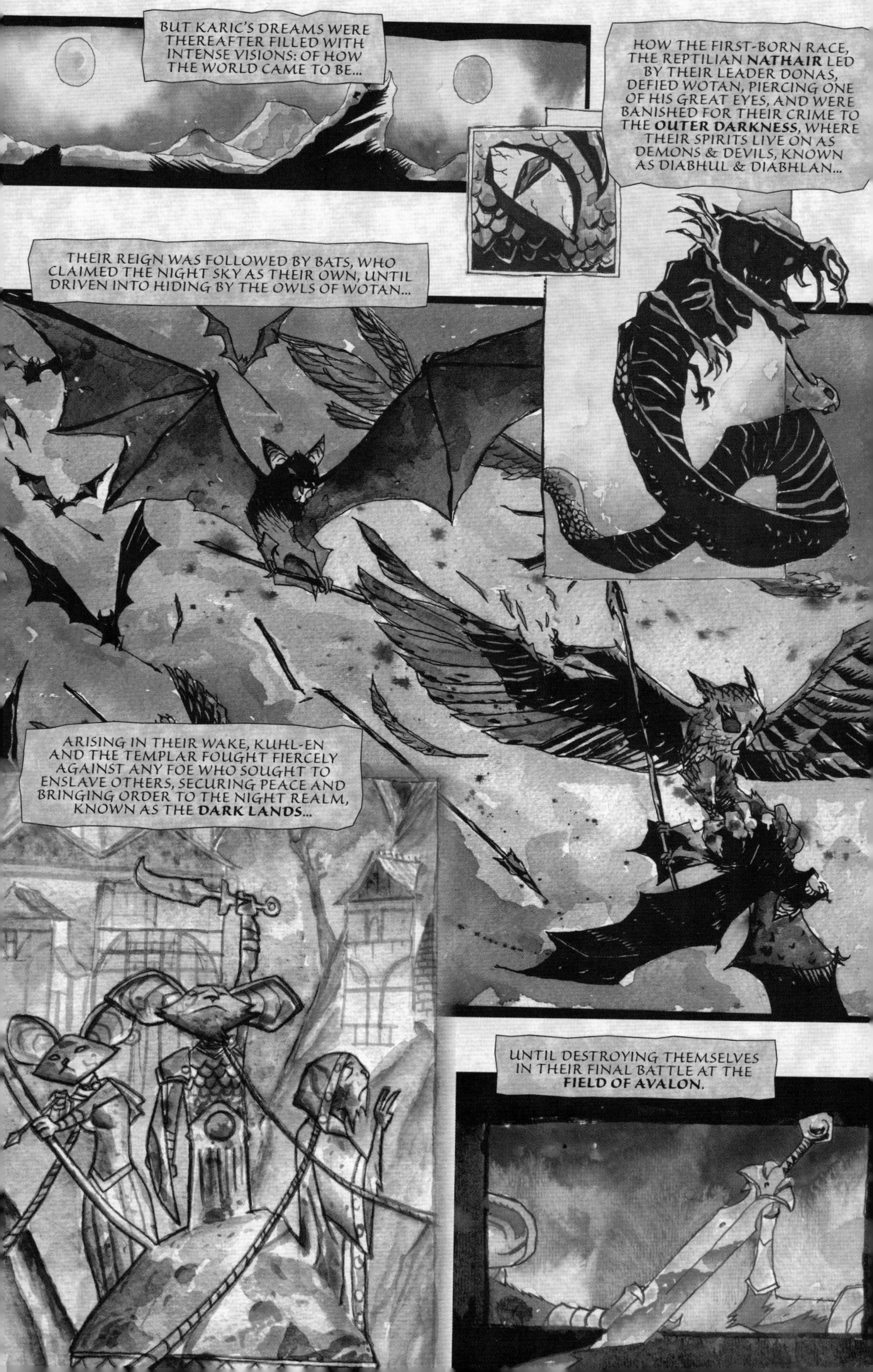
BUT KARIC'S DREAMS WERE THEREAFTER FILLED WITH INTENSE VISIONS: OF HOW THE WORLD CAME TO BE...
HOW THE FIRST-BORN RACE, THE REPTILIAN **NATHAIR** LED BY THEIR LEADER DONAS, DEFIED WOTAN, PIERCING ONE OF HIS GREAT EYES, AND WERE BANISHED FOR THEIR CRIME TO THE **OUTER DARKNESS**, WHERE THEIR SPIRITS LIVE ON AS DEMONS & DEVILS, KNOWN AS DIABHUL & DIABHLAN...
THEIR REIGN WAS FOLLOWED BY BATS, WHO CLAIMED THE NIGHT SKY AS THEIR OWN, UNTIL DRIVEN INTO HIDING BY THE OWLS OF WOTAN...
ARISING IN THEIR WAKE, KUHL-EN AND THE TEMPLAR FOUGHT FIERCELY AGAINST ANY FOE WHO SOUGHT TO ENSLAVE OTHERS, SECURING PEACE AND BRINGING ORDER TO THE NIGHT REALM, KNOWN AS THE **DARK LANDS**...
UNTIL DESTROYING THEMSELVES IN THEIR FINAL BATTLE AT THE **FIELD OF AVALON**.

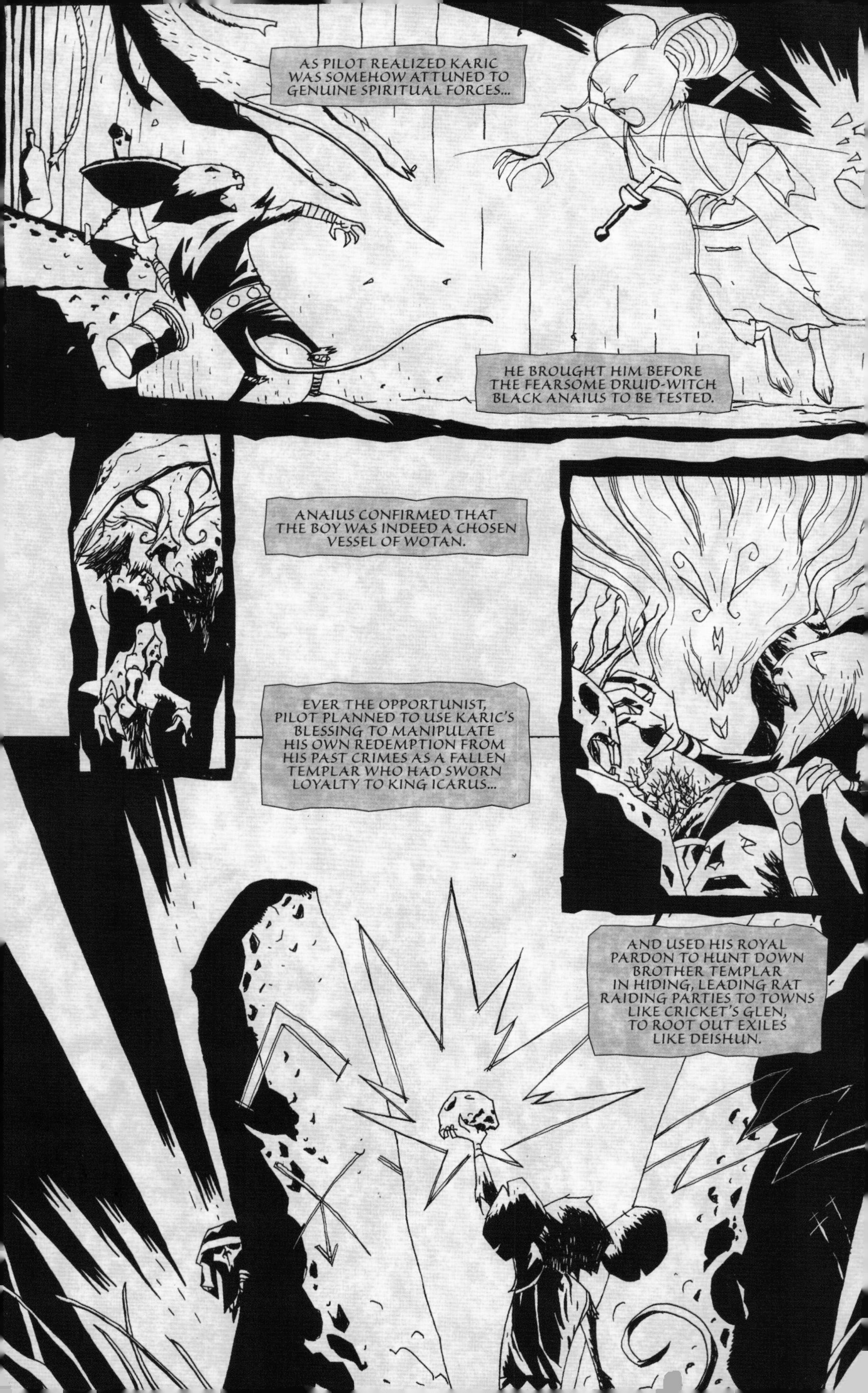
AS PILOT REALIZED KARIC WAS SOMEHOW ATTUNED TO GENUINE SPIRITUAL FORCES...
HE BROUGHT HIM BEFORE THE FEARSOME DRUID-WITCH BLACK ANAIUS TO BE TESTED.
ANAIUS CONFIRMED THAT THE BOY WAS INDEED A CHOSEN VESSEL OF WOTAN.
EVER THE OPPORTUNIST, PILOT PLANNED TO USE KARIC'S BLESSING TO MANIPULATE HIS OWN REDEMPTION FROM HIS PAST CRIMES AS A FALLEN TEMPLAR WHO HAD SWORN LOYALTY TO KING ICARUS...
AND USED HIS ROYAL PARDON TO HUNT DOWN BROTHER TEMPLAR IN HIDING, LEADING RAT RAIDING PARTIES TO TOWNS LIKE CRICKET'S GLEN, TO ROOT OUT EXILES LIKE DEISHUN.

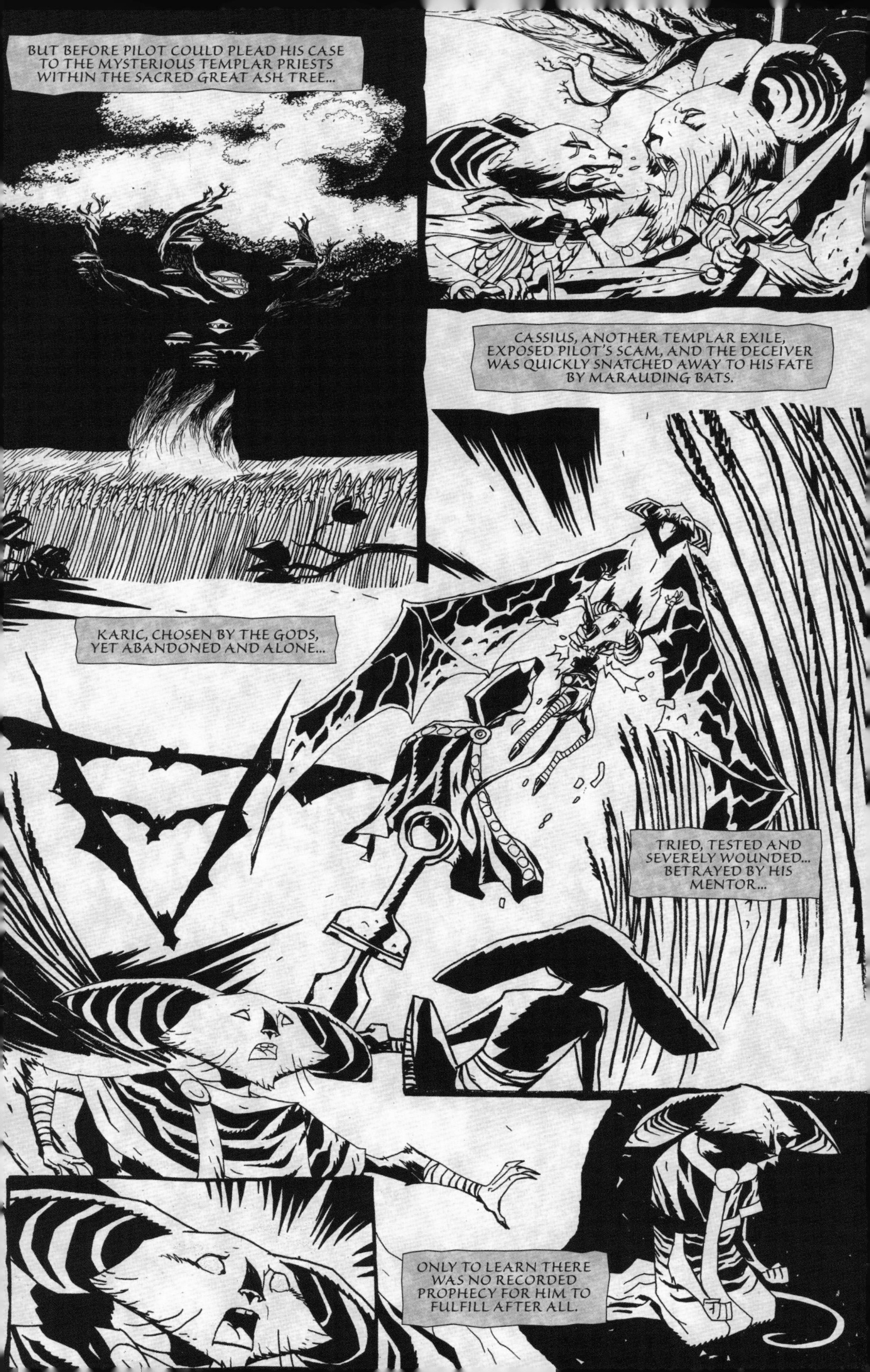
BUT BEFORE PILOT COULD PLEAD HIS CASE TO THE MYSTERIOUS TEMPLAR PRIESTS WITHIN THE SACRED GREAT ASH TREE...
CASSIUS, ANOTHER TEMPLAR EXILE, EXPOSED PILOT'S SCAM, AND THE DECEIVER WAS QUICKLY SNATCHED AWAY TO HIS FATE BY MARAUDING BATS.
KARIC, CHOSEN BY THE GODS, YET ABANDONED AND ALONE...
TRIED, TESTED AND SEVERELY WOUNDED... BETRAYED BY HIS MENTOR...
ONLY TO LEARN THERE WAS NO RECORDED PROPHECY FOR HIM TO FULFILL AFTER ALL.

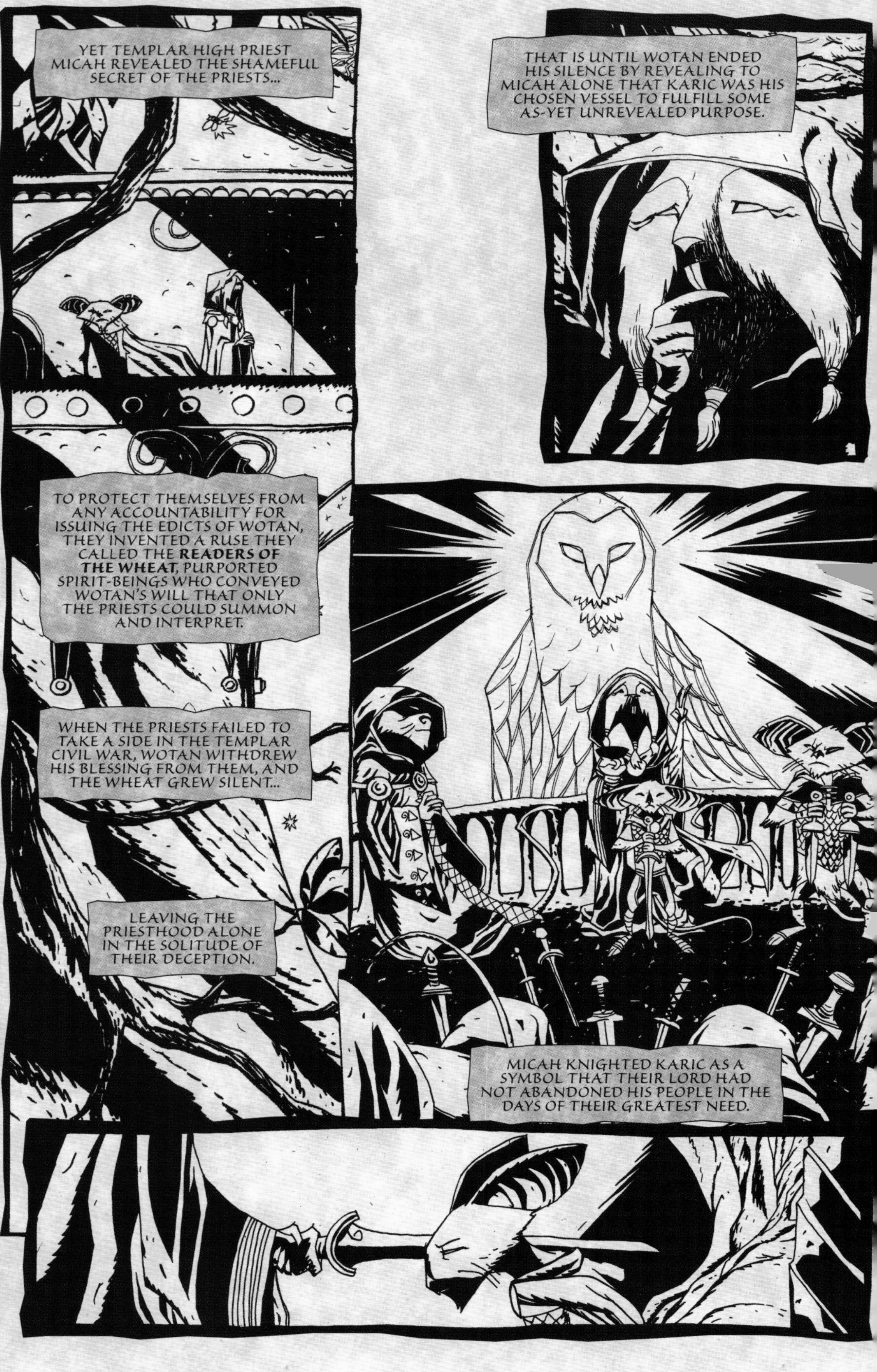
YET TEMPLAR HIGH PRIEST MICAH REVEALED THE SHAMEFUL SECRET OF THE PRIESTS...
TO PROTECT THEMSELVES FROM ANY ACCOUNTABILITY FOR ISSUING THE EDICTS OF WOTAN, THEY INVENTED A RUSE THEY CALLED THE **READERS OF THE WHEAT**, PURPORTED SPIRIT-BEINGS WHO CONVEYED WOTAN'S WILL THAT ONLY THE PRIESTS COULD SUMMON AND INTERPRET.
WHEN THE PRIESTS FAILED TO TAKE A SIDE IN THE TEMPLAR CIVIL WAR, WOTAN WITHDREW HIS BLESSING FROM THEM, AND THE WHEAT GREW SILENT...
LEAVING THE PRIESTHOOD ALONE IN THE SOLITUDE OF THEIR DECEPTION.
THAT IS UNTIL WOTAN ENDED HIS SILENCE BY REVEALING TO MICAH ALONE THAT KARIC WAS HIS CHOSEN VESSEL TO FULFILL SOME AS-YET UNREVEALED PURPOSE.
MICAH KNIGHTED KARIC AS A SYMBOL THAT THEIR LORD HAD NOT ABANDONED HIS PEOPLE IN THE DAYS OF THEIR GREATEST NEED.

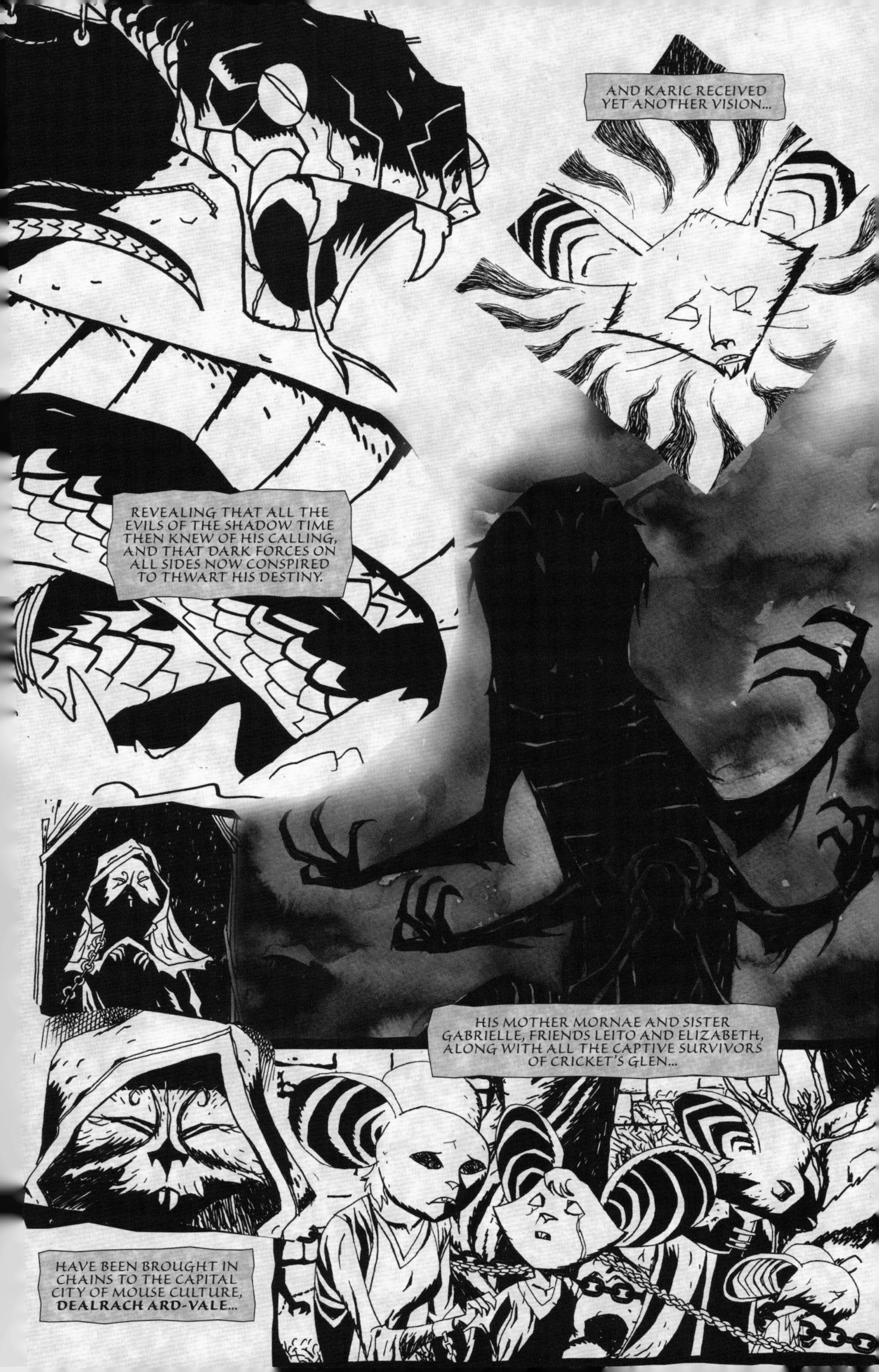
AND KARIC RECEIVED YET ANOTHER VISION...
REVEALING THAT ALL THE EVILS OF THE SHADOW TIME THEN KNEW OF HIS CALLING, AND THAT DARK FORCES ON ALL SIDES NOW CONSPIRED TO THWART HIS DESTINY.
HIS MOTHER MORNAE AND SISTER GABRIELLE, FRIENDS LEITO AND ELIZABETH, ALONG WITH ALL THE CAPTIVE SURVIVORS OF CRICKET'S GLEN...
HAVE BEEN BROUGHT IN CHAINS TO THE CAPITAL CITY OF MOUSE CULTURE, **DEALRACH ARD-VALE...**

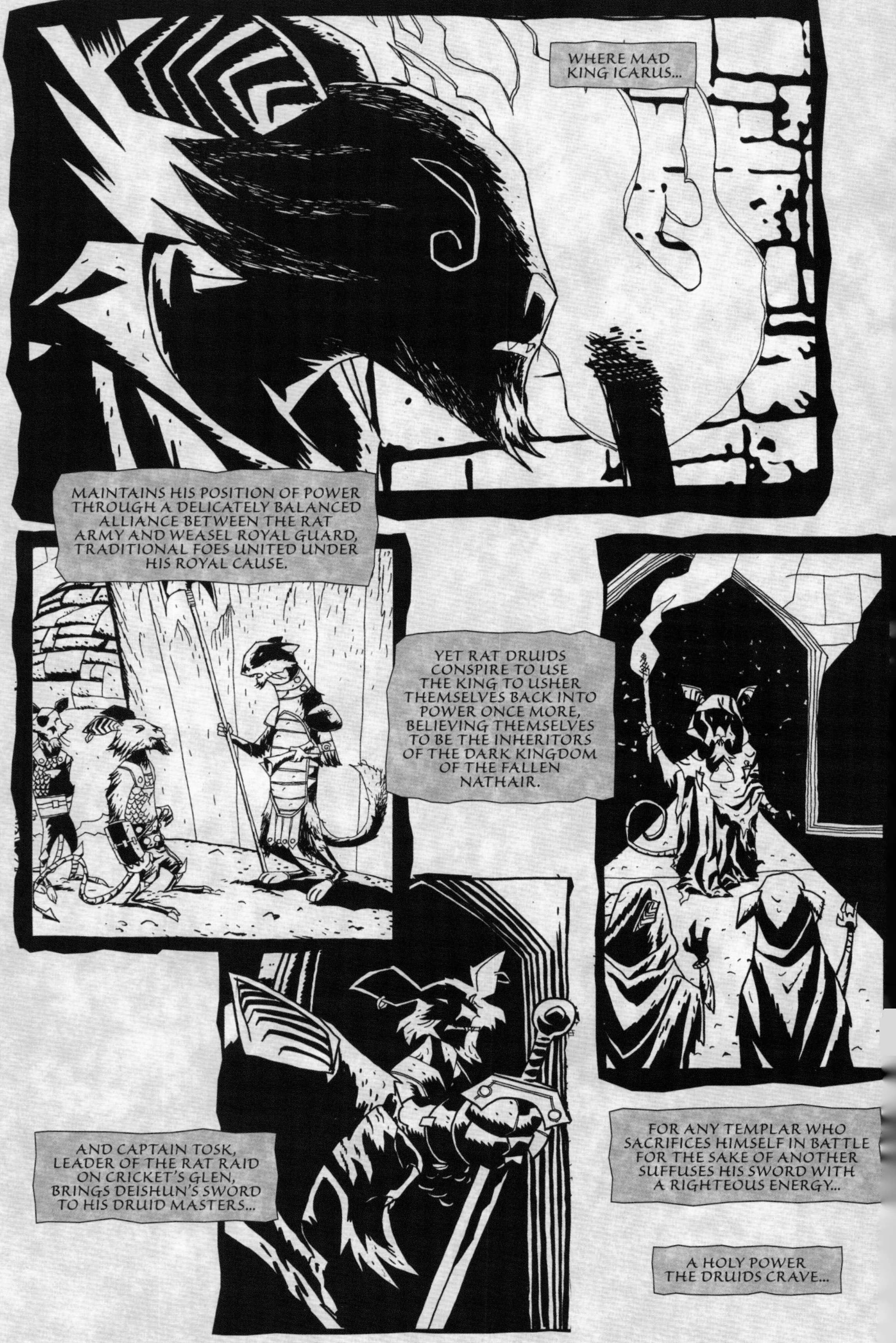
WHERE MAD KING ICARUS...
MAINTAINS HIS POSITION OF POWER THROUGH A DELICATELY BALANCED ALLIANCE BETWEEN THE RAT ARMY AND WEASEL ROYAL GUARD, TRADITIONAL FOES UNITED UNDER HIS ROYAL CAUSE.
YET RAT DRUIDS CONSPIRE TO USE THE KING TO USHER THEMSELVES BACK INTO POWER ONCE MORE, BELIEVING THEMSELVES TO BE THE INHERITORS OF THE DARK KINGDOM OF THE FALLEN NATHAIR.
AND CAPTAIN TOSK, LEADER OF THE RAT RAID ON CRICKET'S GLEN, BRINGS DEISHUN'S SWORD TO HIS DRUID MASTERS...
FOR ANY TEMPLAR WHO SACRIFICES HIMSELF IN BATTLE FOR THE SAKE OF ANOTHER SUFFUSES HIS SWORD WITH A RIGHTEOUS ENERGY...
A HOLY POWER THE DRUIDS CRAVE...

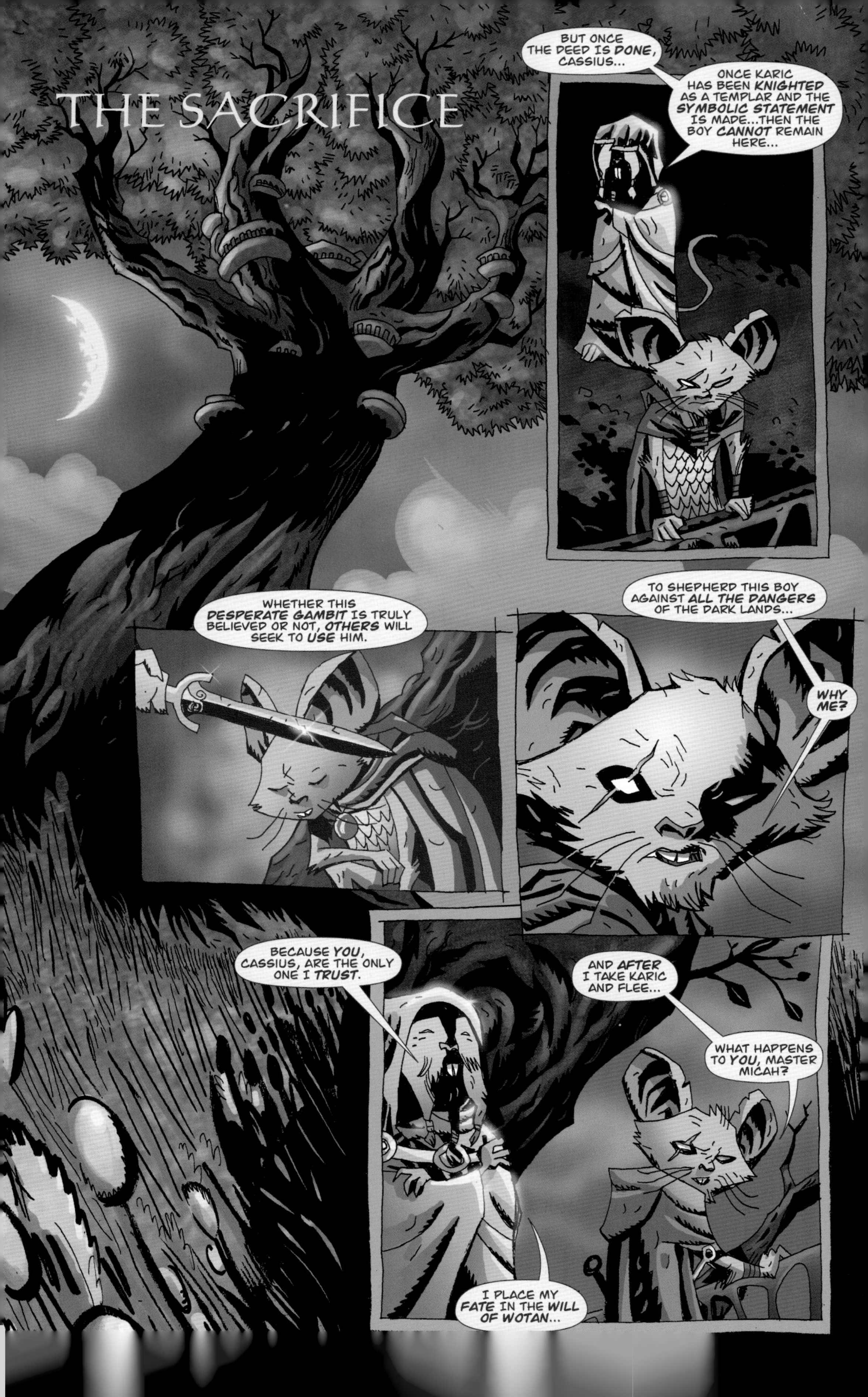
THE SACRIFICE
BUT ONCE THE DEED IS DONE, CASSIUS...
ONCE KARIC HAS BEEN KNIGHTED AS A TEMPLAR AND THE SYMBOLIC STATEMENT IS MADE...THEN THE BOY CANNOT REMAIN HERE...
WHETHER THIS DESPERATE GAMBIT IS TRULY BELIEVED OR NOT, OTHERS WILL SEEK TO USE HIM.
TO SHEPHERD THIS BOY AGAINST ALL THE DANGERS OF THE DARK LANDS...
WHY ME?
BECAUSE YOU, CASSIUS, ARE THE ONLY ONE I TRUST.
AND AFTER I TAKE KARIC AND FLEE...
WHAT HAPPENS TO YOU, MASTER MICAH?
I PLACE MY FATE IN THE WILL OF WOTAN...

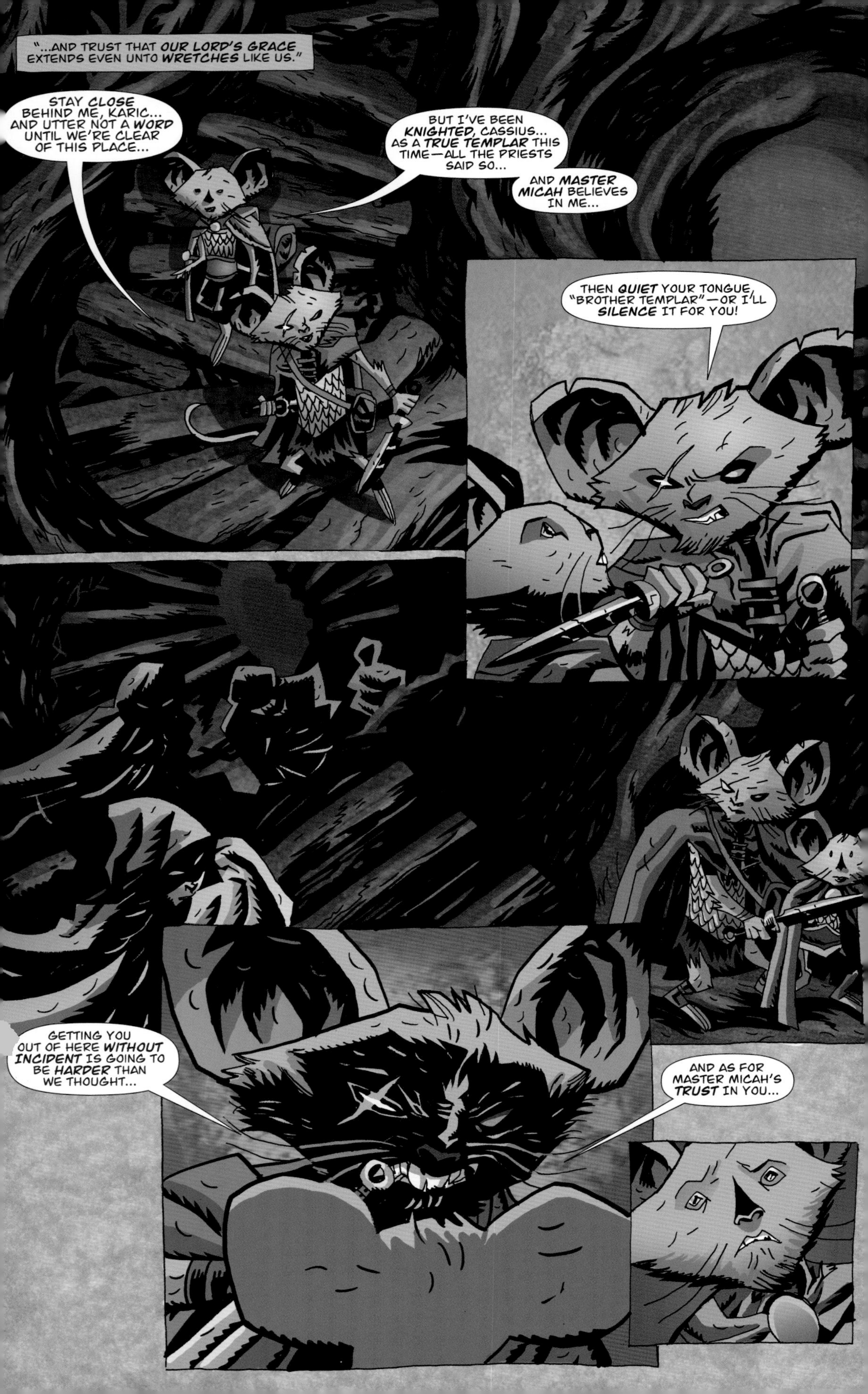
"...AND TRUST THAT OUR LORD'S GRACE EXTENDS EVEN UNTO WRETCHES LIKE US."
STAY CLOSE BEHIND ME, KARIC... AND UTTER NOT A WORD UNTIL WE'RE CLEAR OF THIS PLACE...
BUT I'VE BEEN KNIGHTED, CASSIUS... AS A TRUE TEMPLAR THIS TIME—ALL THE PRIESTS SAID SO...
AND MASTER MICAH BELIEVES IN ME...
THEN QUIET YOUR TONGUE, "BROTHER TEMPLAR"—OR I'LL SILENCE IT FOR YOU!
GETTING YOU OUT OF HERE WITHOUT INCIDENT IS GOING TO BE HARDER THAN WE THOUGHT...
AND AS FOR MASTER MICAH'S TRUST IN YOU...

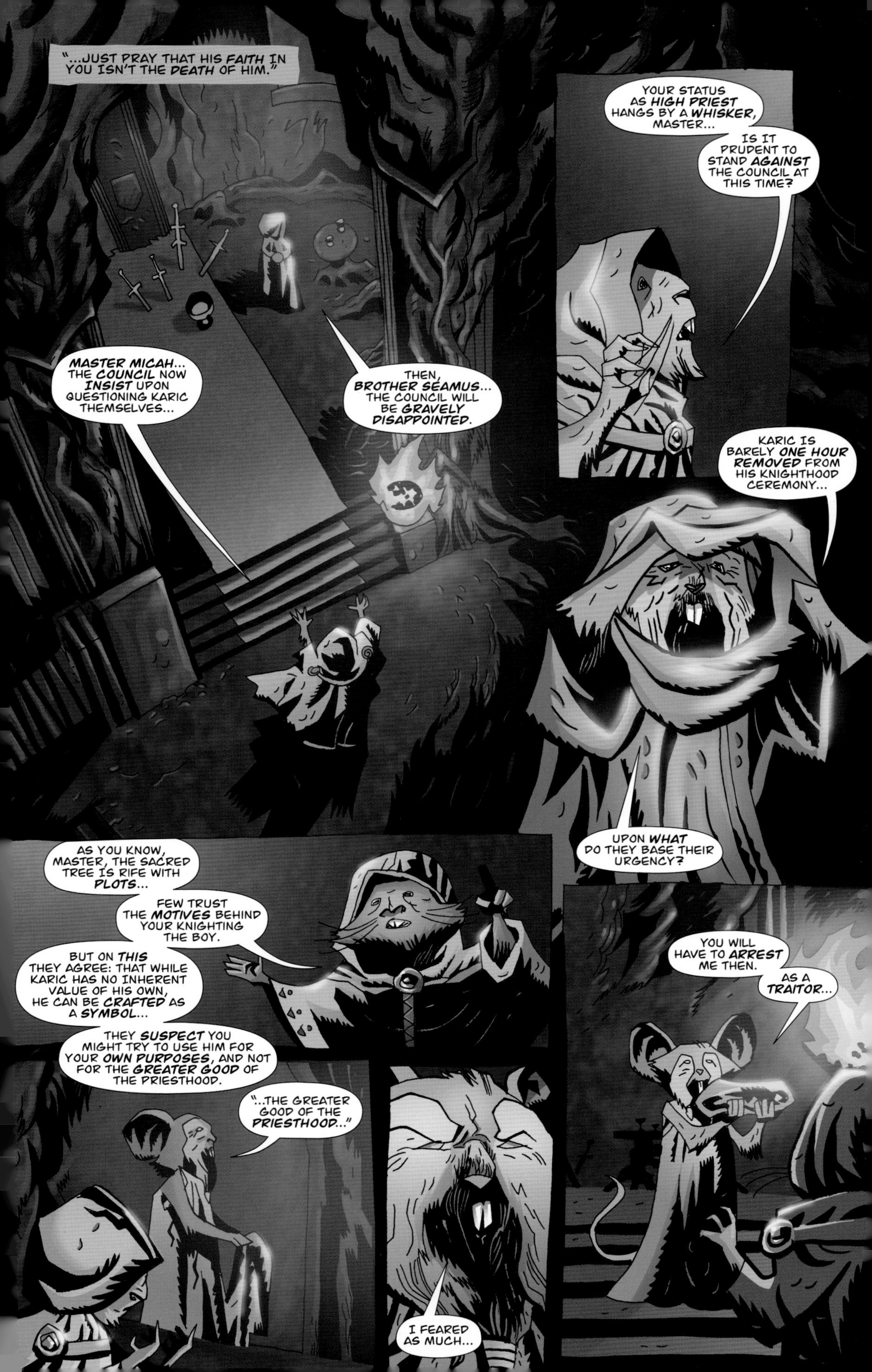
"...JUST PRAY THAT HIS FAITH IN YOU ISN'T THE DEATH OF HIM."
YOUR STATUS AS HIGH PRIEST HANGS BY A WHISKER, MASTER...
IS IT PRUDENT TO STAND AGAINST THE COUNCIL AT THIS TIME?
MASTER MICAH... THE COUNCIL NOW INSIST UPON QUESTIONING KARIC THEMSELVES...
THEN, BROTHER SEAMUS... THE COUNCIL WILL BE GRAVELY DISAPPOINTED.
KARIC IS BARELY ONE HOUR REMOVED FROM HIS KNIGHTHOOD CEREMONY...
UPON WHAT DO THEY BASE THEIR URGENCY?
AS YOU KNOW, MASTER, THE SACRED TREE IS RIFE WITH PLOTS...
FEW TRUST THE MOTIVES BEHIND YOUR KNIGHTING THE BOY.
BUT ON THIS THEY AGREE: THAT WHILE KARIC HAS NO INHERENT VALUE OF HIS OWN, HE CAN BE CRAFTED AS A SYMBOL...
THEY SUSPECT YOU MIGHT TRY TO USE HIM FOR YOUR OWN PURPOSES, AND NOT FOR THE GREATER GOOD OF THE PRIESTHOOD.
"...THE GREATER GOOD OF THE PRIESTHOOD..."
I FEARED AS MUCH...
YOU WILL HAVE TO ARREST ME THEN.
AS A TRAITOR...

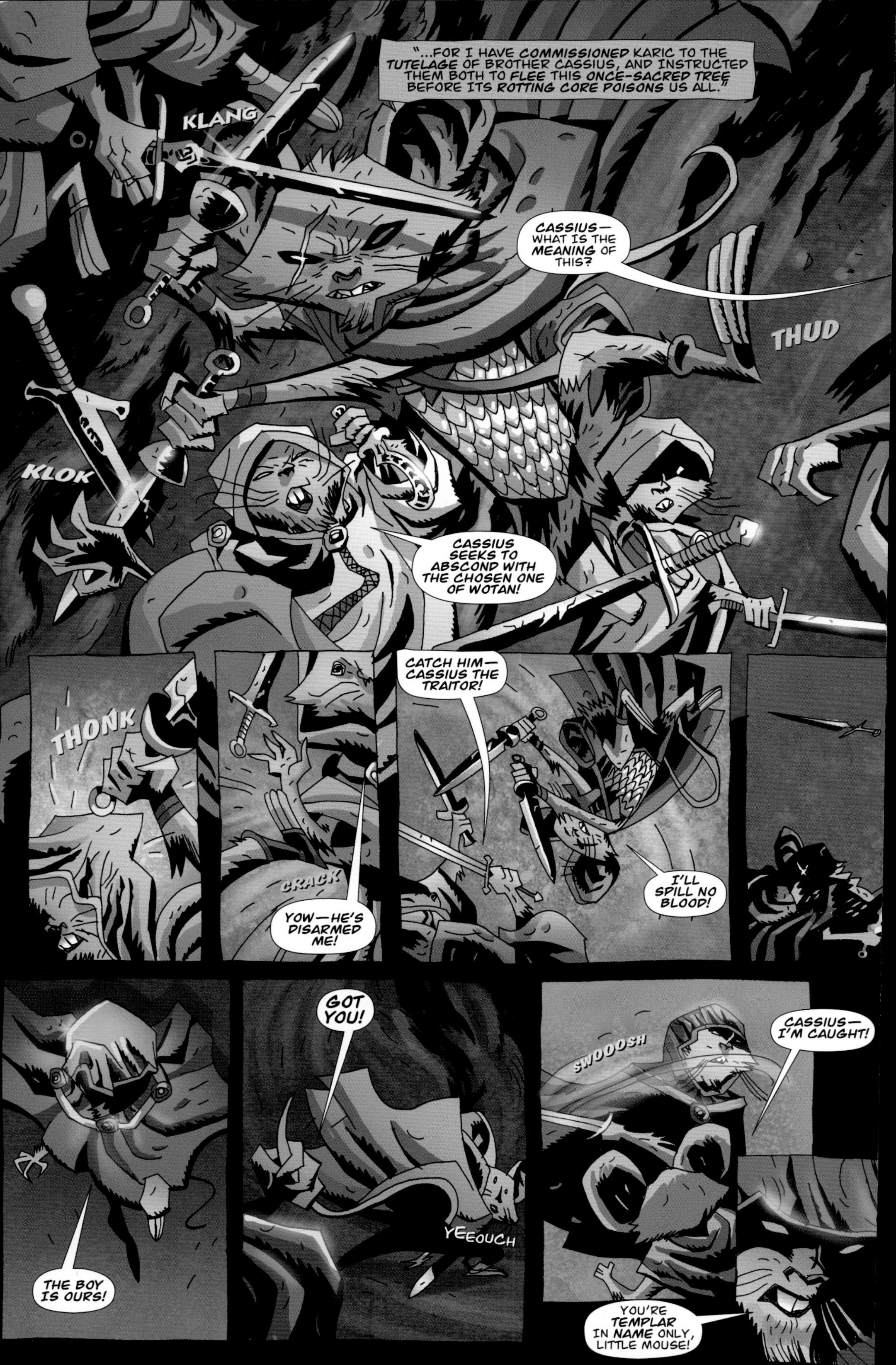
"...FOR I HAVE COMMISSIONED KARIC TO THE TUTELAGE OF BROTHER CASSIUS, AND INSTRUCTED THEM BOTH TO FLEE THIS ONCE-SACRED TREE BEFORE ITS ROTTING CORE POISONS US ALL."
KLANG
CASSIUS—WHAT IS THE MEANING OF THIS?
THUD
KLOK
CASSIUS SEEKS TO ABSCOND WITH THE CHOSEN ONE OF WOTAN!
THONK
CRACK
YOW—HE'S DISARMED ME!
CATCH HIM—CASSIUS THE TRAITOR!
I'LL SPILL NO BLOOD!
THE BOY IS OURS!
GOT YOU!
YEEOUCH
SWOOOSH
CASSIUS—I'M CAUGHT!
YOU'RE TEMPLAR IN NAME ONLY, LITTLE MOUSE!

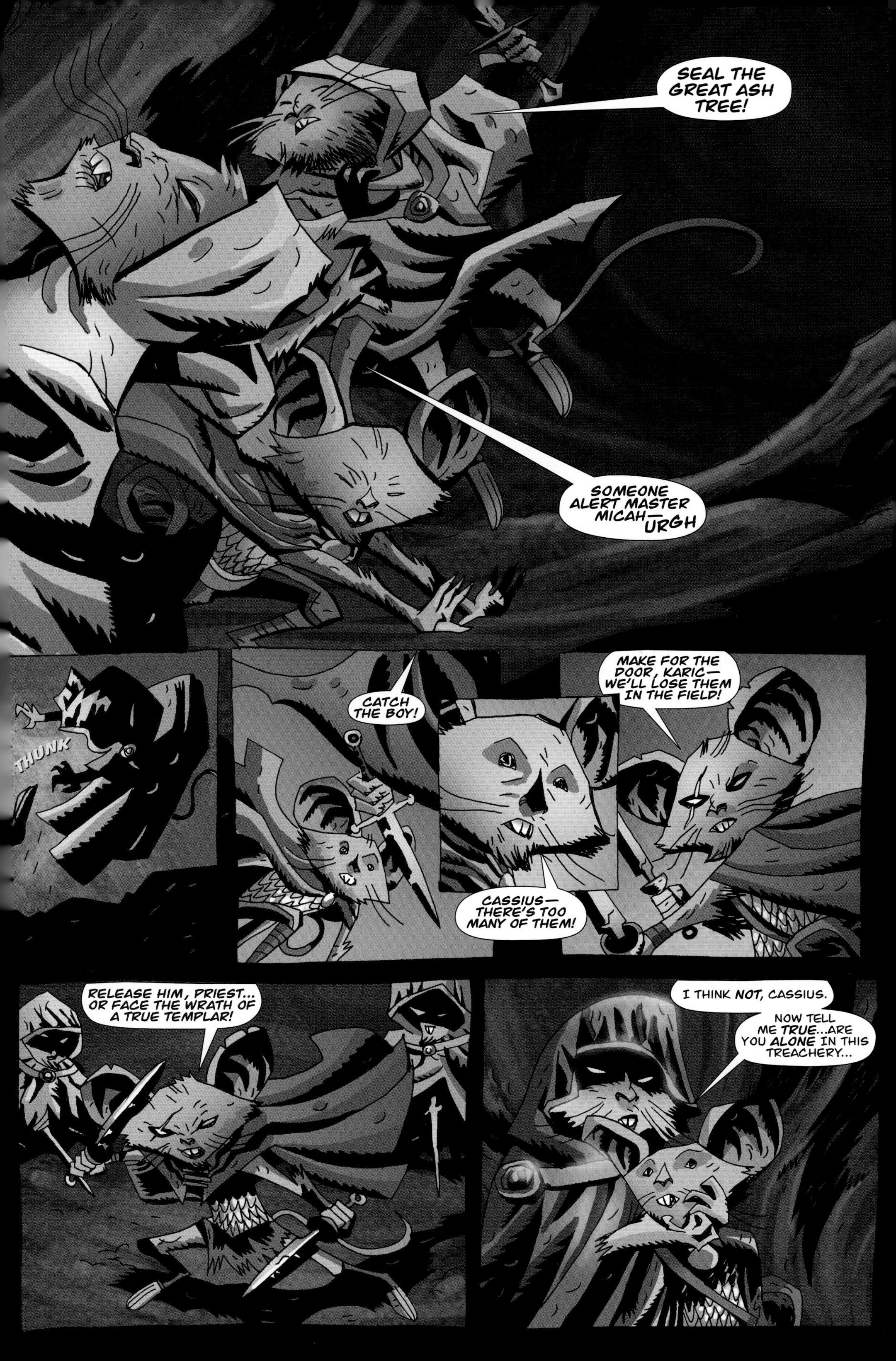
SEAL THE GREAT ASH TREE!
SOMEONE ALERT MASTER MICAH—URGH
THUNK
CATCH THE BOY!
MAKE FOR THE DOOR, KARIC— WE'LL LOSE THEM IN THE FIELD!
CASSIUS— THERE'S TOO MANY OF THEM!
RELEASE HIM, PRIEST... OR FACE THE WRATH OF A TRUE TEMPLAR!
I THINK NOT, CASSIUS.
NOW TELL ME TRUE...ARE YOU ALONE IN THIS TREACHERY...

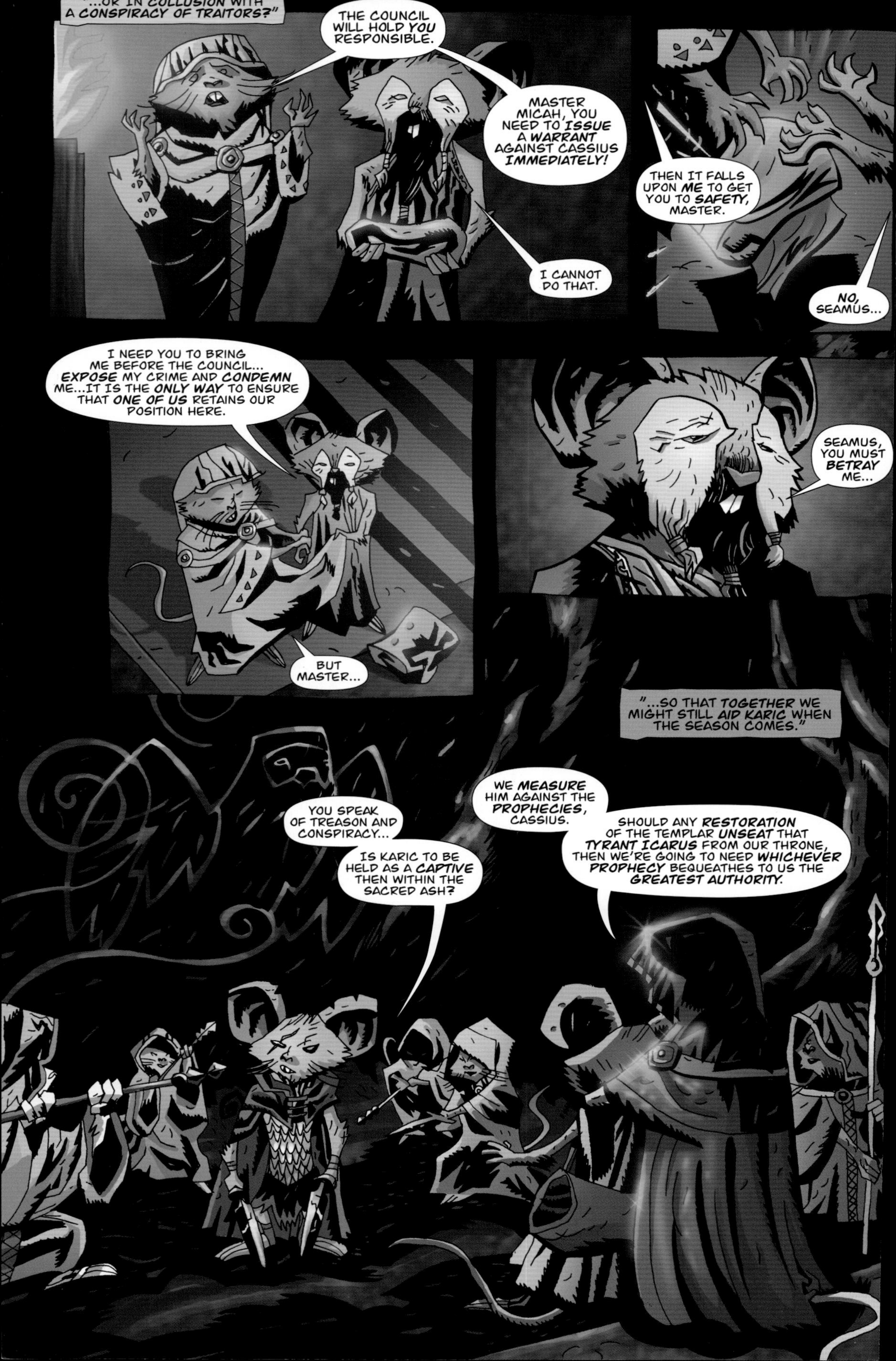
"...OR IN COLLUSION WITH A CONSPIRACY OF TRAITORS?"
THE COUNCIL WILL HOLD YOU RESPONSIBLE.
MASTER MICAH, YOU NEED TO ISSUE A WARRANT AGAINST CASSIUS IMMEDIATELY!
I CANNOT DO THAT.
THEN IT FALLS UPON ME TO GET YOU TO SAFETY, MASTER.
NO, SEAMUS...
I NEED YOU TO BRING ME BEFORE THE COUNCIL... EXPOSE MY CRIME AND CONDEMN ME...IT IS THE ONLY WAY TO ENSURE THAT ONE OF US RETAINS OUR POSITION HERE.
BUT MASTER...
SEAMUS, YOU MUST BETRAY ME...
"...SO THAT TOGETHER WE MIGHT STILL AID KARIC WHEN THE SEASON COMES."
YOU SPEAK OF TREASON AND CONSPIRACY...
IS KARIC TO BE HELD AS A CAPTIVE THEN WITHIN THE SACRED ASH?
WE MEASURE HIM AGAINST THE PROPHECIES, CASSIUS.
SHOULD ANY RESTORATION OF THE TEMPLAR UNSEAT THAT TYRANT ICARUS FROM OUR THRONE, THEN WE'RE GOING TO NEED WHICHEVER PROPHECY BEQUEATHES TO US THE GREATEST AUTHORITY.

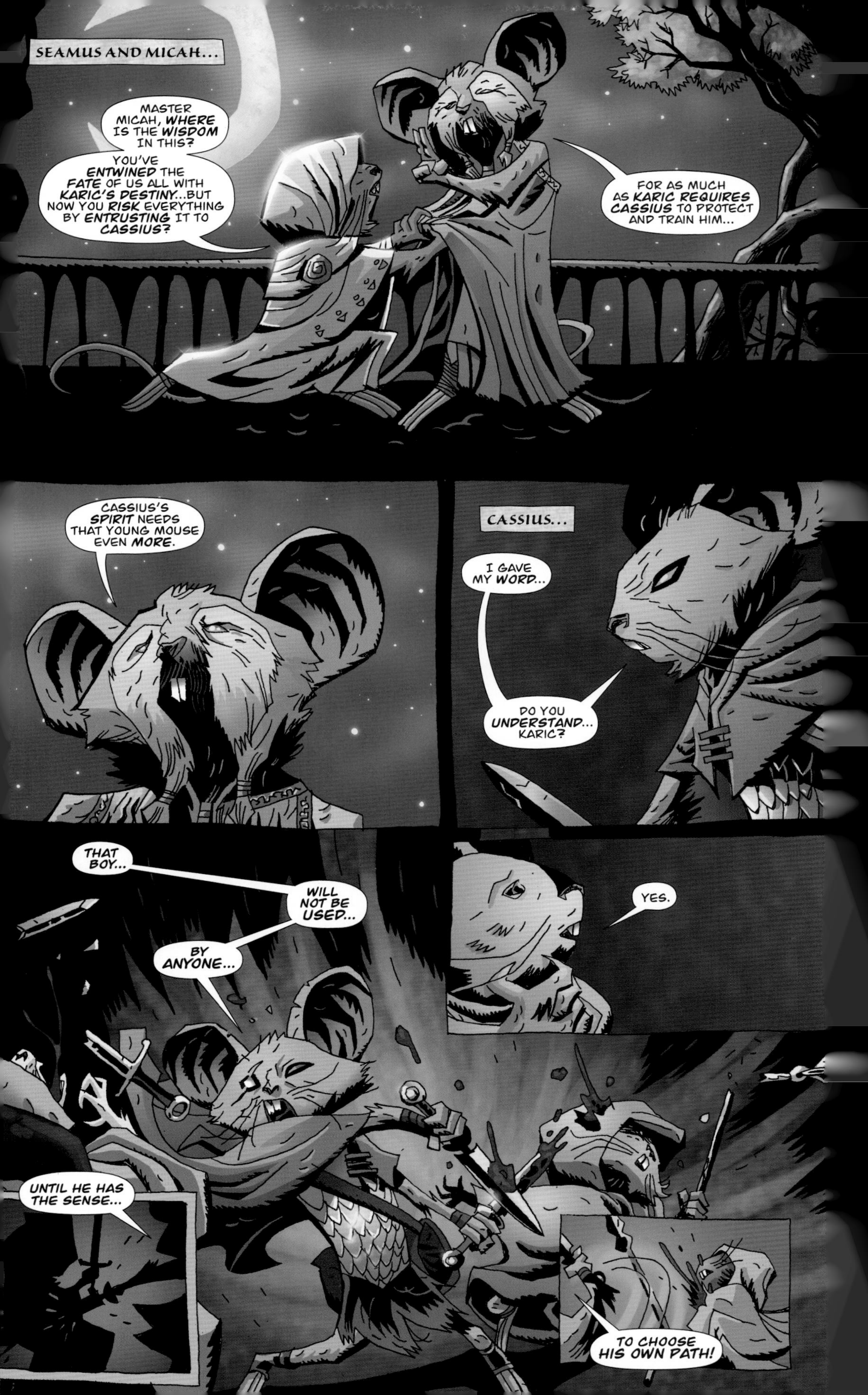
SEAMUS AND MICAH...
MASTER MICAH, WHERE IS THE WISDOM IN THIS?
YOU'VE ENTWINED THE FATE OF US ALL WITH KARIC'S DESTINY...BUT NOW YOU RISK EVERYTHING BY ENTRUSTING IT TO CASSIUS?
FOR AS MUCH AS KARIC REQUIRES CASSIUS TO PROTECT AND TRAIN HIM...
CASSIUS'S SPIRIT NEEDS THAT YOUNG MOUSE EVEN MORE.
CASSIUS...
I GAVE MY WORD...
DO YOU UNDERSTAND... KARIC?
YES.
THAT BOY...
WILL NOT BE USED...
BY ANYONE...
UNTIL HE HAS THE SENSE...
TO CHOOSE HIS OWN PATH!

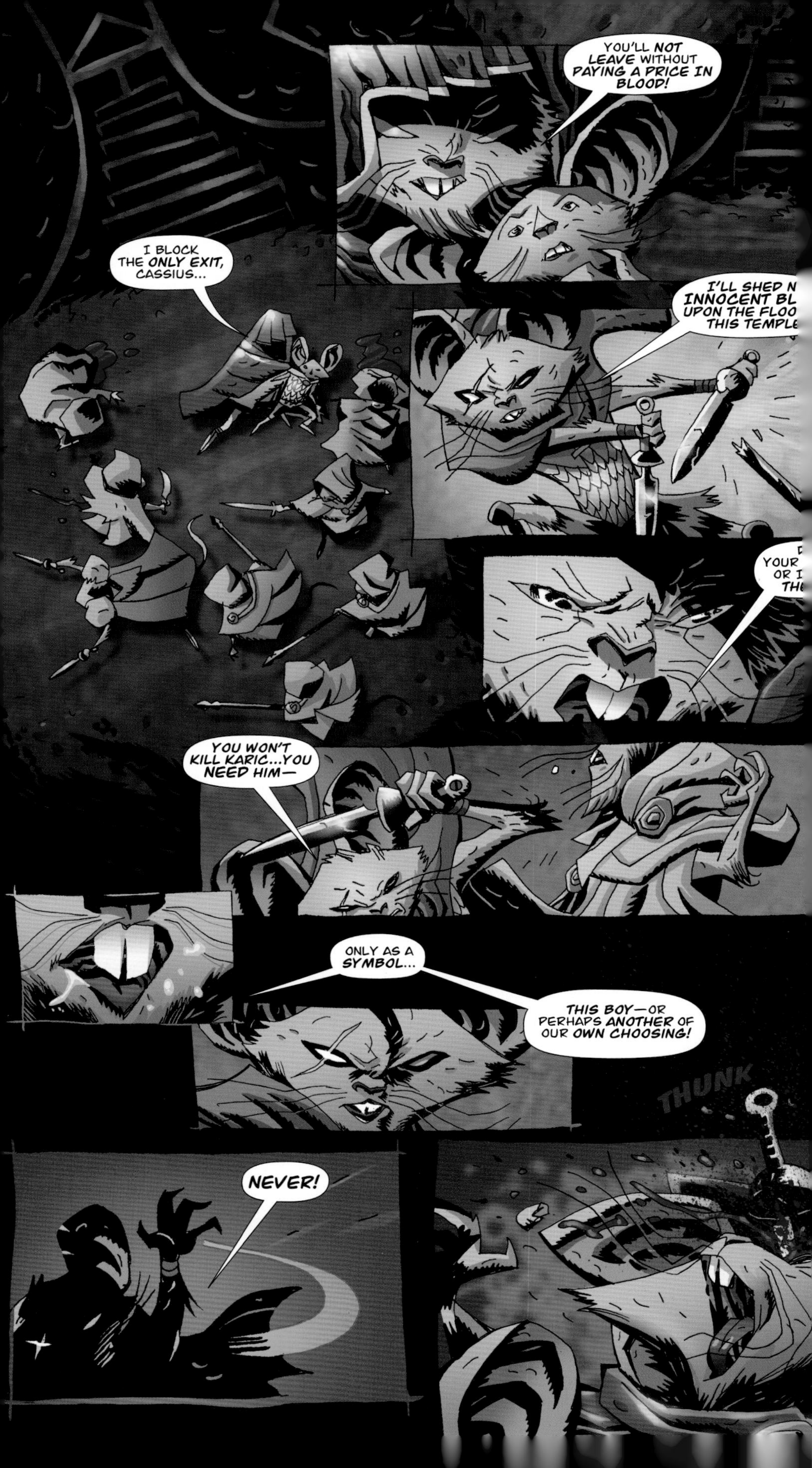
YOU'LL NOT LEAVE WITHOUT PAYING A PRICE IN BLOOD!
I BLOCK THE ONLY EXIT, CASSIUS...
I'LL SHED N
INNOCENT BL
UPON THE FLOO
THIS TEMPLE
YOU WON'T KILL KARIC...YOU NEED HIM—
ONLY AS A SYMBOL...
THIS BOY—OR PERHAPS ANOTHER OF OUR OWN CHOOSING!
THUNK
NEVER!

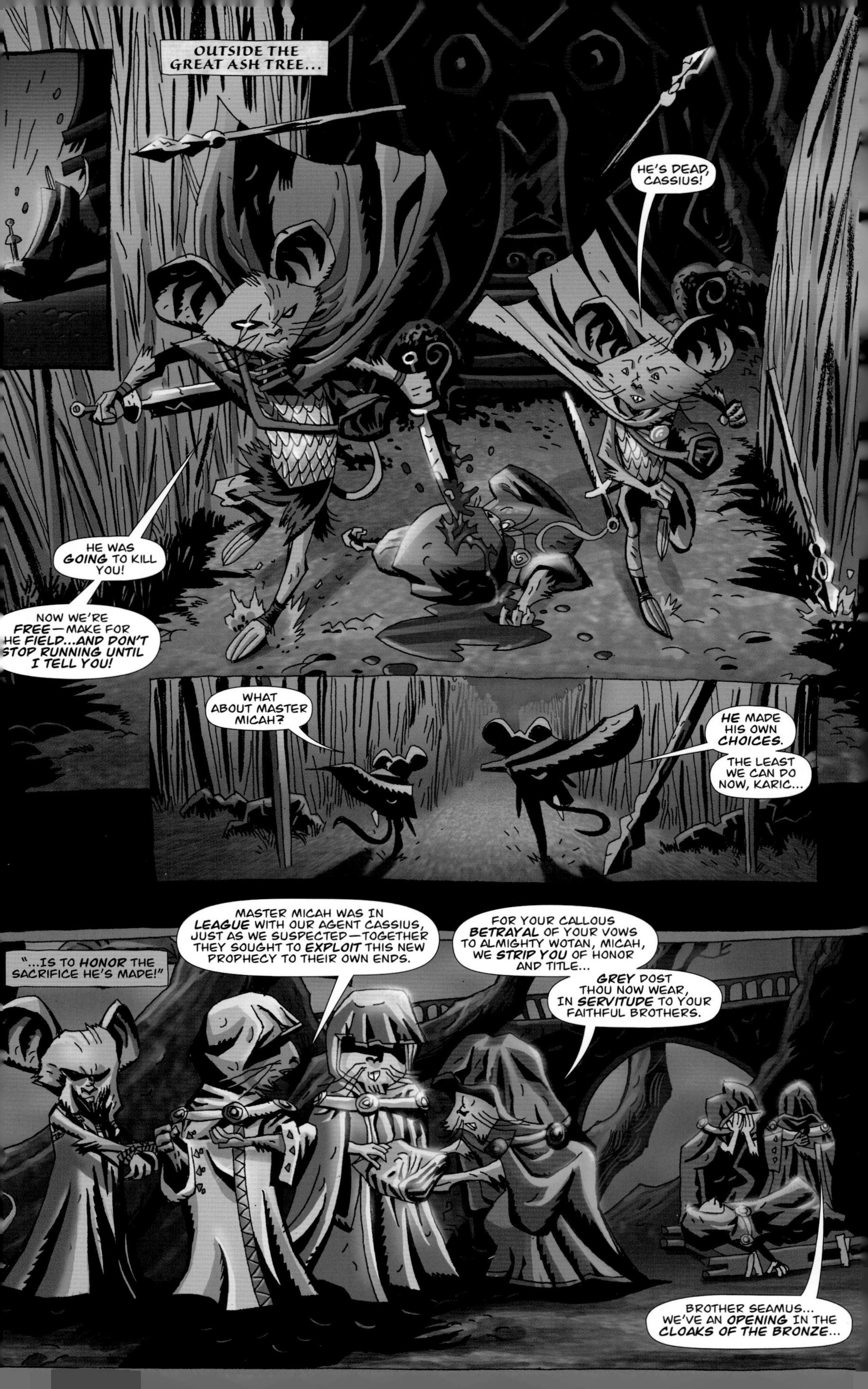
OUTSIDE THE GREAT ASH TREE...
HE'S DEAD, CASSIUS!
HE WAS GOING TO KILL YOU!
NOW WE'RE FREE—MAKE FOR HE FIELD...AND DON'T STOP RUNNING UNTIL I TELL YOU!
WHAT ABOUT MASTER MICAH?
HE MADE HIS OWN CHOICES.
THE LEAST WE CAN DO NOW, KARIC...
"...IS TO HONOR THE SACRIFICE HE'S MADE!"
MASTER MICAH WAS IN LEAGUE WITH OUR AGENT CASSIUS, JUST AS WE SUSPECTED—TOGETHER THEY SOUGHT TO EXPLOIT THIS NEW PROPHECY TO THEIR OWN ENDS.
FOR YOUR CALLOUS BETRAYAL OF YOUR VOWS TO ALMIGHTY WOTAN, MICAH, WE STRIP YOU OF HONOR AND TITLE...
GREY DOST THOU NOW WEAR, IN SERVITUDE TO YOUR FAITHFUL BROTHERS.
BROTHER SEAMUS... WE'VE AN OPENING IN THE CLOAKS OF THE BRONZE...

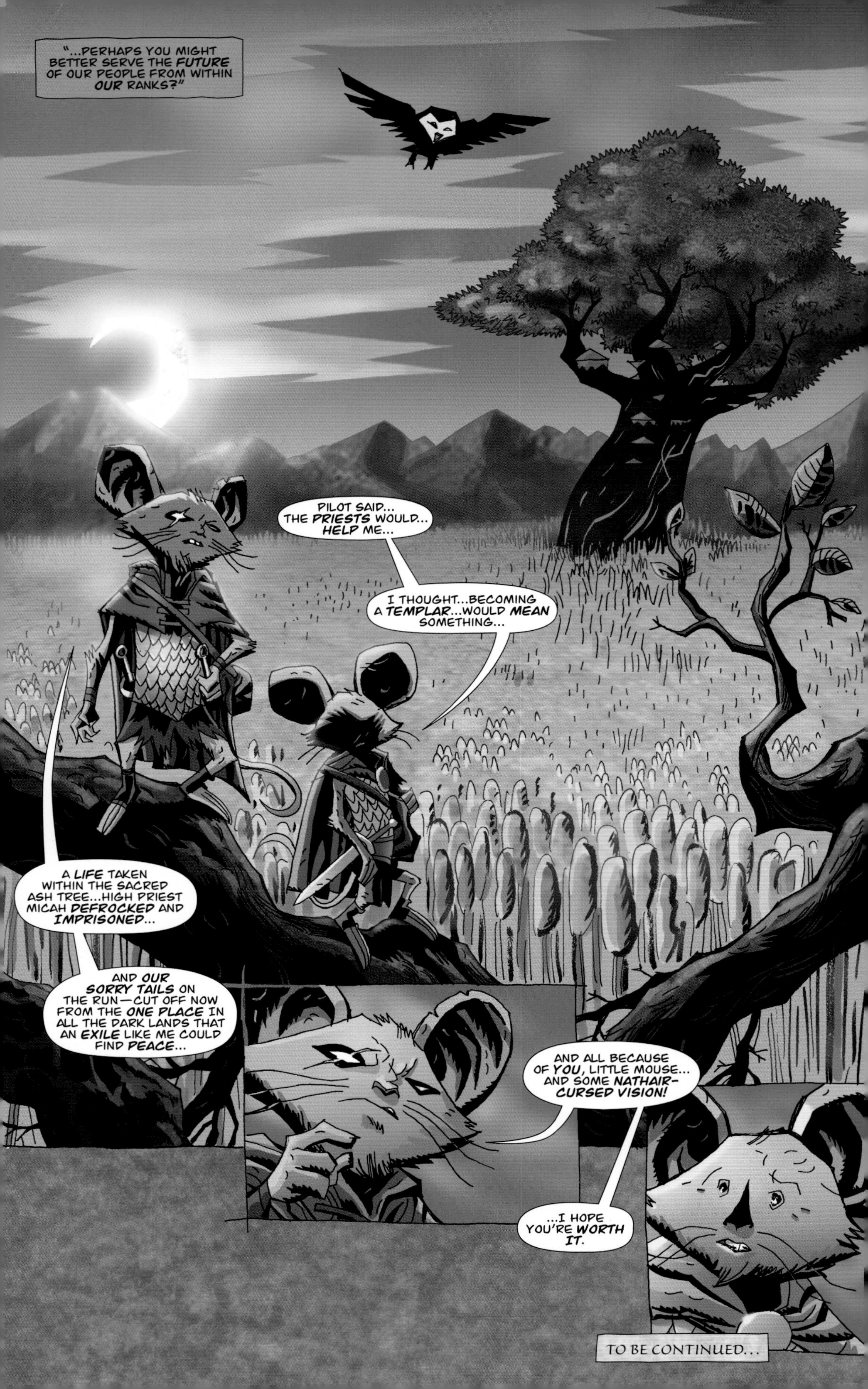
"...PERHAPS YOU MIGHT BETTER SERVE THE FUTURE OF OUR PEOPLE FROM WITHIN OUR RANKS?"
PILOT SAID... THE PRIESTS WOULD... HELP ME...
I THOUGHT...BECOMING A TEMPLAR...WOULD MEAN SOMETHING...
A LIFE TAKEN WITHIN THE SACRED ASH TREE...HIGH PRIEST MICAH DEFROCKED AND IMPRISONED...
AND OUR SORRY TAILS ON THE RUN—CUT OFF NOW FROM THE ONE PLACE IN ALL THE DARK LANDS THAT AN EXILE LIKE ME COULD FIND PEACE...
AND ALL BECAUSE OF YOU, LITTLE MOUSE... AND SOME NATHAIR-CURSED VISION!
...I HOPE YOU'RE WORTH IT.
TO BE CONTINUED...

CHAPTER ONE
THE HAUNTED WOOD

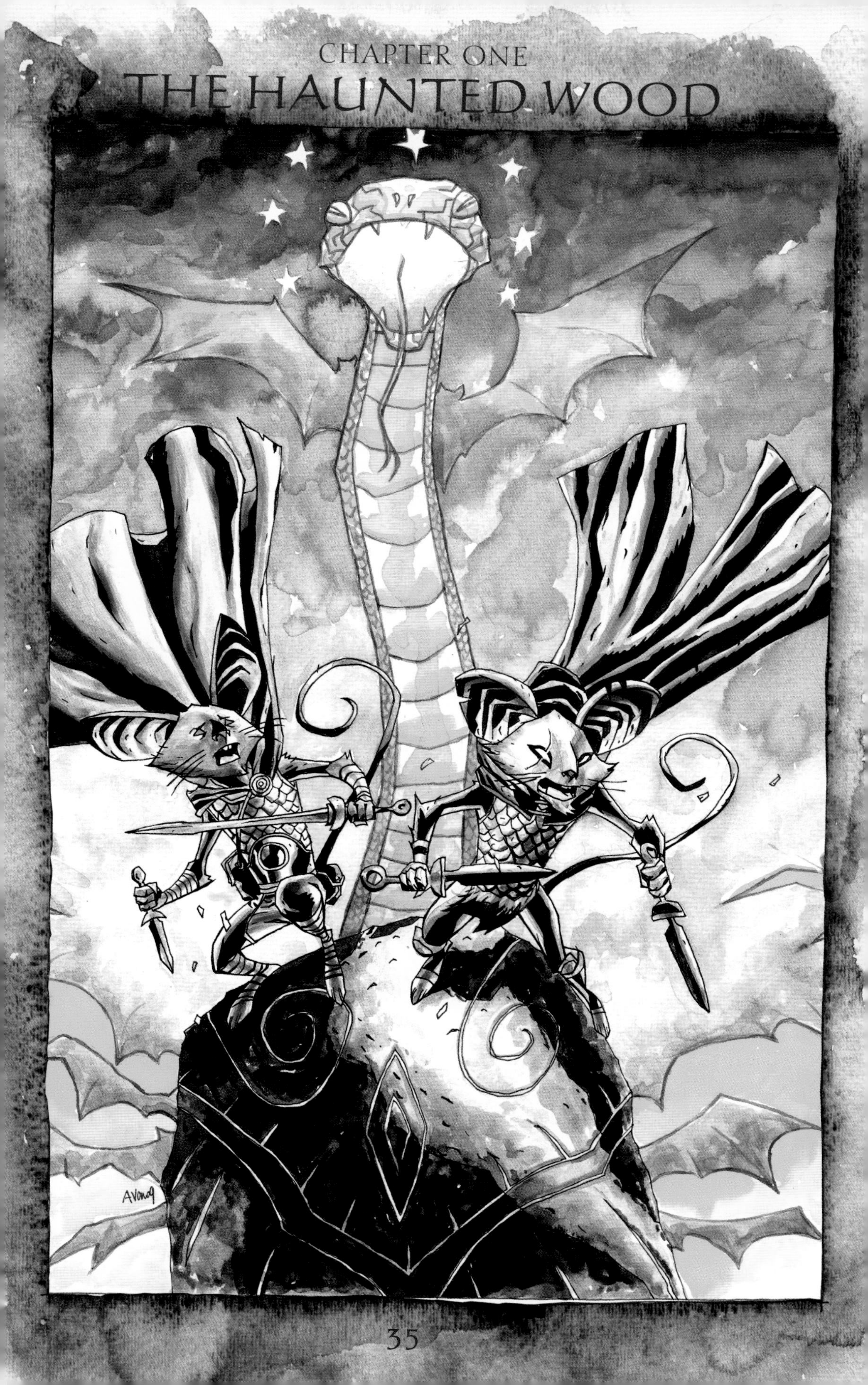

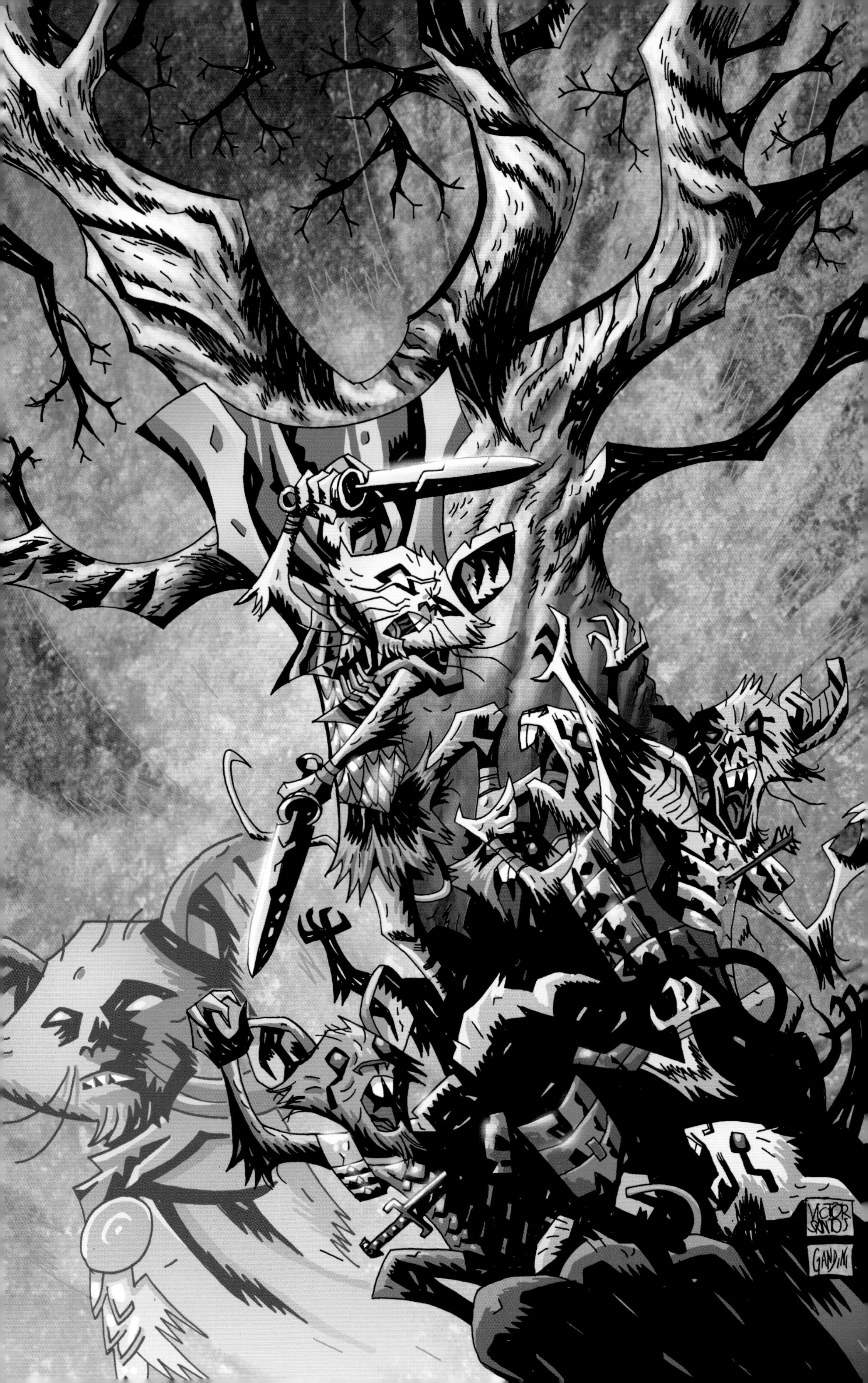
VICTOR SANTOS
GANDINI

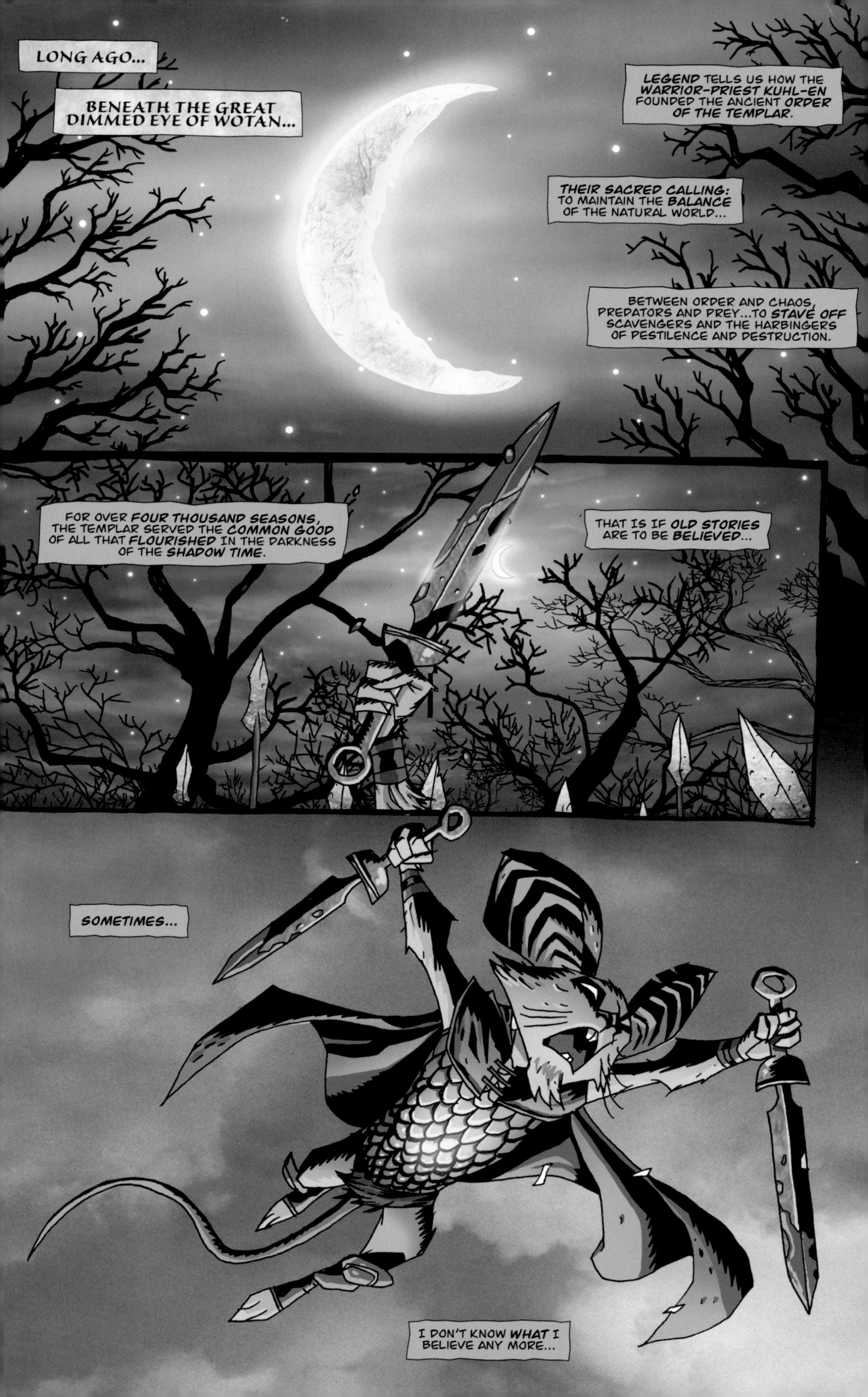
LONG AGO...
BENEATH THE GREAT DIMMED EYE OF WOTAN...
LEGEND TELLS US HOW THE WARRIOR-PRIEST KUHL-EN FOUNDED THE ANCIENT ORDER OF THE TEMPLAR.
THEIR SACRED CALLING: TO MAINTAIN THE BALANCE OF THE NATURAL WORLD...
BETWEEN ORDER AND CHAOS, PREDATORS AND PREY...TO STAVE OFF SCAVENGERS AND THE HARBINGERS OF PESTILENCE AND DESTRUCTION.
FOR OVER FOUR THOUSAND SEASONS, THE TEMPLAR SERVED THE COMMON GOOD OF ALL THAT FLOURISHED IN THE DARKNESS OF THE SHADOW TIME.
THAT IS IF OLD STORIES ARE TO BE BELIEVED...
SOMETIMES...
I DON'T KNOW WHAT I BELIEVE ANY MORE...

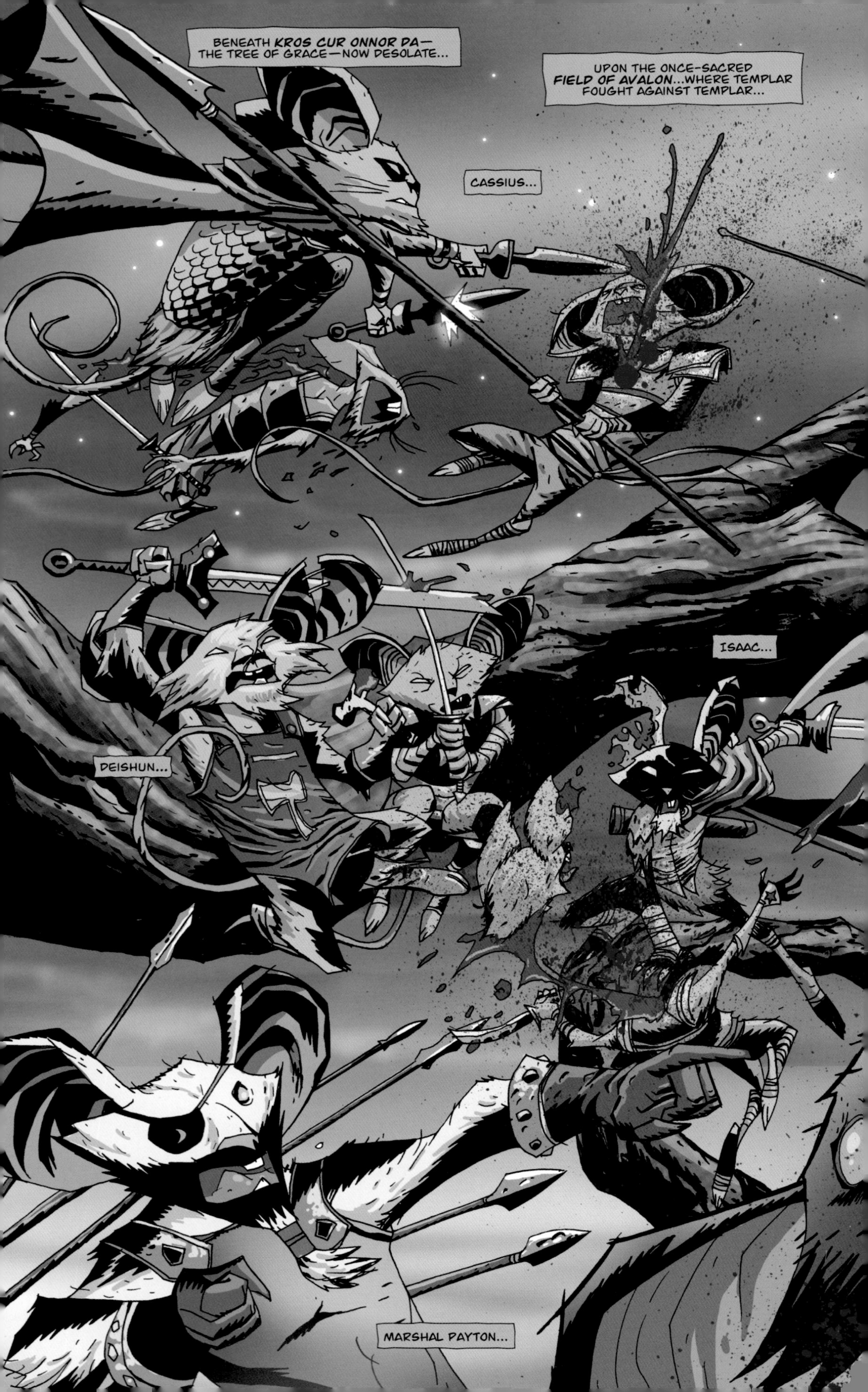

BENEATH KROS CUR ONNOR DA— THE TREE OF GRACE—NOW DESOLATE...
UPON THE ONCE-SACRED FIELD OF AVALON...WHERE TEMPLAR FOUGHT AGAINST TEMPLAR...
CASSIUS...
ISAAC...
DEISHUN...
MARSHAL PAYTON...

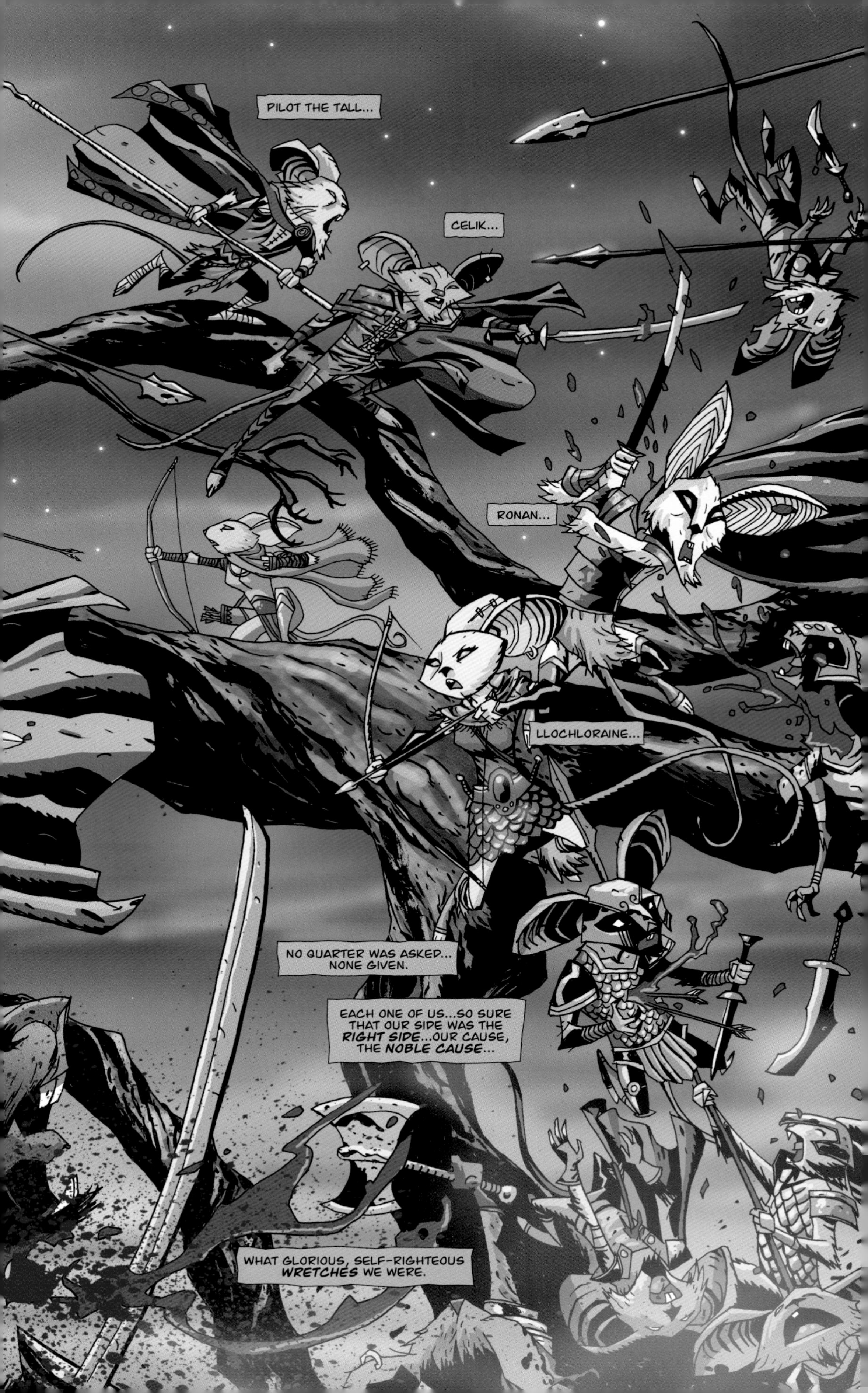
PILOT THE TALL...
CELIK...
RONAN...
LLOCHLORAINE...
NO QUARTER WAS ASKED... NONE GIVEN.
EACH ONE OF US...SO SURE THAT OUR SIDE WAS THE RIGHT SIDE...OUR CAUSE, THE NOBLE CAUSE...
WHAT GLORIOUS, SELF-RIGHTEOUS WRETCHES WE WERE.

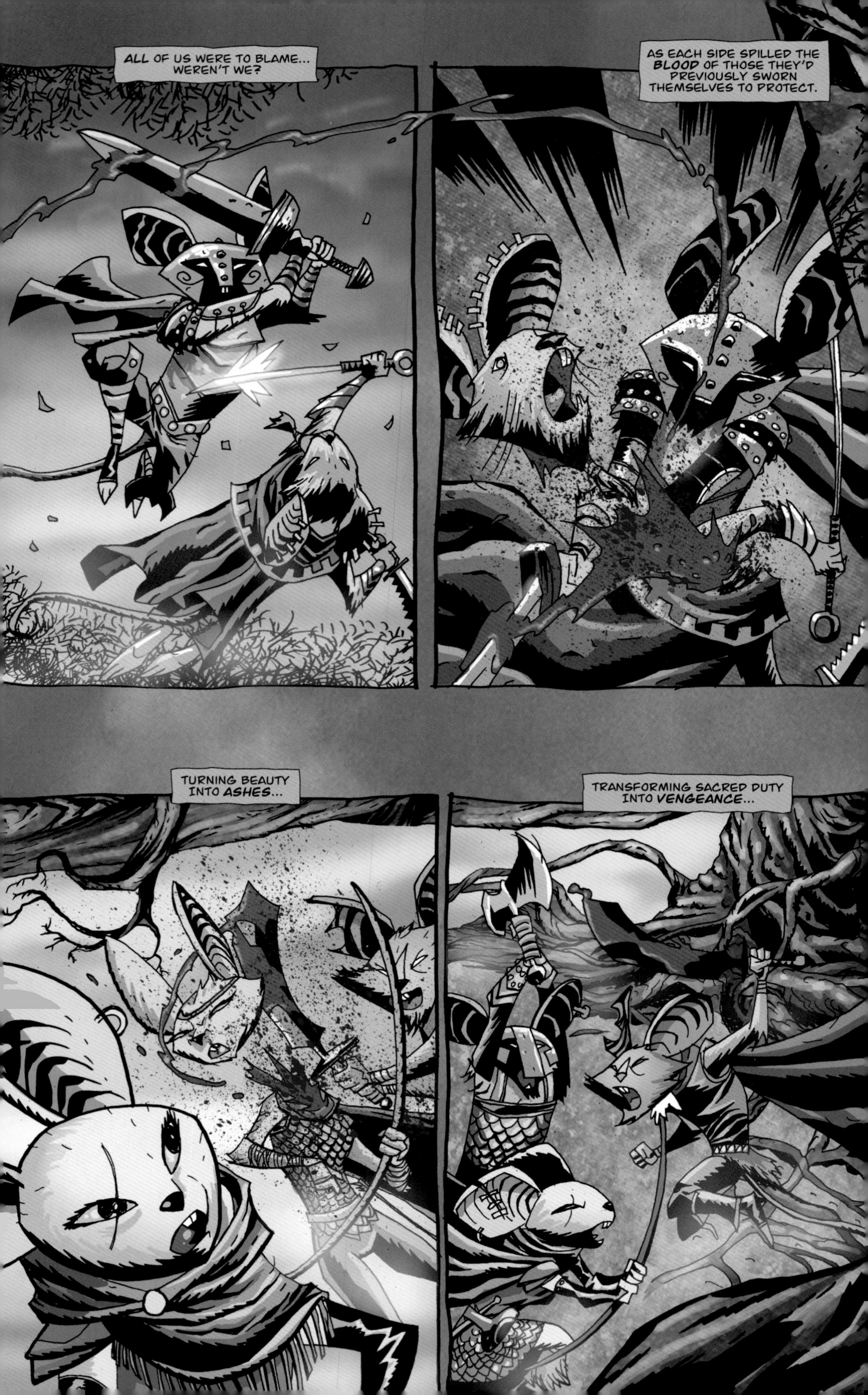
ALL OF US WERE TO BLAME... WEREN'T WE?
AS EACH SIDE SPILLED THE BLOOD OF THOSE THEY'D PREVIOUSLY SWORN THEMSELVES TO PROTECT.
TURNING BEAUTY INTO ASHES...
TRANSFORMING SACRED DUTY INTO VENGEANCE...

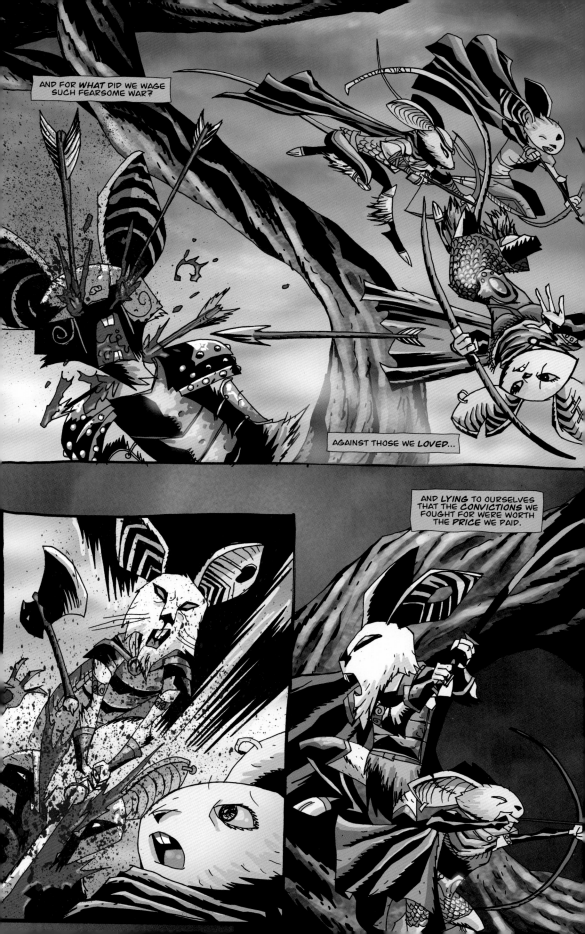

AND FOR **WHAT** DID WE WAGE SUCH FEARSOME WAR?

AGAINST THOSE WE **LOVED**...

AND **LYING** TO OURSELVES THAT THE **CONVICTIONS** WE FOUGHT FOR WERE WORTH THE **PRICE** WE PAID.

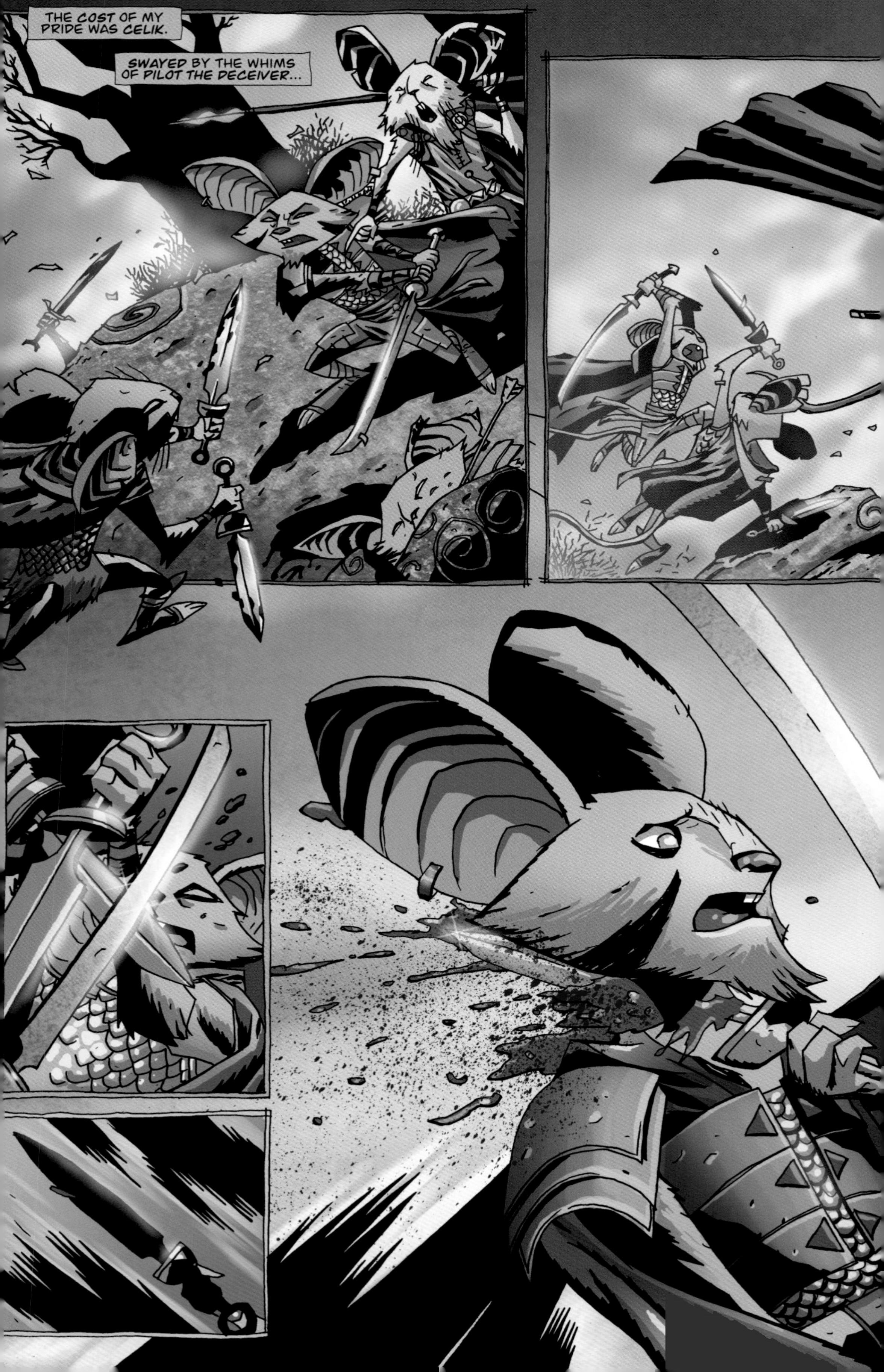
THE COST OF MY PRIDE WAS CELIK.
SWAYED BY THE WHIMS OF PILOT THE DECEIVER...

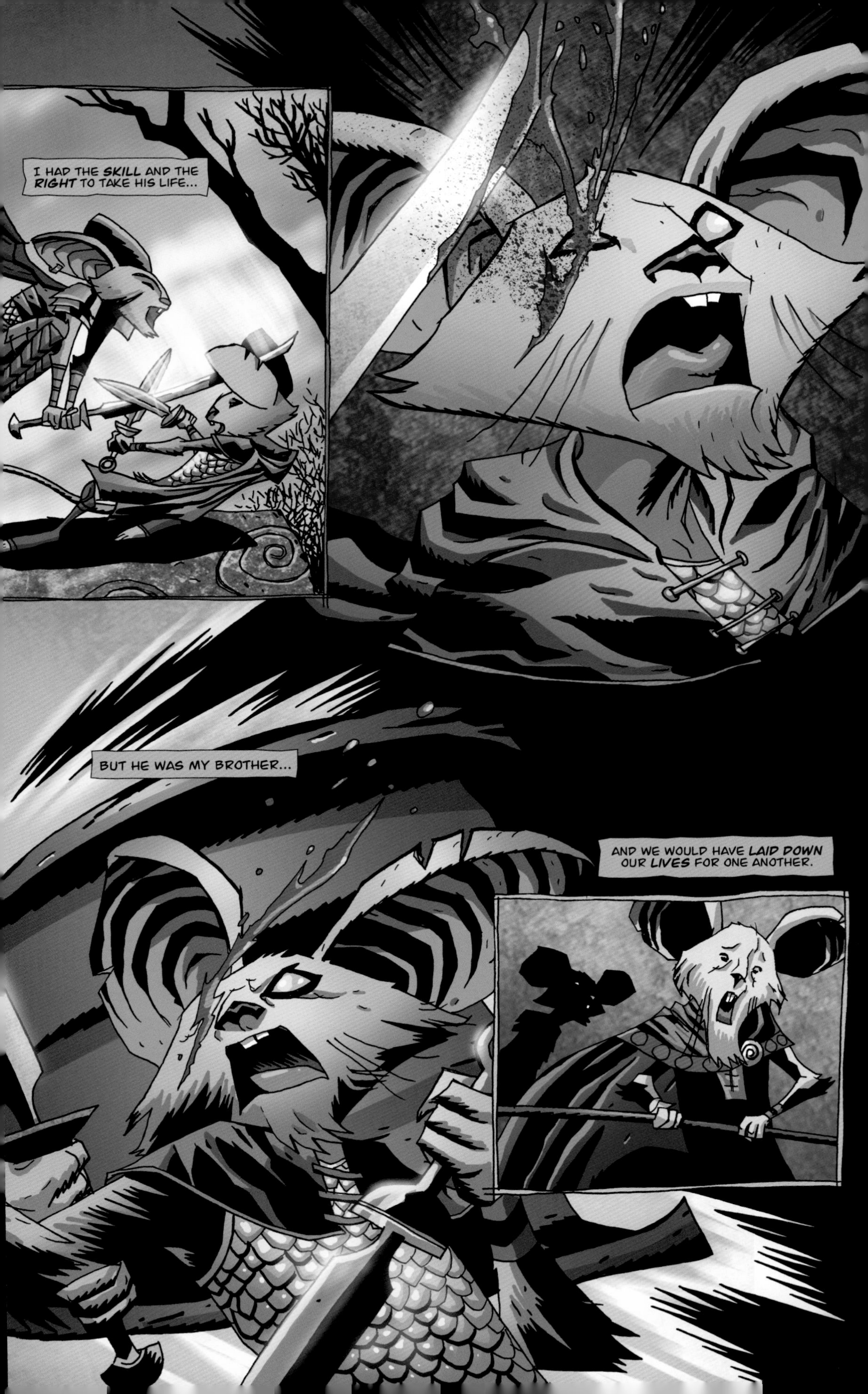
I HAD THE SKILL AND THE RIGHT TO TAKE HIS LIFE...
BUT HE WAS MY BROTHER...
AND WE WOULD HAVE LAID DOWN OUR LIVES FOR ONE ANOTHER.

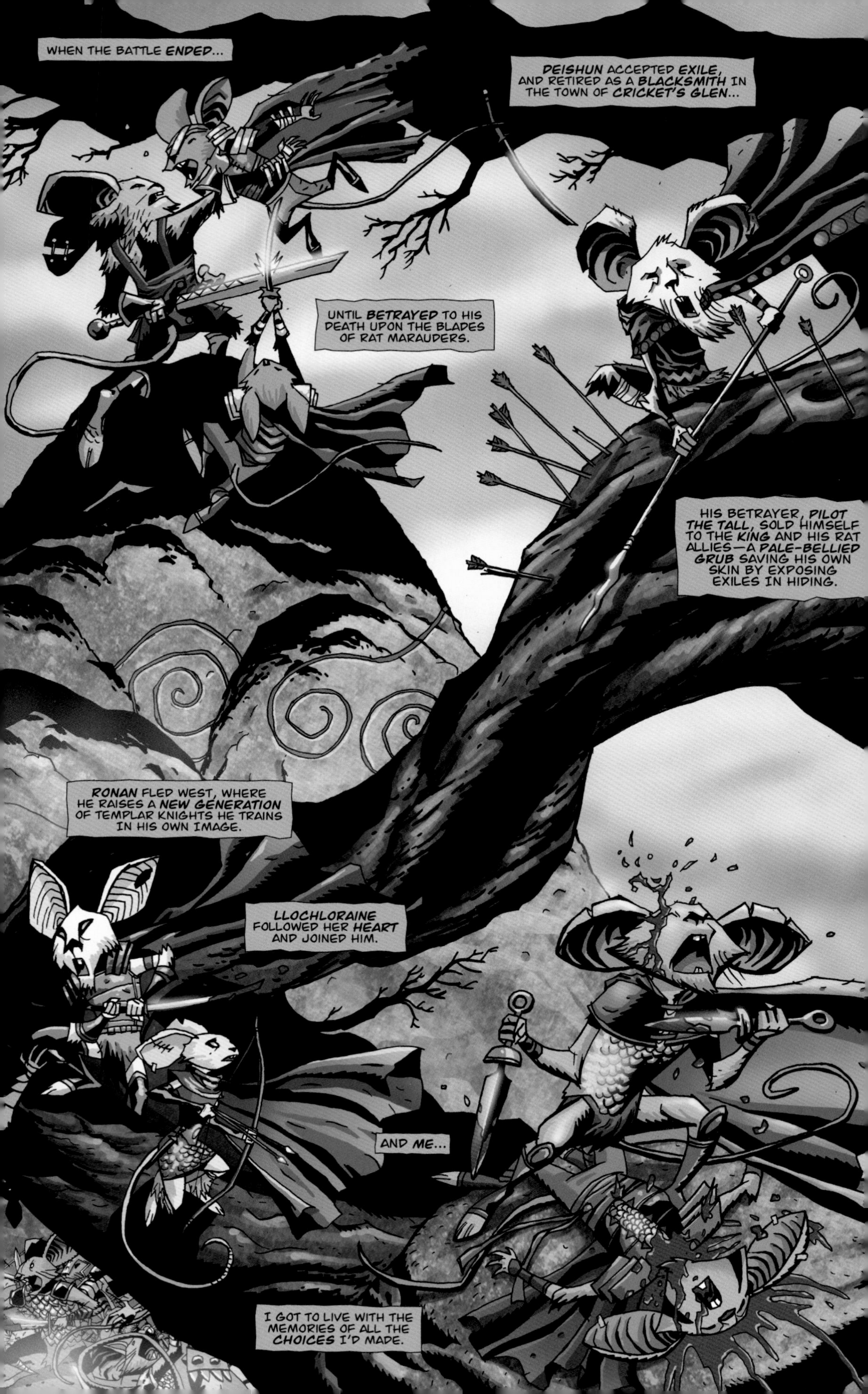
WHEN THE BATTLE ENDED...
DEISHUN ACCEPTED EXILE, AND RETIRED AS A BLACKSMITH IN THE TOWN OF CRICKET'S GLEN...
UNTIL BETRAYED TO HIS DEATH UPON THE BLADES OF RAT MARAUDERS.
HIS BETRAYER, PILOT THE TALL, SOLD HIMSELF TO THE KING AND HIS RAT ALLIES—A PALE-BELLIED GRUB SAVING HIS OWN SKIN BY EXPOSING EXILES IN HIDING.
RONAN FLED WEST, WHERE HE RAISES A NEW GENERATION OF TEMPLAR KNIGHTS HE TRAINS IN HIS OWN IMAGE.
LLOCHLORAINE FOLLOWED HER HEART AND JOINED HIM.
AND ME...
I GOT TO LIVE WITH THE MEMORIES OF ALL THE CHOICES I'D MADE.

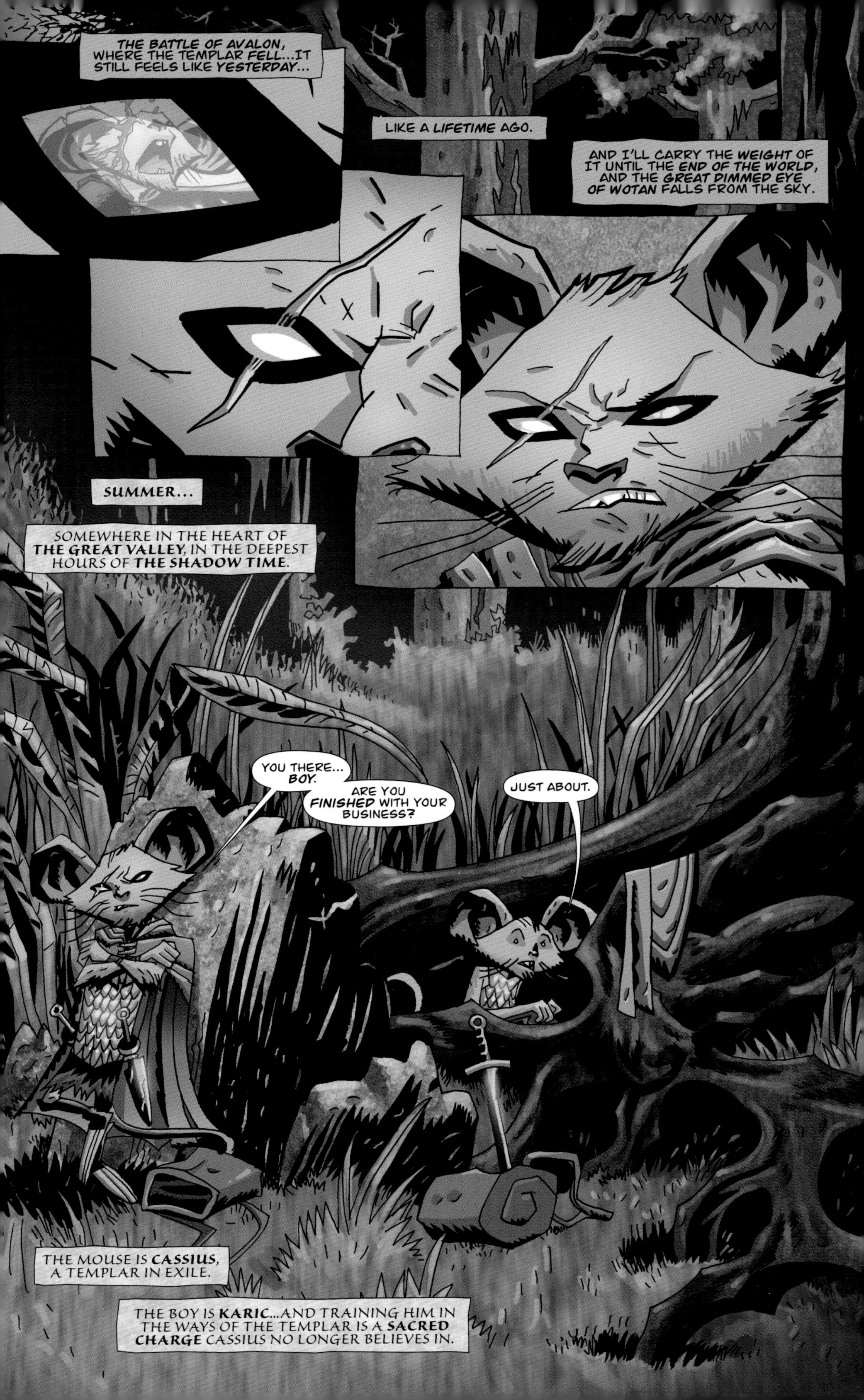
THE BATTLE OF AVALON, WHERE THE TEMPLAR FELL...IT STILL FEELS LIKE YESTERDAY...
LIKE A LIFETIME AGO.
AND I'LL CARRY THE WEIGHT OF IT UNTIL THE END OF THE WORLD, AND THE GREAT DIMMED EYE OF WOTAN FALLS FROM THE SKY.
SUMMER...
SOMEWHERE IN THE HEART OF THE GREAT VALLEY, IN THE DEEPEST HOURS OF THE SHADOW TIME.
YOU THERE... BOY.
ARE YOU FINISHED WITH YOUR BUSINESS?
JUST ABOUT.
THE MOUSE IS CASSIUS, A TEMPLAR IN EXILE.
THE BOY IS KARIC...AND TRAINING HIM IN THE WAYS OF THE TEMPLAR IS A SACRED CHARGE CASSIUS NO LONGER BELIEVES IN.

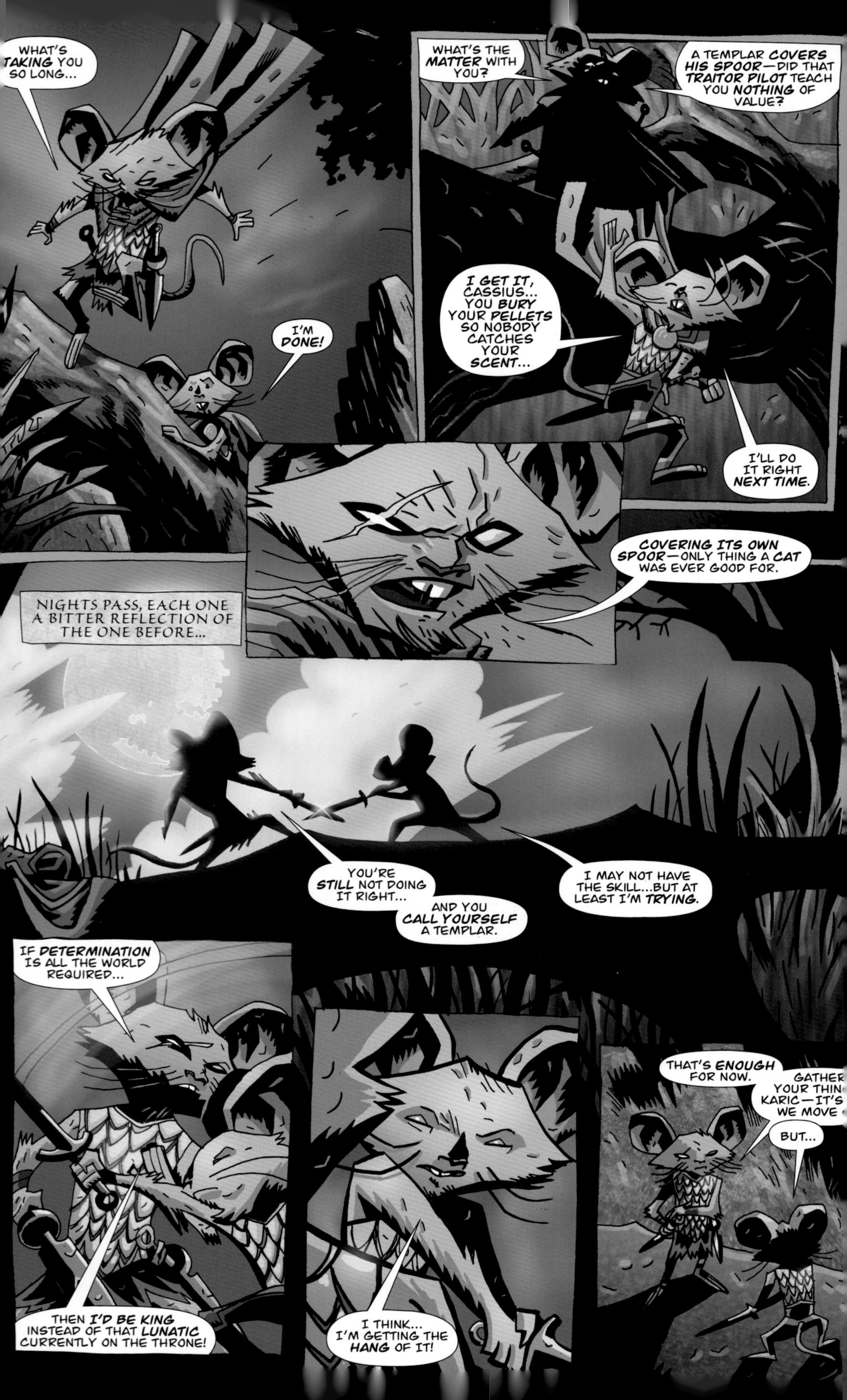
WHAT'S TAKING YOU SO LONG...
I'M DONE!
WHAT'S THE MATTER WITH YOU?
A TEMPLAR COVERS HIS SPOOR—DID THAT TRAITOR PILOT TEACH YOU NOTHING OF VALUE?
I GET IT, CASSIUS... YOU BURY YOUR PELLETS SO NOBODY CATCHES YOUR SCENT...
I'LL DO IT RIGHT NEXT TIME.
COVERING ITS OWN SPOOR—ONLY THING A CAT WAS EVER GOOD FOR.
NIGHTS PASS, EACH ONE A BITTER REFLECTION OF THE ONE BEFORE...
YOU'RE STILL NOT DOING IT RIGHT...
AND YOU CALL YOURSELF A TEMPLAR.
I MAY NOT HAVE THE SKILL...BUT AT LEAST I'M TRYING.
IF DETERMINATION IS ALL THE WORLD REQUIRED...
THEN I'D BE KING INSTEAD OF THAT LUNATIC CURRENTLY ON THE THRONE!
I THINK... I'M GETTING THE HANG OF IT!
THAT'S ENOUGH FOR NOW.
GATHER YOUR THIN KARIC—IT'S WE MOVE
BUT...

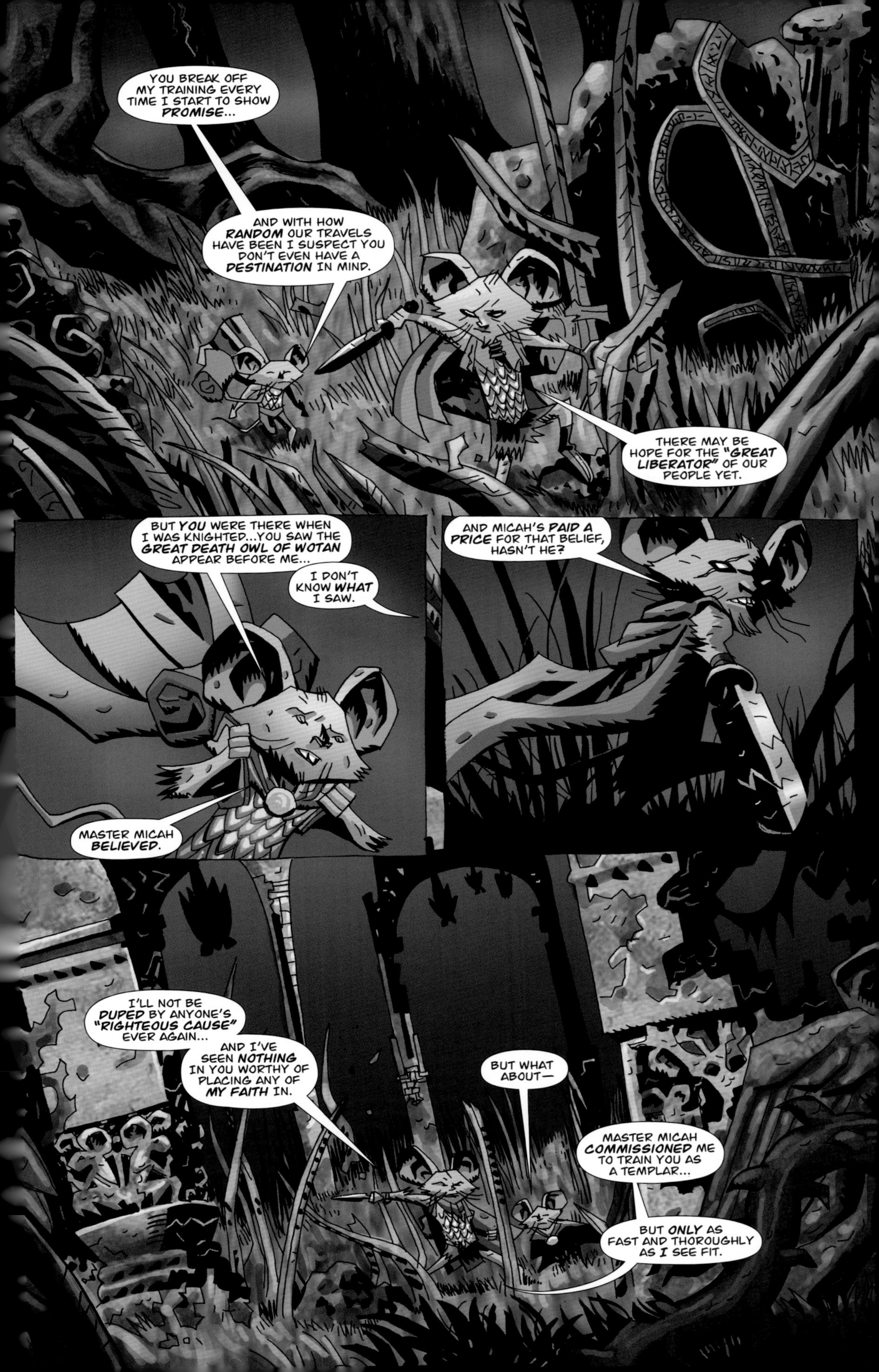
YOU BREAK OFF MY TRAINING EVERY TIME I START TO SHOW PROMISE...
AND WITH HOW RANDOM OUR TRAVELS HAVE BEEN I SUSPECT YOU DON'T EVEN HAVE A DESTINATION IN MIND.
THERE MAY BE HOPE FOR THE "GREAT LIBERATOR" OF OUR PEOPLE YET.
BUT YOU WERE THERE WHEN I WAS KNIGHTED...YOU SAW THE GREAT DEATH OWL OF WOTAN APPEAR BEFORE ME...
I DON'T KNOW WHAT I SAW.
MASTER MICAH BELIEVED.
AND MICAH'S PAID A PRICE FOR THAT BELIEF, HASN'T HE?
I'LL NOT BE DUPED BY ANYONE'S "RIGHTEOUS CAUSE" EVER AGAIN...
AND I'VE SEEN NOTHING IN YOU WORTHY OF PLACING ANY OF MY FAITH IN.
BUT WHAT ABOUT—
MASTER MICAH COMMISSIONED ME TO TRAIN YOU AS A TEMPLAR...
BUT ONLY AS FAST AND THOROUGHLY AS I SEE FIT.

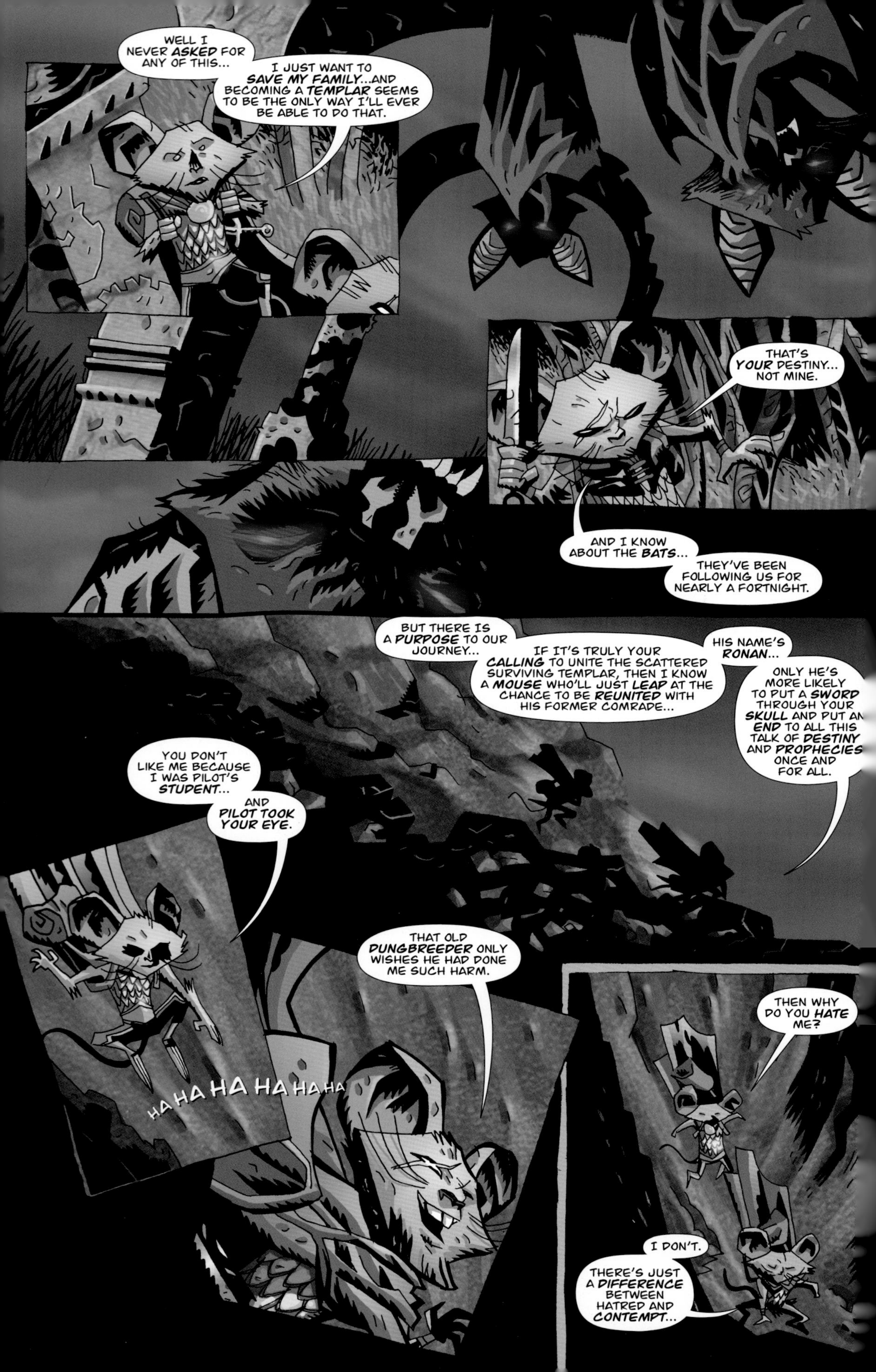

WELL I NEVER ASKED FOR ANY OF THIS...
I JUST WANT TO SAVE MY FAMILY...AND BECOMING A TEMPLAR SEEMS TO BE THE ONLY WAY I'LL EVER BE ABLE TO DO THAT.
THAT'S YOUR DESTINY... NOT MINE.
AND I KNOW ABOUT THE BATS...
THEY'VE BEEN FOLLOWING US FOR NEARLY A FORTNIGHT.
BUT THERE IS A PURPOSE TO OUR JOURNEY...
IF IT'S TRULY YOUR CALLING TO UNITE THE SCATTERED SURVIVING TEMPLAR, THEN I KNOW A MOUSE WHO'LL JUST LEAP AT THE CHANCE TO BE REUNITED WITH HIS FORMER COMRADE...
HIS NAME'S RONAN...
ONLY HE'S MORE LIKELY TO PUT A SWORD THROUGH YOUR SKULL AND PUT AN END TO ALL THIS TALK OF DESTINY AND PROPHECIES ONCE AND FOR ALL.
YOU DON'T LIKE ME BECAUSE I WAS PILOT'S STUDENT...
AND PILOT TOOK YOUR EYE.
HA HA HA HA HA HA
THAT OLD DUNGBREEDER ONLY WISHES HE HAD DONE ME SUCH HARM.
THEN WHY DO YOU HATE ME?
I DON'T.
THERE'S JUST A DIFFERENCE BETWEEN HATRED AND CONTEMPT...

"...AND I'VE LEARNED TO DESPISE THE RECKLESSNESS OF YOUTH."
THEIR JOURNEY CONTINUES, NIGHT AFTER NIGHT, UNTIL A LEGENDARY IMPEDIMENT BLOCKS THEIR COURSE...
CASSIUS...
WE KEEP SKIRTING THE EDGE OF THIS FOREST...SHOULDN'T WE JUST CUT THROUGH IT IF OUR DESTINATION IS TRULY ON THE OTHER SIDE?
TIME FOR ANOTHER LESSON, KARIC...
THIS IS THE HAUNTED WOOD.
AND NO SANE MOUSE SHOULD EVER CROSS ITS THRESHOLD...

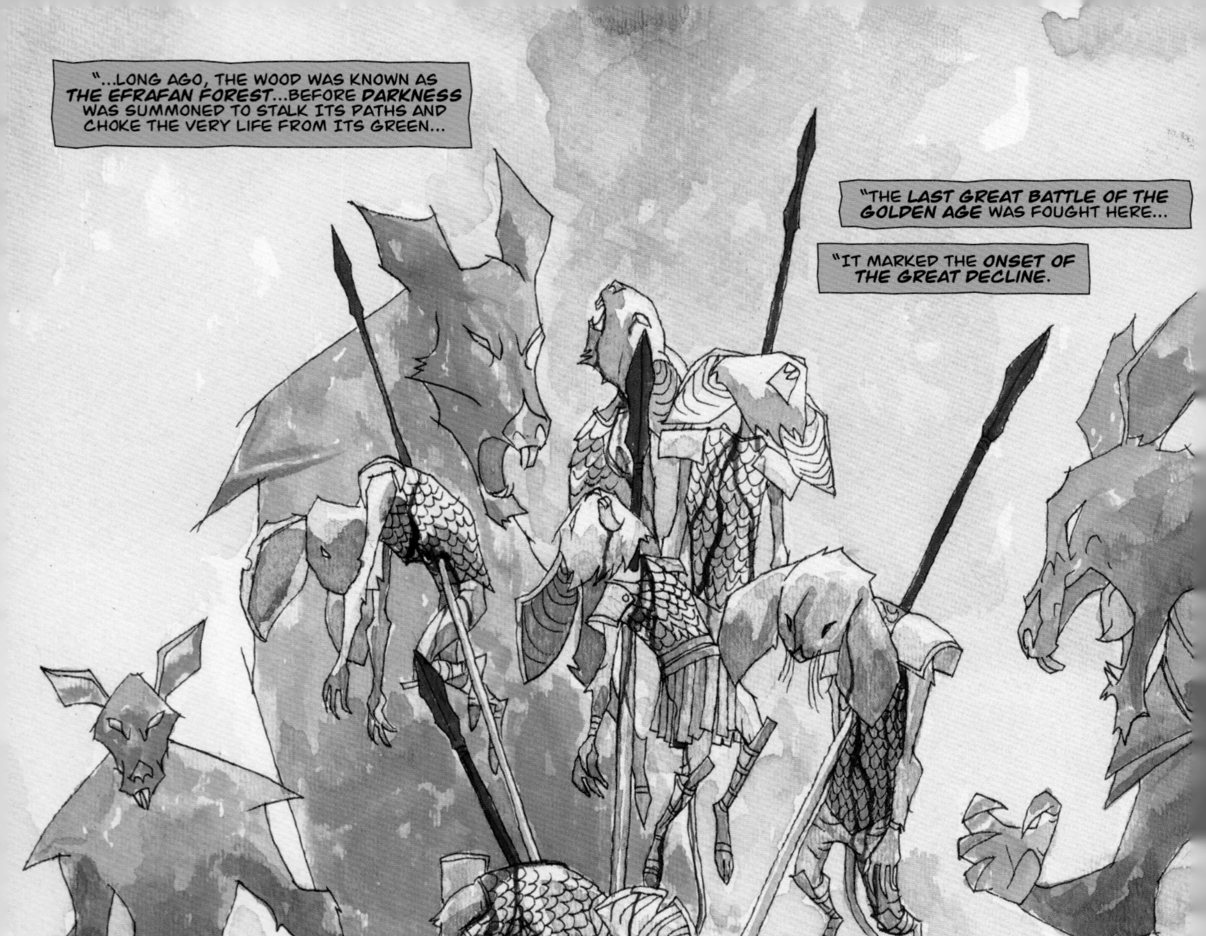
"...LONG AGO, THE WOOD WAS KNOWN AS THE EFRAFAN FOREST...BEFORE DARKNESS WAS SUMMONED TO STALK ITS PATHS AND CHOKE THE VERY LIFE FROM ITS GREEN...
"THE LAST GREAT BATTLE OF THE GOLDEN AGE WAS FOUGHT HERE...
"IT MARKED THE ONSET OF THE GREAT DECLINE.
"IT BEGAN WHEN AN ENTIRE DIVISION OF TEMPLAR ELITE WAS SLAUGHTERED BY A RAT ARMY IMBUED WITH DIABHUL POWER CONJURED INTO THEM BY THEIR DRUID MASTERS.
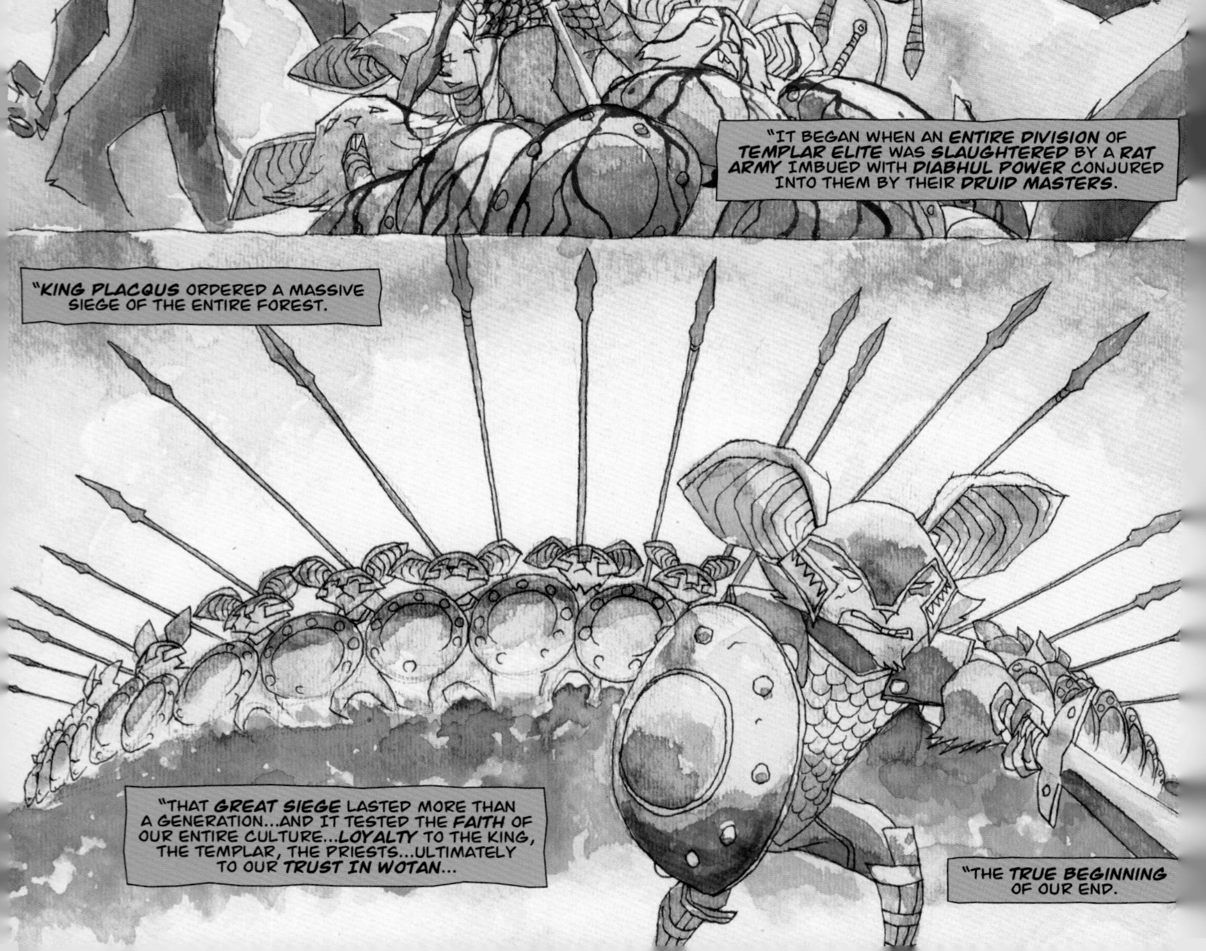
"KING PLACQUS ORDERED A MASSIVE SIEGE OF THE ENTIRE FOREST.
"THAT GREAT SIEGE LASTED MORE THAN A GENERATION...AND IT TESTED THE FAITH OF OUR ENTIRE CULTURE...LOYALTY TO THE KING, THE TEMPLAR, THE PRIESTS...ULTIMATELY TO OUR TRUST IN WOTAN...
"THE TRUE BEGINNING OF OUR END.

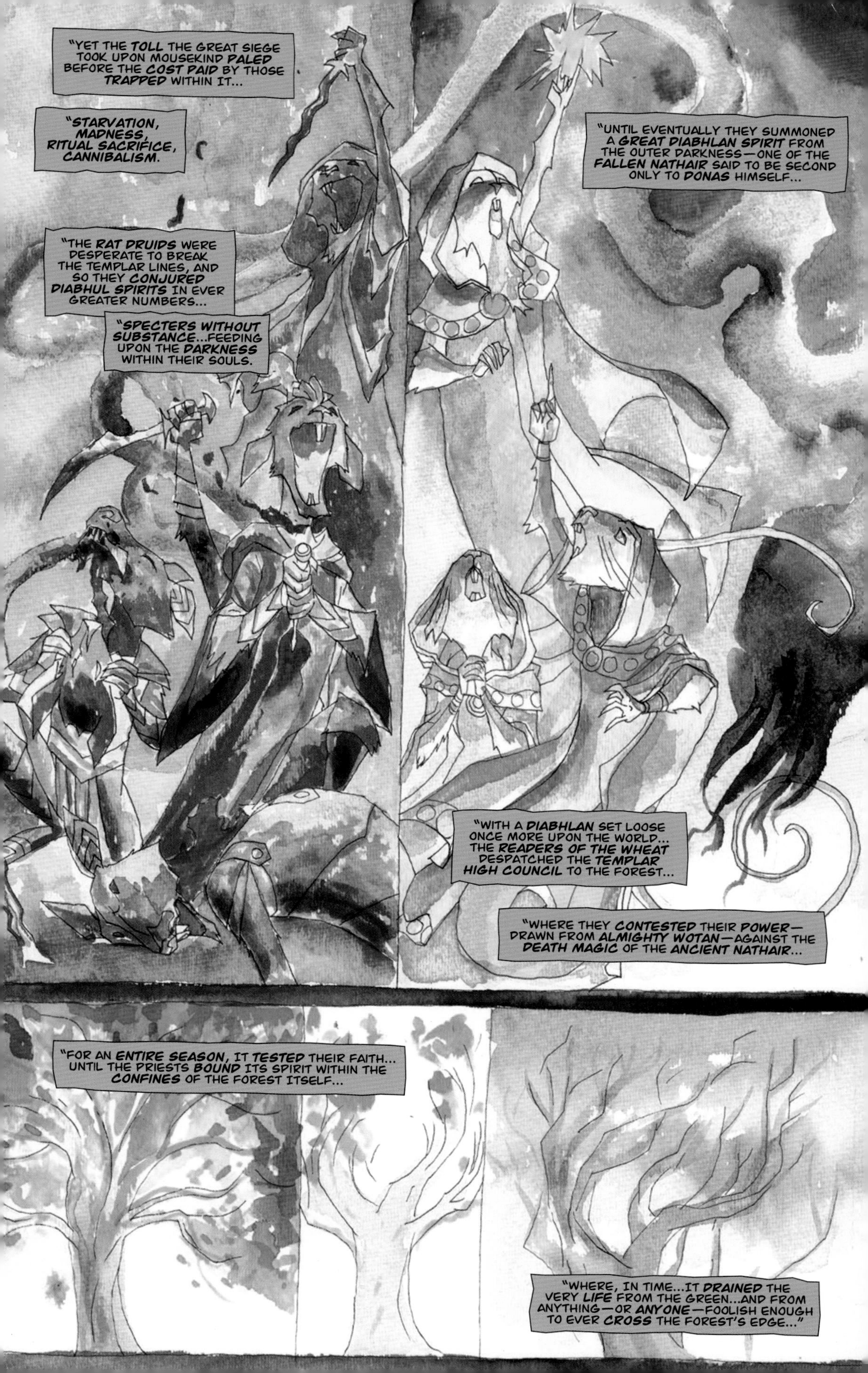
"YET THE TOLL THE GREAT SIEGE TOOK UPON MOUSEKIND PALED BEFORE THE COST PAID BY THOSE TRAPPED WITHIN IT...
"STARVATION, MADNESS, RITUAL SACRIFICE, CANNIBALISM.
"THE RAT DRUIDS WERE DESPERATE TO BREAK THE TEMPLAR LINES, AND SO THEY CONJURED DIABHUL SPIRITS IN EVER GREATER NUMBERS...
"SPECTERS WITHOUT SUBSTANCE...FEEDING UPON THE DARKNESS WITHIN THEIR SOULS.
"UNTIL EVENTUALLY THEY SUMMONED A GREAT DIABHLAN SPIRIT FROM THE OUTER DARKNESS—ONE OF THE FALLEN NATHAIR SAID TO BE SECOND ONLY TO DONAS HIMSELF...
"WITH A DIABHLAN SET LOOSE ONCE MORE UPON THE WORLD... THE READERS OF THE WHEAT DESPATCHED THE TEMPLAR HIGH COUNCIL TO THE FOREST...
"WHERE THEY CONTESTED THEIR POWER—DRAWN FROM ALMIGHTY WOTAN—AGAINST THE DEATH MAGIC OF THE ANCIENT NATHAIR...
"FOR AN ENTIRE SEASON, IT TESTED THEIR FAITH... UNTIL THE PRIESTS BOUND ITS SPIRIT WITHIN THE CONFINES OF THE FOREST ITSELF...
"WHERE, IN TIME...IT DRAINED THE VERY LIFE FROM THE GREEN...AND FROM ANYTHING—OR ANYONE—FOOLISH ENOUGH TO EVER CROSS THE FOREST'S EDGE..."

BUT ALL OF THAT WAS A LONG, LONG TIME AGO...
SOME SUSPECT THAT A PRIEST TOOK A SLIVER OF THAT SPIRIT BACK WITH HIM TO THE GREAT ASH TREE... WHERE IT FED UPON THE ROOTS AND CORRUPTED THE HEART OF THE ORDER...
SOME BELIEVE THAT'S WHY THE READERS DID NOTHING WHEN THE TEMPLAR TURNED UPON THEMSELVES.
WHEN WE TORE OURSELVES APART.
SO...YOU'RE SAYING A MIGHTY TEMPLAR WARRIOR LIKE YOURSELF...
IS TOO AFRAID TO PASS THROUGH SOME FOREST THE PRIESTS CLEARED OUT LONG BEFORE YOU WERE BORN?
GIVE ME YOUR BLADE.
MY SWORD!
THUNK-K-K-K
THERE...

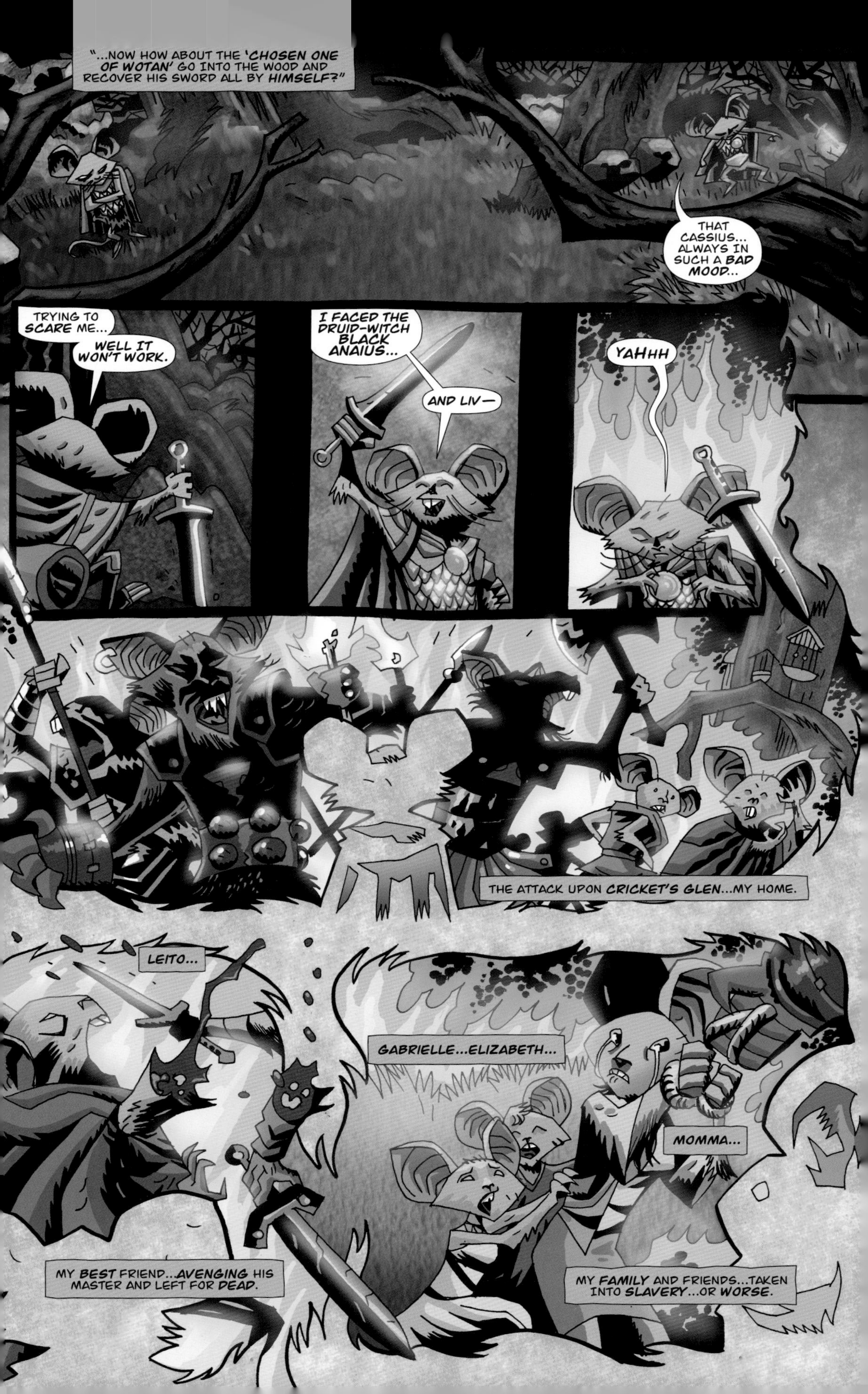
"...NOW HOW ABOUT THE 'CHOSEN ONE OF WOTAN' GO INTO THE WOOD AND RECOVER HIS SWORD ALL BY HIMSELF?"
THAT CASSIUS... ALWAYS IN SUCH A BAD MOOD...
TRYING TO SCARE ME...
WELL IT WON'T WORK.
I FACED THE DRUID-WITCH BLACK ANAIUS...
AND LIV—
YAHHH
THE ATTACK UPON CRICKET'S GLEN...MY HOME.
LEITO...
GABRIELLE...ELIZABETH...
MOMMA...
MY BEST FRIEND...AVENGING HIS MASTER AND LEFT FOR DEAD.
MY FAMILY AND FRIENDS...TAKEN INTO SLAVERY...OR WORSE.

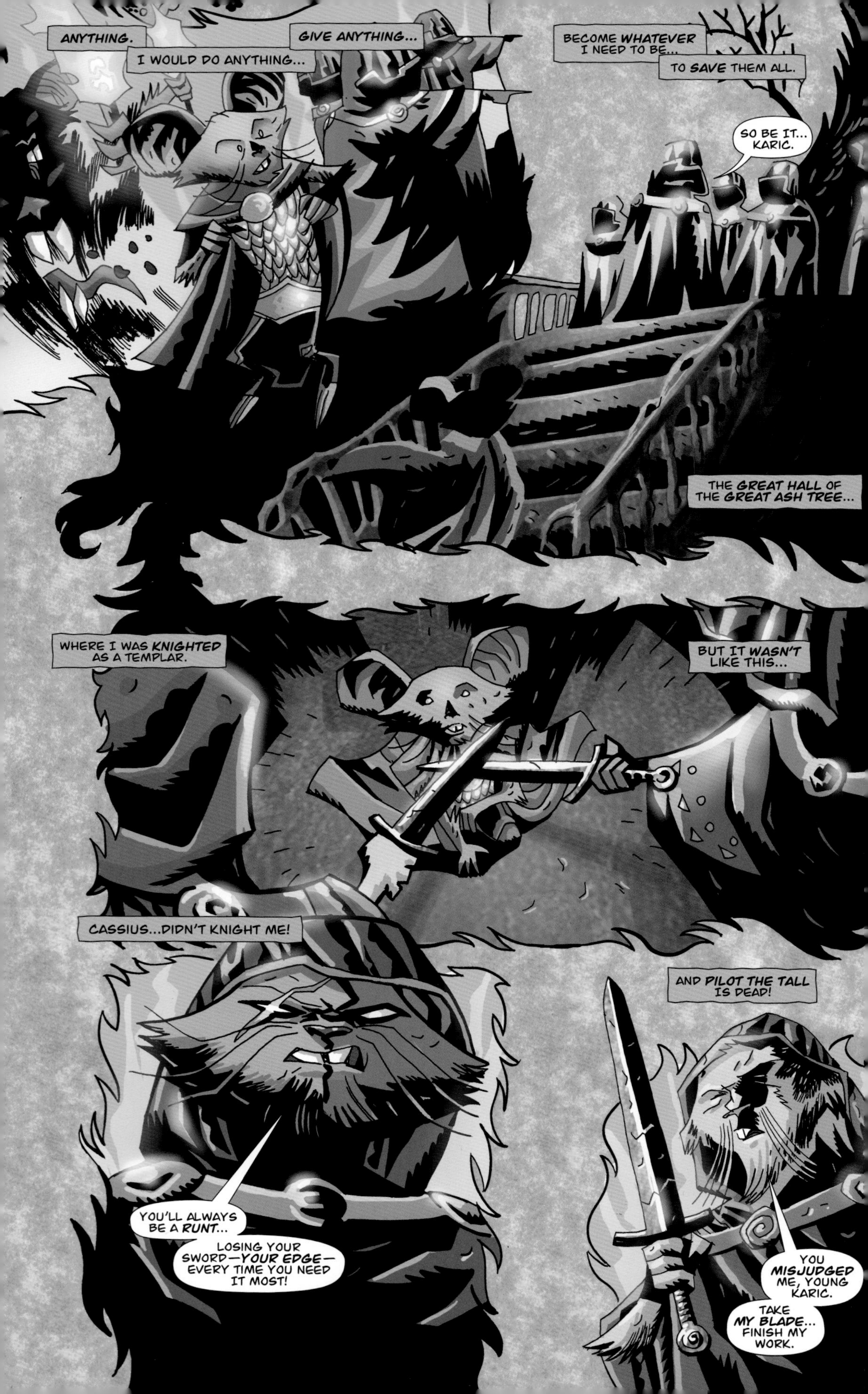
ANYTHING.
I WOULD DO ANYTHING...
GIVE ANYTHING...
BECOME WHATEVER I NEED TO BE...
TO SAVE THEM ALL.
SO BE IT... KARIC.
THE GREAT HALL OF THE GREAT ASH TREE...
WHERE I WAS KNIGHTED AS A TEMPLAR.
BUT IT WASN'T LIKE THIS...
CASSIUS...DIDN'T KNIGHT ME!
YOU'LL ALWAYS BE A RUNT...
LOSING YOUR SWORD—YOUR EDGE—EVERY TIME YOU NEED IT MOST!
AND PILOT THE TALL IS DEAD!
YOU MISJUDGED ME, YOUNG KARIC.
TAKE MY BLADE... FINISH MY WORK.

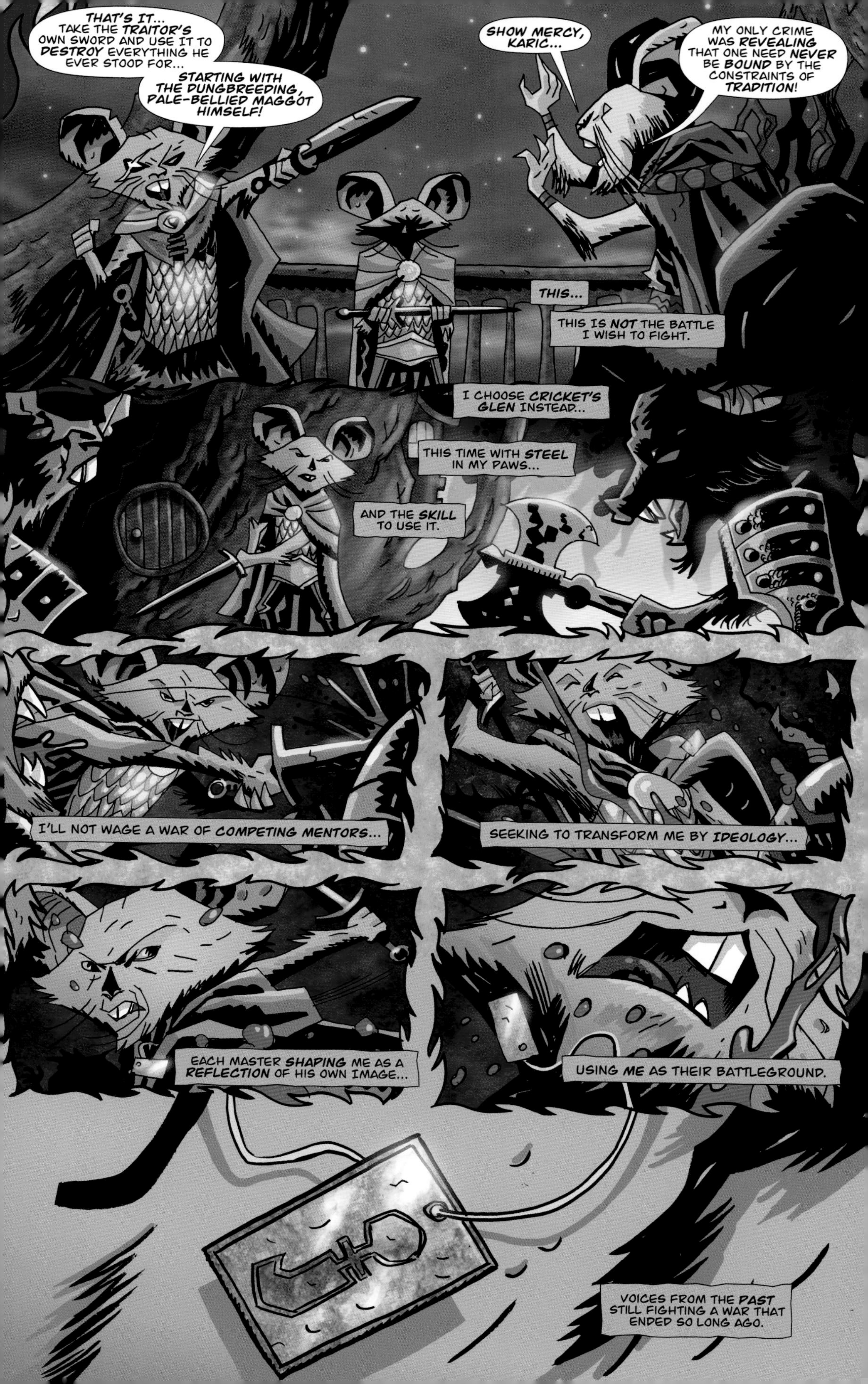
THAT'S IT... TAKE THE TRAITOR'S OWN SWORD AND USE IT TO DESTROY EVERYTHING HE EVER STOOD FOR...
STARTING WITH THE DUNGBREEDING, PALE-BELLIED MAGGOT HIMSELF!
SHOW MERCY, KARIC...
MY ONLY CRIME WAS REVEALING THAT ONE NEED NEVER BE BOUND BY THE CONSTRAINTS OF TRADITION!
THIS...
THIS IS NOT THE BATTLE I WISH TO FIGHT.
I CHOOSE CRICKET'S GLEN INSTEAD...
THIS TIME WITH STEEL IN MY PAWS...
AND THE SKILL TO USE IT.
I'LL NOT WAGE A WAR OF COMPETING MENTORS...
SEEKING TO TRANSFORM ME BY IDEOLOGY...
EACH MASTER SHAPING ME AS A REFLECTION OF HIS OWN IMAGE...
USING ME AS THEIR BATTLEGROUND.
VOICES FROM THE PAST STILL FIGHTING A WAR THAT ENDED SO LONG AGO.

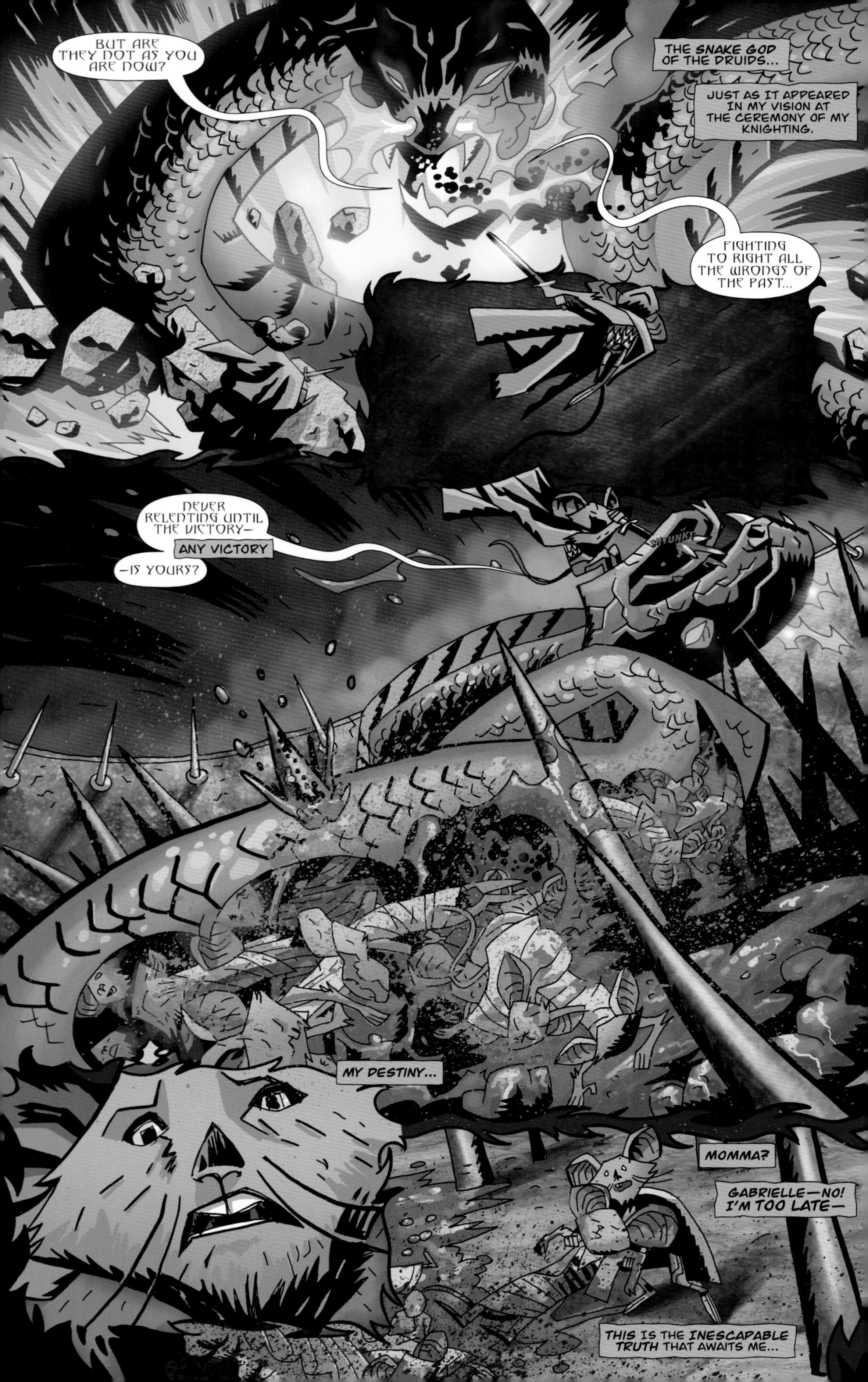

BUT ARE THEY NOT AS YOU ARE NOW?
THE SNAKE GOD OF THE DRUIDS...
JUST AS IT APPEARED IN MY VISION AT THE CEREMONY OF MY KNIGHTING.
FIGHTING TO RIGHT ALL THE WRONGS OF THE PAST...
NEVER RELENTING UNTIL THE VICTORY—
ANY VICTORY
—IS YOURS?
SHUNK!
MY DESTINY...
MOMMA?
GABRIELLE—NO! I'M TOO LATE—
THIS IS THE INESCAPABLE TRUTH THAT AWAITS ME...

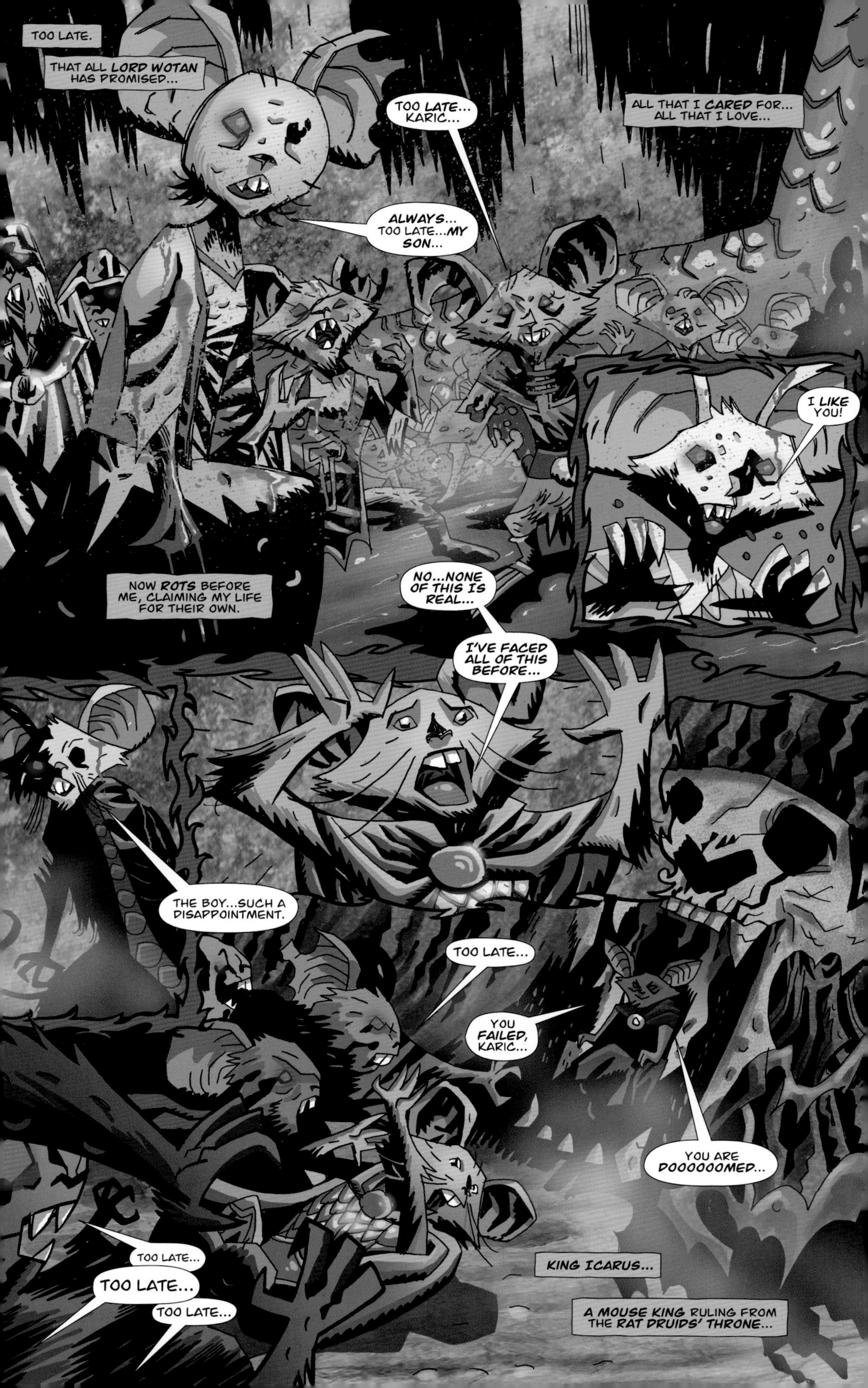
TOO LATE.
THAT ALL LORD WOTAN HAS PROMISED...
TOO LATE... KARIC...
ALL THAT I CARED FOR... ALL THAT I LOVE...
ALWAYS... TOO LATE...MY SON...
I LIKE YOU!
NOW ROTS BEFORE ME, CLAIMING MY LIFE FOR THEIR OWN.
NO...NONE OF THIS IS REAL...
I'VE FACED ALL OF THIS BEFORE...
THE BOY...SUCH A DISAPPOINTMENT.
TOO LATE...
YOU FAILED, KARIC...
YOU ARE DOOOOOOMED...
TOO LATE...
TOO LATE...
TOO LATE...
KING ICARUS...
A MOUSE KING RULING FROM THE RAT DRUIDS' THRONE...

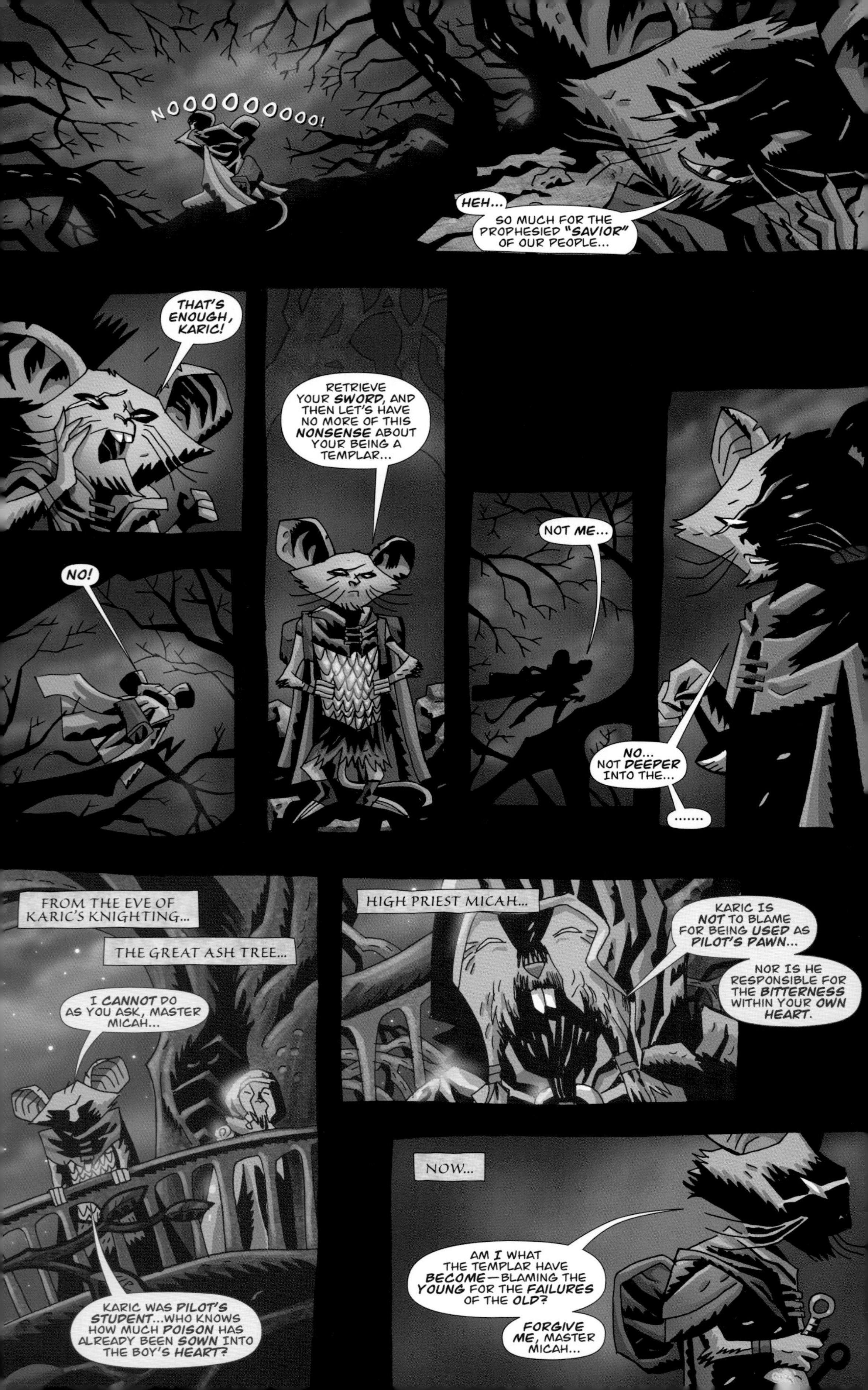

NOOOOOOOOOO!
HEH... SO MUCH FOR THE PROPHESIED "SAVIOR" OF OUR PEOPLE...
THAT'S ENOUGH, KARIC!
NO!
RETRIEVE YOUR SWORD, AND THEN LET'S HAVE NO MORE OF THIS NONSENSE ABOUT YOUR BEING A TEMPLAR...
NOT ME...
NO... NOT DEEPER INTO THE...
....
FROM THE EVE OF KARIC'S KNIGHTING...
THE GREAT ASH TREE...
I CANNOT DO AS YOU ASK, MASTER MICAH...
KARIC WAS PILOT'S STUDENT...WHO KNOWS HOW MUCH POISON HAS ALREADY BEEN SOWN INTO THE BOY'S HEART?
HIGH PRIEST MICAH...
KARIC IS NOT TO BLAME FOR BEING USED AS PILOT'S PAWN...
NOR IS HE RESPONSIBLE FOR THE BITTERNESS WITHIN YOUR OWN HEART.
NOW...
AM I WHAT THE TEMPLAR HAVE BECOME—BLAMING THE YOUNG FOR THE FAILURES OF THE OLD?
FORGIVE ME, MASTER MICAH...

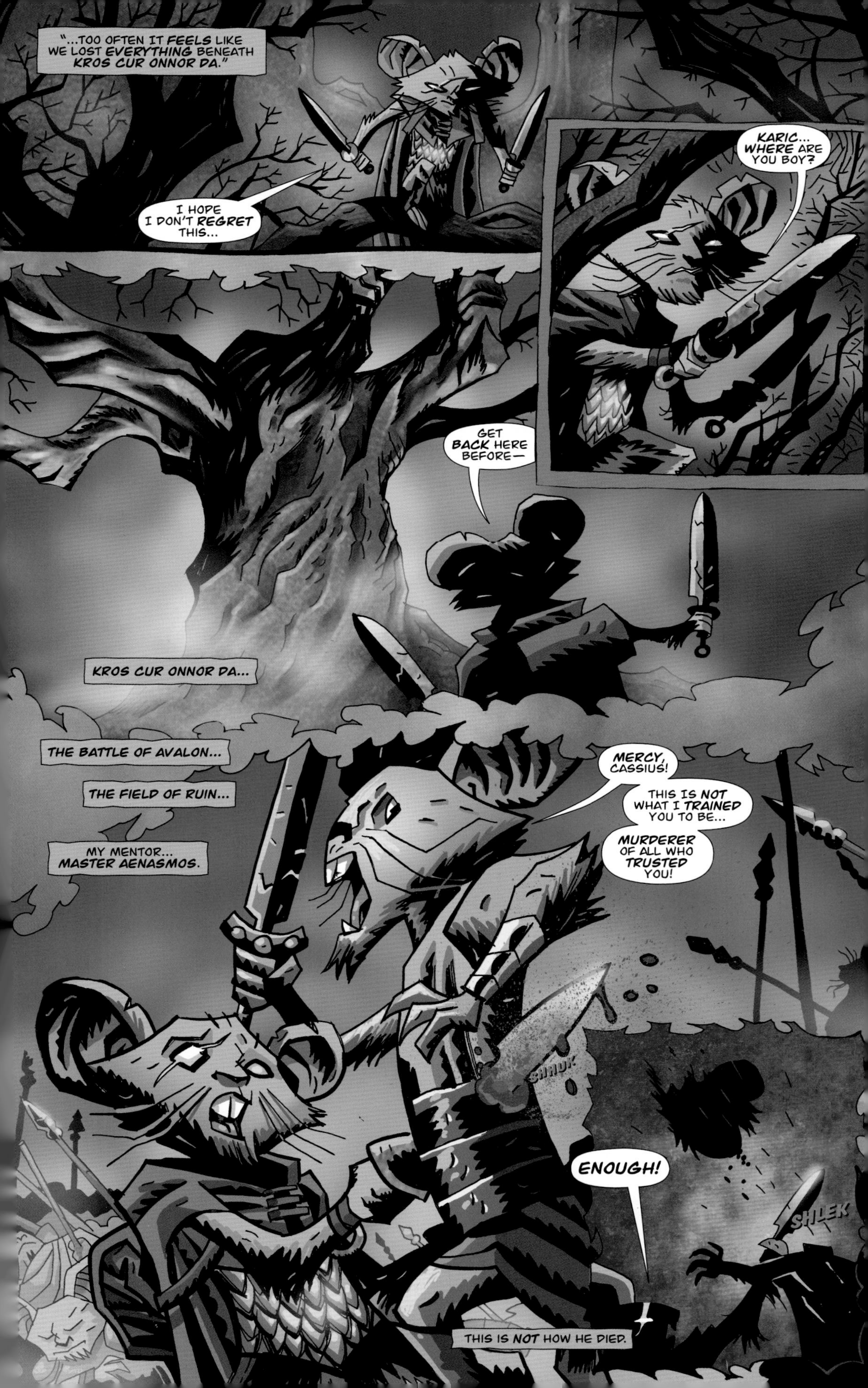
"...TOO OFTEN IT FEELS LIKE WE LOST EVERYTHING BENEATH KROS CUR ONNOR DA."
I HOPE I DON'T REGRET THIS...
KARIC... WHERE ARE YOU BOY?
GET BACK HERE BEFORE—
KROS CUR ONNOR DA...
THE BATTLE OF AVALON...
THE FIELD OF RUIN...
MY MENTOR... MASTER AENASMOS.
MERCY, CASSIUS!
THIS IS NOT WHAT I TRAINED YOU TO BE...
MURDERER OF ALL WHO TRUSTED YOU!
SHRUK
ENOUGH!
SHLEK
THIS IS NOT HOW HE DIED.

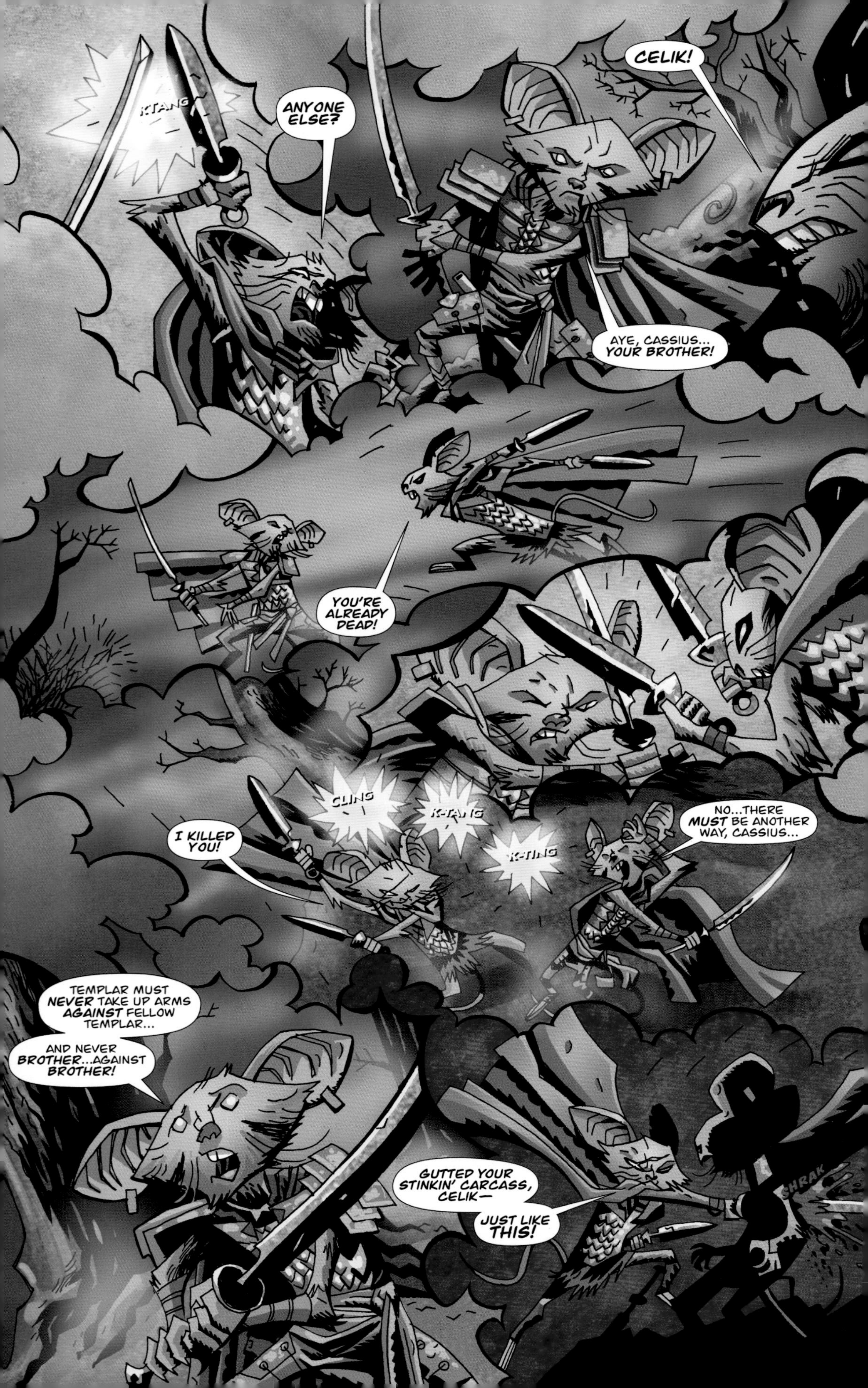
KTANG
ANYONE ELSE?
CELIK!
AYE, CASSIUS... YOUR BROTHER!
YOU'RE ALREADY DEAD!
CLING
K-TANG
K-TING
I KILLED YOU!
NO...THERE MUST BE ANOTHER WAY, CASSIUS...
TEMPLAR MUST NEVER TAKE UP ARMS AGAINST FELLOW TEMPLAR...
AND NEVER BROTHER...AGAINST BROTHER!
GUTTED YOUR STINKIN' CARCASS, CELIK—
JUST LIKE THIS!
SHRAK

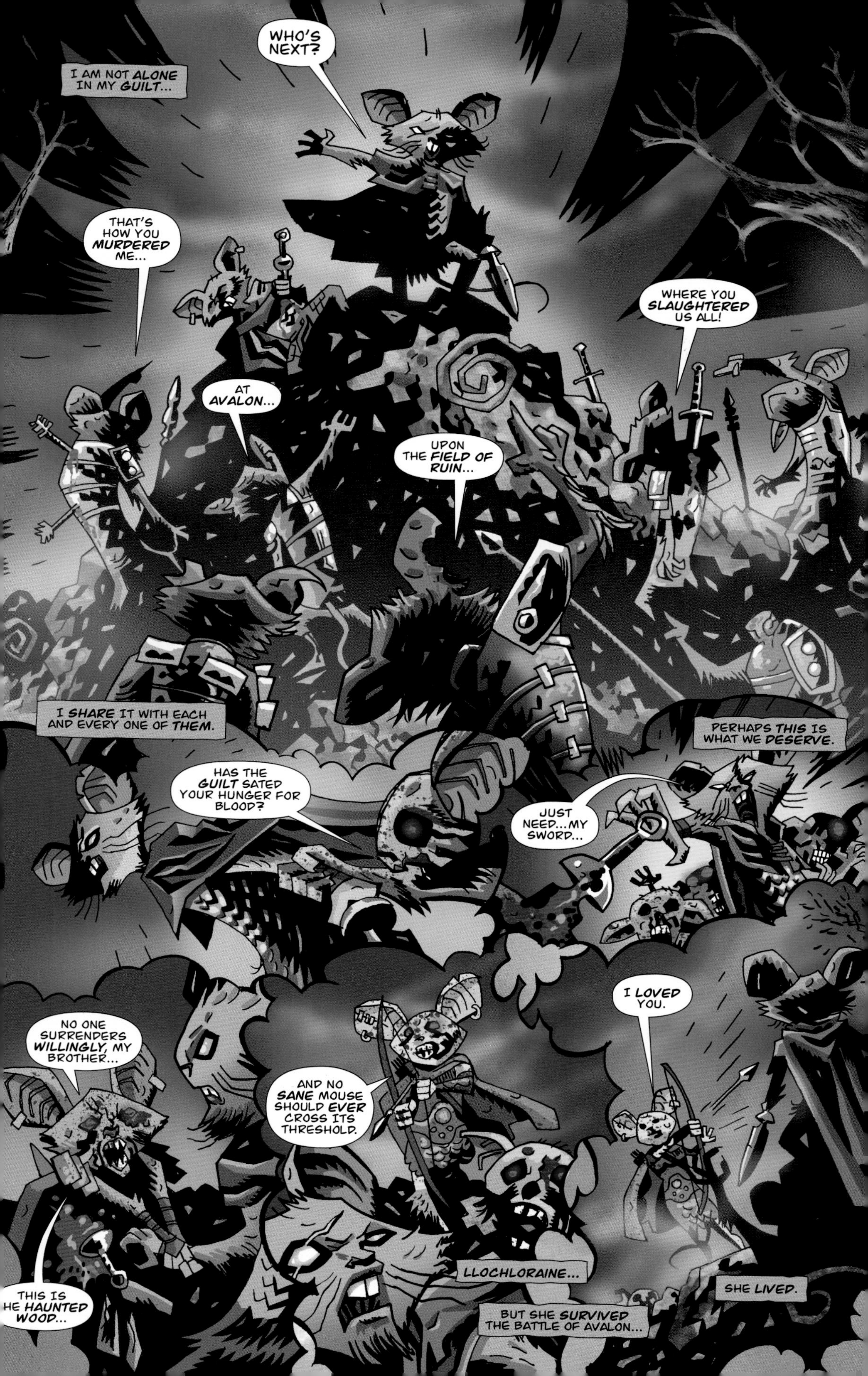
I AM NOT ALONE IN MY GUILT...
WHO'S NEXT?
THAT'S HOW YOU MURDERED ME...
AT AVALON...
UPON THE FIELD OF RUIN...
WHERE YOU SLAUGHTERED US ALL!
I SHARE IT WITH EACH AND EVERY ONE OF THEM.
PERHAPS THIS IS WHAT WE DESERVE.
HAS THE GUILT SATED YOUR HUNGER FOR BLOOD?
JUST NEED...MY SWORD...
NO ONE SURRENDERS WILLINGLY, MY BROTHER...
AND NO SANE MOUSE SHOULD EVER CROSS ITS THRESHOLD.
I LOVED YOU.
THIS IS HE HAUNTED WOOD...
LLOCHLORAINE...
BUT SHE SURVIVED THE BATTLE OF AVALON...
SHE LIVED.

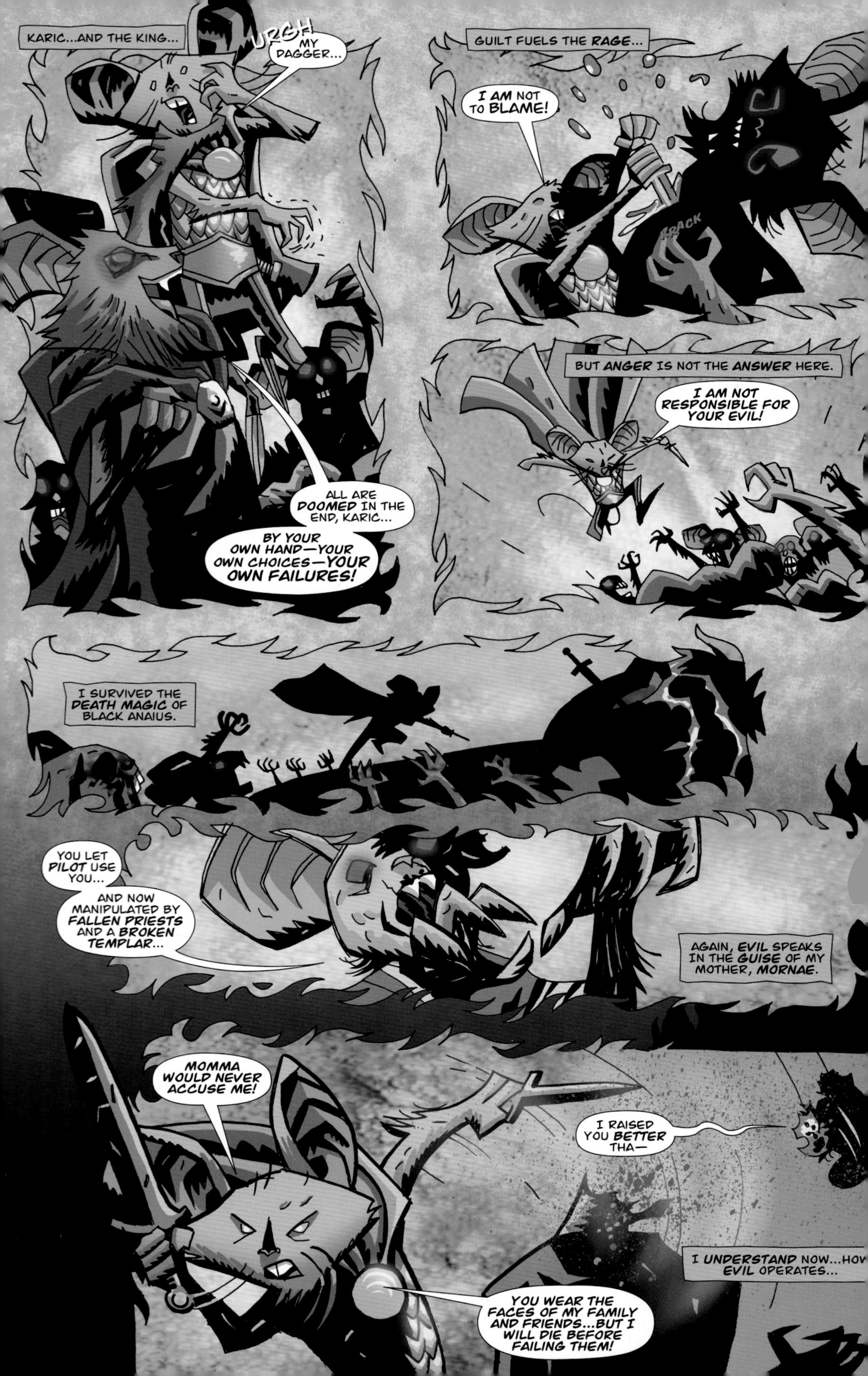
KARIC...AND THE KING...
URGH
MY DAGGER...
ALL ARE DOOMED IN THE END, KARIC...
BY YOUR OWN HAND—YOUR OWN CHOICES—YOUR OWN FAILURES!
GUILT FUELS THE RAGE...
I AM NOT TO BLAME!
KRACK
BUT ANGER IS NOT THE ANSWER HERE.
I AM NOT RESPONSIBLE FOR YOUR EVIL!
I SURVIVED THE DEATH MAGIC OF BLACK ANAIUS.
YOU LET PILOT USE YOU...
AND NOW MANIPULATED BY FALLEN PRIESTS AND A BROKEN TEMPLAR...
AGAIN, EVIL SPEAKS IN THE GUISE OF MY MOTHER, MORNAE.
MOMMA WOULD NEVER ACCUSE ME!
I RAISED YOU BETTER THA—
I UNDERSTAND NOW...HOW EVIL OPERATES...
YOU WEAR THE FACES OF MY FAMILY AND FRIENDS...BUT I WILL DIE BEFORE FAILING THEM!

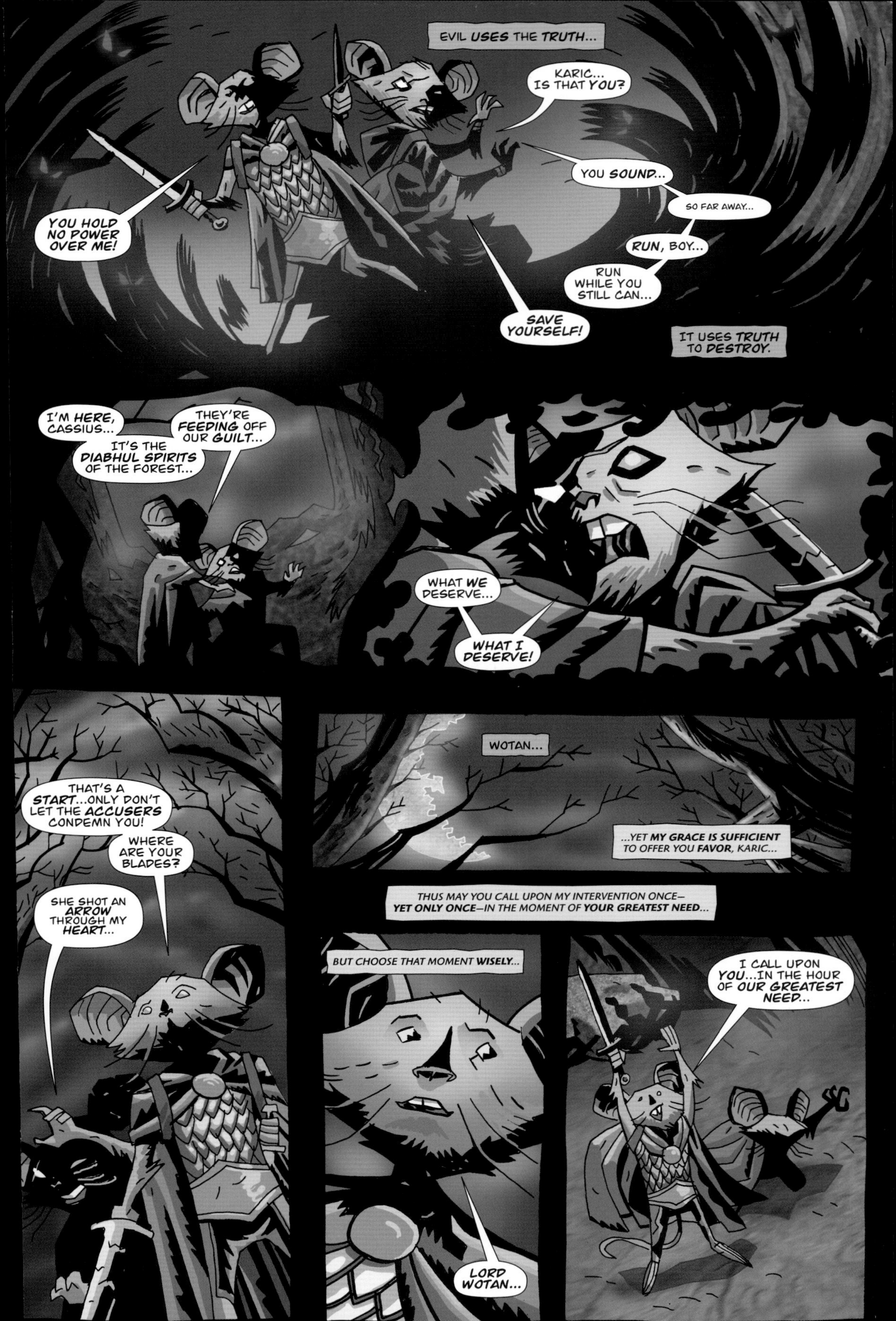
EVIL USES THE TRUTH...
KARIC... IS THAT YOU?
YOU HOLD NO POWER OVER ME!
YOU SOUND...
SO FAR AWAY...
RUN, BOY...
RUN WHILE YOU STILL CAN...
SAVE YOURSELF!
IT USES TRUTH TO DESTROY.
I'M HERE, CASSIUS...
IT'S THE DIABHUL SPIRITS OF THE FOREST...
THEY'RE FEEDING OFF OUR GUILT...
WHAT WE DESERVE...
WHAT I DESERVE!
THAT'S A START...ONLY DON'T LET THE ACCUSERS CONDEMN YOU!
WHERE ARE YOUR BLADES?
SHE SHOT AN ARROW THROUGH MY HEART...
WOTAN...
...YET MY GRACE IS SUFFICIENT TO OFFER YOU FAVOR, KARIC...
THUS MAY YOU CALL UPON MY INTERVENTION ONCE—
YET ONLY ONCE—IN THE MOMENT OF YOUR GREATEST NEED...
BUT CHOOSE THAT MOMENT WISELY...
LORD WOTAN...
I CALL UPON YOU...IN THE HOUR OF OUR GREATEST NEED...

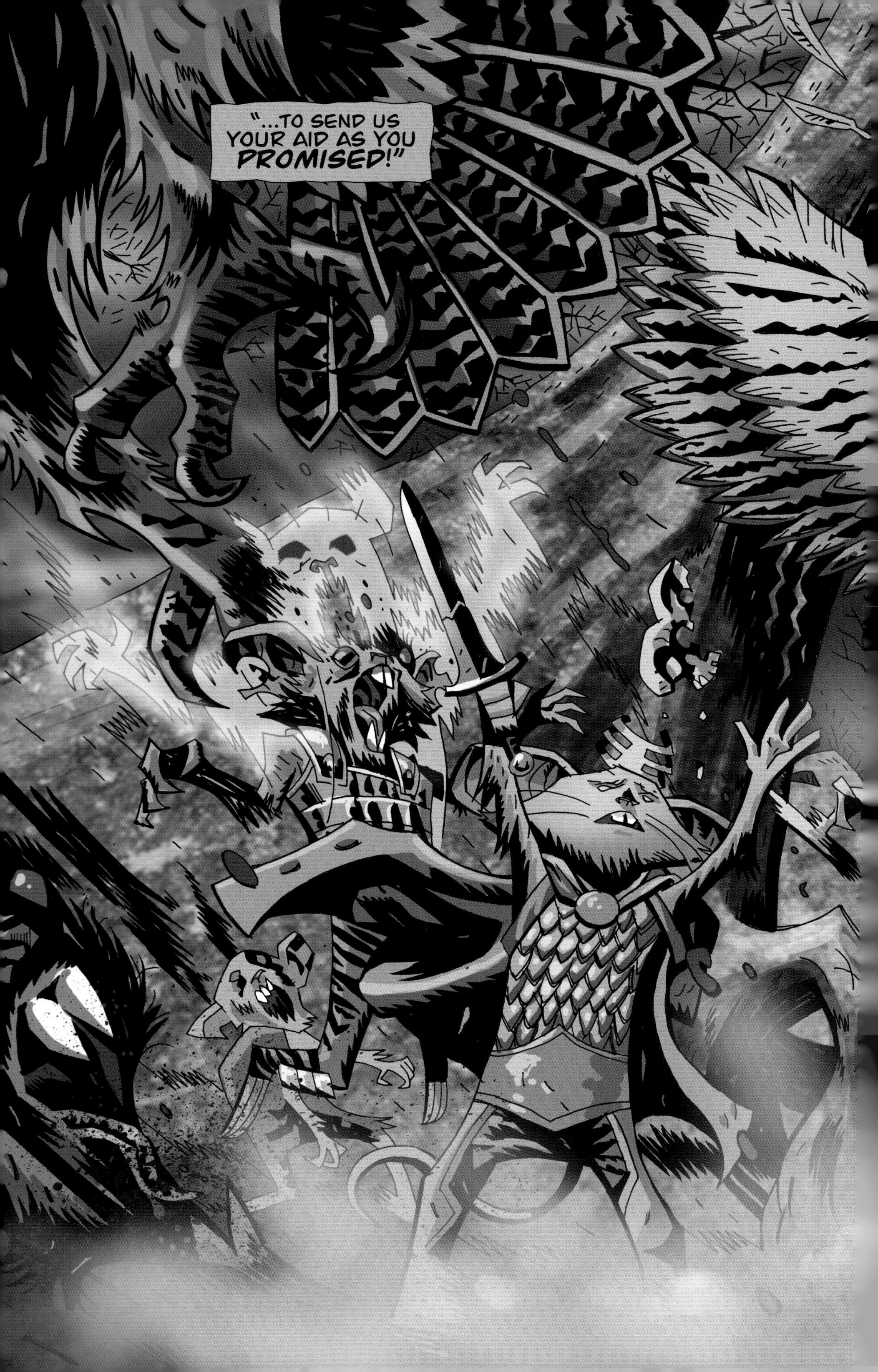
"...TO SEND US YOUR AID AS YOU PROMISED!"

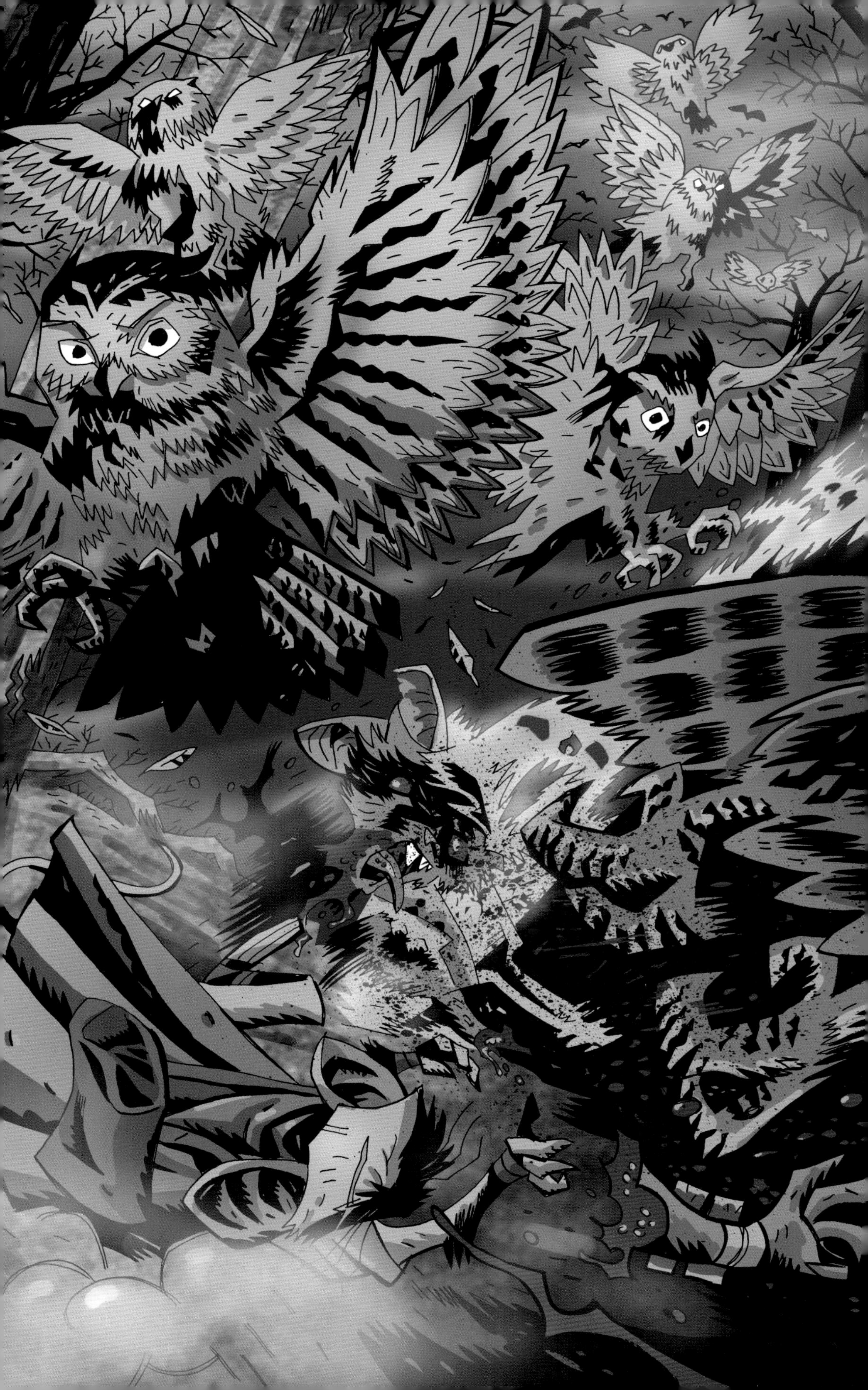

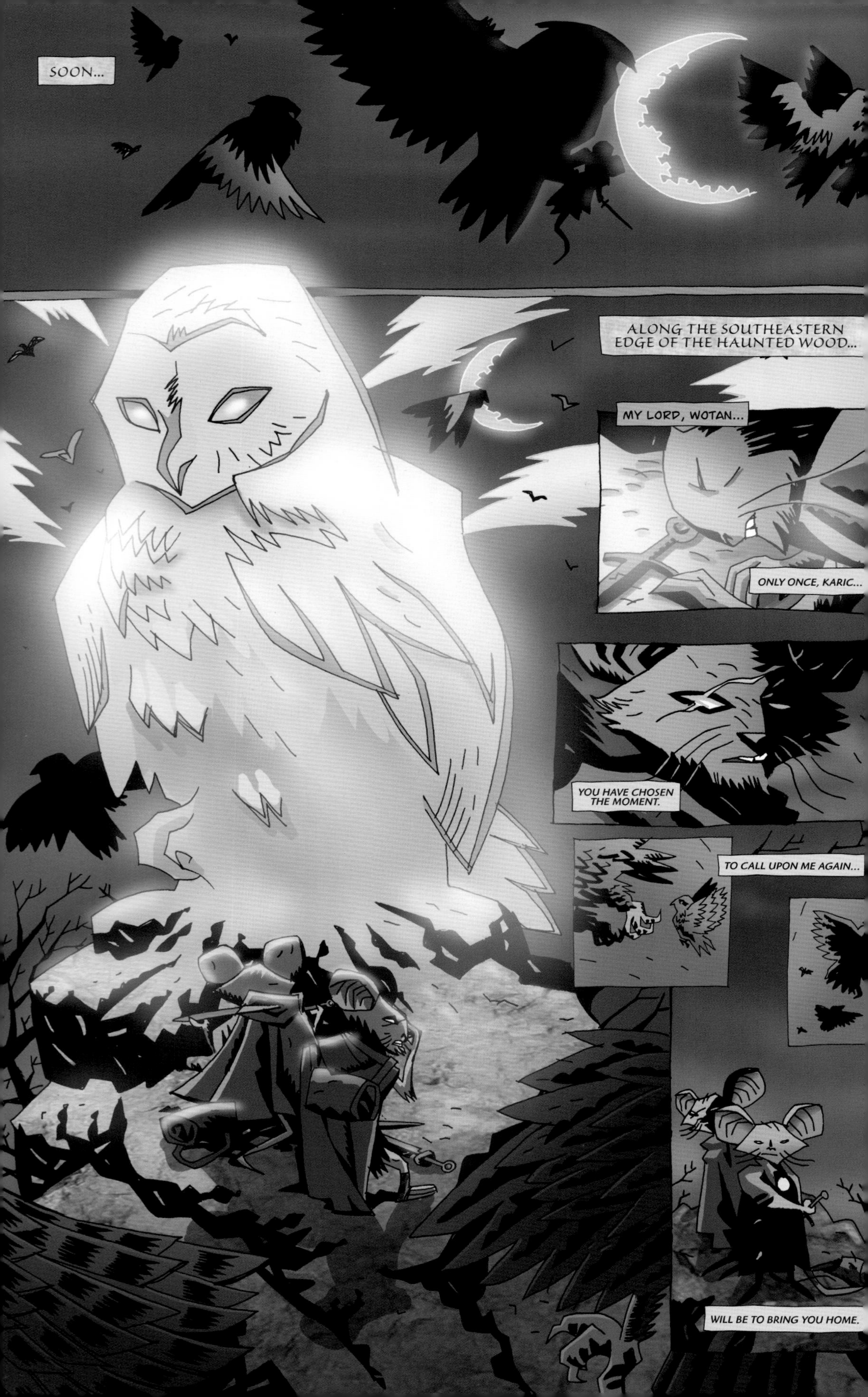
SOON...
ALONG THE SOUTHEASTERN EDGE OF THE HAUNTED WOOD...
MY LORD, WOTAN...
ONLY ONCE, KARIC...
YOU HAVE CHOSEN THE MOMENT.
TO CALL UPON ME AGAIN...
WILL BE TO BRING YOU HOME.

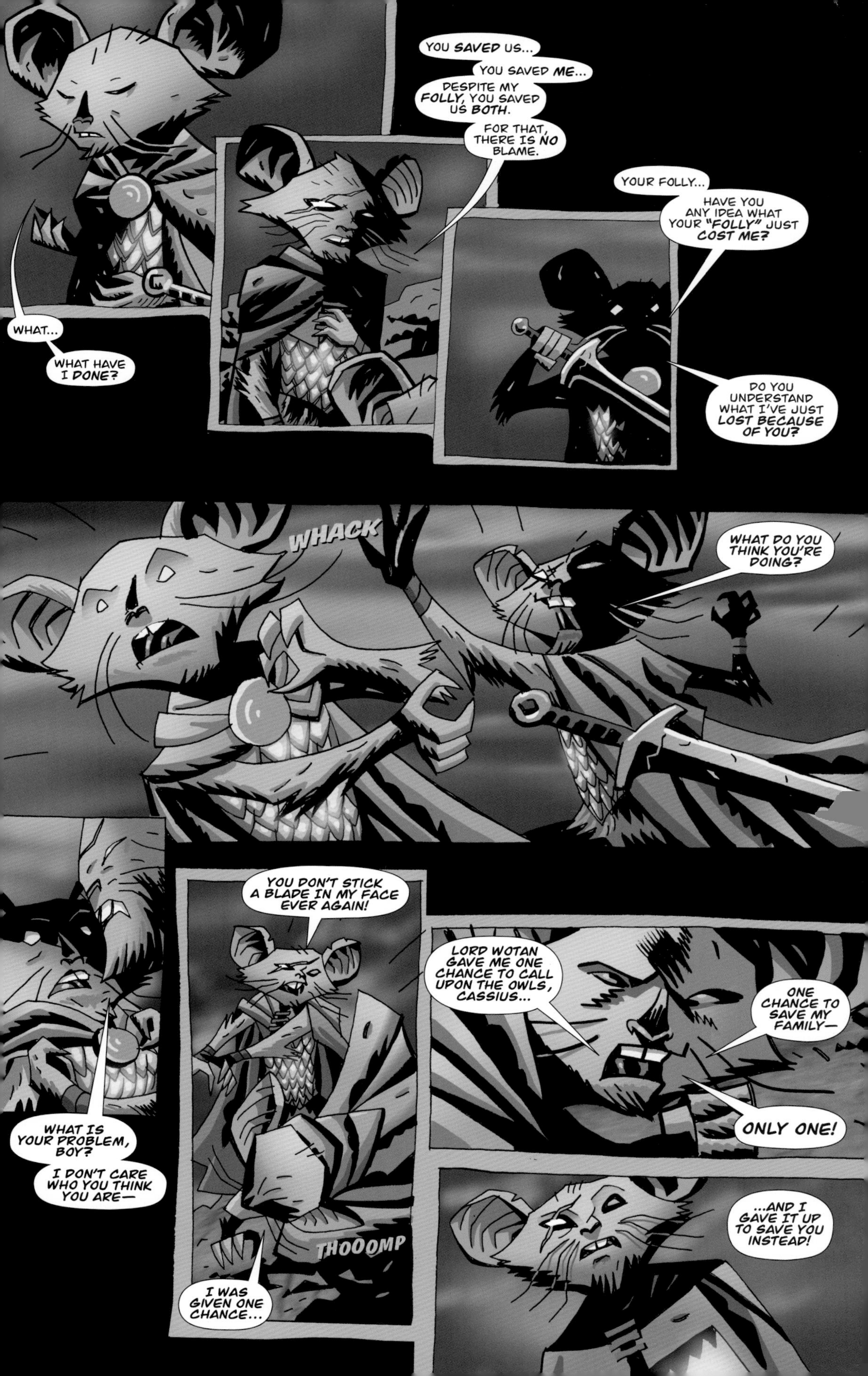

YOU SAVED US...
YOU SAVED ME...
DESPITE MY FOLLY, YOU SAVED US BOTH.
FOR THAT, THERE IS NO BLAME.
WHAT...
WHAT HAVE I DONE?
YOUR FOLLY...
HAVE YOU ANY IDEA WHAT YOUR "FOLLY" JUST COST ME?
DO YOU UNDERSTAND WHAT I'VE JUST LOST BECAUSE OF YOU?
WHACK
WHAT DO YOU THINK YOU'RE DOING?
WHAT IS YOUR PROBLEM, BOY?
I DON'T CARE WHO YOU THINK YOU ARE—
YOU DON'T STICK A BLADE IN MY FACE EVER AGAIN!
THOOOMP
I WAS GIVEN ONE CHANCE...
LORD WOTAN GAVE ME ONE CHANCE TO CALL UPON THE OWLS, CASSIUS...
ONE CHANCE TO SAVE MY FAMILY—
ONLY ONE!
...AND I GAVE IT UP TO SAVE YOU INSTEAD!

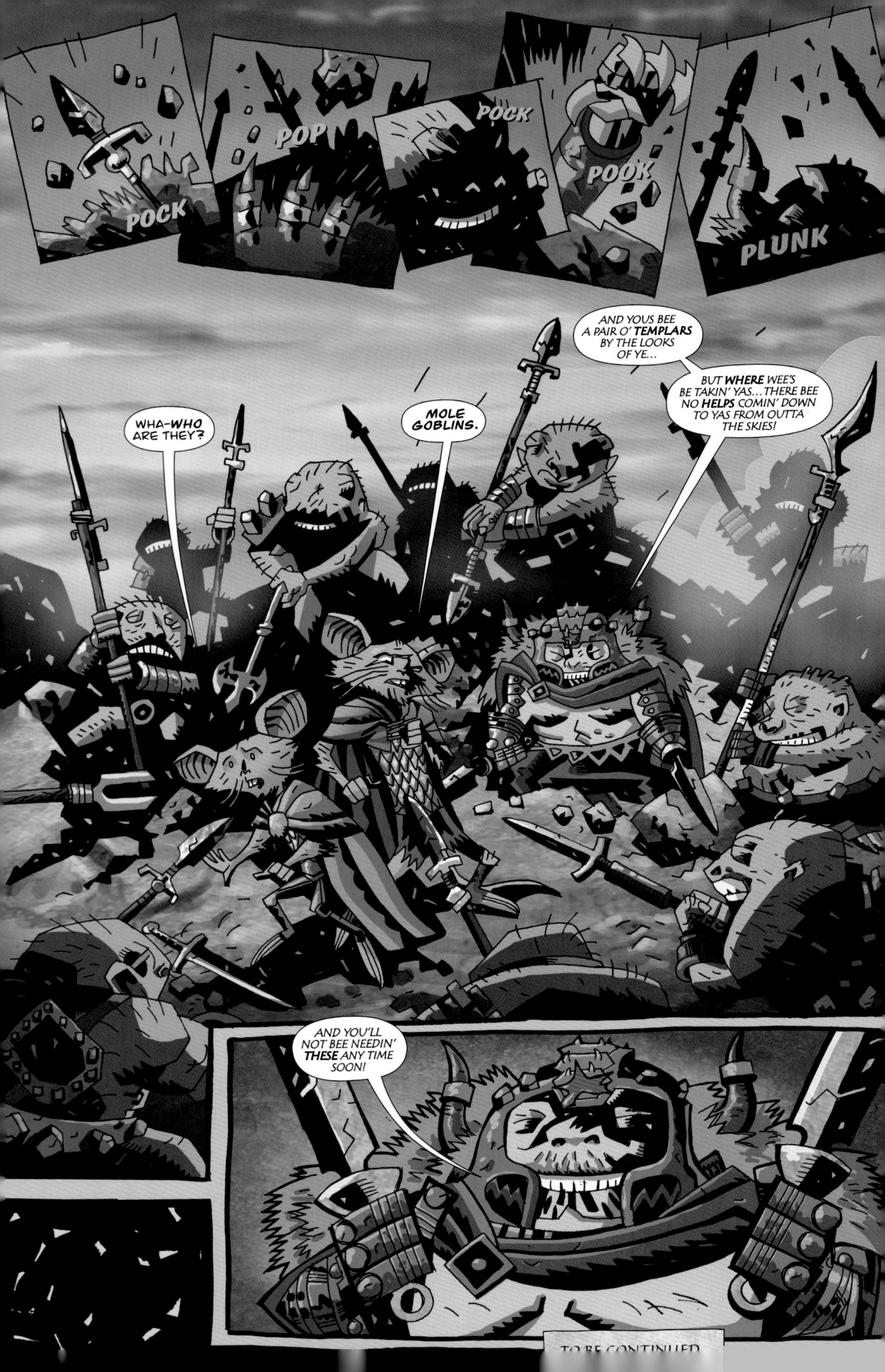
POCK
POP
POCK
POOK
PLUNK
WHA-WHO ARE THEY?
MOLE GOBLINS.
AND YOUS BEE A PAIR O' TEMPLARS BY THE LOOKS OF YE...
BUT WHERE WEE'S BE TAKIN' YAS...THERE BEE NO HELPS COMIN' DOWN TO YAS FROM OUTTA THE SKIES!
AND YOU'LL NOT BEE NEEDIN' THESE ANY TIME SOON!

CHAPTER TWO

IN THE BOWELS OF THE EARTH

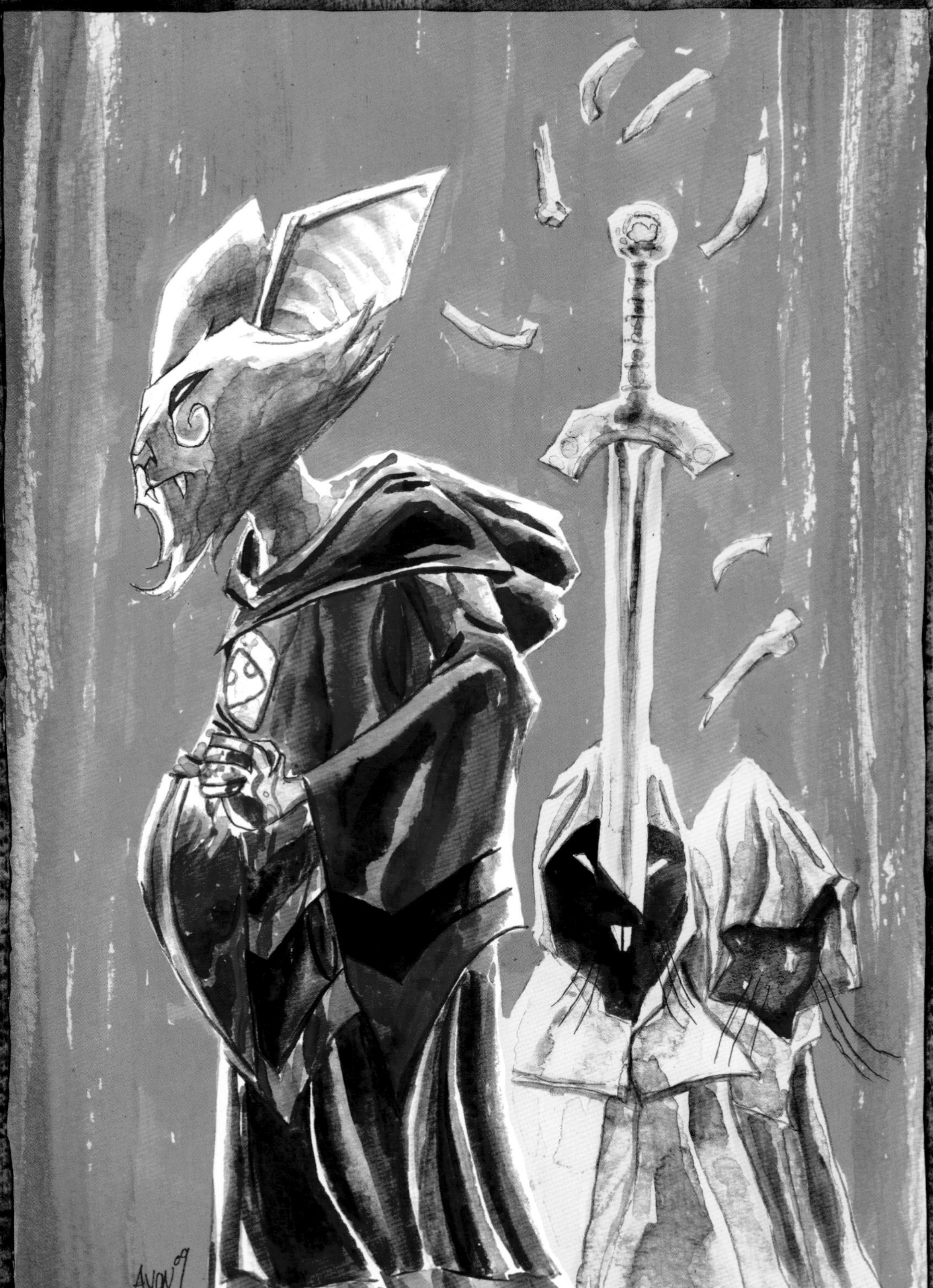

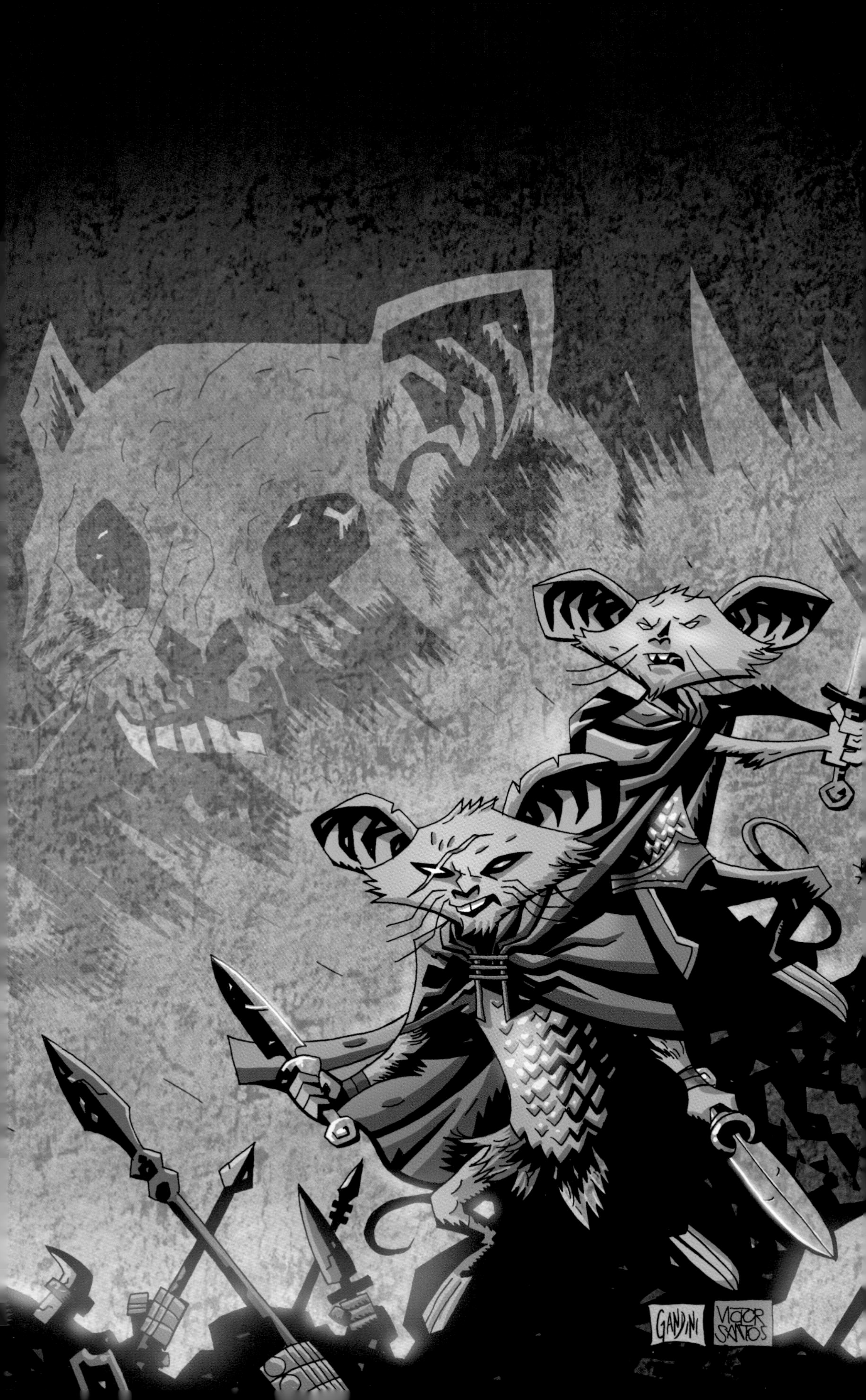
GANDINI
VICTOR SANTOS

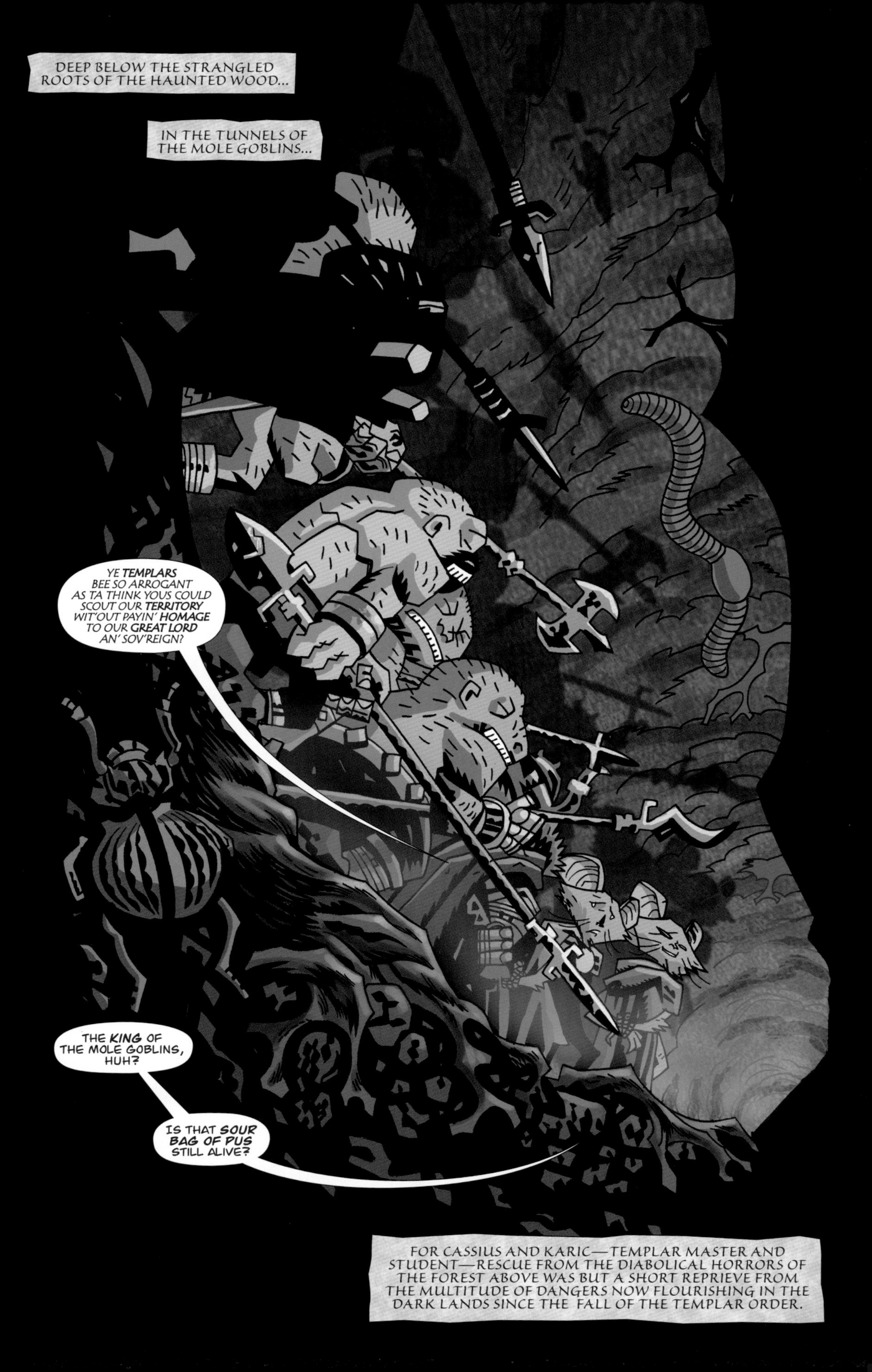

DEEP BELOW THE STRANGLED ROOTS OF THE HAUNTED WOOD...
IN THE TUNNELS OF THE MOLE GOBLINS...
YE TEMPLARS BEE SO ARROGANT AS TA THINK YOUS COULD SCOUT OUR TERRITORY WIT'OUT PAYIN' HOMAGE TO OUR GREAT LORD AN' SOV'REIGN?
THE KING OF THE MOLE GOBLINS, HUH?
IS THAT SOUR BAG OF PUS STILL ALIVE?
FOR CASSIUS AND KARIC—TEMPLAR MASTER AND STUDENT—RESCUE FROM THE DIABOLICAL HORRORS OF THE FOREST ABOVE WAS BUT A SHORT REPRIEVE FROM THE MULTITUDE OF DANGERS NOW FLOURISHING IN THE DARK LANDS SINCE THE FALL OF THE TEMPLAR ORDER.

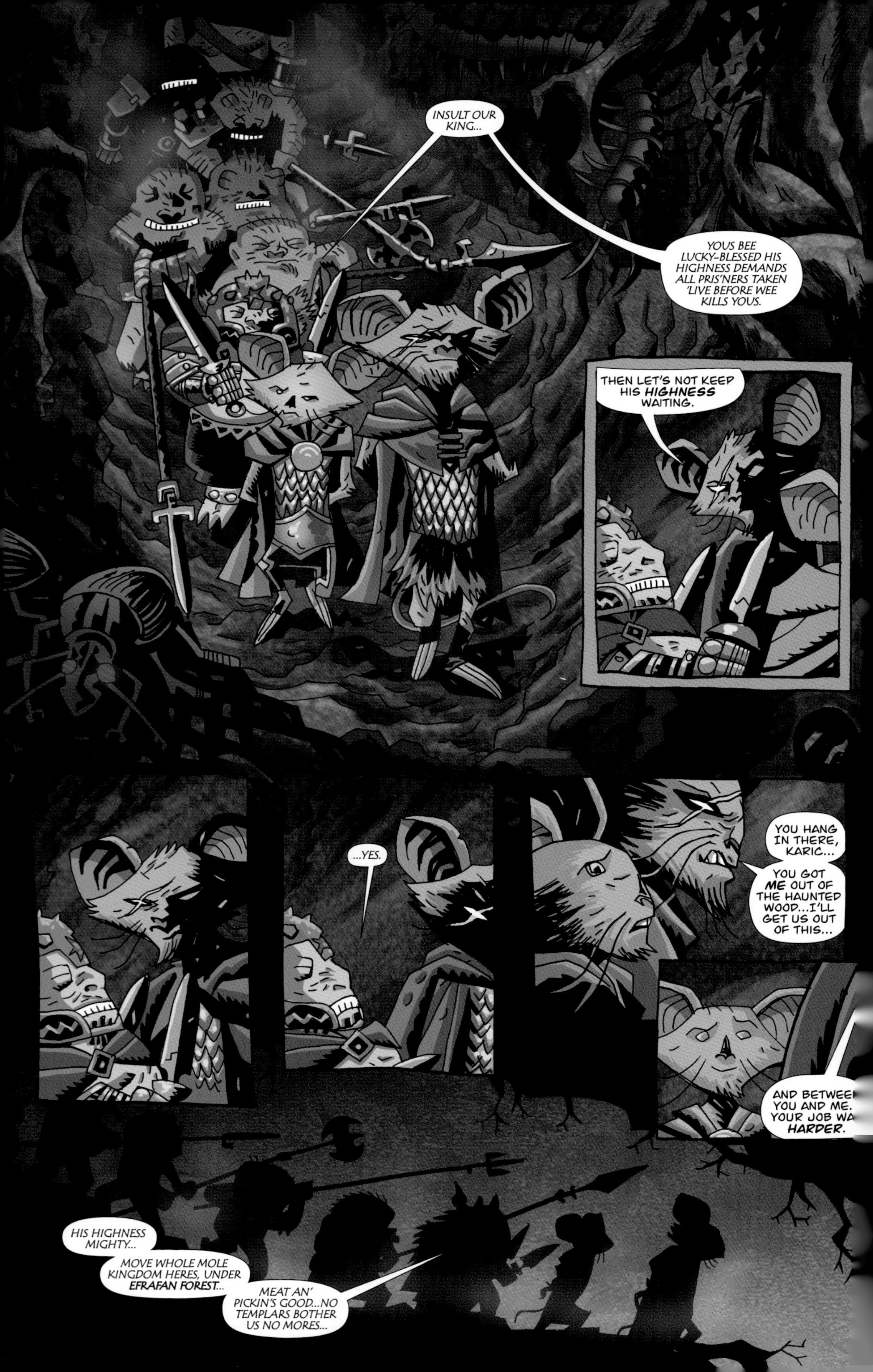
INSULT OUR KING...
YOUS BEE LUCKY-BLESSED HIS HIGHNESS DEMANDS ALL PRIS'NERS TAKEN 'LIVE BEFORE WEE KILLS YOUS.
THEN LET'S NOT KEEP HIS **HIGHNESS** WAITING.
...YES.
YOU HANG IN THERE, KARIC...
YOU GOT **ME** OUT OF THE HAUNTED WOOD...I'LL GET US OUT OF THIS...
AND BETWEEN YOU AND ME. YOUR JOB WA **HARDER**.
HIS HIGHNESS MIGHTY...
MOVE WHOLE MOLE KINGDOM HERES, UNDER **EFRAFAN FOREST**...
MEAT AN' PICKIN'S GOOD...NO TEMPLARS BOTHER US NO MORES...

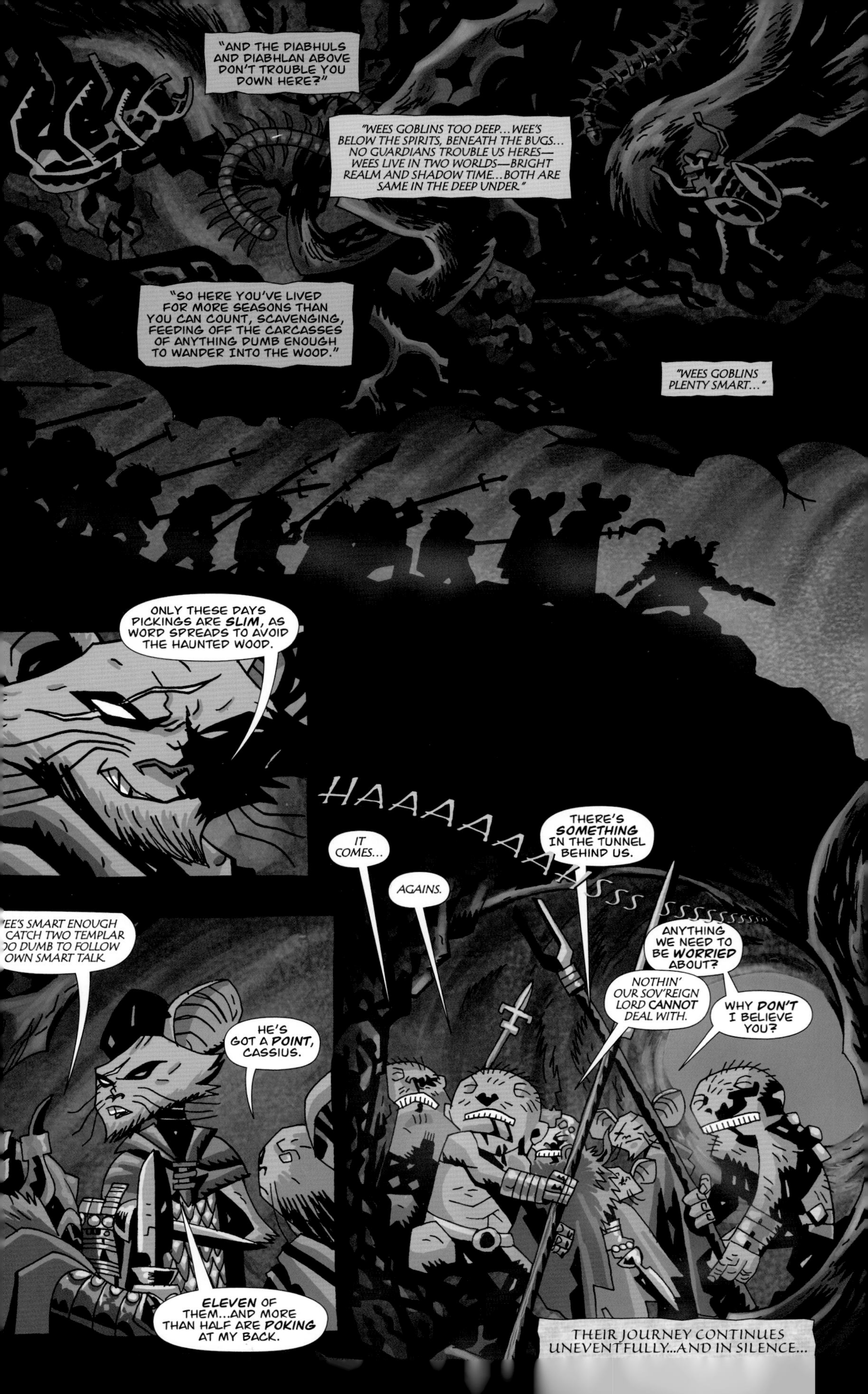
"AND THE DIABHULS AND DIABHLAN ABOVE DON'T TROUBLE YOU DOWN HERE?"
"WEES GOBLINS TOO DEEP...WEE'S BELOW THE SPIRITS, BENEATH THE BUGS... NO GUARDIANS TROUBLE US HERES— WEES LIVE IN TWO WORLDS—BRIGHT REALM AND SHADOW TIME...BOTH ARE SAME IN THE DEEP UNDER."
"SO HERE YOU'VE LIVED FOR MORE SEASONS THAN YOU CAN COUNT, SCAVENGING, FEEDING OFF THE CARCASSES OF ANYTHING DUMB ENOUGH TO WANDER INTO THE WOOD."
"WEES GOBLINS PLENTY SMART..."
ONLY THESE DAYS PICKINGS ARE SLIM, AS WORD SPREADS TO AVOID THE HAUNTED WOOD.
HAAAAAAAHSSSSSSSSSSS
IT COMES...
AGAINS.
THERE'S SOMETHING IN THE TUNNEL BEHIND US.
ANYTHING WE NEED TO BE WORRIED ABOUT?
NOTHIN' OUR SOV'REIGN LORD CANNOT DEAL WITH.
WHY DON'T I BELIEVE YOU?
EE'S SMART ENOUGH CATCH TWO TEMPLAR OO DUMB TO FOLLOW OWN SMART TALK.
HE'S GOT A POINT, CASSIUS.
ELEVEN OF THEM...AND MORE THAN HALF ARE POKING AT MY BACK.
THEIR JOURNEY CONTINUES UNEVENTFULLY...AND IN SILENCE...

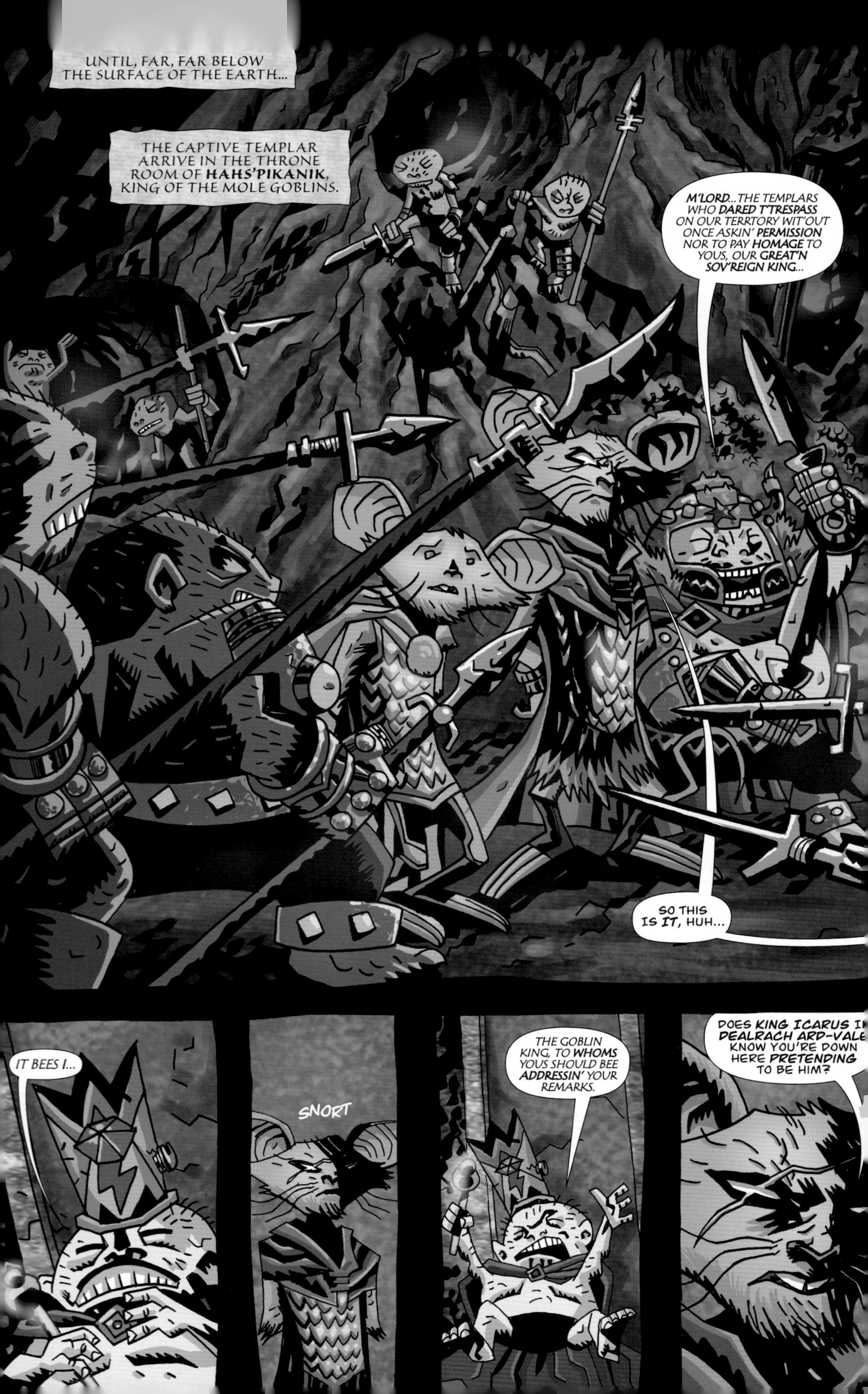
UNTIL, FAR, FAR BELOW THE SURFACE OF THE EARTH...
THE CAPTIVE TEMPLAR ARRIVE IN THE THRONE ROOM OF **HAHS'PIKANIK**, KING OF THE MOLE GOBLINS.
*M'LORD...THE TEMPLARS WHO **DARED T'TRESPASS** ON OUR TERRTORY WIT'OUT ONCE ASKIN' **PERMISSION** NOR TO PAY **HOMAGE** TO YOUS, OUR **GREAT'N SOV'REIGN KING**...*
SO THIS IS ***IT***, HUH...
IT BEES I...
SNORT
*THE GOBLIN KING, TO **WHOMS** YOUS SHOULD BEE **ADDRESSIN'** YOUR REMARKS.*
DOES **KING ICARUS I** **DEALRACH ARD-VALE** KNOW YOU'RE DOWN HERE ***PRETENDING*** TO BE HIM?

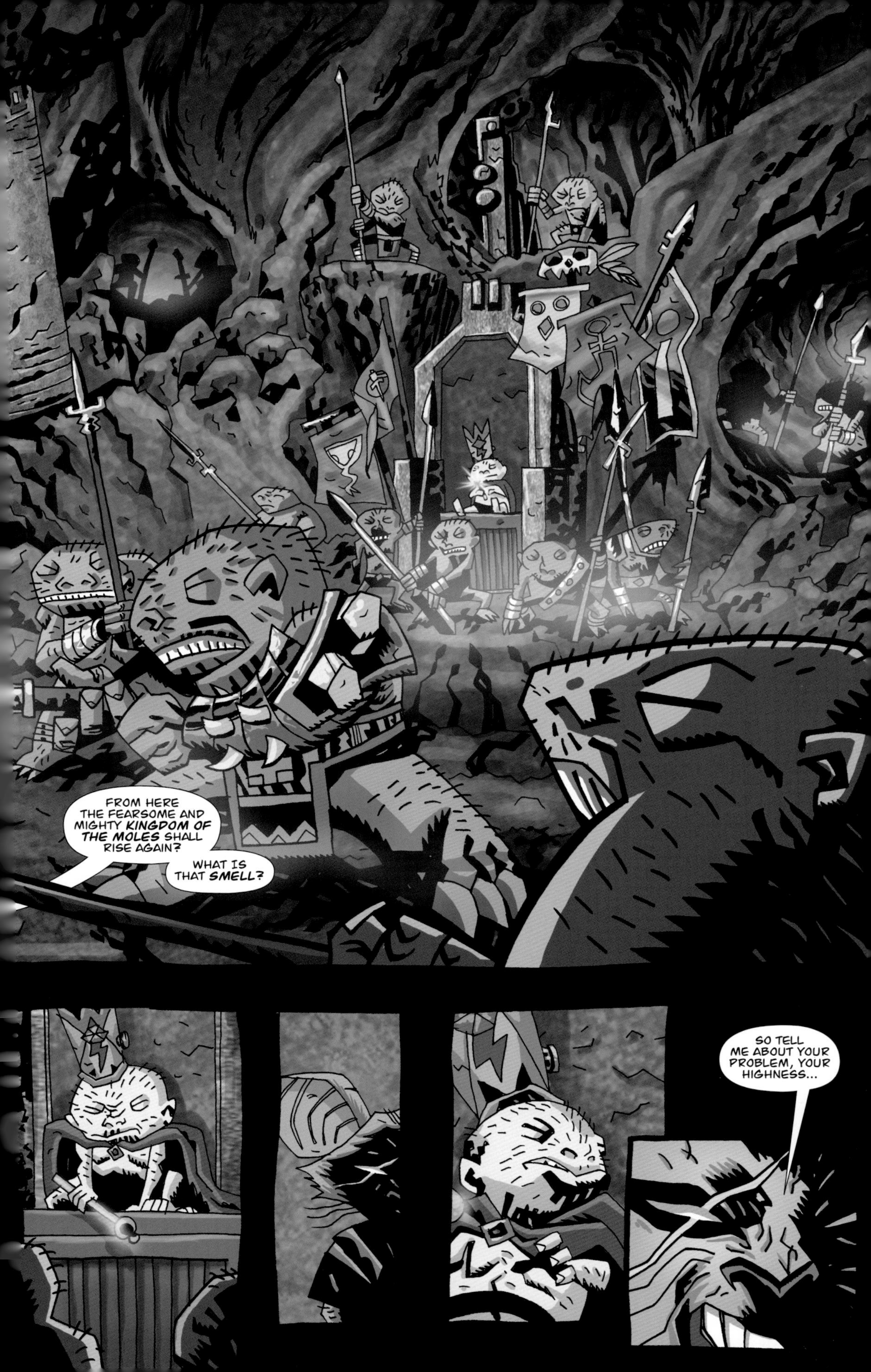
FROM HERE THE FEARSOME AND MIGHTY KINGDOM OF THE MOLES SHALL RISE AGAIN?
WHAT IS THAT SMELL?
SO TELL ME ABOUT YOUR PROBLEM, YOUR HIGHNESS...

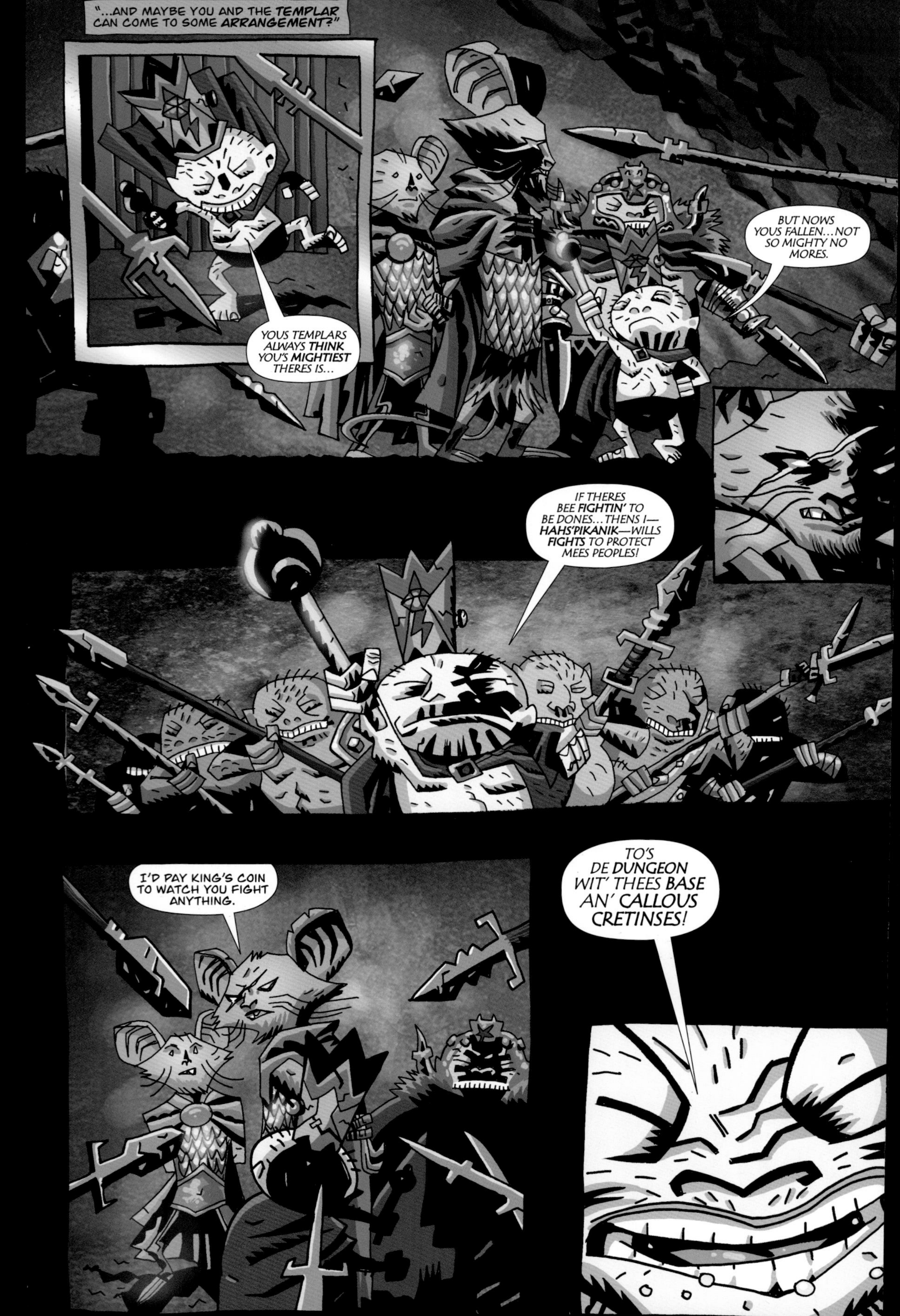
"...AND MAYBE YOU AND THE TEMPLAR CAN COME TO SOME ARRANGEMENT?"
YOUS TEMPLARS ALWAYS THINK YOU'S MIGHTIEST THERES IS...
BUT NOWS YOUS FALLEN...NOT SO MIGHTY NO MORES.
IF THERES BEE FIGHTIN' TO BE DONES...THENS I—HAHS'PIKANIK—WILLS FIGHTS TO PROTECT MEES PEOPLES!
I'D PAY KING'S COIN TO WATCH YOU FIGHT ANYTHING.
TO'S DE DUNGEON WIT' THEES BASE AN' CALLOUS CRETINSES!

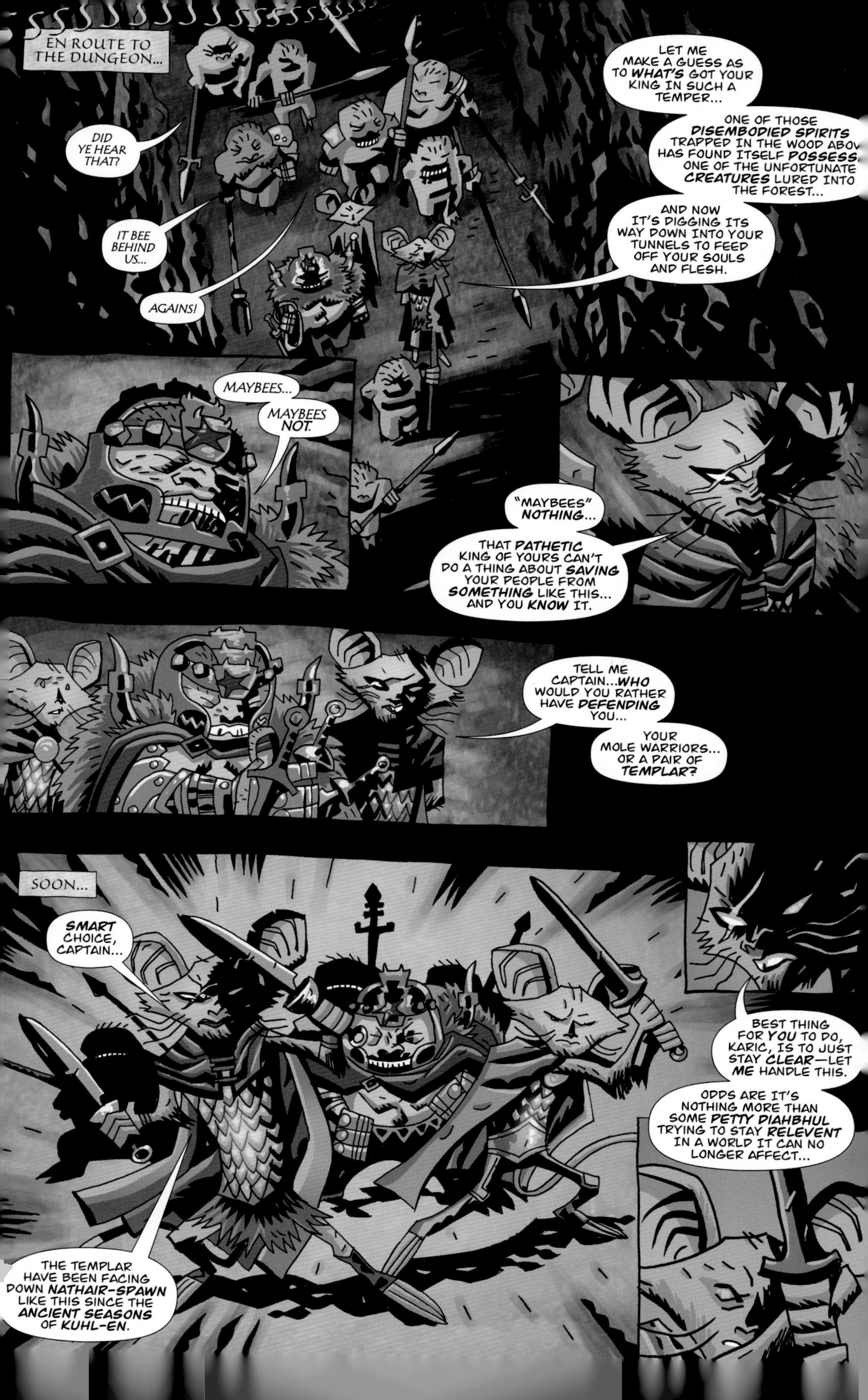
EN ROUTE TO THE DUNGEON...
DID YE HEAR THAT?
IT BEE BEHIND US...
AGAINS!
LET ME MAKE A GUESS AS TO WHAT'S GOT YOUR KING IN SUCH A TEMPER...
ONE OF THOSE DISEMBODIED SPIRITS TRAPPED IN THE WOOD ABOVE HAS FOUND ITSELF POSSESSING ONE OF THE UNFORTUNATE CREATURES LURED INTO THE FOREST...
AND NOW IT'S DIGGING ITS WAY DOWN INTO YOUR TUNNELS TO FEED OFF YOUR SOULS AND FLESH.
MAYBEES...
MAYBEES NOT.
"MAYBEES" NOTHING...
THAT PATHETIC KING OF YOURS CAN'T DO A THING ABOUT SAVING YOUR PEOPLE FROM SOMETHING LIKE THIS... AND YOU KNOW IT.
TELL ME CAPTAIN...WHO WOULD YOU RATHER HAVE DEFENDING YOU...
YOUR MOLE WARRIORS... OR A PAIR OF TEMPLAR?
SOON...
SMART CHOICE, CAPTAIN...
THE TEMPLAR HAVE BEEN FACING DOWN NATHAIR-SPAWN LIKE THIS SINCE THE ANCIENT SEASONS OF KUHL-EN.
BEST THING FOR YOU TO DO, KARIC, IS TO JUST STAY CLEAR—LET ME HANDLE THIS.
ODDS ARE IT'S NOTHING MORE THAN SOME PETTY DIAHBHUL TRYING TO STAY RELEVENT IN A WORLD IT CAN NO LONGER AFFECT...

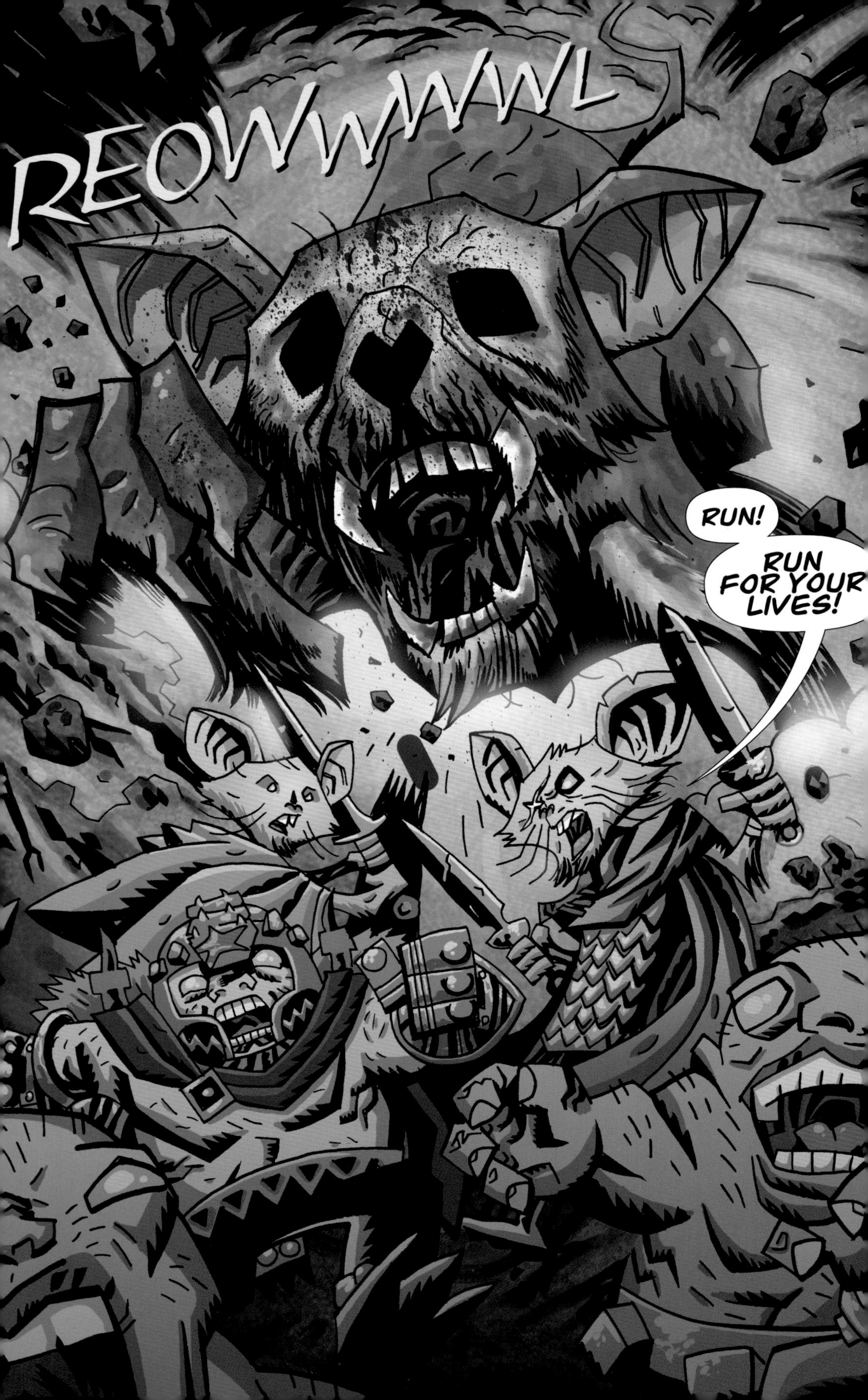
REOWWWWL
RUN!
RUN FOR YOUR LIVES!

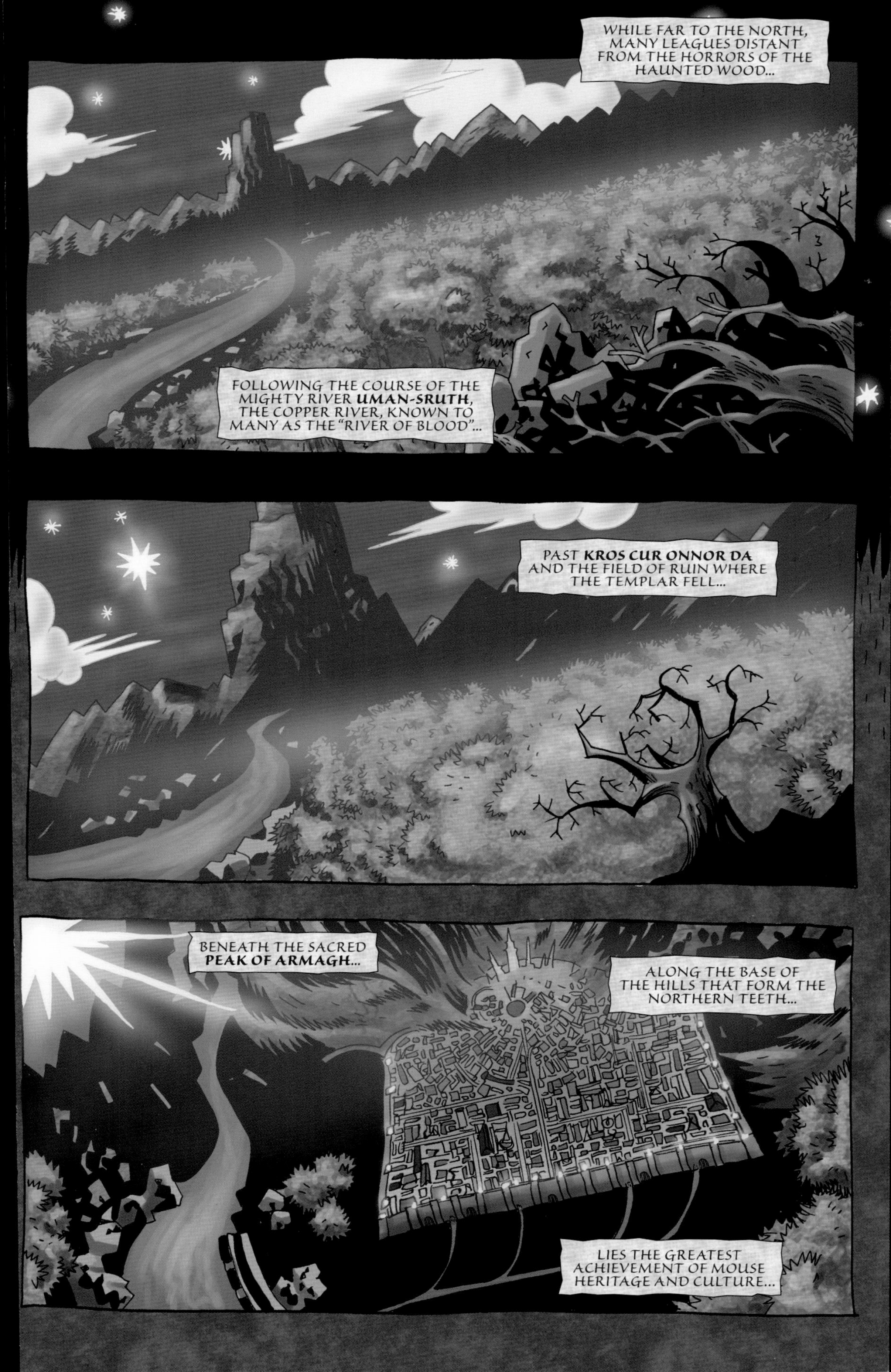
WHILE FAR TO THE NORTH, MANY LEAGUES DISTANT FROM THE HORRORS OF THE HAUNTED WOOD...
FOLLOWING THE COURSE OF THE MIGHTY RIVER **UMAN-SRUTH**, THE COPPER RIVER, KNOWN TO MANY AS THE "RIVER OF BLOOD"...
PAST **KROS CUR ONNOR DA** AND THE FIELD OF RUIN WHERE THE TEMPLAR FELL...
BENEATH THE SACRED **PEAK OF ARMAGH**...
ALONG THE BASE OF THE HILLS THAT FORM THE NORTHERN TEETH...
LIES THE GREATEST ACHIEVEMENT OF MOUSE HERITAGE AND CULTURE...

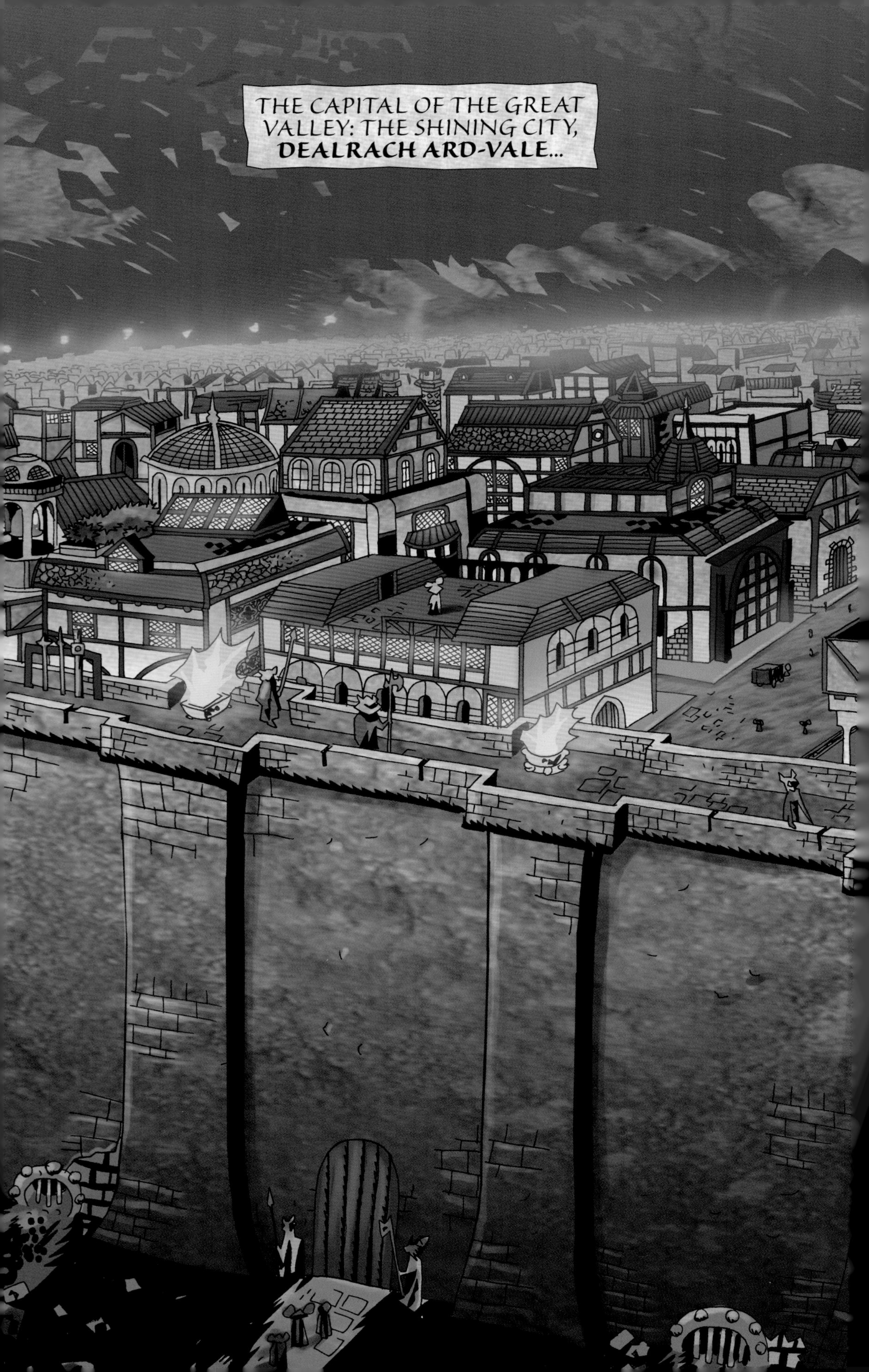
THE CAPITAL OF THE GREAT VALLEY: THE SHINING CITY, DEALRACH ARD-VALE...

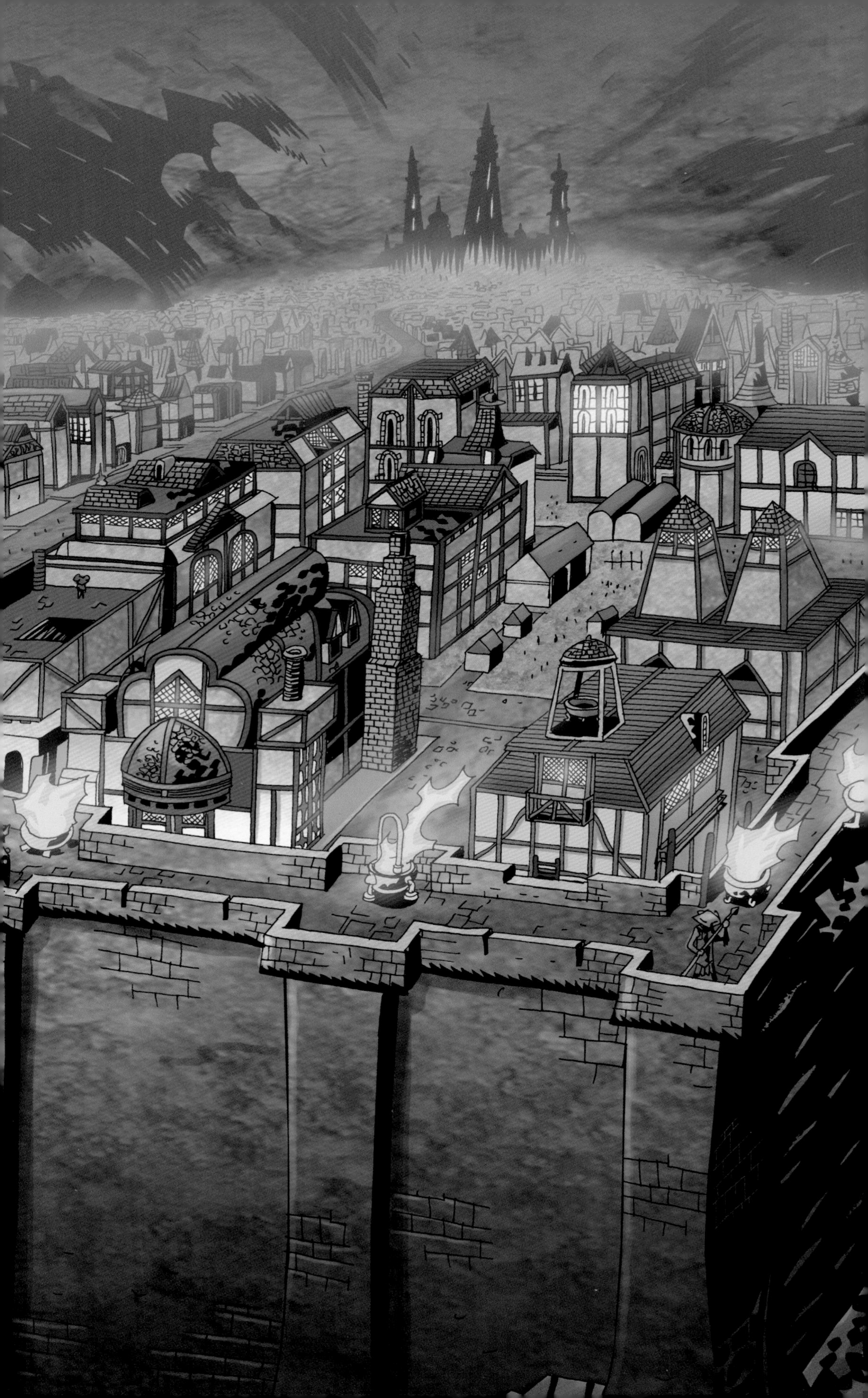

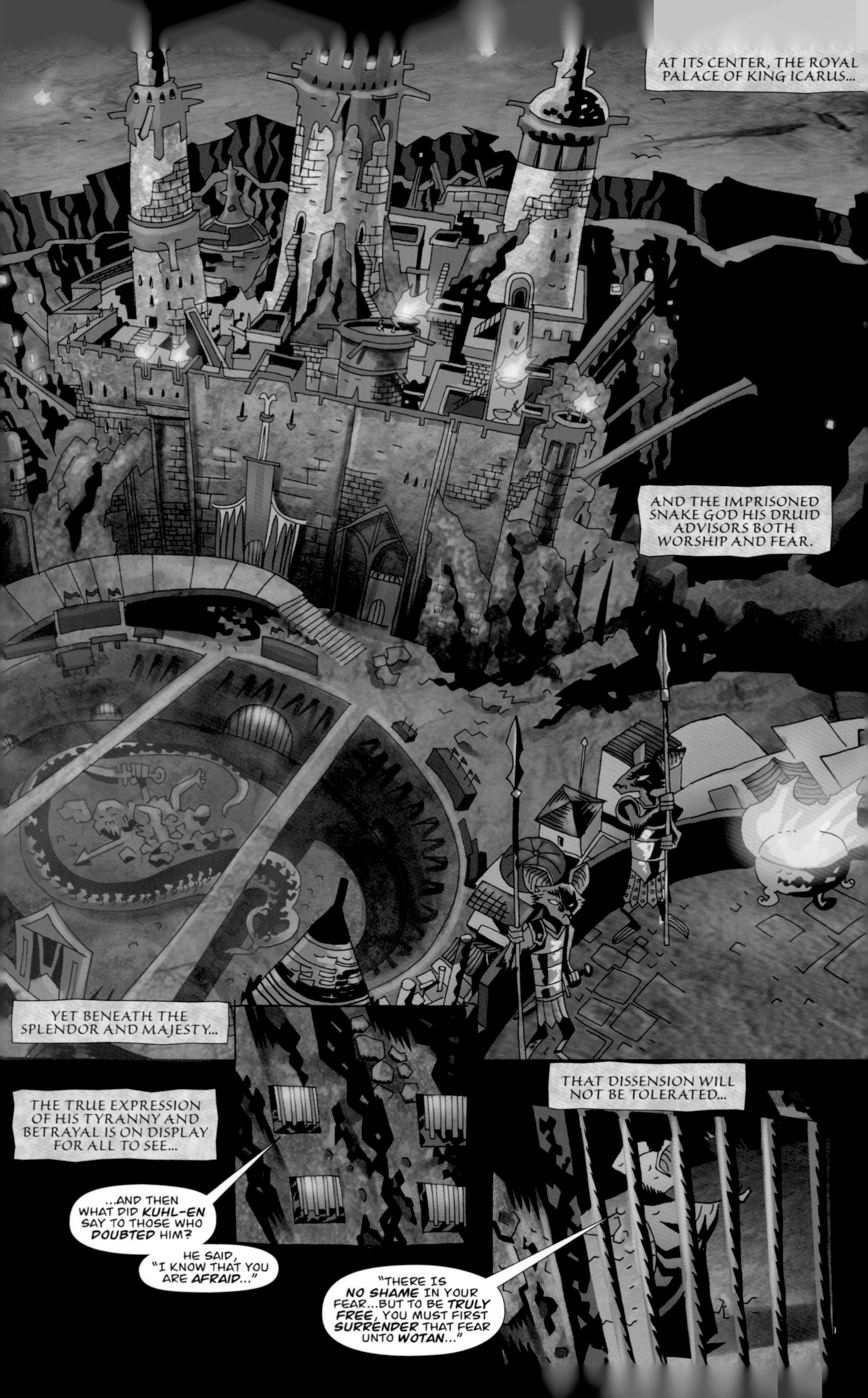
AT ITS CENTER, THE ROYAL PALACE OF KING ICARUS...
AND THE IMPRISONED SNAKE GOD HIS DRUID ADVISORS BOTH WORSHIP AND FEAR.
YET BENEATH THE SPLENDOR AND MAJESTY...
THE TRUE EXPRESSION OF HIS TYRANNY AND BETRAYAL IS ON DISPLAY FOR ALL TO SEE...
...AND THEN WHAT DID KUHL-EN SAY TO THOSE WHO DOUBTED HIM?
HE SAID, "I KNOW THAT YOU ARE AFRAID..."
THAT DISSENSION WILL NOT BE TOLERATED...
"THERE IS NO SHAME IN YOUR FEAR...BUT TO BE TRULY FREE, YOU MUST FIRST SURRENDER THAT FEAR UNTO WOTAN..."

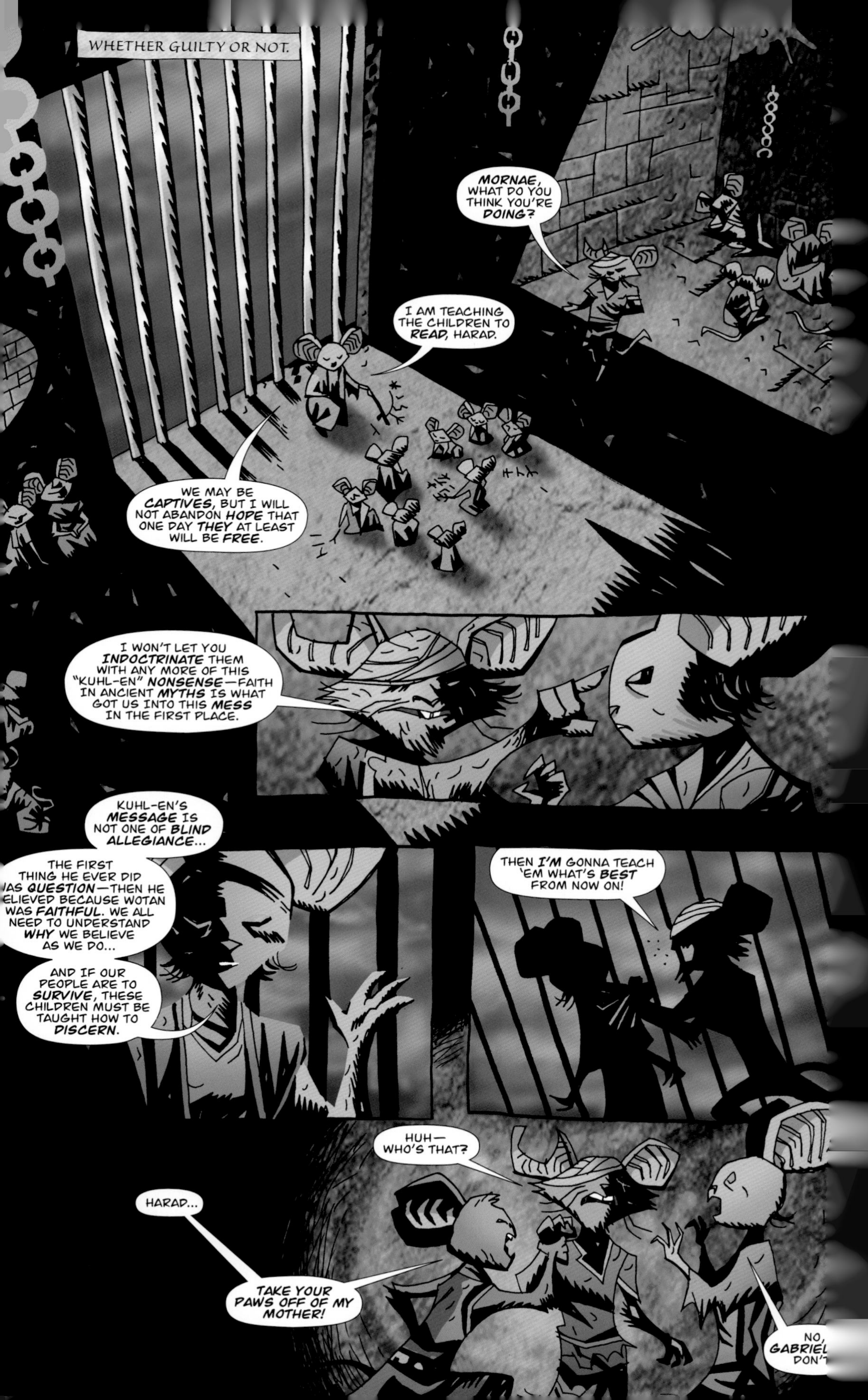
WHETHER GUILTY OR NOT.
MORNAE, WHAT DO YOU THINK YOU'RE DOING?
I AM TEACHING THE CHILDREN TO READ, HARAD.
WE MAY BE CAPTIVES, BUT I WILL NOT ABANDON HOPE THAT ONE DAY THEY AT LEAST WILL BE FREE.
I WON'T LET YOU INDOCTRINATE THEM WITH ANY MORE OF THIS "KUHL-EN" NONSENSE—FAITH IN ANCIENT MYTHS IS WHAT GOT US INTO THIS MESS IN THE FIRST PLACE.
KUHL-EN'S MESSAGE IS NOT ONE OF BLIND ALLEGIANCE...
THE FIRST THING HE EVER DID WAS QUESTION—THEN HE BELIEVED BECAUSE WOTAN WAS FAITHFUL. WE ALL NEED TO UNDERSTAND WHY WE BELIEVE AS WE DO...
AND IF OUR PEOPLE ARE TO SURVIVE, THESE CHILDREN MUST BE TAUGHT HOW TO DISCERN.
THEN I'M GONNA TEACH 'EM WHAT'S BEST FROM NOW ON!
HUH— WHO'S THAT?
HARAD...
TAKE YOUR PAWS OFF OF MY MOTHER!
NO, GABRIEL DON'T

WHAP
AAAHGH
WHAT'S THE PROBLEM HERE?
NOTHING I CAN'T HANDLE, LEITO— AND IF HARAD GETS UP, I'LL JUST KNOCK HIM DOWN AGAIN!
IF IT ISN'T THE TEMPLAR WANNABE COMIN' TO SAVE THE DAY... TOO LATE AS USUAL.
DON'T YOU EVER TOUCH MY MOTHER AGAIN, YOU...YOU...
DUNGBREEDER!
THAT'S ENOUGH, GABRIELLE...
YOU'D BEST PUT A LEASH ON THAT UPPITY LITTLE "MAEVEN" OF YOURS... BEFORE I PUT HER DOWN HARD!
DON'T WE HAVE ENOUGH ENEMIES OUTSIDE THESE BARS TO BE MAKING THEM OF OURSELVES WITHIN?
BUT THEN...

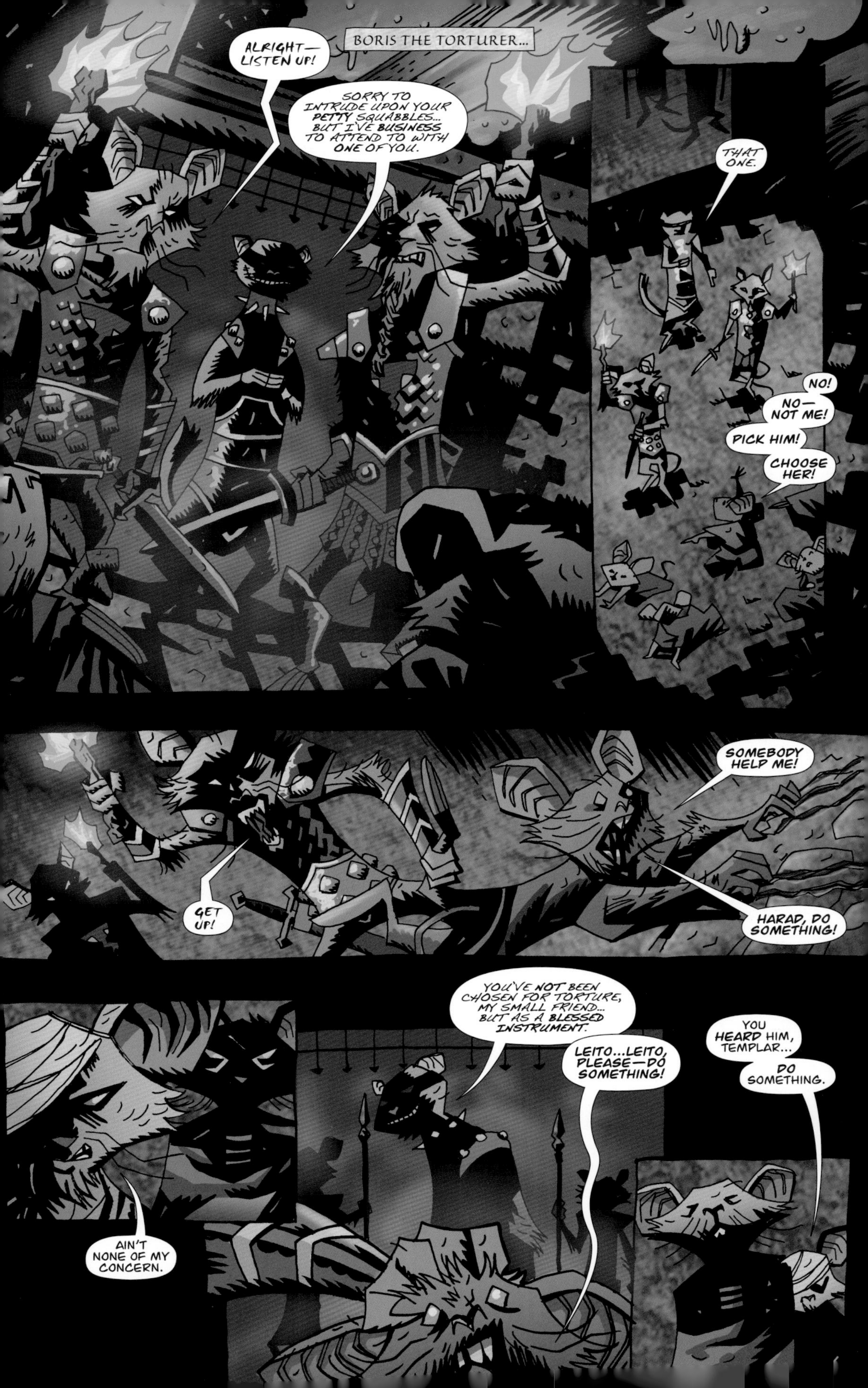
BORIS THE TORTURER...
ALRIGHT— LISTEN UP!
SORRY TO INTRUDE UPON YOUR PETTY SQUABBLES... BUT I'VE BUSINESS TO ATTEND TO WITH ONE OF YOU.
THAT ONE.
NO!
NO— NOT ME!
PICK HIM!
CHOOSE HER!
SOMEBODY HELP ME!
GET UP!
HARAD, DO SOMETHING!
YOU'VE NOT BEEN CHOSEN FOR TORTURE, MY SMALL FRIEND... BUT AS A BLESSED INSTRUMENT.
LEITO...LEITO, PLEASE—DO SOMETHING!
YOU HEARD HIM, TEMPLAR...
DO SOMETHING.
AIN'T NONE OF MY CONCERN.

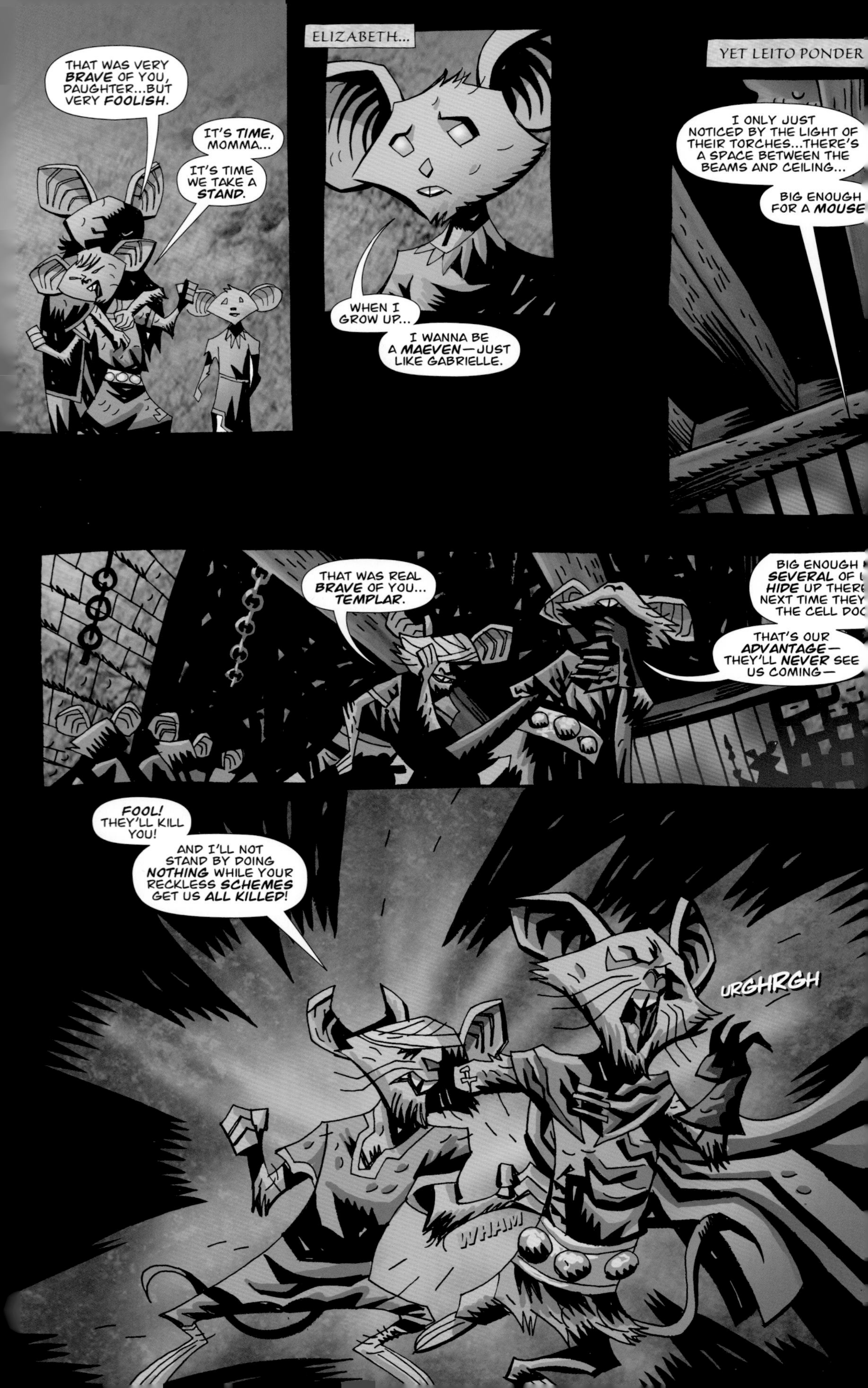
THAT WAS VERY BRAVE OF YOU, DAUGHTER...BUT VERY FOOLISH.
IT'S TIME, MOMMA...
IT'S TIME WE TAKE A STAND.
ELIZABETH...
WHEN I GROW UP...
I WANNA BE A MAEVEN—JUST LIKE GABRIELLE.
YET LEITO PONDER
I ONLY JUST NOTICED BY THE LIGHT OF THEIR TORCHES...THERE'S A SPACE BETWEEN THE BEAMS AND CEILING...
BIG ENOUGH FOR A MOUSE
THAT WAS REAL BRAVE OF YOU... TEMPLAR.
BIG ENOUGH SEVERAL OF HIDE UP THER NEXT TIME THEY THE CELL DO
THAT'S OUR ADVANTAGE—THEY'LL NEVER SEE US COMING—
FOOL! THEY'LL KILL YOU!
AND I'LL NOT STAND BY DOING NOTHING WHILE YOUR RECKLESS SCHEMES GET US ALL KILLED!
URGHRGH
WHAM

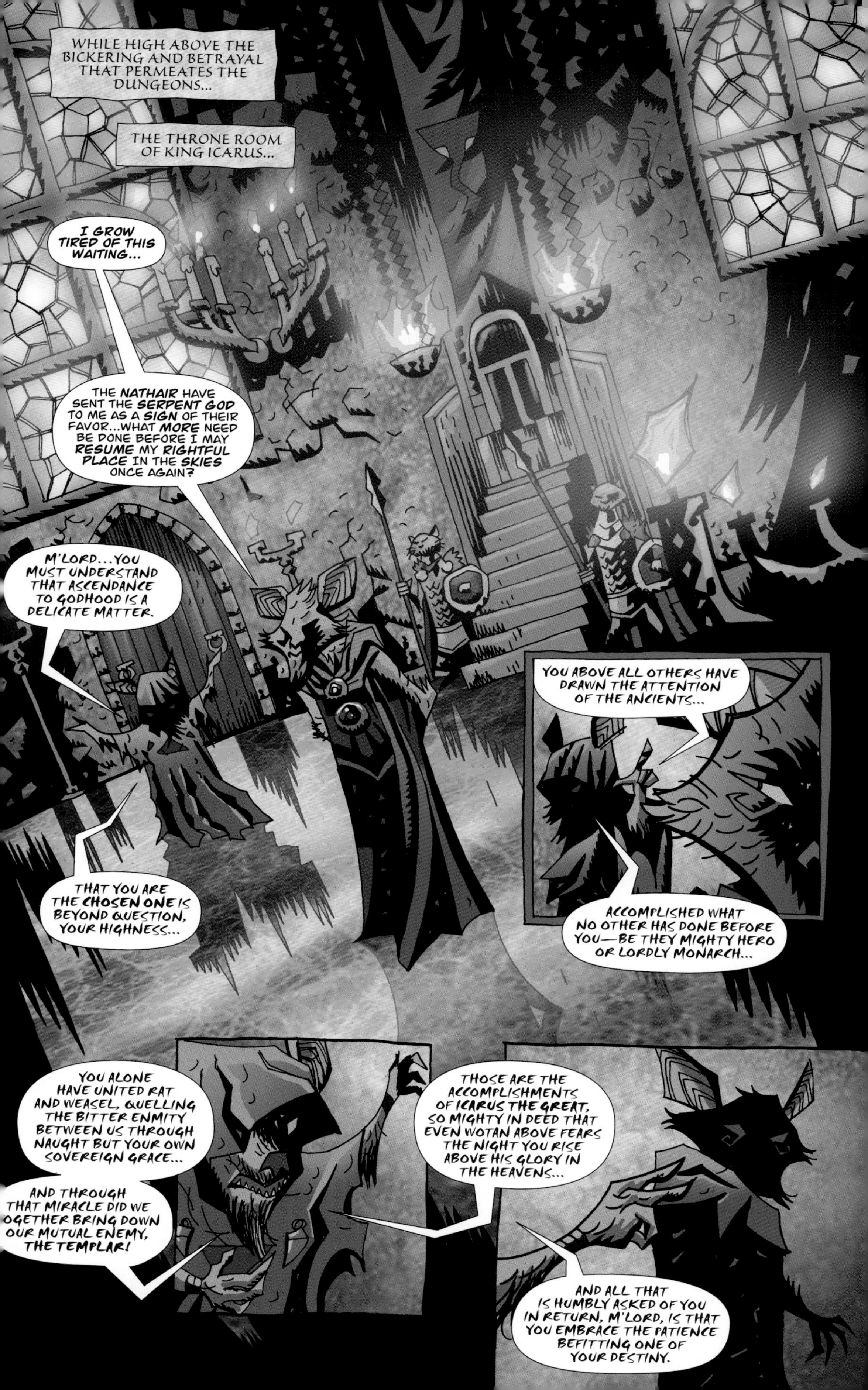

WHILE HIGH ABOVE THE BICKERING AND BETRAYAL THAT PERMEATES THE DUNGEONS...
THE THRONE ROOM OF KING ICARUS...
I GROW TIRED OF THIS WAITING...
THE NATHAIR HAVE SENT THE SERPENT GOD TO ME AS A SIGN OF THEIR FAVOR...WHAT MORE NEED BE DONE BEFORE I MAY RESUME MY RIGHTFUL PLACE IN THE SKIES ONCE AGAIN?
M'LORD...YOU MUST UNDERSTAND THAT ASCENDANCE TO GODHOOD IS A DELICATE MATTER.
THAT YOU ARE THE CHOSEN ONE IS BEYOND QUESTION, YOUR HIGHNESS...
YOU ABOVE ALL OTHERS HAVE DRAWN THE ATTENTION OF THE ANCIENTS...
ACCOMPLISHED WHAT NO OTHER HAS DONE BEFORE YOU—BE THEY MIGHTY HERO OR LORDLY MONARCH...
YOU ALONE HAVE UNITED RAT AND WEASEL, QUELLING THE BITTER ENMITY BETWEEN US THROUGH NAUGHT BUT YOUR OWN SOVEREIGN GRACE...
AND THROUGH THAT MIRACLE DID WE TOGETHER BRING DOWN OUR MUTUAL ENEMY, THE TEMPLAR!
THOSE ARE THE ACCOMPLISHMENTS OF ICARUS THE GREAT, SO MIGHTY IN DEED THAT EVEN WOTAN ABOVE FEARS THE NIGHT YOU RISE ABOVE HIS GLORY IN THE HEAVENS...
AND ALL THAT IS HUMBLY ASKED OF YOU IN RETURN, M'LORD, IS THAT YOU EMBRACE THE PATIENCE BEFITTING ONE OF YOUR DESTINY.

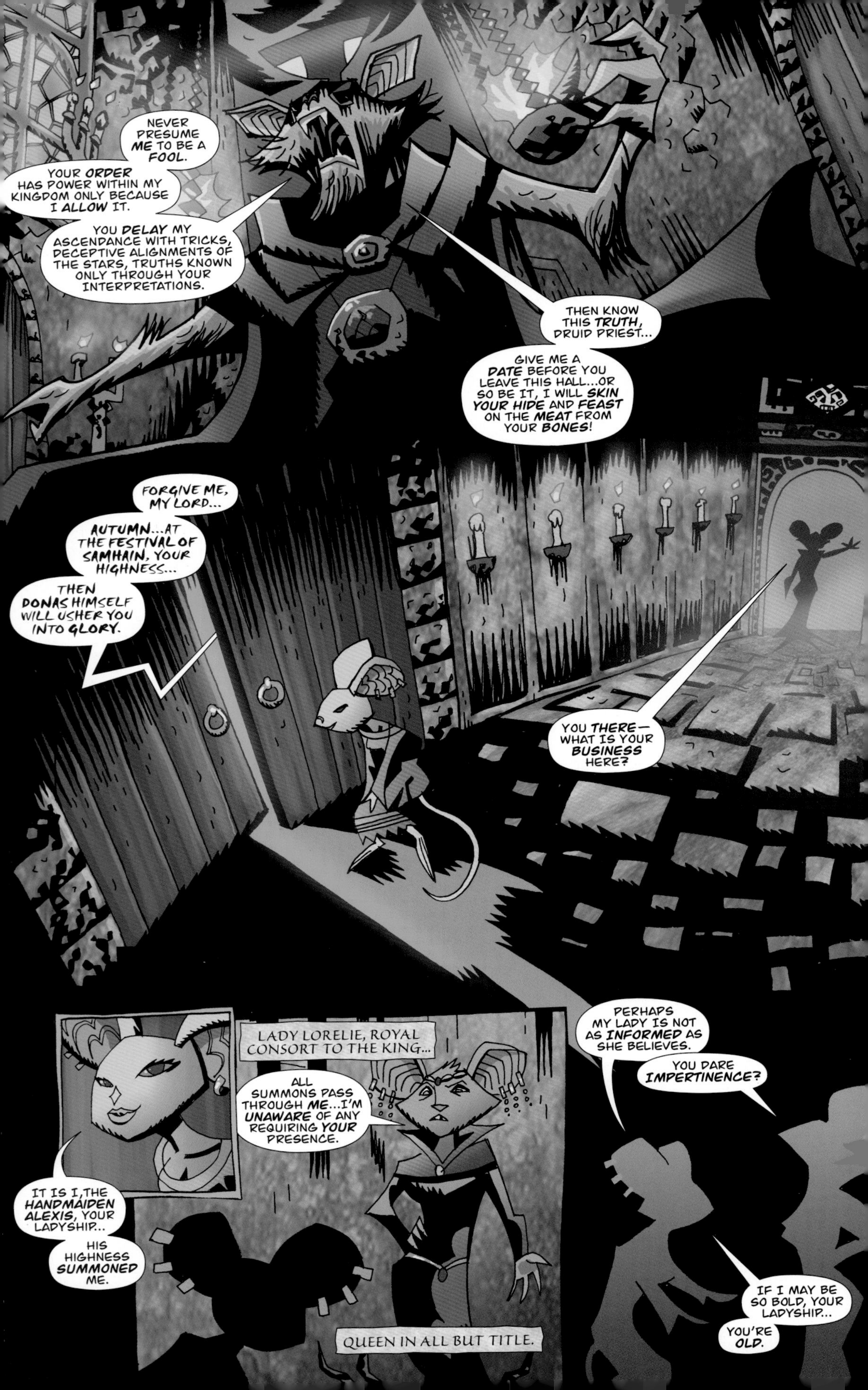
NEVER PRESUME ME TO BE A FOOL.
YOUR ORDER HAS POWER WITHIN MY KINGDOM ONLY BECAUSE I ALLOW IT.
YOU DELAY MY ASCENDANCE WITH TRICKS, DECEPTIVE ALIGNMENTS OF THE STARS, TRUTHS KNOWN ONLY THROUGH YOUR INTERPRETATIONS.
THEN KNOW THIS TRUTH, DRUID PRIEST...
GIVE ME A DATE BEFORE YOU LEAVE THIS HALL...OR SO BE IT, I WILL SKIN YOUR HIDE AND FEAST ON THE MEAT FROM YOUR BONES!
FORGIVE ME, MY LORD...
AUTUMN...AT THE FESTIVAL OF SAMHAIN, YOUR HIGHNESS...
THEN DONAS HIMSELF WILL USHER YOU INTO GLORY.
YOU THERE—WHAT IS YOUR BUSINESS HERE?
LADY LORELIE, ROYAL CONSORT TO THE KING...
IT IS I, THE HANDMAIDEN ALEXIS, YOUR LADYSHIP...
HIS HIGHNESS SUMMONED ME.
ALL SUMMONS PASS THROUGH ME...I'M UNAWARE OF ANY REQUIRING YOUR PRESENCE.
QUEEN IN ALL BUT TITLE.
PERHAPS MY LADY IS NOT AS INFORMED AS SHE BELIEVES.
YOU DARE IMPERTINENCE?
IF I MAY BE SO BOLD, YOUR LADYSHIP...
YOU'RE OLD.

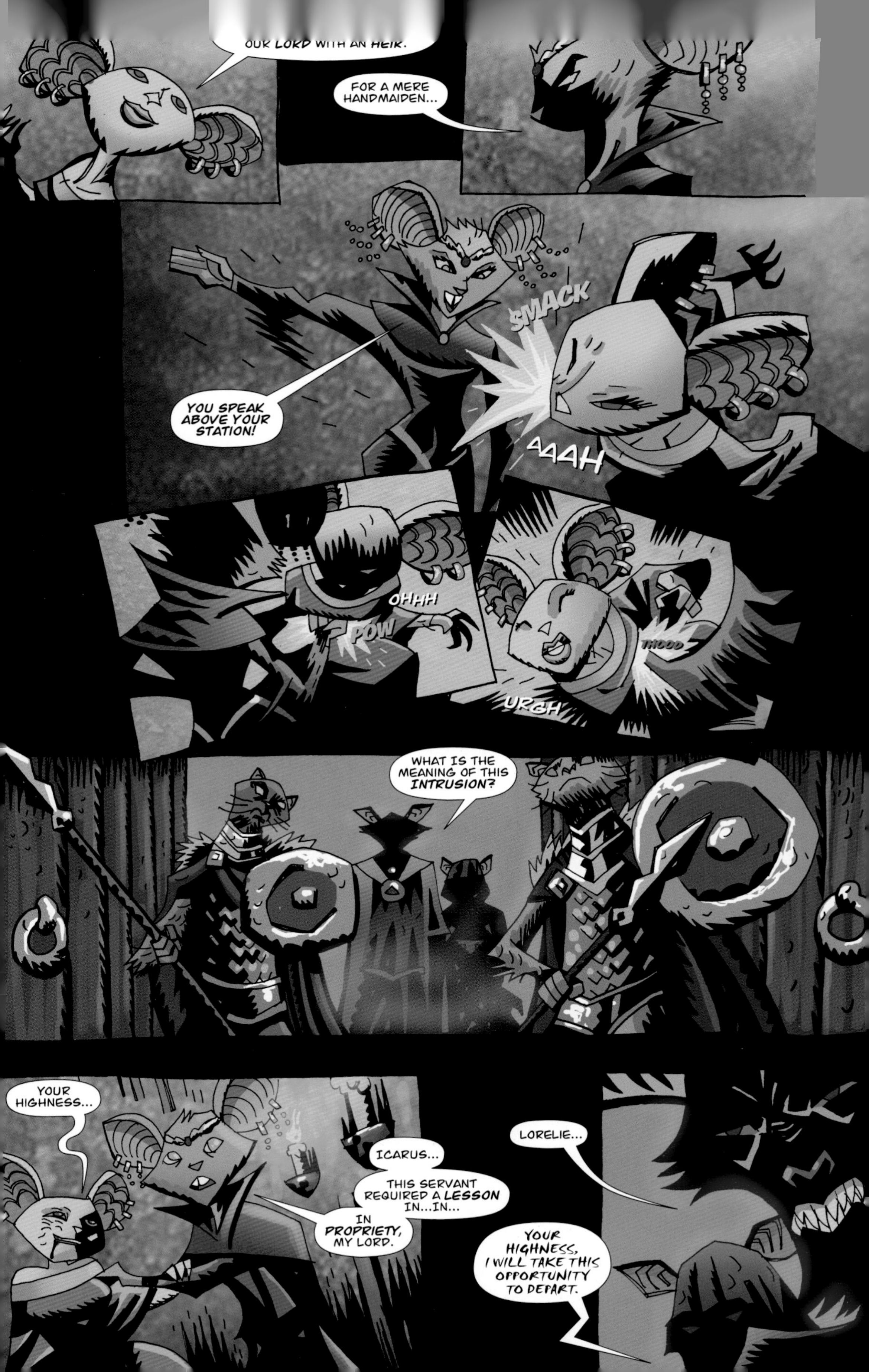
OUR LORD WITH AN HEIR.
FOR A MERE HANDMAIDEN...
SMACK
YOU SPEAK ABOVE YOUR STATION!
AAAH
OHHH
POW
THOOD
URGH
WHAT IS THE MEANING OF THIS INTRUSION?
YOUR HIGHNESS...
ICARUS...
THIS SERVANT REQUIRED A LESSON IN...IN...
IN PROPRIETY, MY LORD.
LORELIE...
YOUR HIGHNESS, I WILL TAKE THIS OPPORTUNITY TO DEPART.

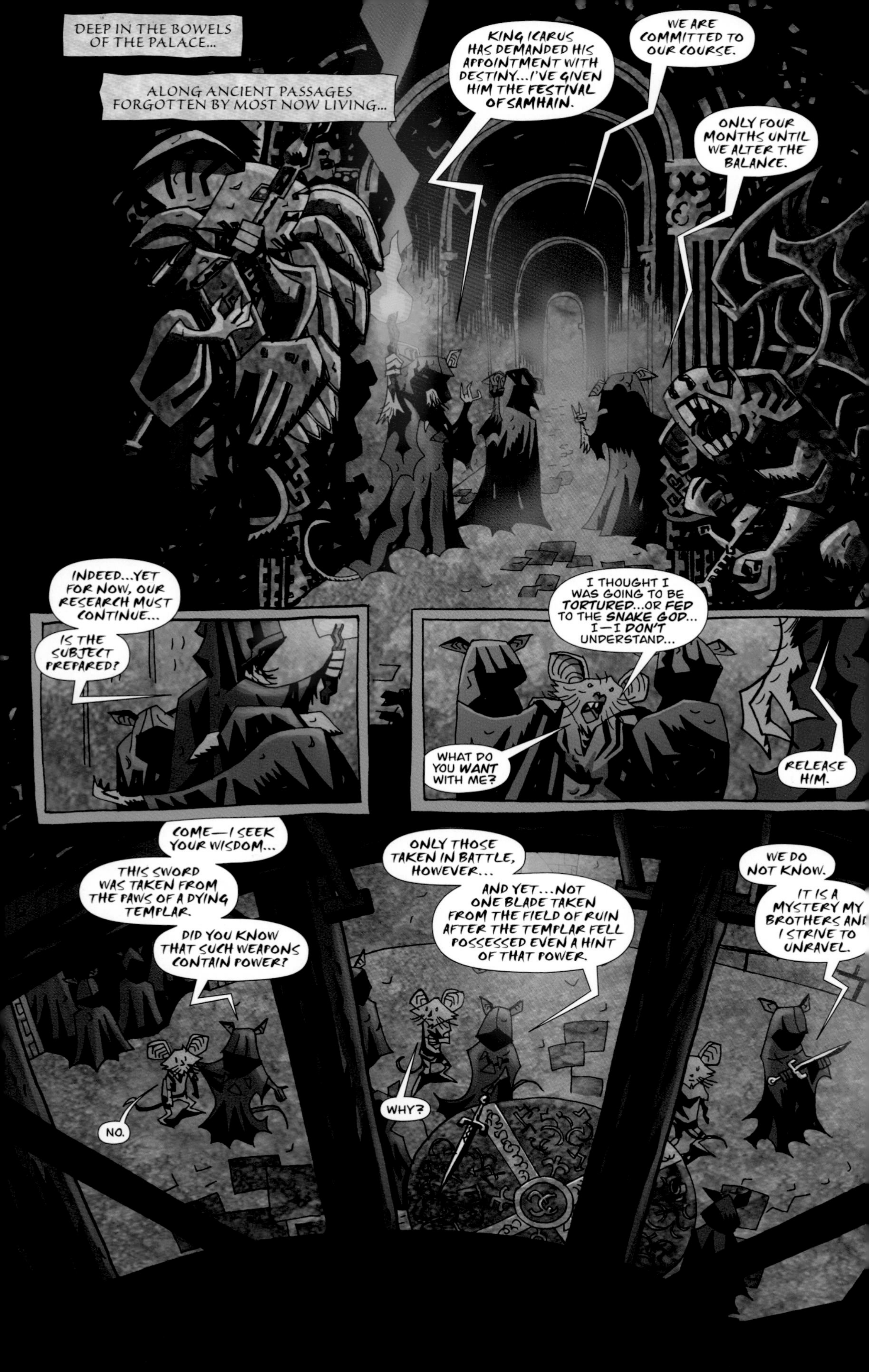
DEEP IN THE BOWELS OF THE PALACE...
ALONG ANCIENT PASSAGES FORGOTTEN BY MOST NOW LIVING...
KING ICARUS HAS DEMANDED HIS APPOINTMENT WITH DESTINY...I'VE GIVEN HIM THE FESTIVAL OF SAMHAIN.
WE ARE COMMITTED TO OUR COURSE.
ONLY FOUR MONTHS UNTIL WE ALTER THE BALANCE.
INDEED...YET FOR NOW, OUR RESEARCH MUST CONTINUE...
IS THE SUBJECT PREPARED?
I THOUGHT I WAS GOING TO BE TORTURED...OR FED TO THE SNAKE GOD... I—I DON'T UNDERSTAND...
WHAT DO YOU WANT WITH ME?
RELEASE HIM.
COME—I SEEK YOUR WISDOM...
THIS SWORD WAS TAKEN FROM THE PAWS OF A DYING TEMPLAR.
DID YOU KNOW THAT SUCH WEAPONS CONTAIN POWER?
NO.
ONLY THOSE TAKEN IN BATTLE, HOWEVER...
AND YET...NOT ONE BLADE TAKEN FROM THE FIELD OF RUIN AFTER THE TEMPLAR FELL POSSESSED EVEN A HINT OF THAT POWER.
WHY?
WE DO NOT KNOW.
IT IS A MYSTERY MY BROTHERS AND I STRIVE TO UNRAVEL.

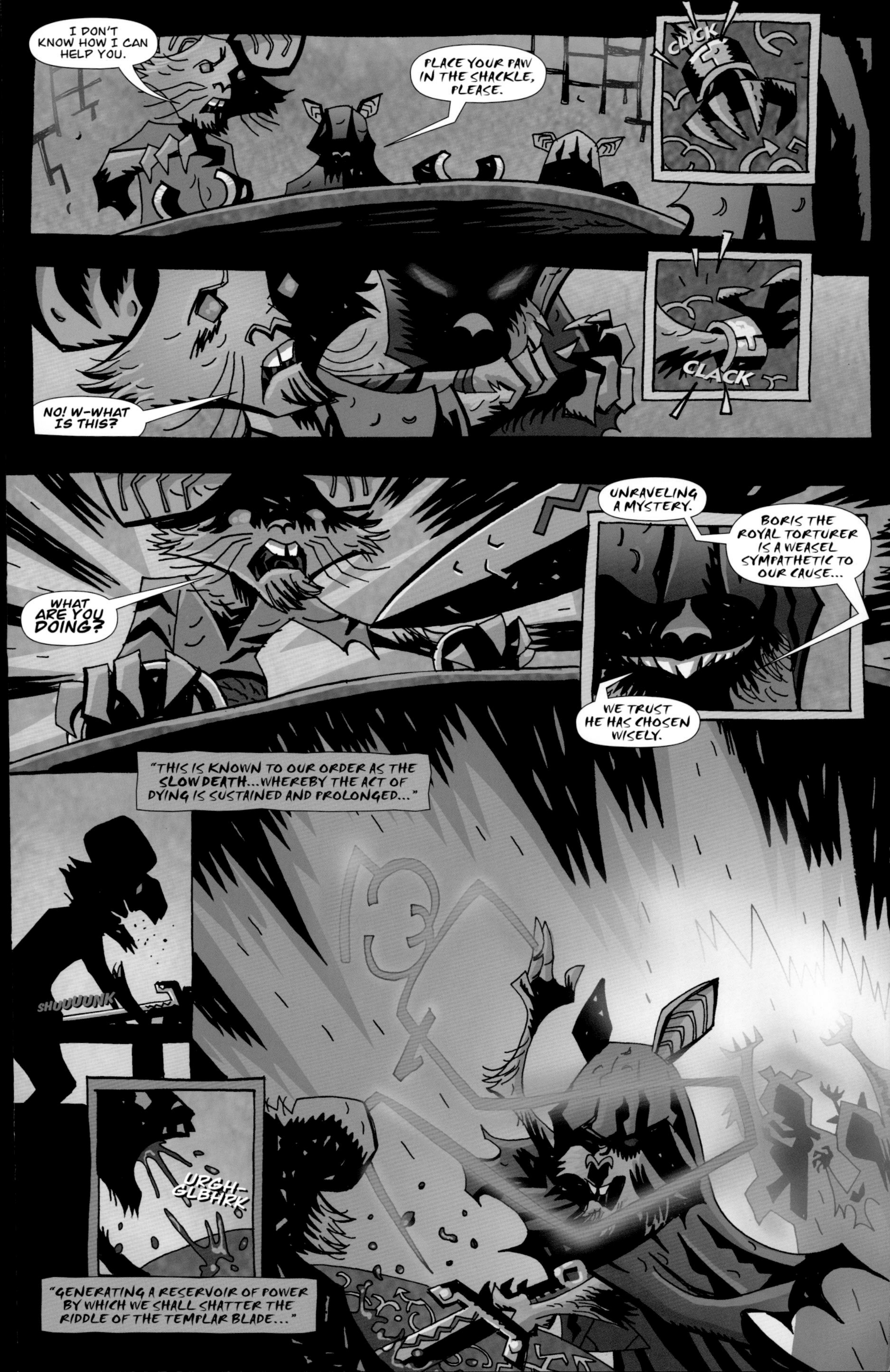
I DON'T KNOW HOW I CAN HELP YOU.
PLACE YOUR PAW IN THE SHACKLE, PLEASE.
CLICK
NO! W-WHAT IS THIS?
CLACK
WHAT ARE YOU DOING?
UNRAVELING A MYSTERY.
BORIS THE ROYAL TORTURER IS A WEASEL SYMPATHETIC TO OUR CAUSE...
WE TRUST HE HAS CHOSEN WISELY.
"THIS IS KNOWN TO OUR ORDER AS THE SLOW DEATH...WHEREBY THE ACT OF DYING IS SUSTAINED AND PROLONGED..."
SHUUUUNK
URGH-GLBHRK
"GENERATING A RESERVOIR OF POWER BY WHICH WE SHALL SHATTER THE RIDDLE OF THE TEMPLAR BLADE..."

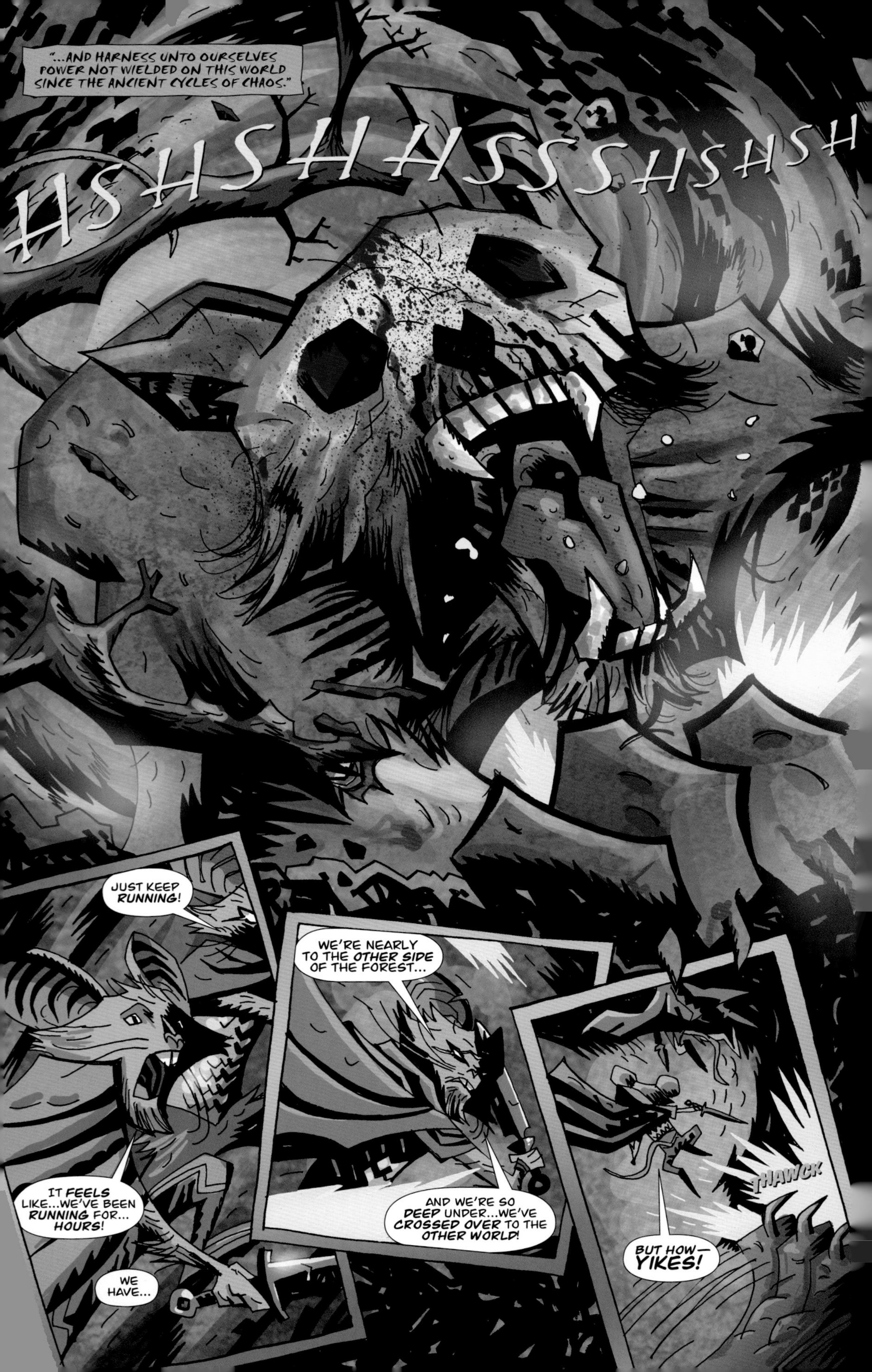
"...AND HARNESS UNTO OURSELVES POWER NOT WIELDED ON THIS WORLD SINCE THE ANCIENT CYCLES OF CHAOS."
HSHSHHSSSSHSHSH
JUST KEEP RUNNING!
IT FEELS LIKE...WE'VE BEEN RUNNING FOR... HOURS!
WE HAVE...
WE'RE NEARLY TO THE OTHER SIDE OF THE FOREST...
AND WE'RE SO DEEP UNDER...WE'VE CROSSED OVER TO THE OTHER WORLD!
THAWCK
BUT HOW— YIKES!

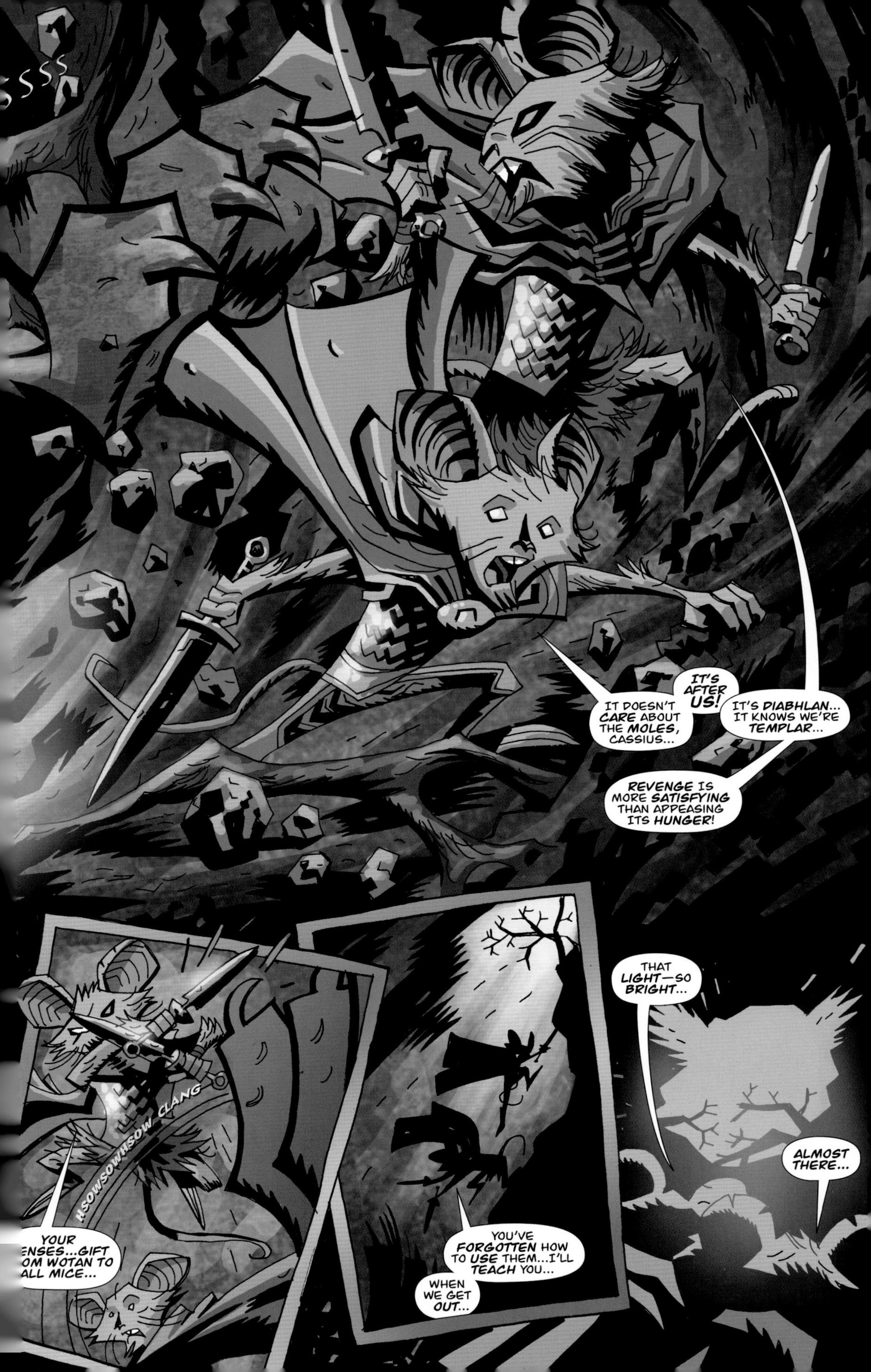

IT DOESN'T CARE ABOUT THE MOLES, CASSIUS...
IT'S AFTER US!
IT'S DIABHLAN... IT KNOWS WE'RE TEMPLAR...
REVENGE IS MORE SATISFYING THAN APPEASING ITS HUNGER!
CLANG
YOUR ENSES...GIFT OM WOTAN TO ALL MICE...
YOU'VE FORGOTTEN HOW TO USE THEM...I'LL TEACH YOU...
WHEN WE GET OUT...
THAT LIGHT—SO BRIGHT...
ALMOST THERE...

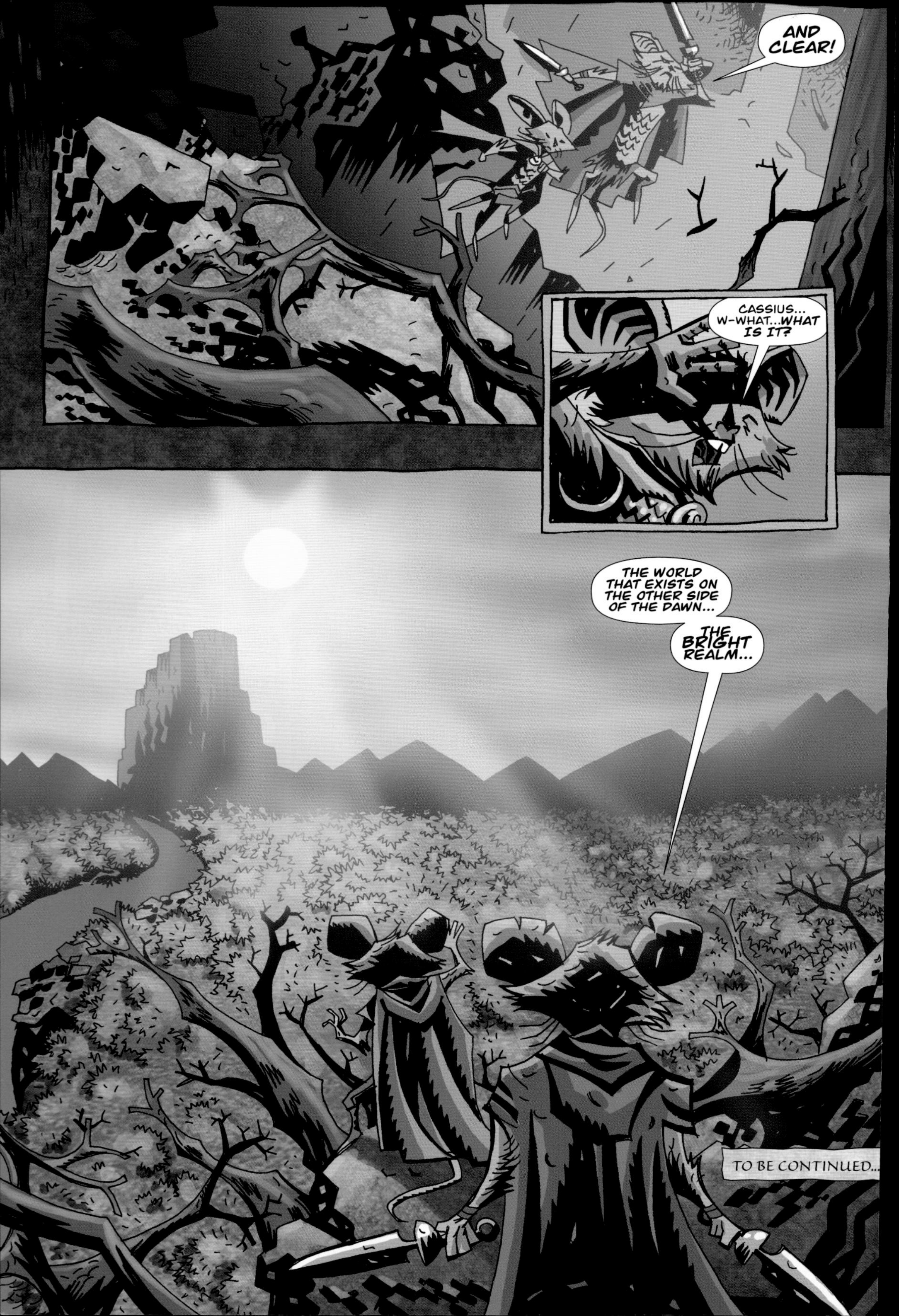
AND CLEAR!
CASSIUS... W-WHAT...WHAT IS IT?
THE WORLD THAT EXISTS ON THE OTHER SIDE OF THE DAWN...
THE BRIGHT REALM...
TO BE CONTINUED...

CHAPTER THREE

THE BRIGHT REALM

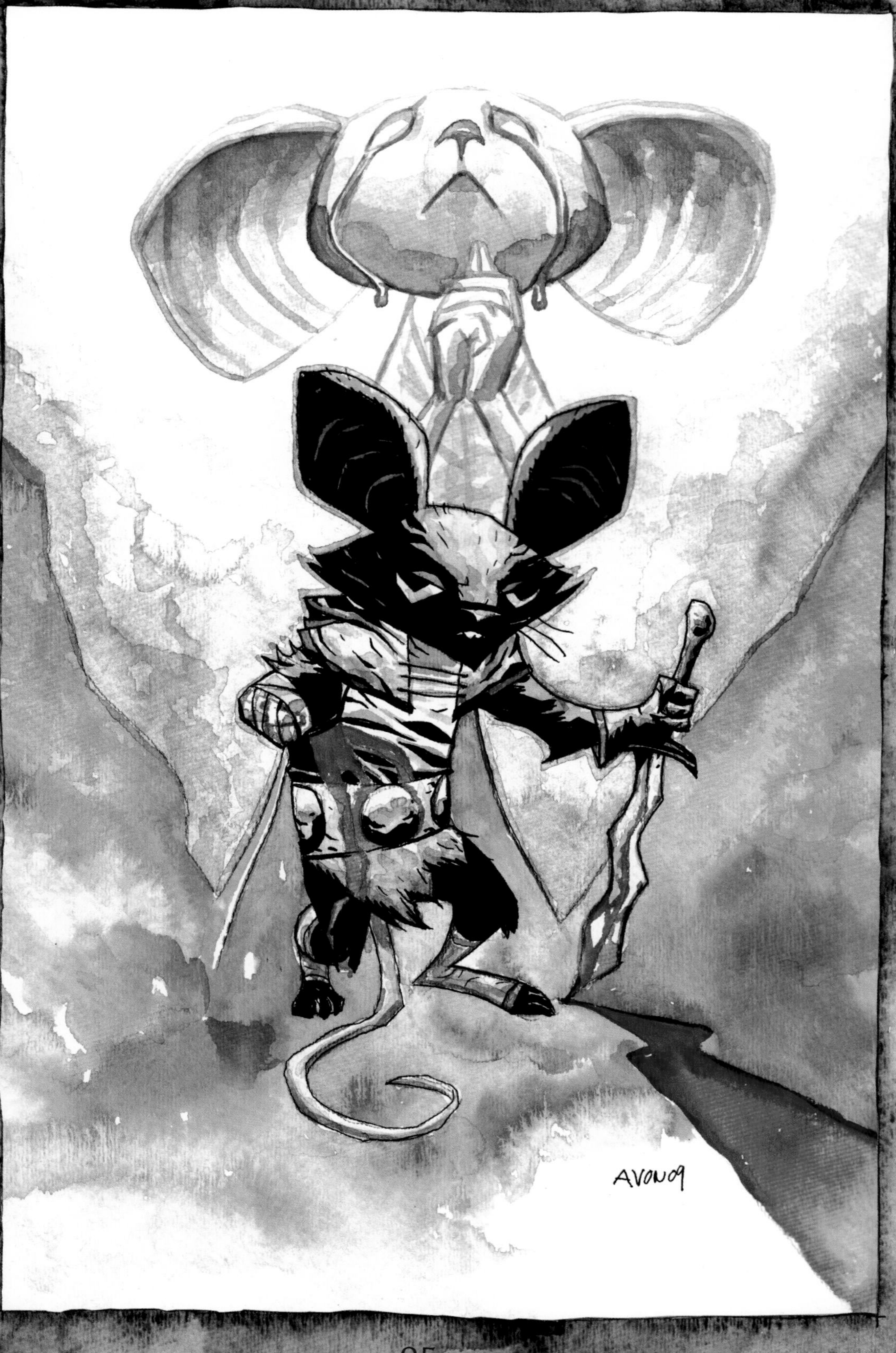
AVON09

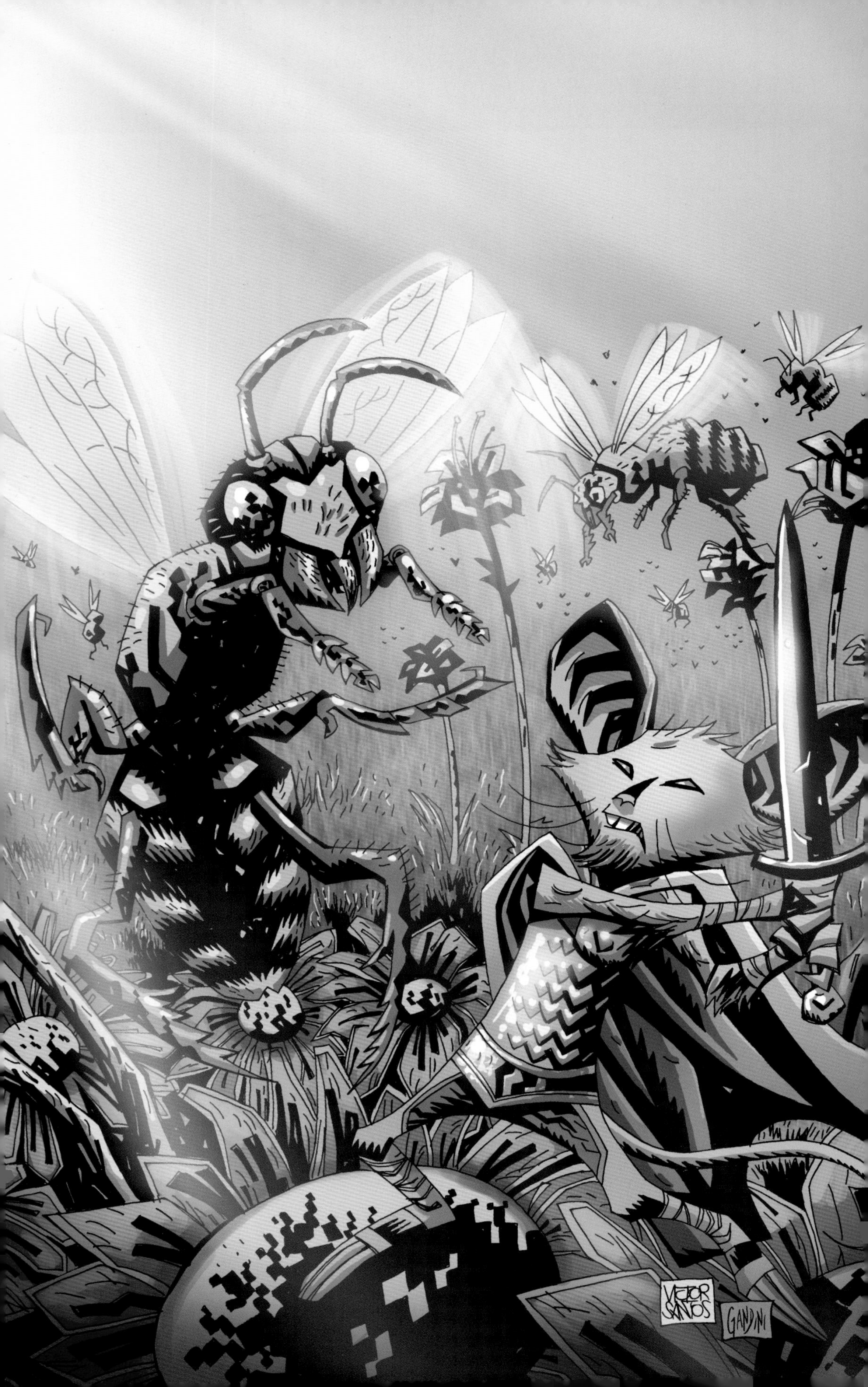
VICTOR SANTOS
GANDINI

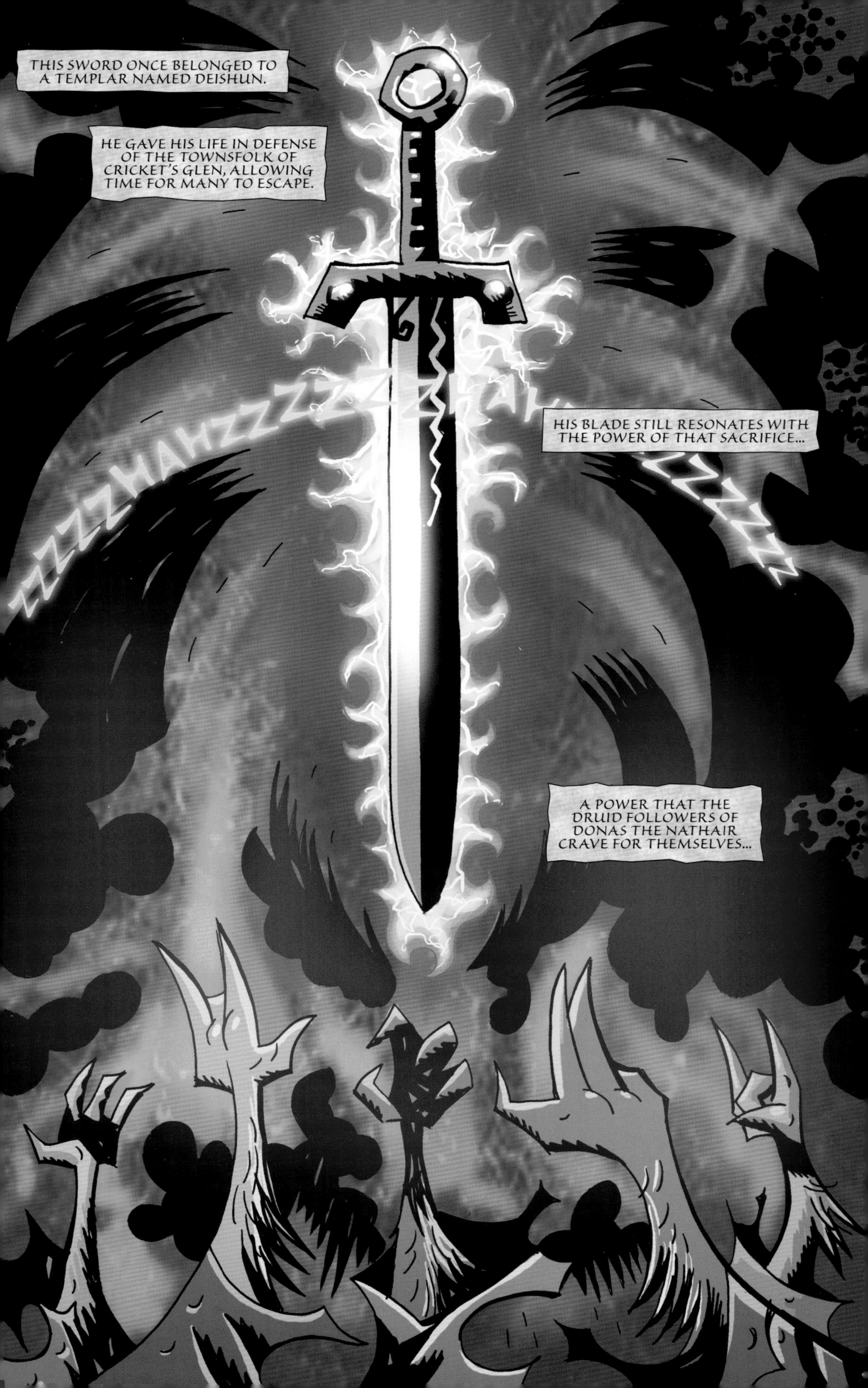
THIS SWORD ONCE BELONGED TO A TEMPLAR NAMED DEISHUN.
HE GAVE HIS LIFE IN DEFENSE OF THE TOWNSFOLK OF CRICKET'S GLEN, ALLOWING TIME FOR MANY TO ESCAPE.
HIS BLADE STILL RESONATES WITH THE POWER OF THAT SACRIFICE...
A POWER THAT THE DRUID FOLLOWERS OF DONAS THE NATHAIR CRAVE FOR THEMSELVES...

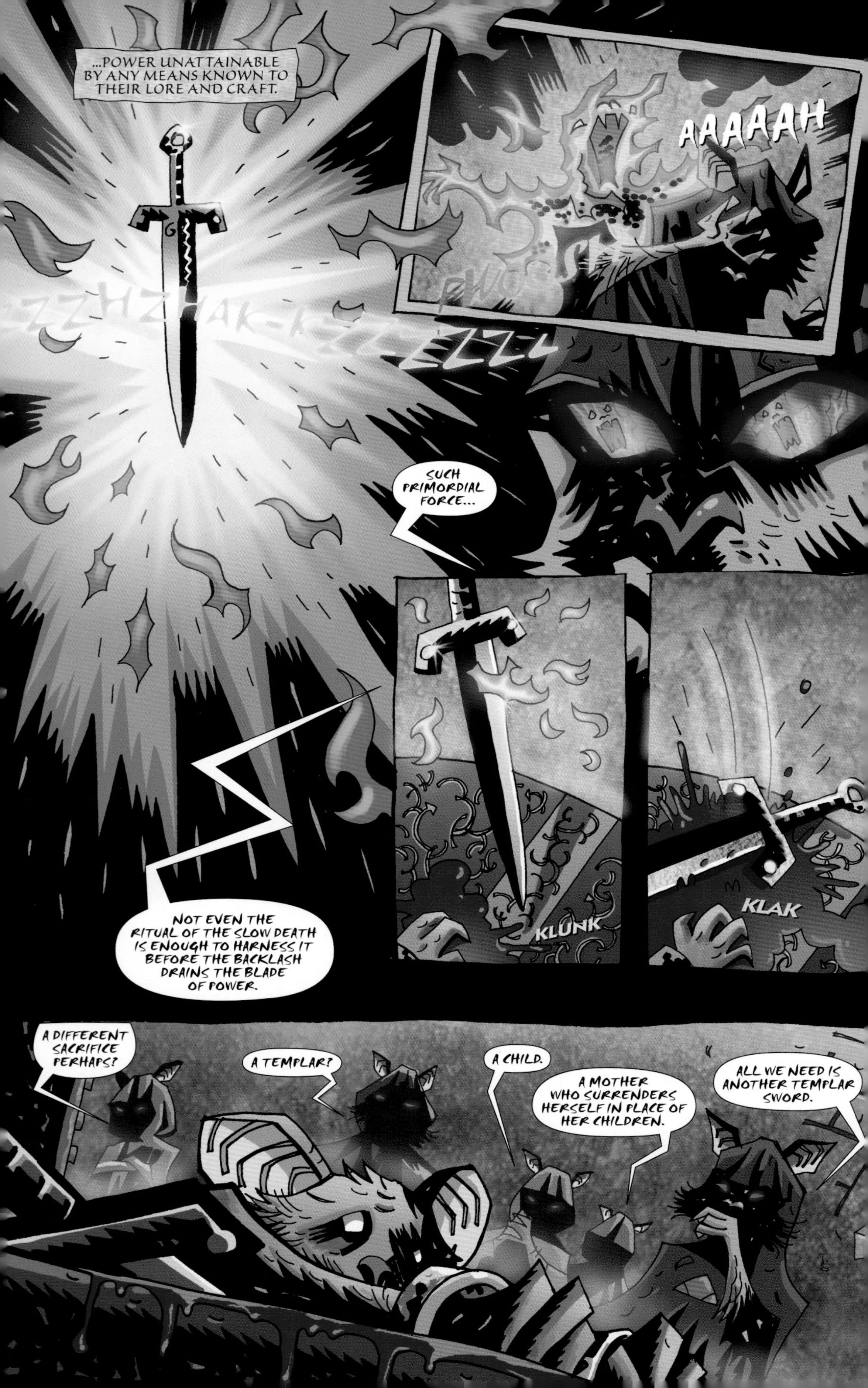
...POWER UNATTAINABLE BY ANY MEANS KNOWN TO THEIR LORE AND CRAFT.
AAAAAH
PWOOSH
ZZZHZHAK-KZZZZZZ
SUCH PRIMORDIAL FORCE...
NOT EVEN THE RITUAL OF THE SLOW DEATH IS ENOUGH TO HARNESS IT BEFORE THE BACKLASH DRAINS THE BLADE OF POWER.
KLUNK
KLAK
A DIFFERENT SACRIFICE PERHAPS?
A TEMPLAR?
A CHILD.
A MOTHER WHO SURRENDERS HERSELF IN PLACE OF HER CHILDREN.
ALL WE NEED IS ANOTHER TEMPLAR SWORD.

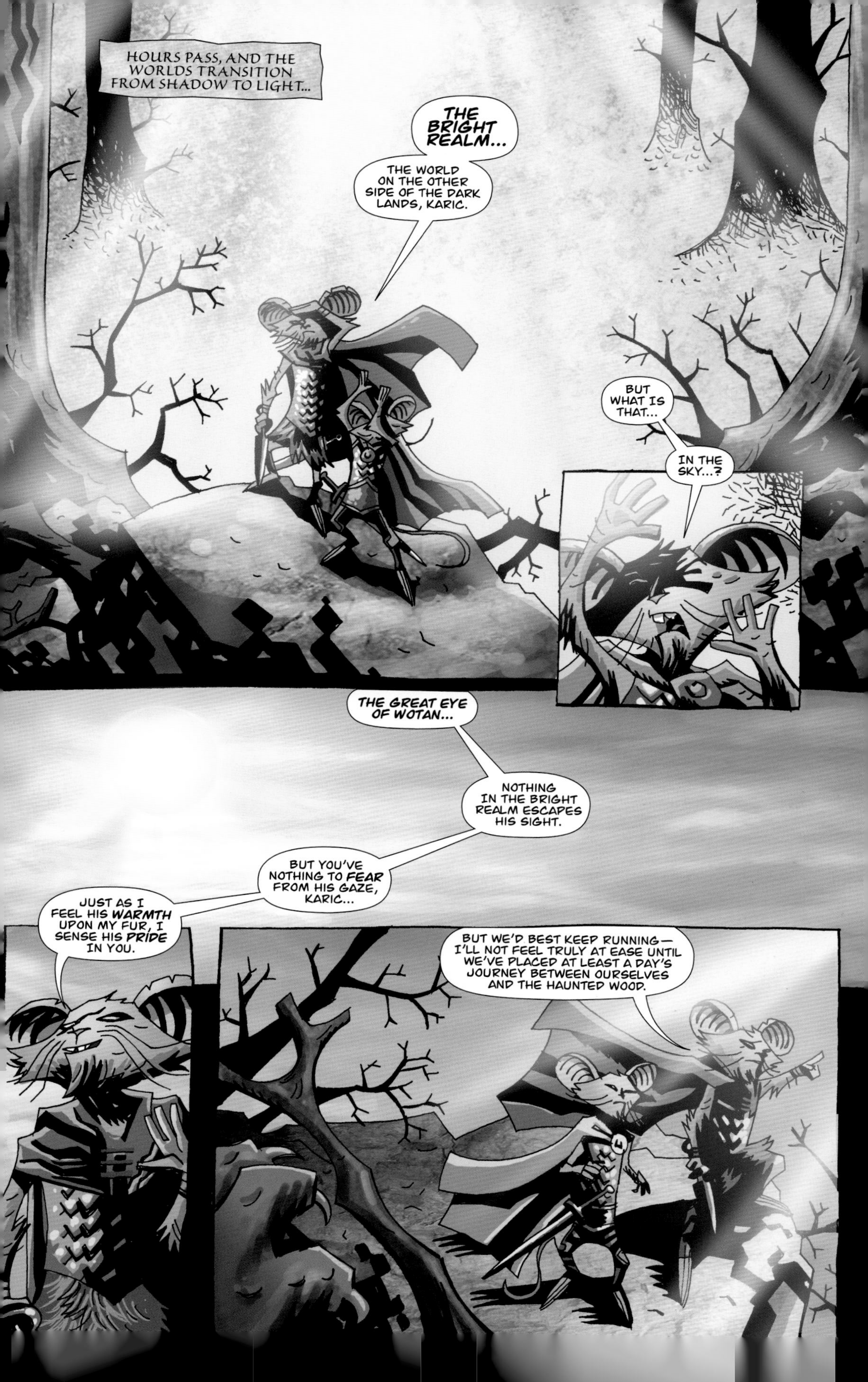
HOURS PASS, AND THE WORLDS TRANSITION FROM SHADOW TO LIGHT...
THE BRIGHT REALM...
THE WORLD ON THE OTHER SIDE OF THE DARK LANDS, KARIC.
BUT WHAT IS THAT...
IN THE SKY...?
THE GREAT EYE OF WOTAN...
NOTHING IN THE BRIGHT REALM ESCAPES HIS SIGHT.
BUT YOU'VE NOTHING TO FEAR FROM HIS GAZE, KARIC...
JUST AS I FEEL HIS WARMTH UPON MY FUR, I SENSE HIS PRIDE IN YOU.
BUT WE'D BEST KEEP RUNNING— I'LL NOT FEEL TRULY AT EASE UNTIL WE'VE PLACED AT LEAST A DAY'S JOURNEY BETWEEN OURSELVES AND THE HAUNTED WOOD.

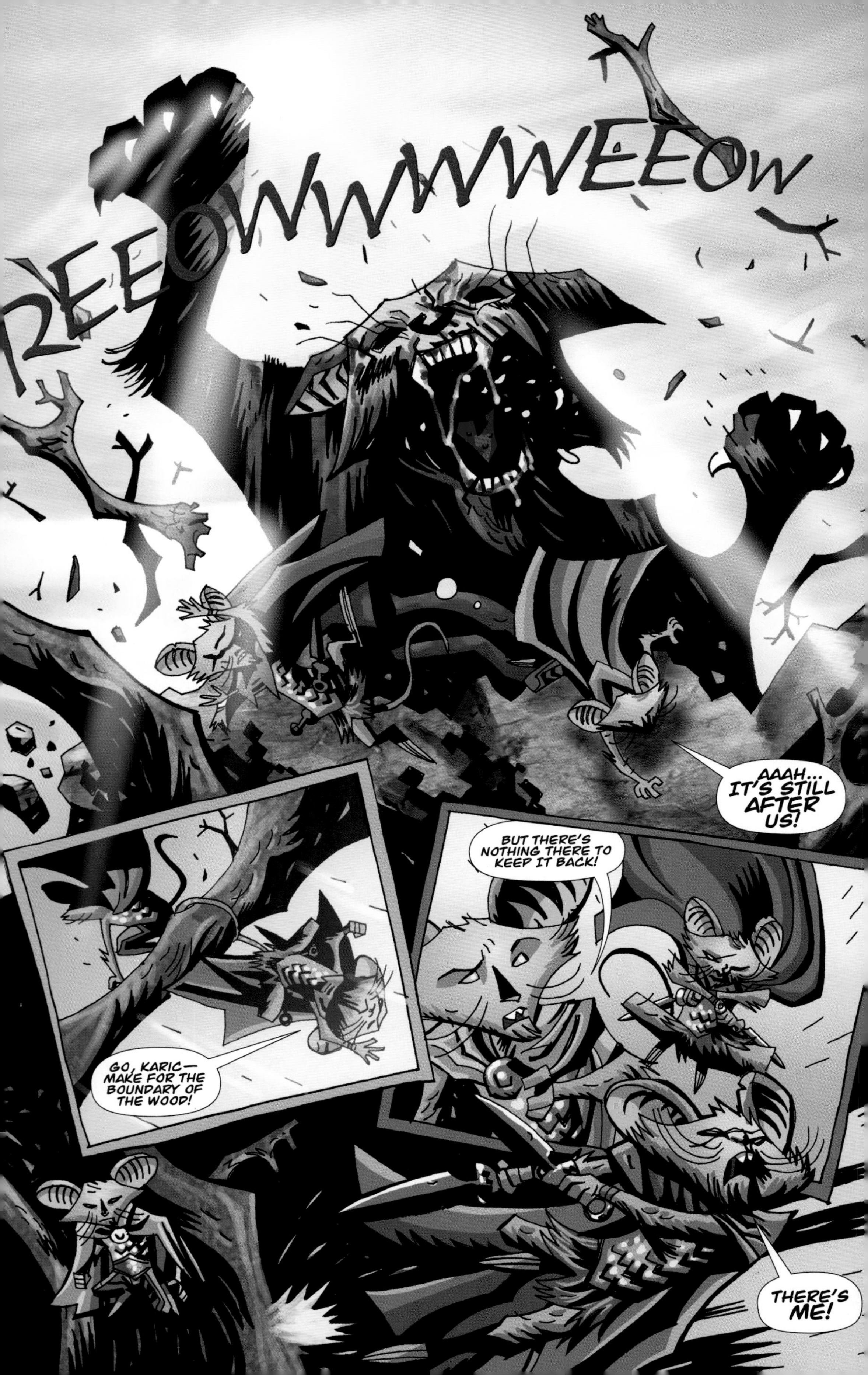
REEOWWWWEEOW
AAAH... IT'S STILL AFTER US!
GO, KARIC— MAKE FOR THE BOUNDARY OF THE WOOD!
BUT THERE'S NOTHING THERE TO KEEP IT BACK!
THERE'S ME!

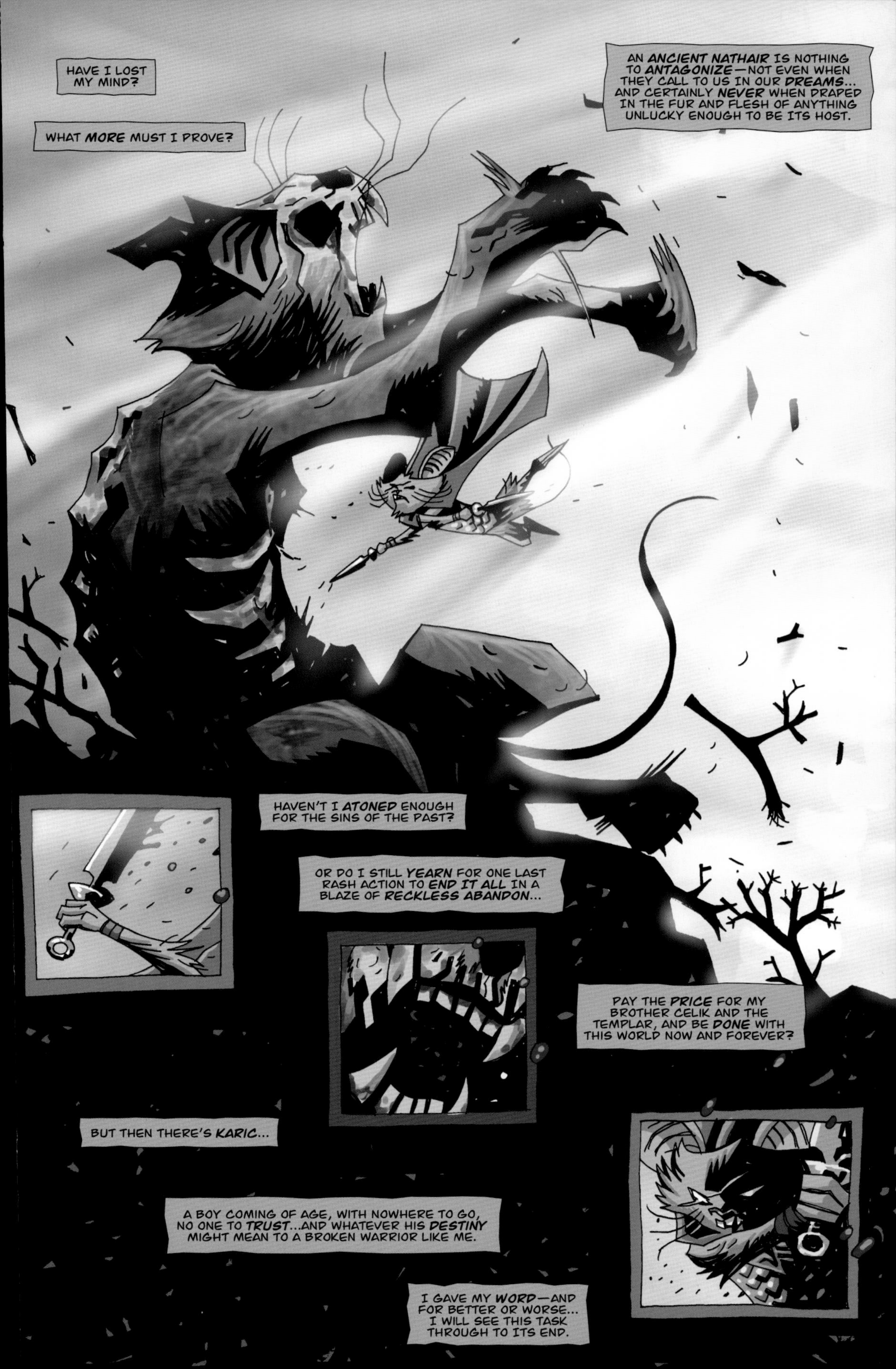

HAVE I LOST MY MIND?
WHAT MORE MUST I PROVE?
AN ANCIENT NATHAIR IS NOTHING TO ANTAGONIZE—NOT EVEN WHEN THEY CALL TO US IN OUR DREAMS... AND CERTAINLY NEVER WHEN DRAPED IN THE FUR AND FLESH OF ANYTHING UNLUCKY ENOUGH TO BE ITS HOST.
HAVEN'T I ATONED ENOUGH FOR THE SINS OF THE PAST?
OR DO I STILL YEARN FOR ONE LAST RASH ACTION TO END IT ALL IN A BLAZE OF RECKLESS ABANDON...
PAY THE PRICE FOR MY BROTHER CELIK AND THE TEMPLAR, AND BE DONE WITH THIS WORLD NOW AND FOREVER?
BUT THEN THERE'S KARIC...
A BOY COMING OF AGE, WITH NOWHERE TO GO, NO ONE TO TRUST...AND WHATEVER HIS DESTINY MIGHT MEAN TO A BROKEN WARRIOR LIKE ME.
I GAVE MY WORD—AND FOR BETTER OR WORSE... I WILL SEE THIS TASK THROUGH TO ITS END.

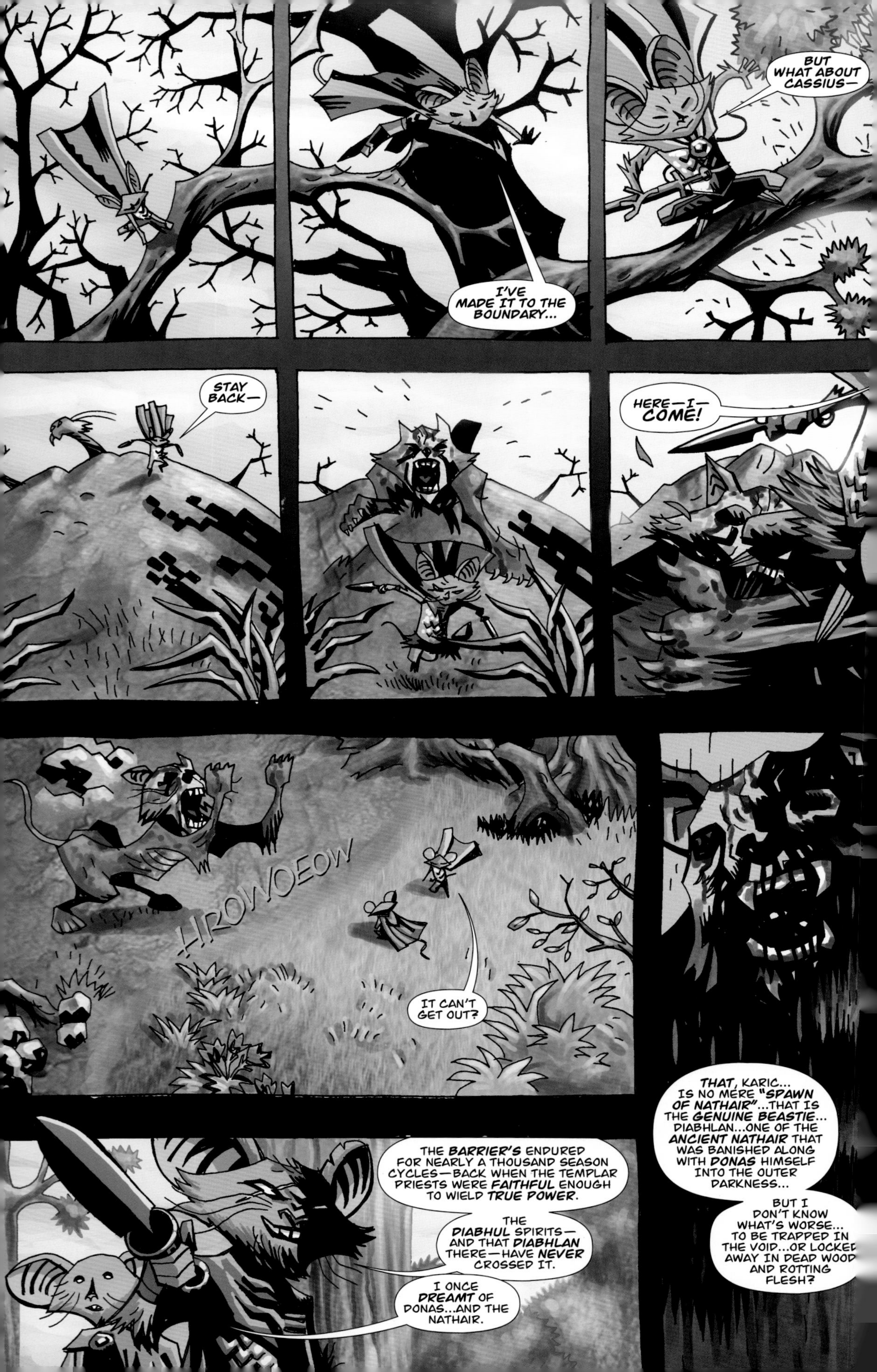
I'VE MADE IT TO THE BOUNDARY...
BUT WHAT ABOUT CASSIUS—
STAY BACK—
HERE—I—COME!
HROWOEOW
IT CAN'T GET OUT?
THAT, KARIC... IS NO MERE "SPAWN OF NATHAIR"...THAT IS THE GENUINE BEASTIE... DIABHLAN...ONE OF THE ANCIENT NATHAIR THAT WAS BANISHED ALONG WITH DONAS HIMSELF INTO THE OUTER DARKNESS...
BUT I DON'T KNOW WHAT'S WORSE... TO BE TRAPPED IN THE VOID...OR LOCKED AWAY IN DEAD WOOD AND ROTTING FLESH?
THE BARRIER'S ENDURED FOR NEARLY A THOUSAND SEASON CYCLES—BACK WHEN THE TEMPLAR PRIESTS WERE FAITHFUL ENOUGH TO WIELD TRUE POWER.
THE DIABHUL SPIRITS—AND THAT DIABHLAN THERE—HAVE NEVER CROSSED IT.
I ONCE DREAMT OF DONAS...AND THE NATHAIR.

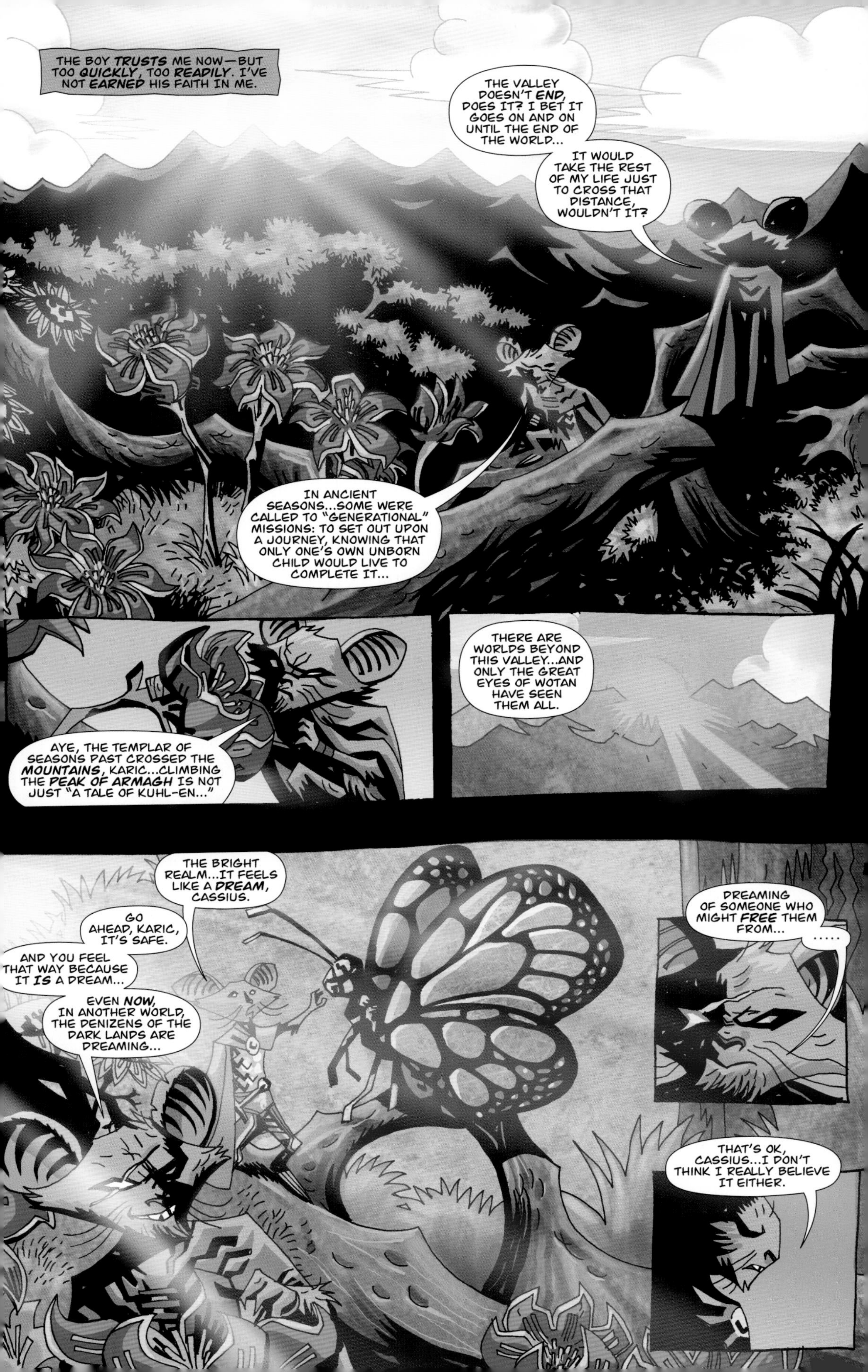
THE BOY TRUSTS ME NOW—BUT TOO QUICKLY, TOO READILY. I'VE NOT EARNED HIS FAITH IN ME.
THE VALLEY DOESN'T END, DOES IT? I BET IT GOES ON AND ON UNTIL THE END OF THE WORLD...
IT WOULD TAKE THE REST OF MY LIFE JUST TO CROSS THAT DISTANCE, WOULDN'T IT?
IN ANCIENT SEASONS...SOME WERE CALLED TO "GENERATIONAL" MISSIONS: TO SET OUT UPON A JOURNEY, KNOWING THAT ONLY ONE'S OWN UNBORN CHILD WOULD LIVE TO COMPLETE IT...
AYE, THE TEMPLAR OF SEASONS PAST CROSSED THE MOUNTAINS, KARIC...CLIMBING THE PEAK OF ARMAGH IS NOT JUST "A TALE OF KUHL-EN..."
THERE ARE WORLDS BEYOND THIS VALLEY...AND ONLY THE GREAT EYES OF WOTAN HAVE SEEN THEM ALL.
THE BRIGHT REALM...IT FEELS LIKE A DREAM, CASSIUS.
GO AHEAD, KARIC, IT'S SAFE.
AND YOU FEEL THAT WAY BECAUSE IT IS A DREAM...
EVEN NOW, IN ANOTHER WORLD, THE DENIZENS OF THE DARK LANDS ARE DREAMING...
DREAMING OF SOMEONE WHO MIGHT FREE THEM FROM...
.....
THAT'S OK, CASSIUS...I DON'T THINK I REALLY BELIEVE IT EITHER.

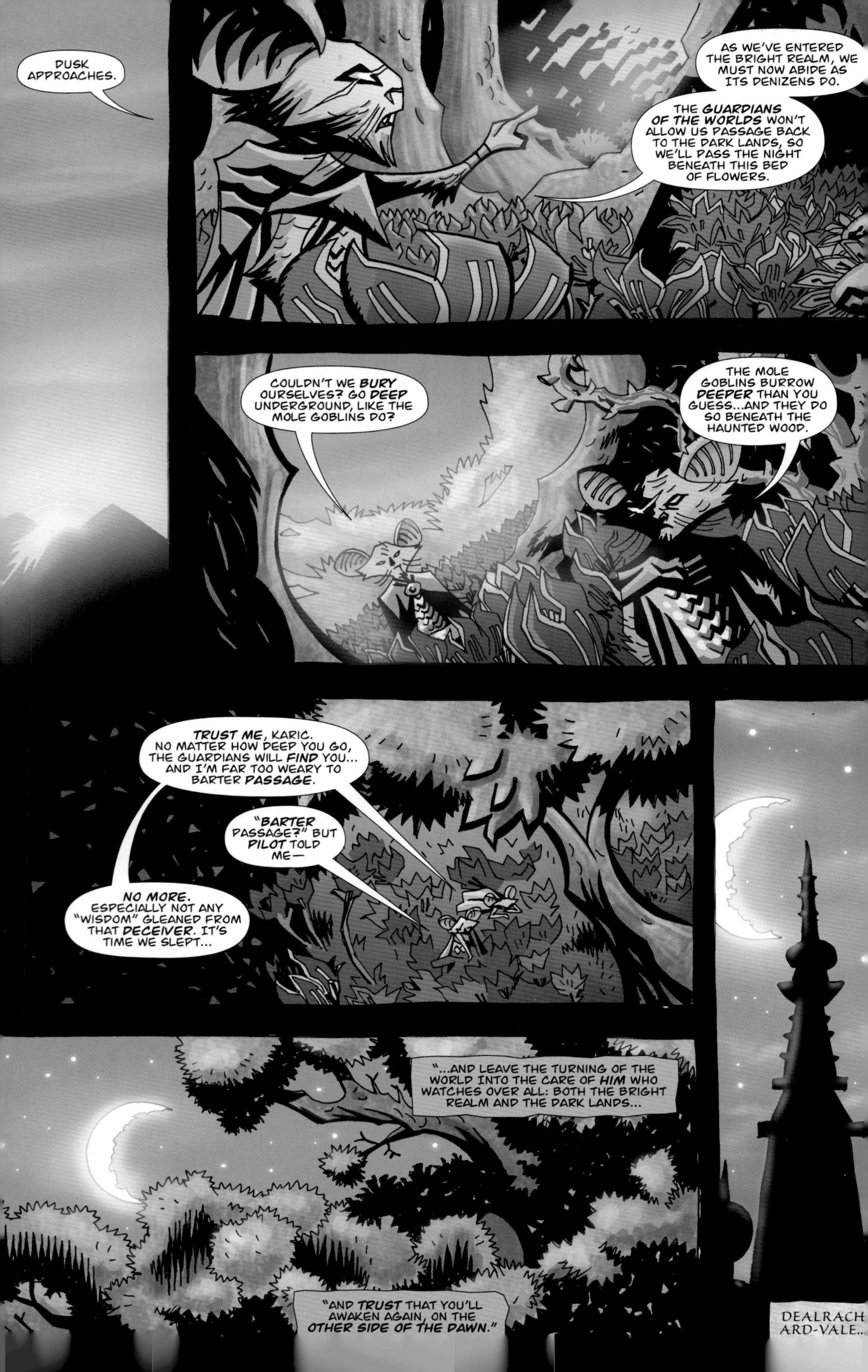
DUSK APPROACHES.
AS WE'VE ENTERED THE BRIGHT REALM, WE MUST NOW ABIDE AS ITS DENIZENS DO.
THE GUARDIANS OF THE WORLDS WON'T ALLOW US PASSAGE BACK TO THE DARK LANDS, SO WE'LL PASS THE NIGHT BENEATH THIS BED OF FLOWERS.
COULDN'T WE BURY OURSELVES? GO DEEP UNDERGROUND, LIKE THE MOLE GOBLINS DO?
THE MOLE GOBLINS BURROW DEEPER THAN YOU GUESS...AND THEY DO SO BENEATH THE HAUNTED WOOD.
TRUST ME, KARIC. NO MATTER HOW DEEP YOU GO, THE GUARDIANS WILL FIND YOU... AND I'M FAR TOO WEARY TO BARTER PASSAGE.
"BARTER PASSAGE?" BUT PILOT TOLD ME—
NO MORE. ESPECIALLY NOT ANY "WISDOM" GLEANED FROM THAT DECEIVER. IT'S TIME WE SLEPT...
"...AND LEAVE THE TURNING OF THE WORLD INTO THE CARE OF HIM WHO WATCHES OVER ALL: BOTH THE BRIGHT REALM AND THE DARK LANDS...
"AND TRUST THAT YOU'LL AWAKEN AGAIN, ON THE OTHER SIDE OF THE DAWN."
DEALRACH ARD-VALE..

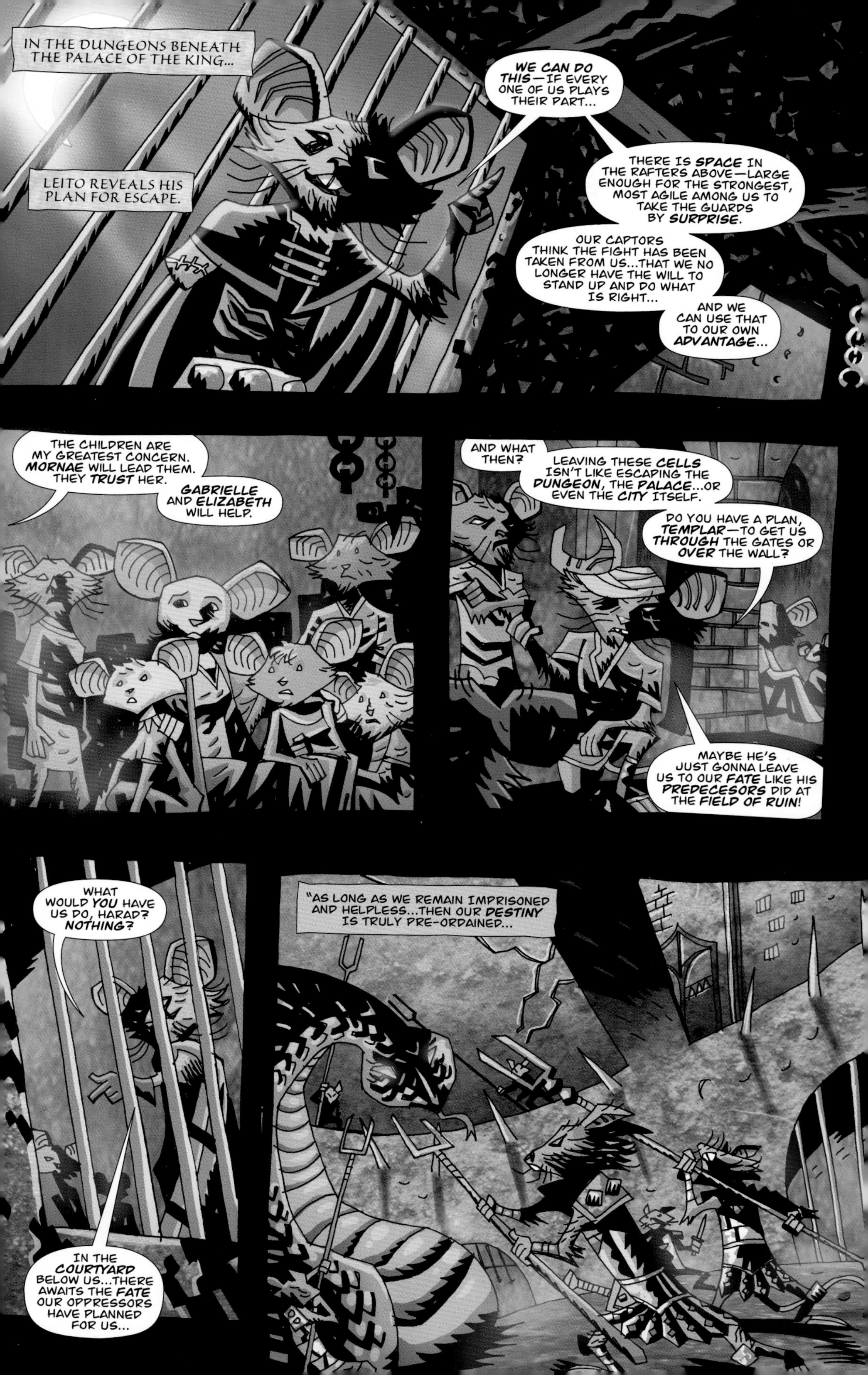
IN THE DUNGEONS BENEATH THE PALACE OF THE KING...
LEITO REVEALS HIS PLAN FOR ESCAPE.
WE CAN DO THIS—IF EVERY ONE OF US PLAYS THEIR PART...
THERE IS SPACE IN THE RAFTERS ABOVE—LARGE ENOUGH FOR THE STRONGEST, MOST AGILE AMONG US TO TAKE THE GUARDS BY SURPRISE.
OUR CAPTORS THINK THE FIGHT HAS BEEN TAKEN FROM US...THAT WE NO LONGER HAVE THE WILL TO STAND UP AND DO WHAT IS RIGHT...
AND WE CAN USE THAT TO OUR OWN ADVANTAGE...
THE CHILDREN ARE MY GREATEST CONCERN. MORNAE WILL LEAD THEM. THEY TRUST HER.
GABRIELLE AND ELIZABETH WILL HELP.
AND WHAT THEN?
LEAVING THESE CELLS ISN'T LIKE ESCAPING THE DUNGEON, THE PALACE...OR EVEN THE CITY ITSELF.
DO YOU HAVE A PLAN, TEMPLAR—TO GET US THROUGH THE GATES OR OVER THE WALL?
MAYBE HE'S JUST GONNA LEAVE US TO OUR FATE LIKE HIS PREDECESORS DID AT THE FIELD OF RUIN!
WHAT WOULD YOU HAVE US DO, HARAD? NOTHING?
IN THE COURTYARD BELOW US...THERE AWAITS THE FATE OUR OPPRESSORS HAVE PLANNED FOR US...
"AS LONG AS WE REMAIN IMPRISONED AND HELPLESS...THEN OUR DESTINY IS TRULY PRE-ORDAINED...

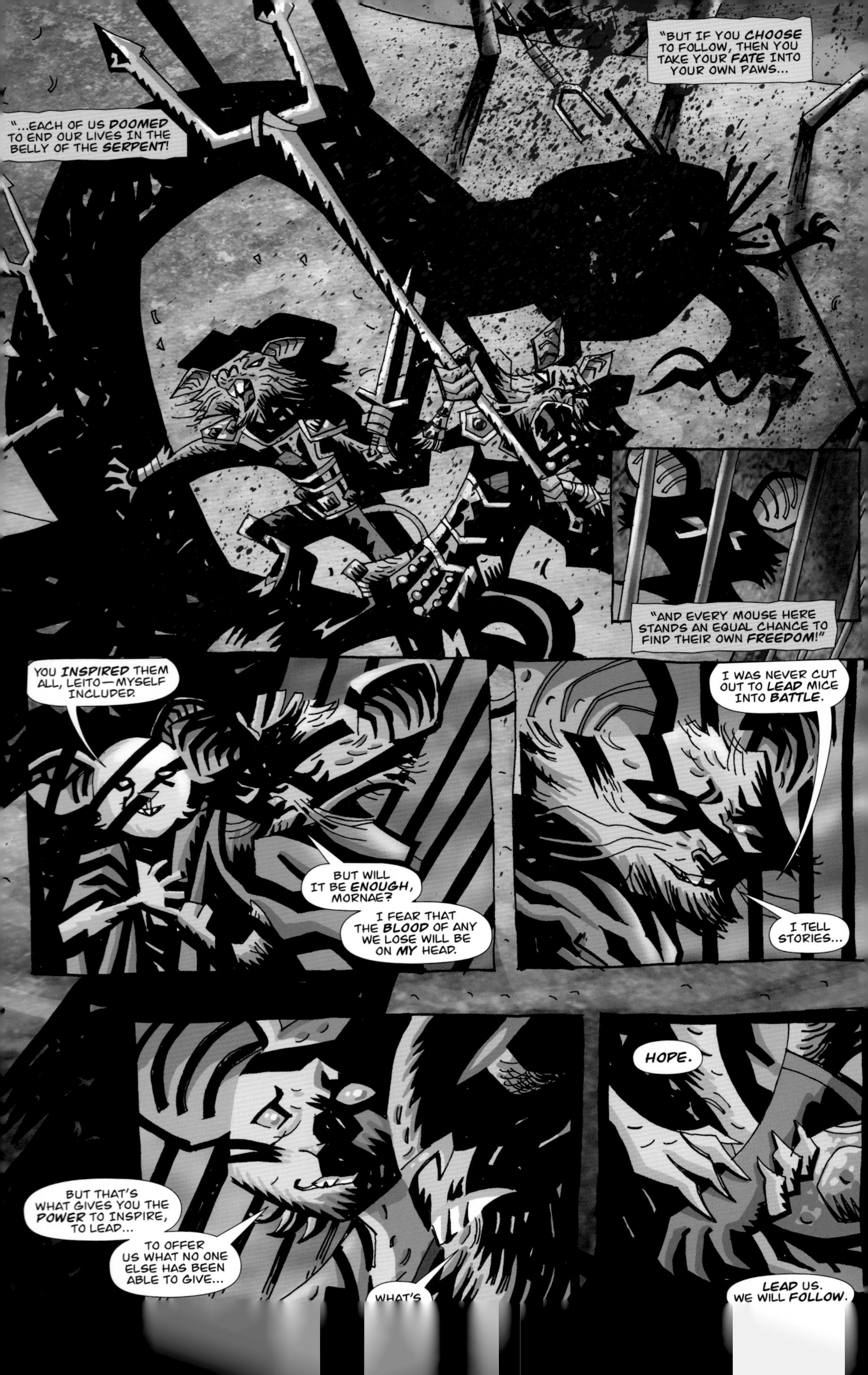
"...EACH OF US DOOMED TO END OUR LIVES IN THE BELLY OF THE SERPENT!
"BUT IF YOU CHOOSE TO FOLLOW, THEN YOU TAKE YOUR FATE INTO YOUR OWN PAWS...
"AND EVERY MOUSE HERE STANDS AN EQUAL CHANCE TO FIND THEIR OWN FREEDOM!"
YOU INSPIRED THEM ALL, LEITO—MYSELF INCLUDED.
BUT WILL IT BE ENOUGH, MORNAE?
I FEAR THAT THE BLOOD OF ANY WE LOSE WILL BE ON MY HEAD.
I WAS NEVER CUT OUT TO LEAD MICE INTO BATTLE.
I TELL STORIES...
BUT THAT'S WHAT GIVES YOU THE POWER TO INSPIRE, TO LEAD...
TO OFFER US WHAT NO ONE ELSE HAS BEEN ABLE TO GIVE...
HOPE.
LEAD US. WE WILL FOLLOW.

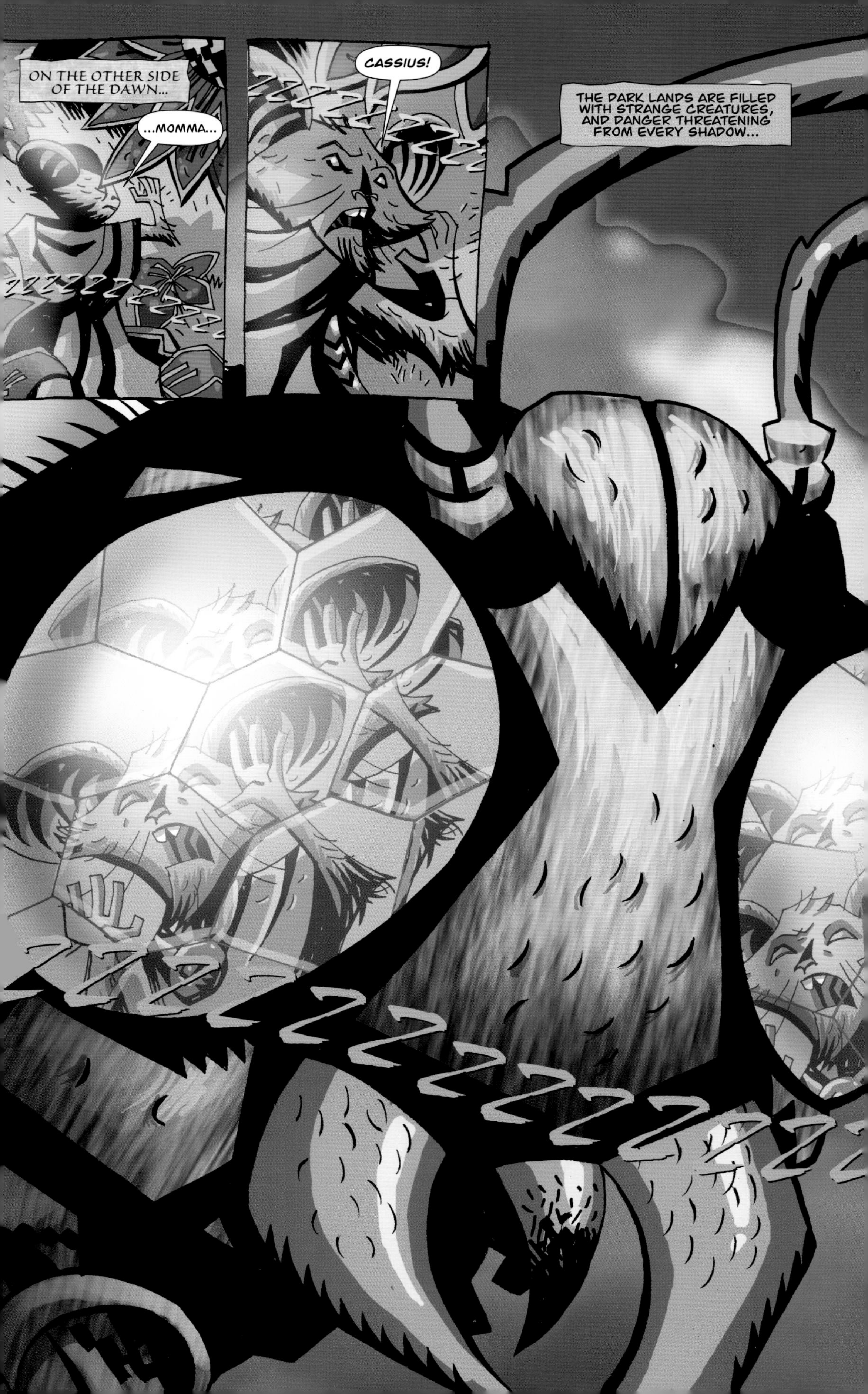
ON THE OTHER SIDE OF THE DAWN...
...MOMMA...
CASSIUS!
THE DARK LANDS ARE FILLED WITH STRANGE CREATURES, AND DANGER THREATENING FROM EVERY SHADOW...

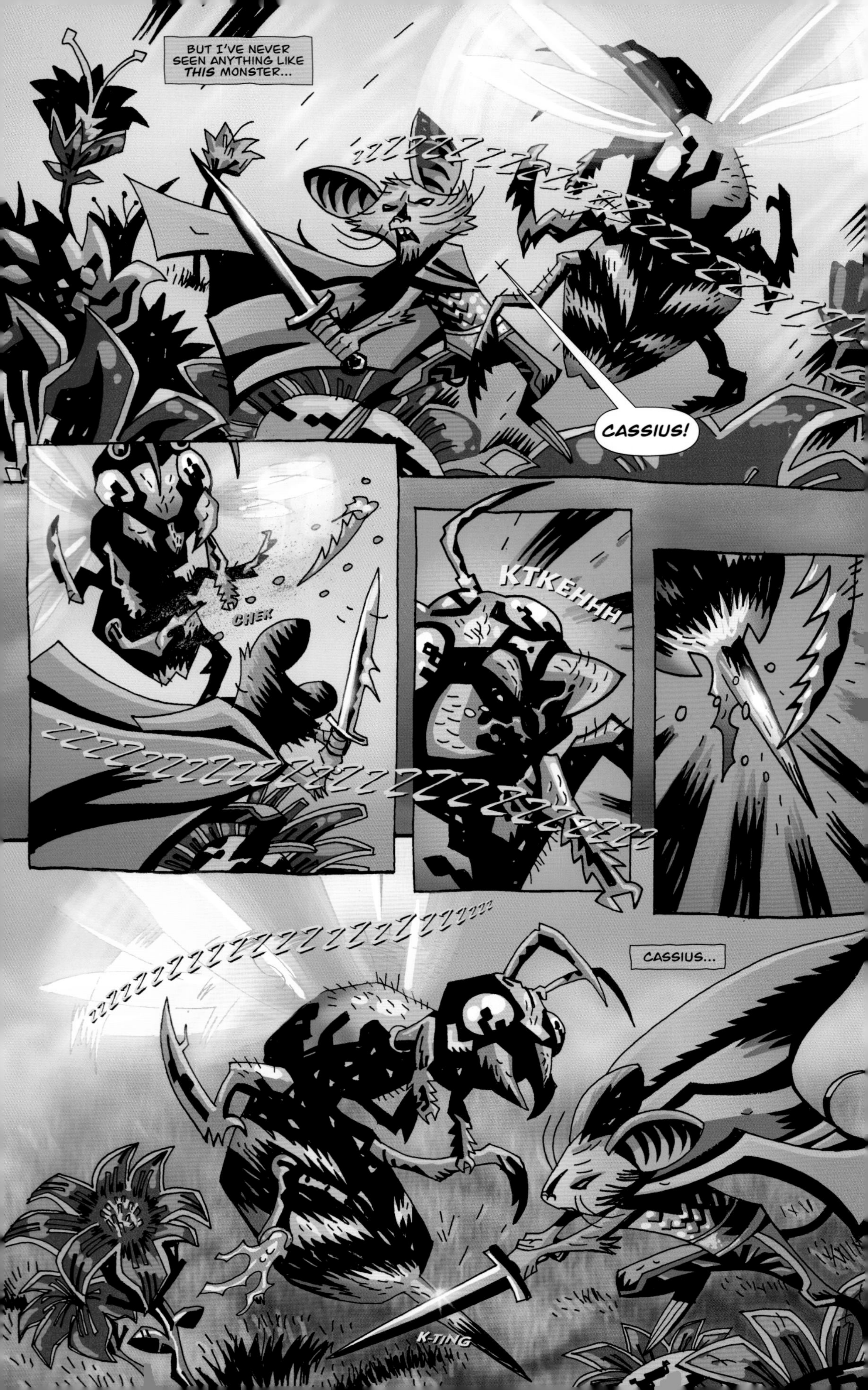
BUT I'VE NEVER SEEN ANYTHING LIKE *THIS* MONSTER...
CASSIUS!
CHEK
KTKEHHH
CASSIUS...
K-TING

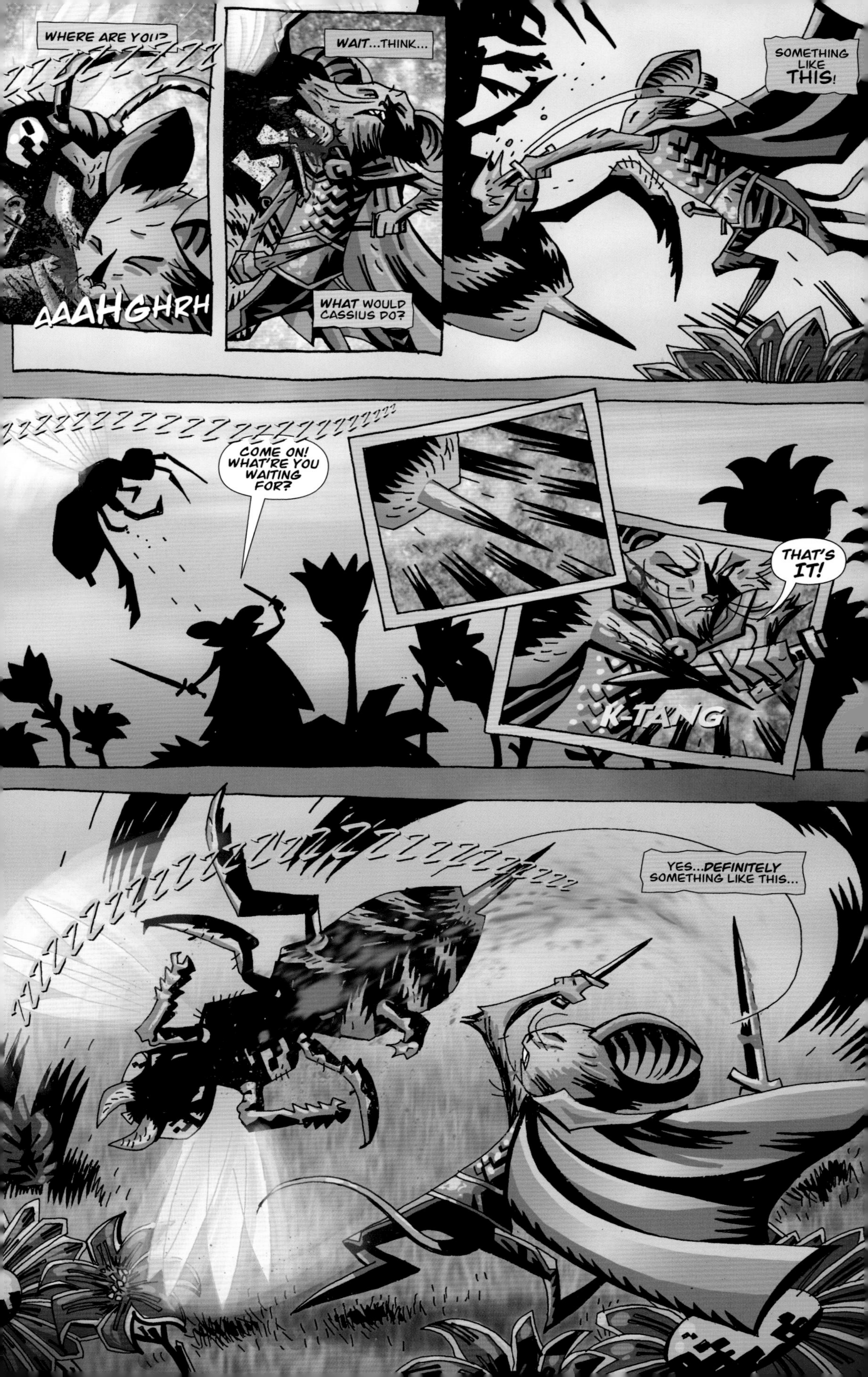
WHERE ARE YOU?
AAAHGHRH
WAIT...THINK...
WHAT WOULD CASSIUS DO?
SOMETHING LIKE THIS!
COME ON! WHAT'RE YOU WAITING FOR?
THAT'S IT!
K-TANG
YES...DEFINITELY SOMETHING LIKE THIS...

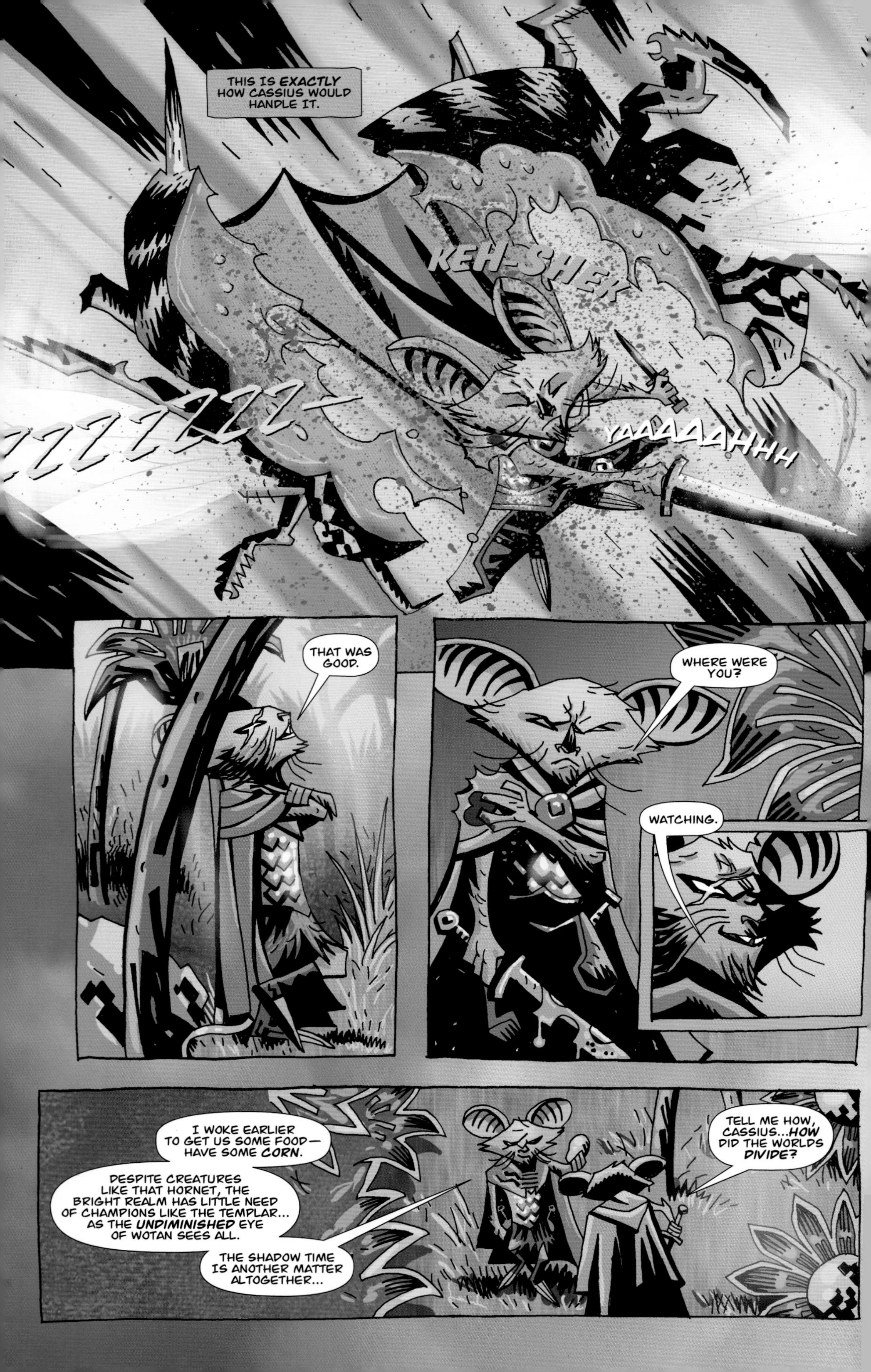
THIS IS EXACTLY HOW CASSIUS WOULD HANDLE IT.
KEH-SHEK
ZZZZZZZZ—
YAAAAAAHHH
THAT WAS GOOD.
WHERE WERE YOU?
WATCHING.
I WOKE EARLIER TO GET US SOME FOOD— HAVE SOME CORN.
DESPITE CREATURES LIKE THAT HORNET, THE BRIGHT REALM HAS LITTLE NEED OF CHAMPIONS LIKE THE TEMPLAR... AS THE UNDIMINISHED EYE OF WOTAN SEES ALL.
THE SHADOW TIME IS ANOTHER MATTER ALTOGETHER...
TELL ME HOW, CASSIUS...HOW DID THE WORLDS DIVIDE?

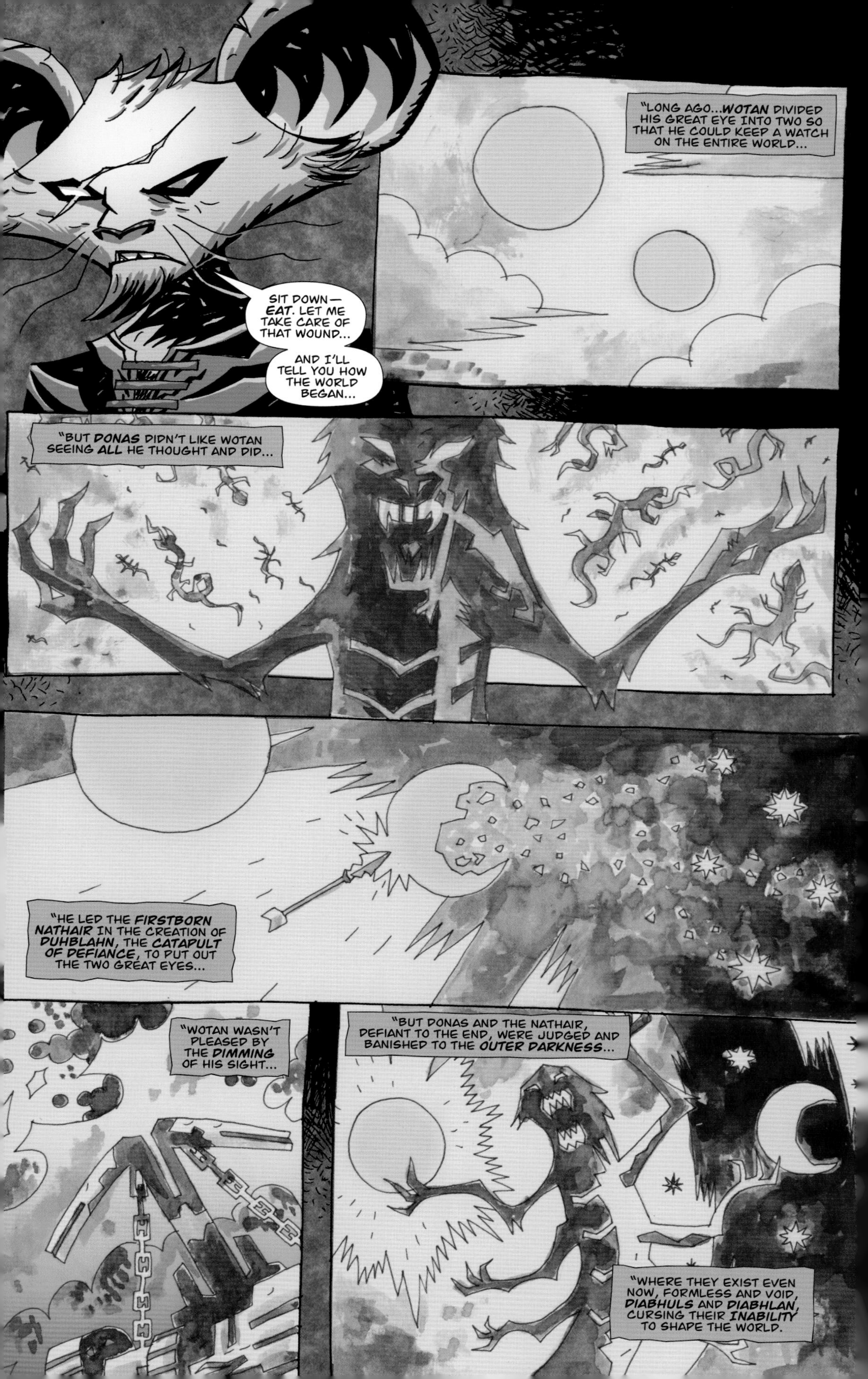
SIT DOWN—EAT. LET ME TAKE CARE OF THAT WOUND...
AND I'LL TELL YOU HOW THE WORLD BEGAN...
"LONG AGO...WOTAN DIVIDED HIS GREAT EYE INTO TWO SO THAT HE COULD KEEP A WATCH ON THE ENTIRE WORLD...
"BUT DONAS DIDN'T LIKE WOTAN SEEING ALL HE THOUGHT AND DID...
"HE LED THE FIRSTBORN NATHAIR IN THE CREATION OF DUHBLAHN, THE CATAPULT OF DEFIANCE, TO PUT OUT THE TWO GREAT EYES...
"WOTAN WASN'T PLEASED BY THE DIMMING OF HIS SIGHT...
"BUT DONAS AND THE NATHAIR, DEFIANT TO THE END, WERE JUDGED AND BANISHED TO THE OUTER DARKNESS...
"WHERE THEY EXIST EVEN NOW, FORMLESS AND VOID, DIABHULS AND DIABHLAN, CURSING THEIR INABILITY TO SHAPE THE WORLD.

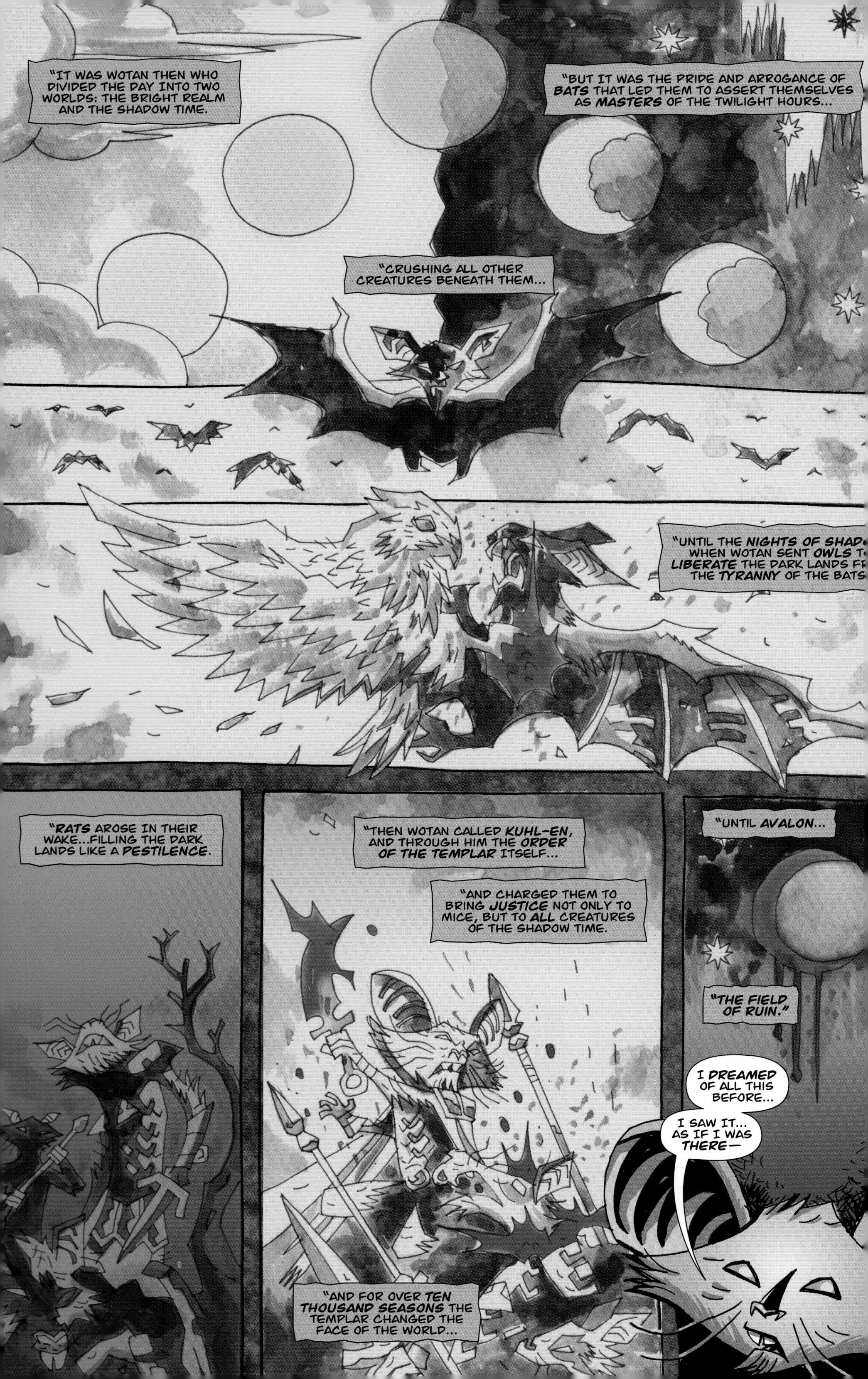
"IT WAS WOTAN THEN WHO DIVIDED THE DAY INTO TWO WORLDS: THE BRIGHT REALM AND THE SHADOW TIME.
"BUT IT WAS THE PRIDE AND ARROGANCE OF BATS THAT LED THEM TO ASSERT THEMSELVES AS MASTERS OF THE TWILIGHT HOURS...
"CRUSHING ALL OTHER CREATURES BENEATH THEM...
"UNTIL THE NIGHTS OF SHAD
WHEN WOTAN SENT OWLS T
LIBERATE THE DARK LANDS FR
THE TYRANNY OF THE BATS
"RATS AROSE IN THEIR WAKE...FILLING THE DARK LANDS LIKE A PESTILENCE.
"THEN WOTAN CALLED KUHL-EN, AND THROUGH HIM THE ORDER OF THE TEMPLAR ITSELF...
"AND CHARGED THEM TO BRING JUSTICE NOT ONLY TO MICE, BUT TO ALL CREATURES OF THE SHADOW TIME.
"AND FOR OVER TEN THOUSAND SEASONS THE TEMPLAR CHANGED THE FACE OF THE WORLD...
"UNTIL AVALON...
"THE FIELD OF RUIN."
I DREAMED OF ALL THIS BEFORE...
I SAW IT... AS IF I WAS THERE—

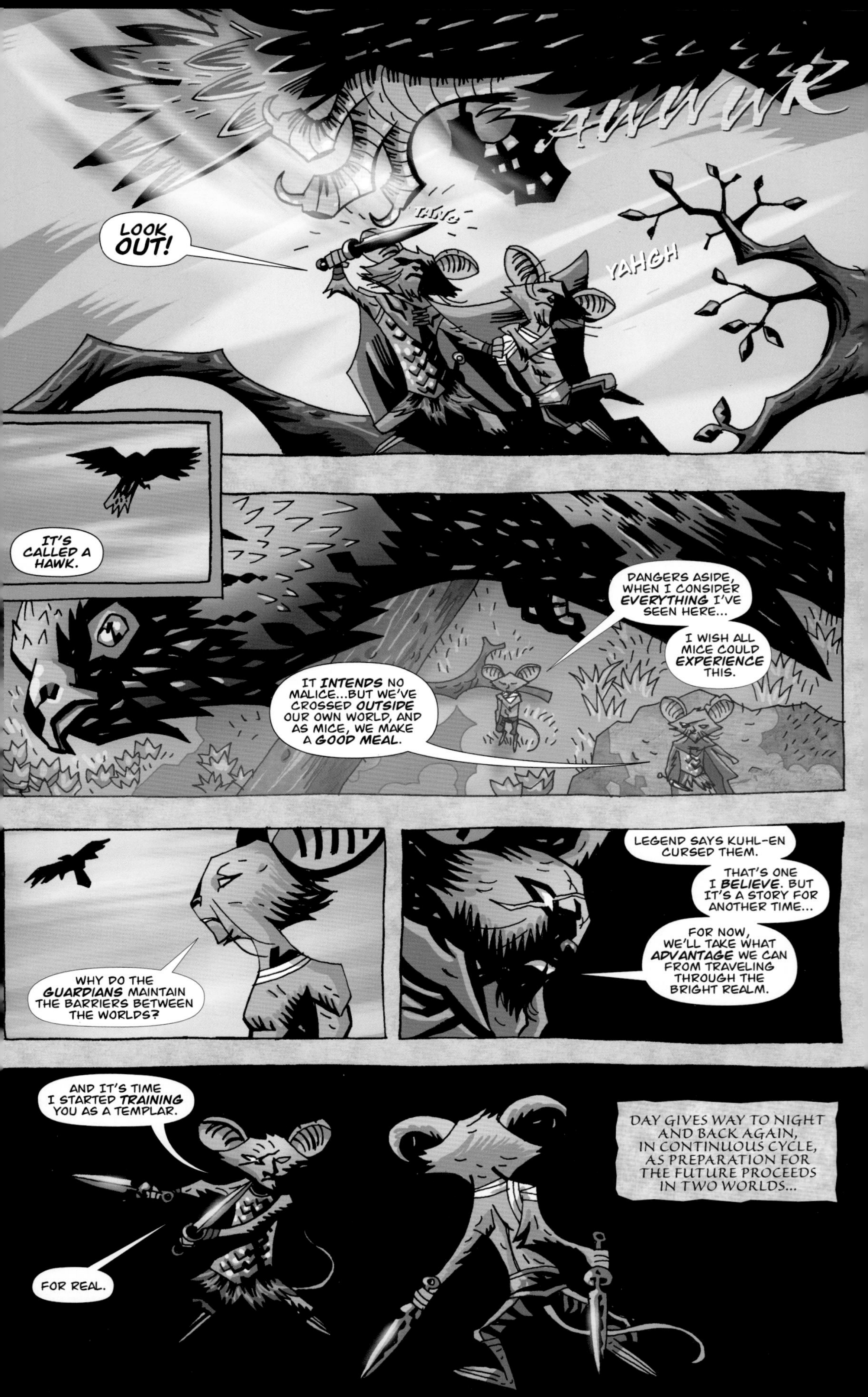
AWWWK
LOOK OUT!
TANG
YAHGH
IT'S CALLED A HAWK.
DANGERS ASIDE, WHEN I CONSIDER EVERYTHING I'VE SEEN HERE...
I WISH ALL MICE COULD EXPERIENCE THIS.
IT INTENDS NO MALICE...BUT WE'VE CROSSED OUTSIDE OUR OWN WORLD, AND AS MICE, WE MAKE A GOOD MEAL.
WHY DO THE GUARDIANS MAINTAIN THE BARRIERS BETWEEN THE WORLDS?
LEGEND SAYS KUHL-EN CURSED THEM.
THAT'S ONE I BELIEVE. BUT IT'S A STORY FOR ANOTHER TIME...
FOR NOW, WE'LL TAKE WHAT ADVANTAGE WE CAN FROM TRAVELING THROUGH THE BRIGHT REALM.
AND IT'S TIME I STARTED TRAINING YOU AS A TEMPLAR.
FOR REAL.
DAY GIVES WAY TO NIGHT AND BACK AGAIN, IN CONTINUOUS CYCLE, AS PREPARATION FOR THE FUTURE PROCEEDS IN TWO WORLDS...

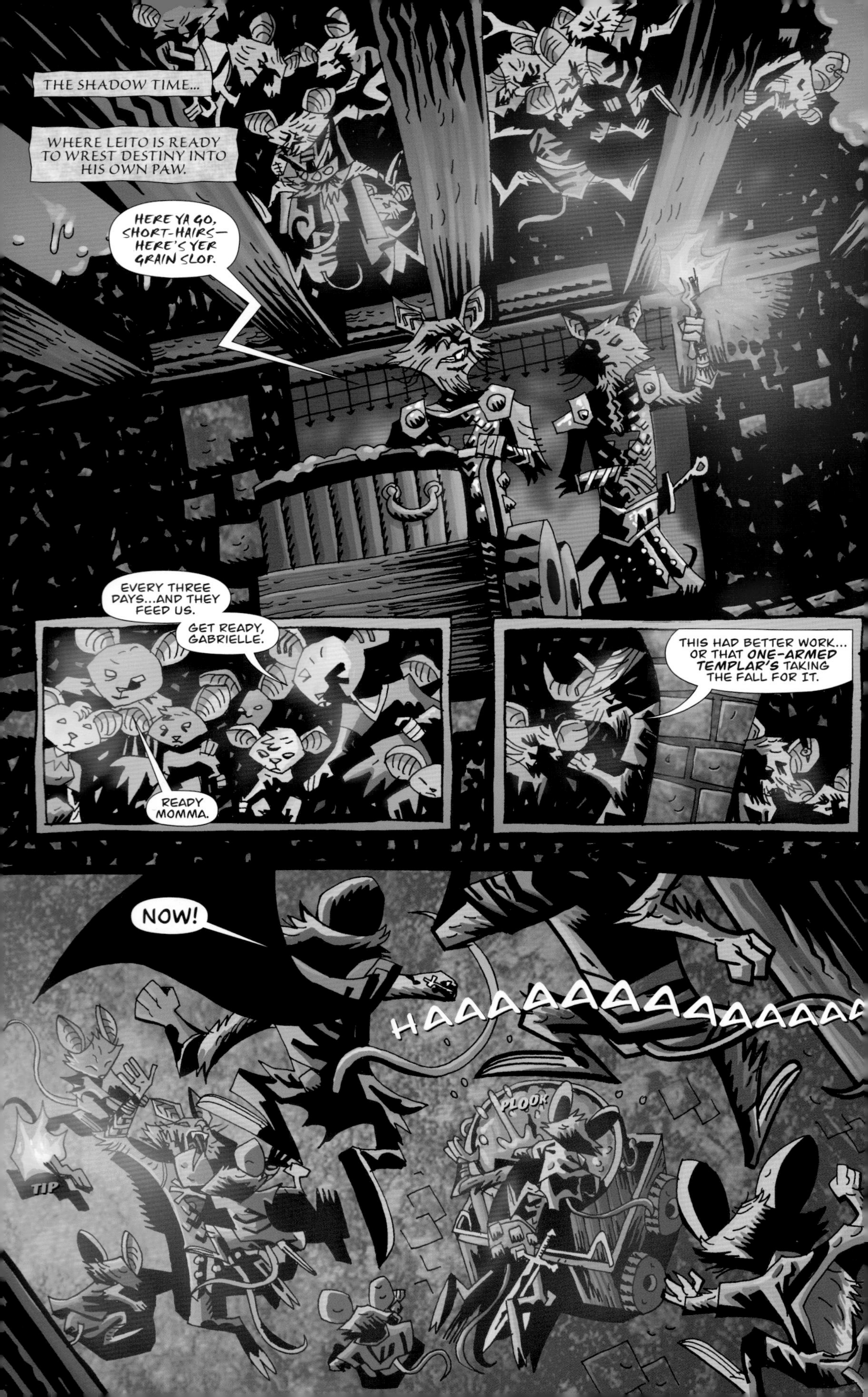
THE SHADOW TIME...
WHERE LEITO IS READY TO WREST DESTINY INTO HIS OWN PAW.
HERE YA GO, SHORT-HAIRS— HERE'S YER GRAIN SLOP.
EVERY THREE DAYS...AND THEY FEED US.
GET READY, GABRIELLE.
READY MOMMA.
THIS HAD BETTER WORK... OR THAT ONE-ARMED TEMPLAR'S TAKING THE FALL FOR IT.
NOW!
HAAAAAAAAAAAAAA
PLOOK
TIP

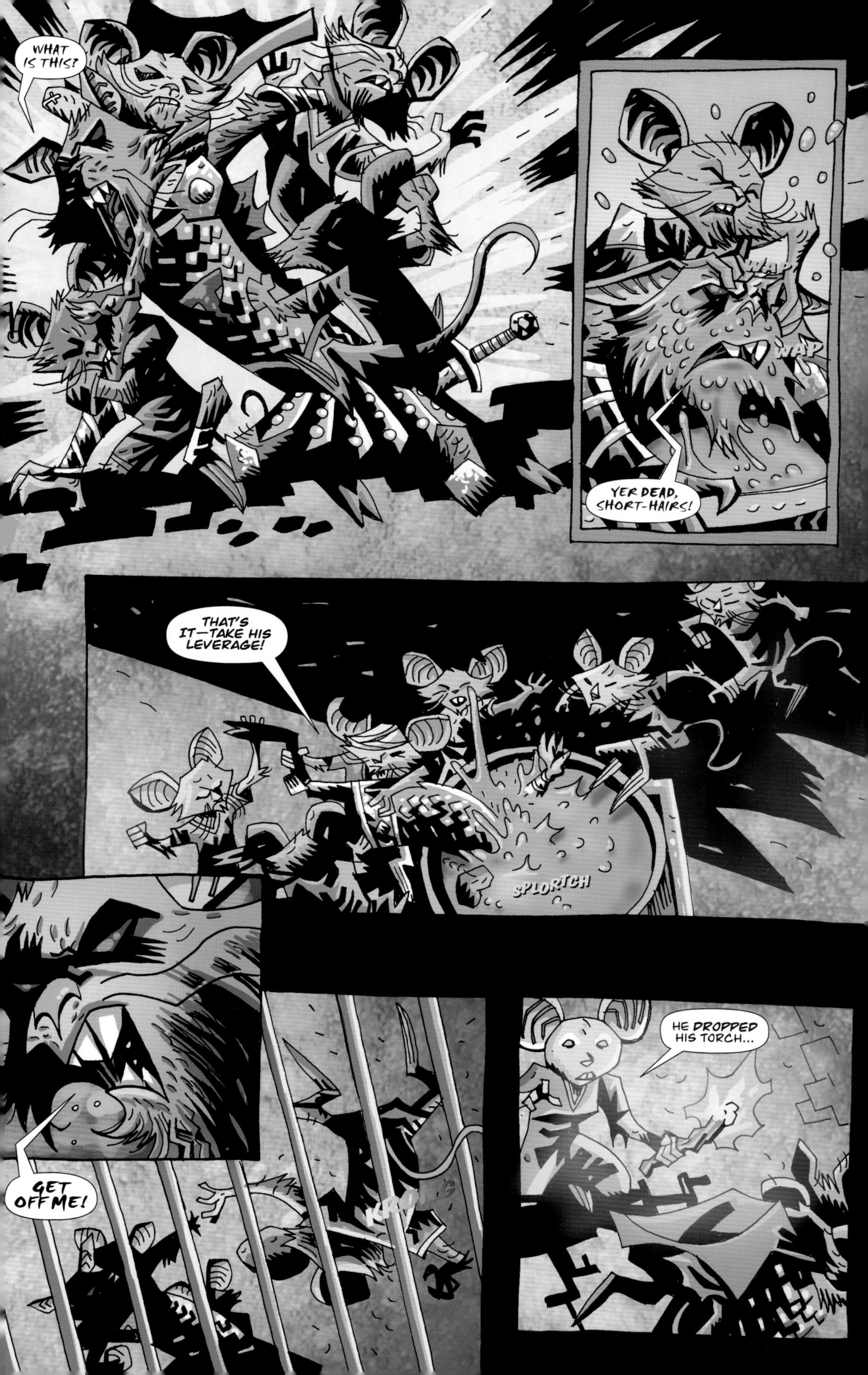

WHAT IS THIS?
WAP
WAP
YER DEAD, SHORT-HAIRS!
THAT'S IT—TAKE HIS LEVERAGE!
SPLORTCH
GET OFF ME!
HE DROPPED HIS TORCH...

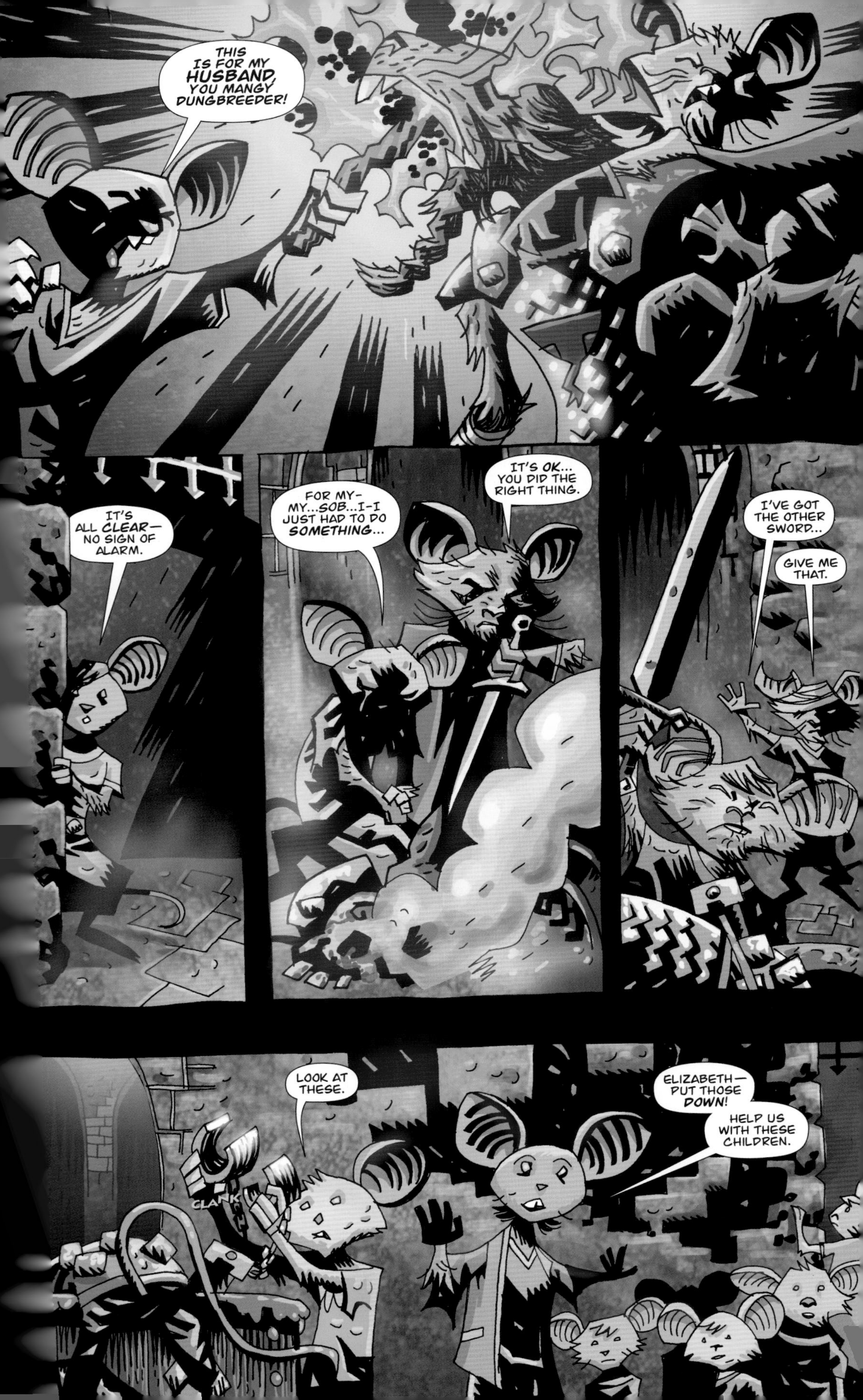

THIS IS FOR MY HUSBAND, YOU MANGY DUNGBREEDER!
IT'S ALL CLEAR— NO SIGN OF ALARM.
FOR MY- MY...SOB...I-I JUST HAD TO DO SOMETHING...
IT'S OK... YOU DID THE RIGHT THING.
I'VE GOT THE OTHER SWORD...
GIVE ME THAT.
LOOK AT THESE.
CLANK
ELIZABETH— PUT THOSE DOWN!
HELP US WITH THESE CHILDREN.

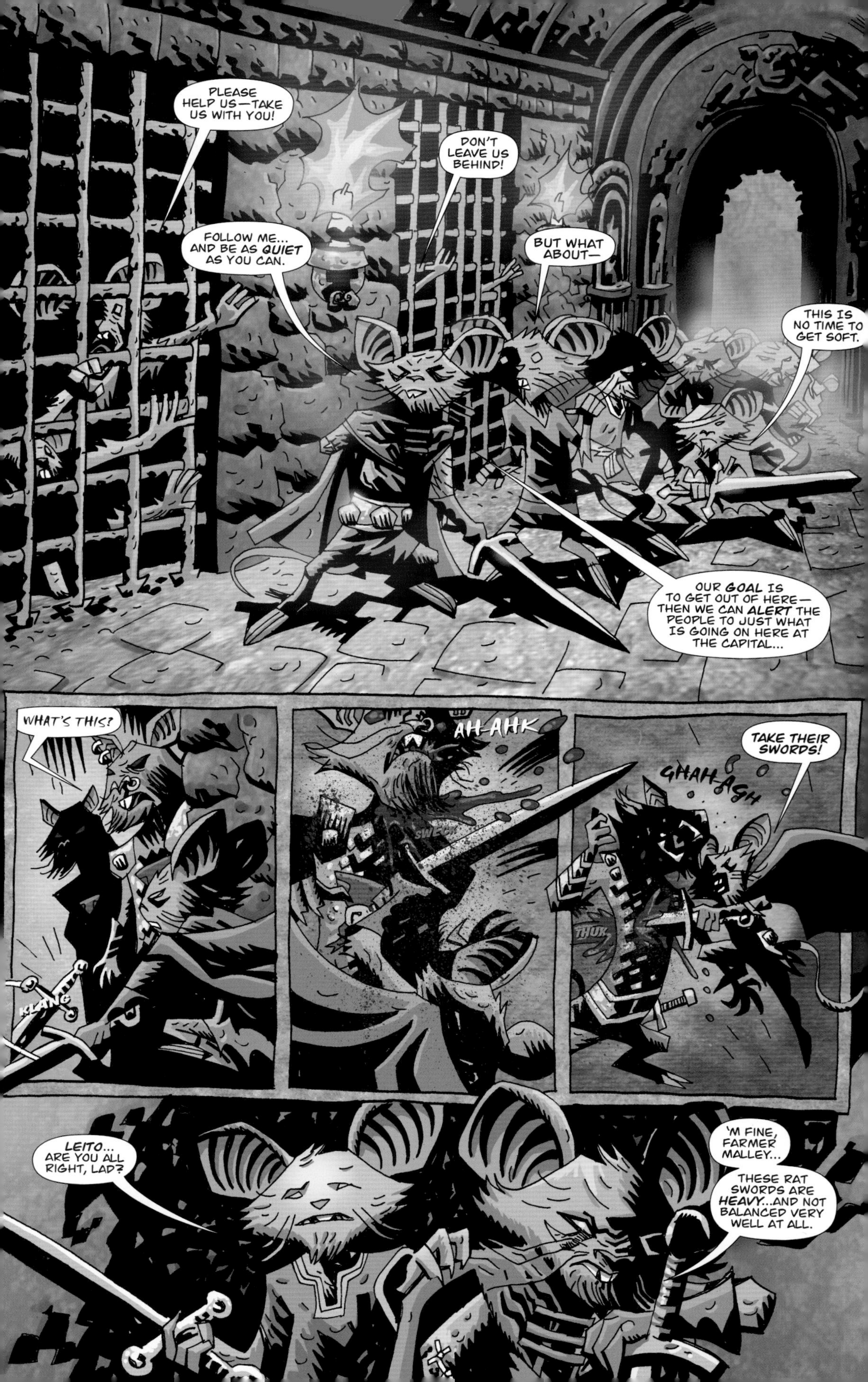
PLEASE HELP US—TAKE US WITH YOU!
DON'T LEAVE US BEHIND!
FOLLOW ME... AND BE AS QUIET AS YOU CAN.
BUT WHAT ABOUT—
THIS IS NO TIME TO GET SOFT.
OUR GOAL IS TO GET OUT OF HERE—THEN WE CAN ALERT THE PEOPLE TO JUST WHAT IS GOING ON HERE AT THE CAPITAL...
WHAT'S THIS?
KLANG
AH-AHK
SWECK
TAKE THEIR SWORDS!
GHAH-AGH
THUK
LEITO... ARE YOU ALL RIGHT, LAD?
'M FINE, FARMER MALLEY...
THESE RAT SWORDS ARE HEAVY...AND NOT BALANCED VERY WELL AT ALL.

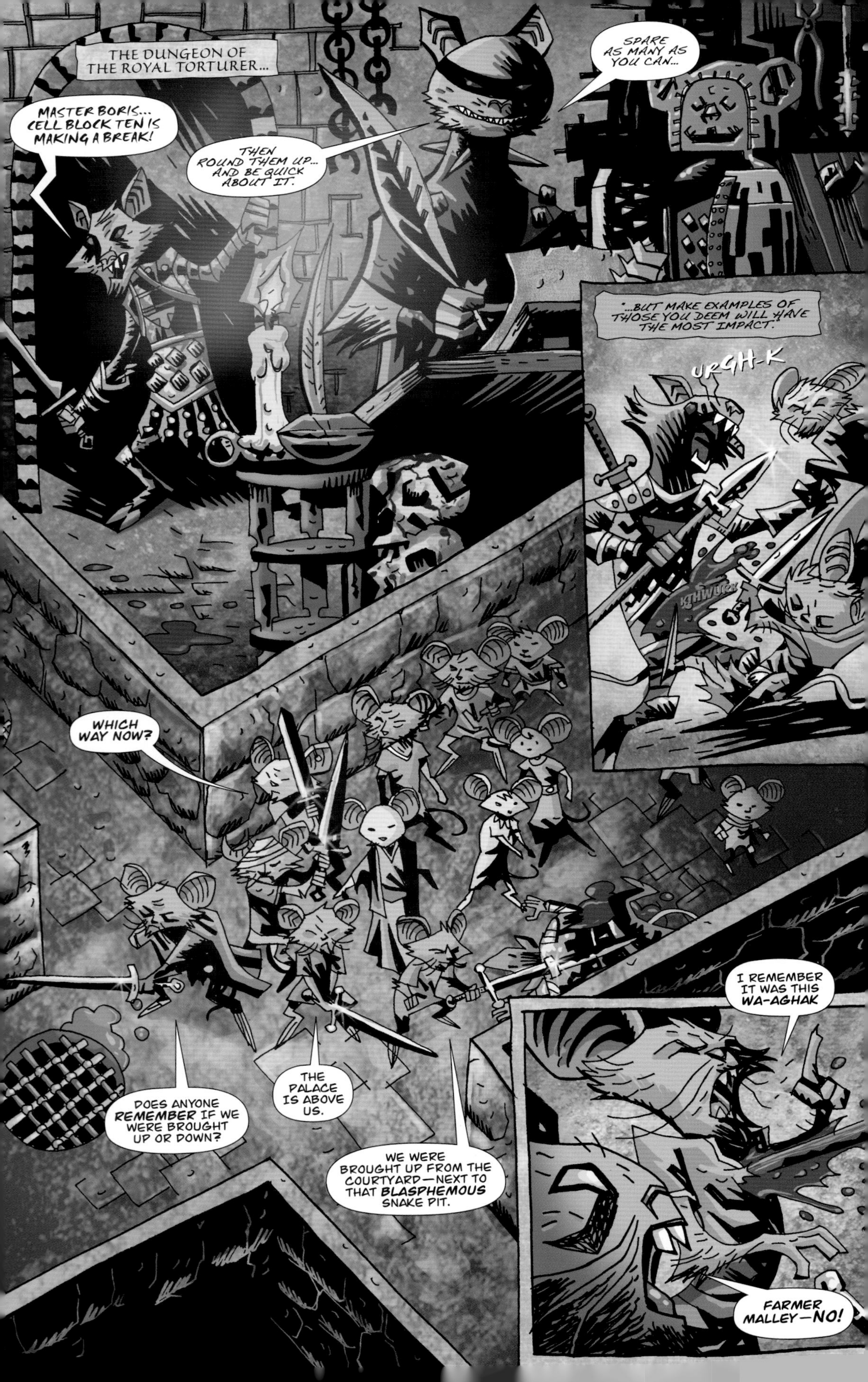
THE DUNGEON OF THE ROYAL TORTURER...
MASTER BORIS... CELL BLOCK TEN IS MAKING A BREAK!
THEN ROUND THEM UP... AND BE QUICK ABOUT IT.
SPARE AS MANY AS YOU CAN...
"...BUT MAKE EXAMPLES OF THOSE YOU DEEM WILL HAVE THE MOST IMPACT."
URGH-K
KTHWURK
WHICH WAY NOW?
DOES ANYONE REMEMBER IF WE WERE BROUGHT UP OR DOWN?
THE PALACE IS ABOVE US.
WE WERE BROUGHT UP FROM THE COURTYARD—NEXT TO THAT BLASPHEMOUS SNAKE PIT.
I REMEMBER IT WAS THIS WA-AGHAK
FARMER MALLEY—NO!

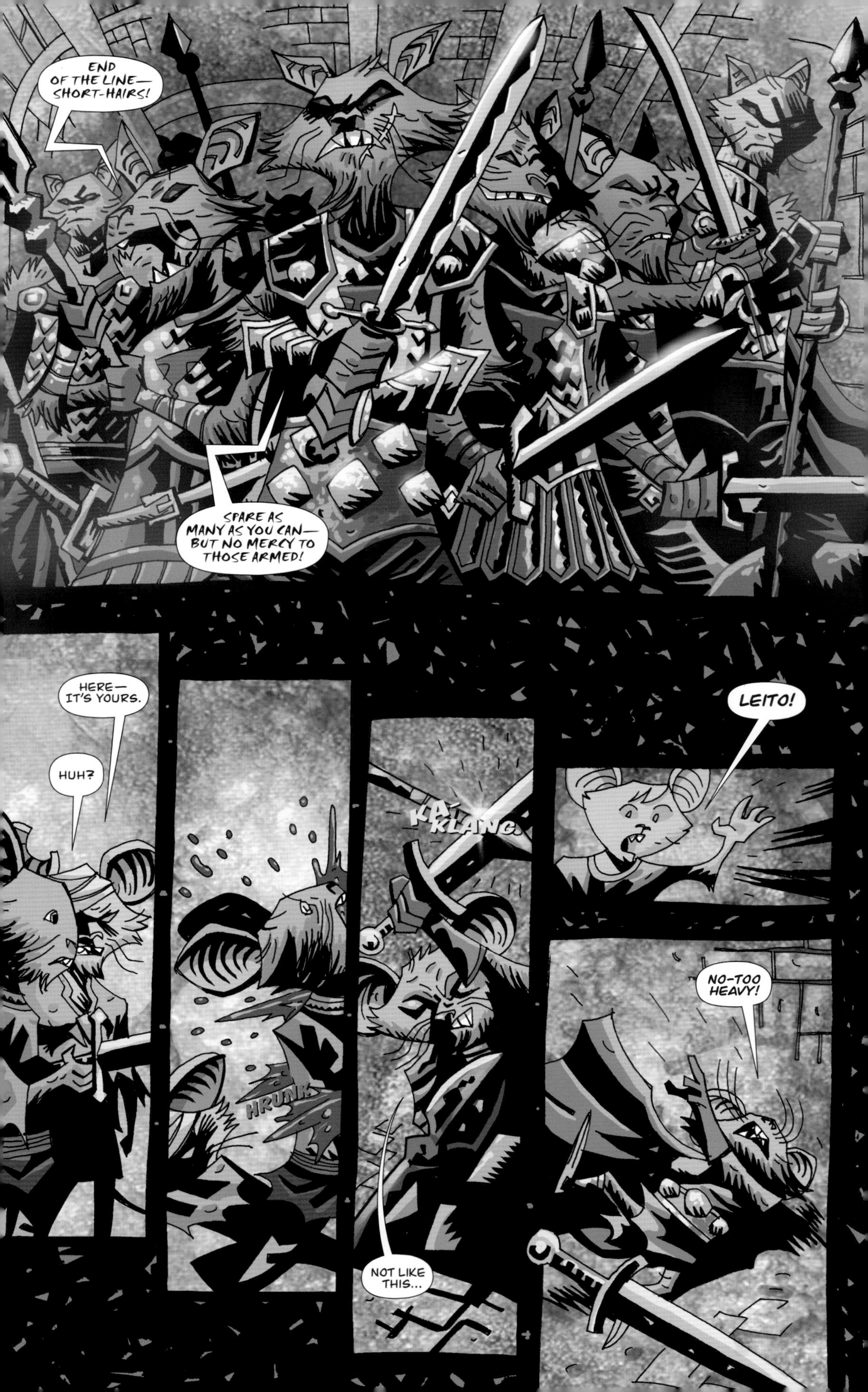
END OF THE LINE—SHORT-HAIRS!
SPARE AS MANY AS YOU CAN—BUT NO MERCY TO THOSE ARMED!
HERE—IT'S YOURS.
HUH?
HRUNK
KA-KLANG
NOT LIKE THIS...
LEITO!
NO-TOO HEAVY!

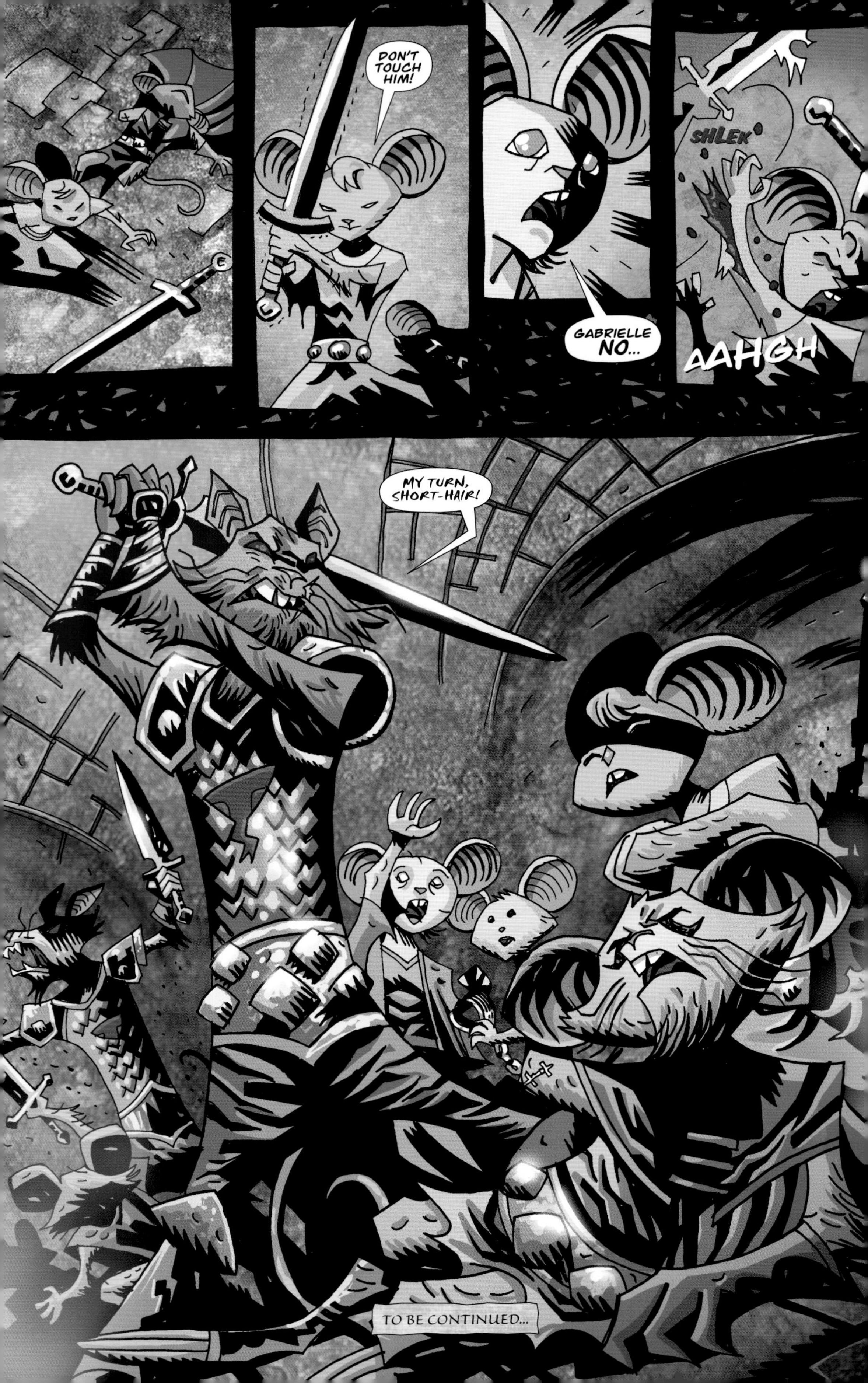
DON'T TOUCH HIM!
GABRIELLE NO...
SHLEK
AAHGH
MY TURN, SHORT-HAIR!
TO BE CONTINUED...

CHAPTER FOUR

A MEASURE OF JUSTICE

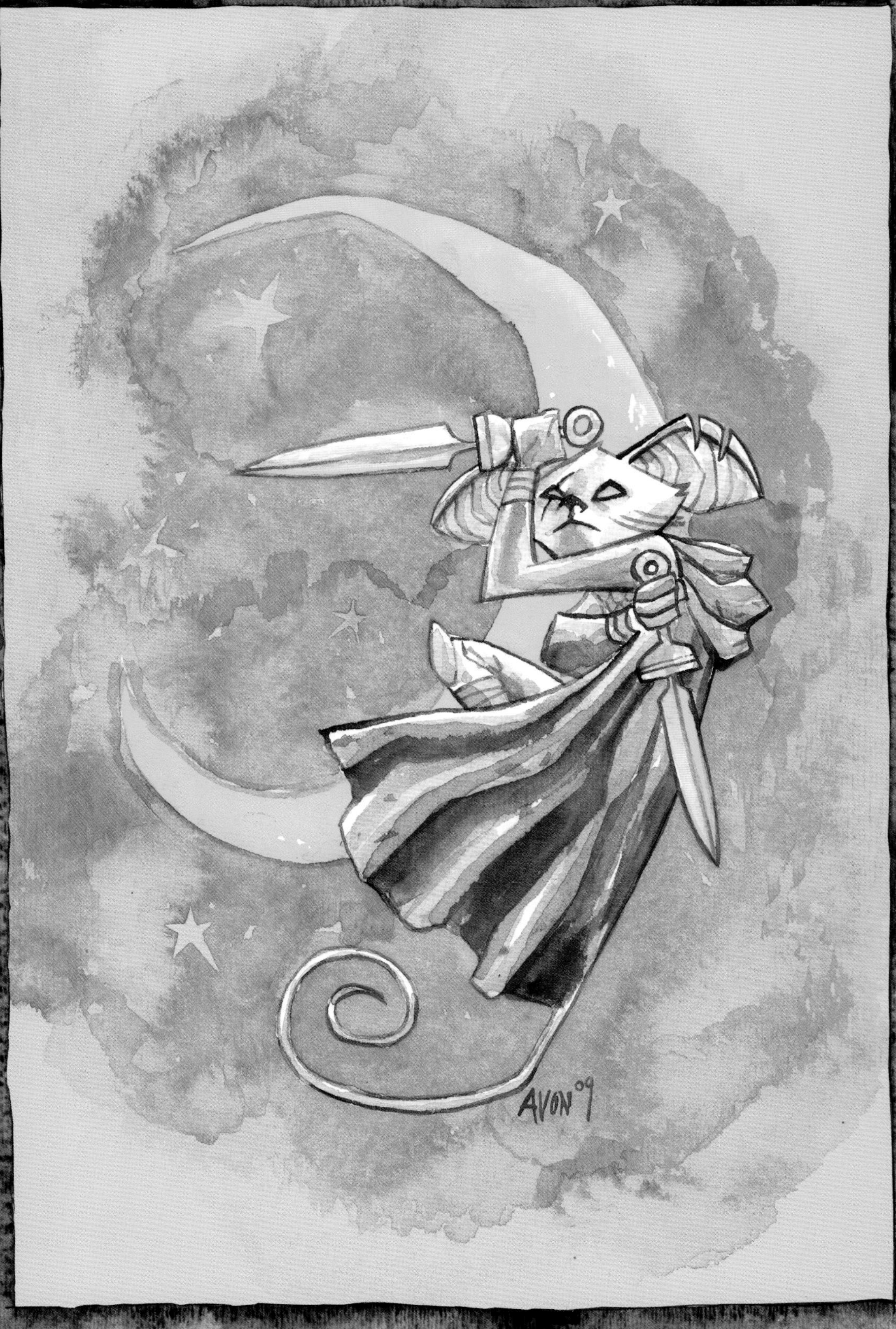
AVON '09

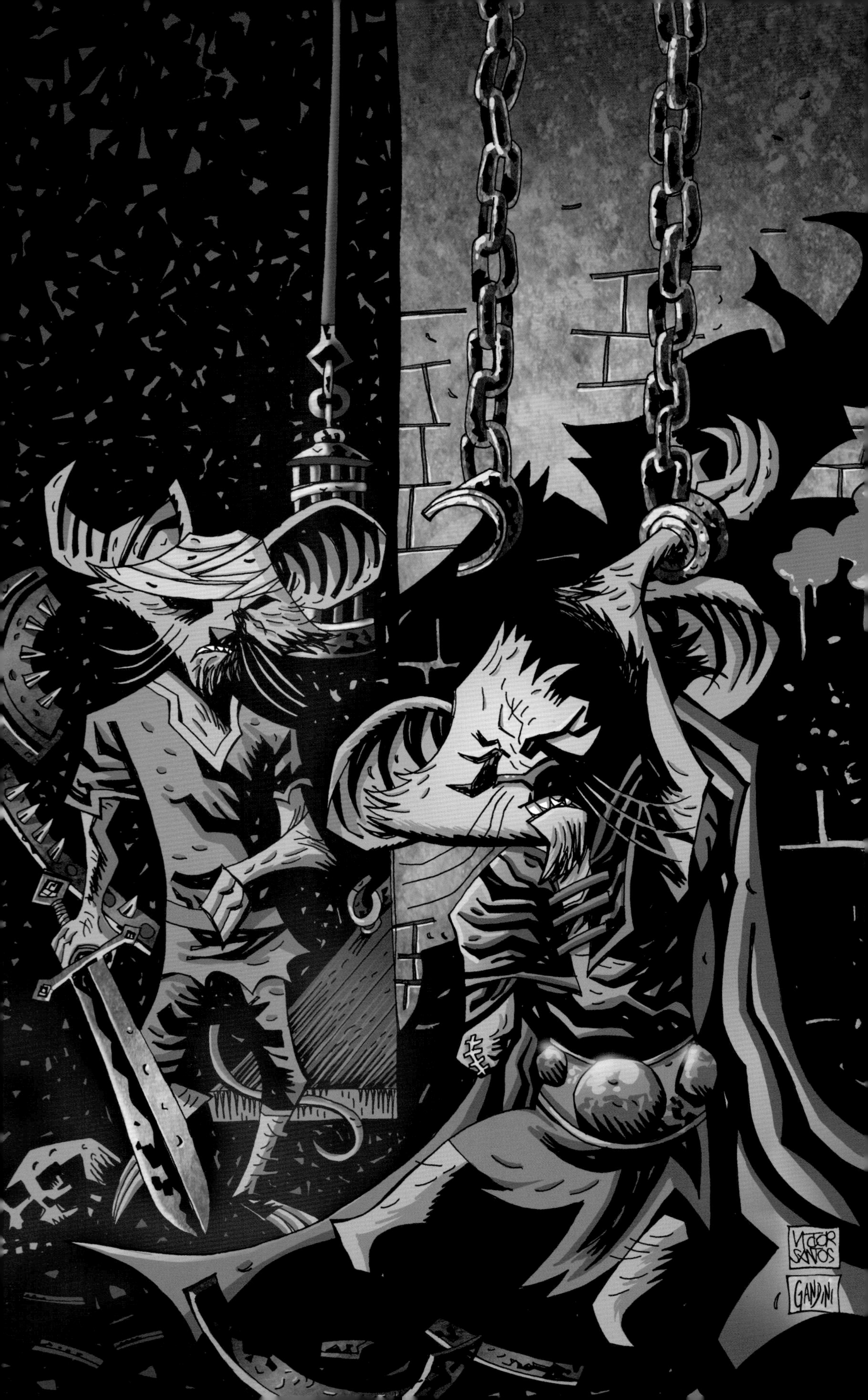
VICTOR SANTOS
GANDINI

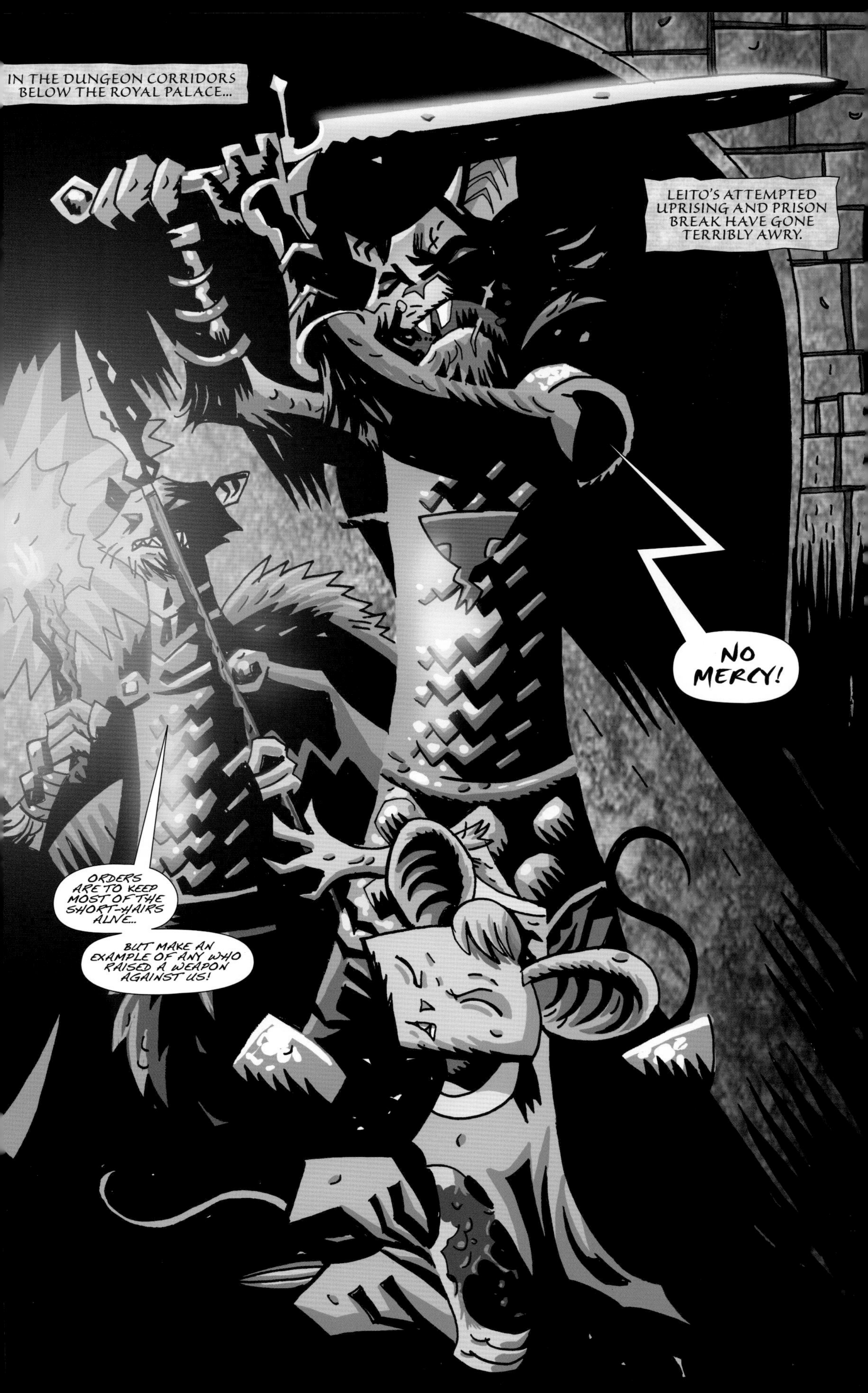
IN THE DUNGEON CORRIDORS BELOW THE ROYAL PALACE...
LEITO'S ATTEMPTED UPRISING AND PRISON BREAK HAVE GONE TERRIBLY AWRY.
NO MERCY!
ORDERS ARE TO KEEP MOST OF THE SHORT-HAIRS ALIVE...
BUT MAKE AN EXAMPLE OF ANY WHO RAISED A WEAPON AGAINST US!

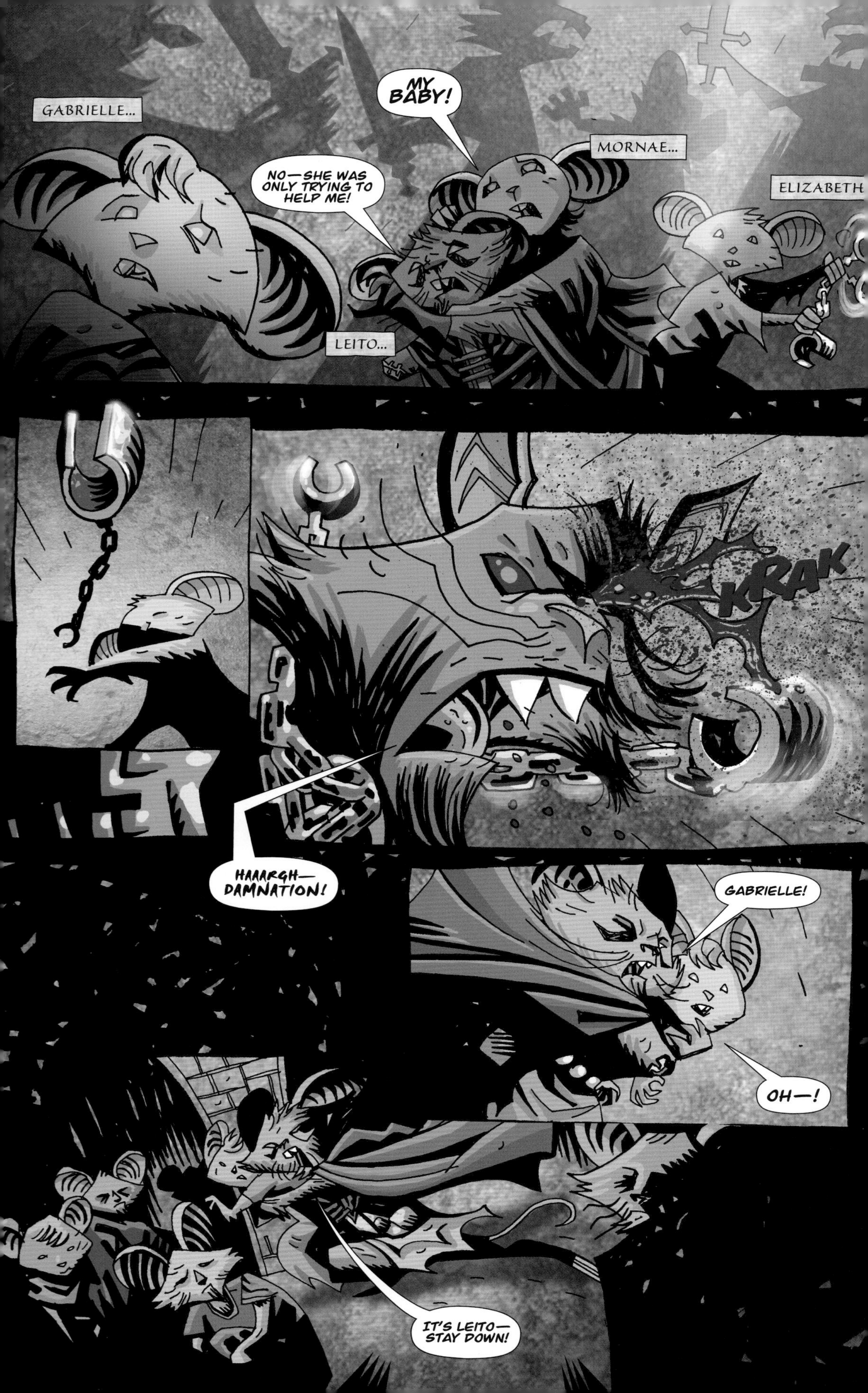
GABRIELLE...
MY BABY!
NO—SHE WAS ONLY TRYING TO HELP ME!
MORNAE...
ELIZABETH
LEITO...
KRAK
HAAARGH—DAMNATION!
GABRIELLE!
OH—!
IT'S LEITO—STAY DOWN!

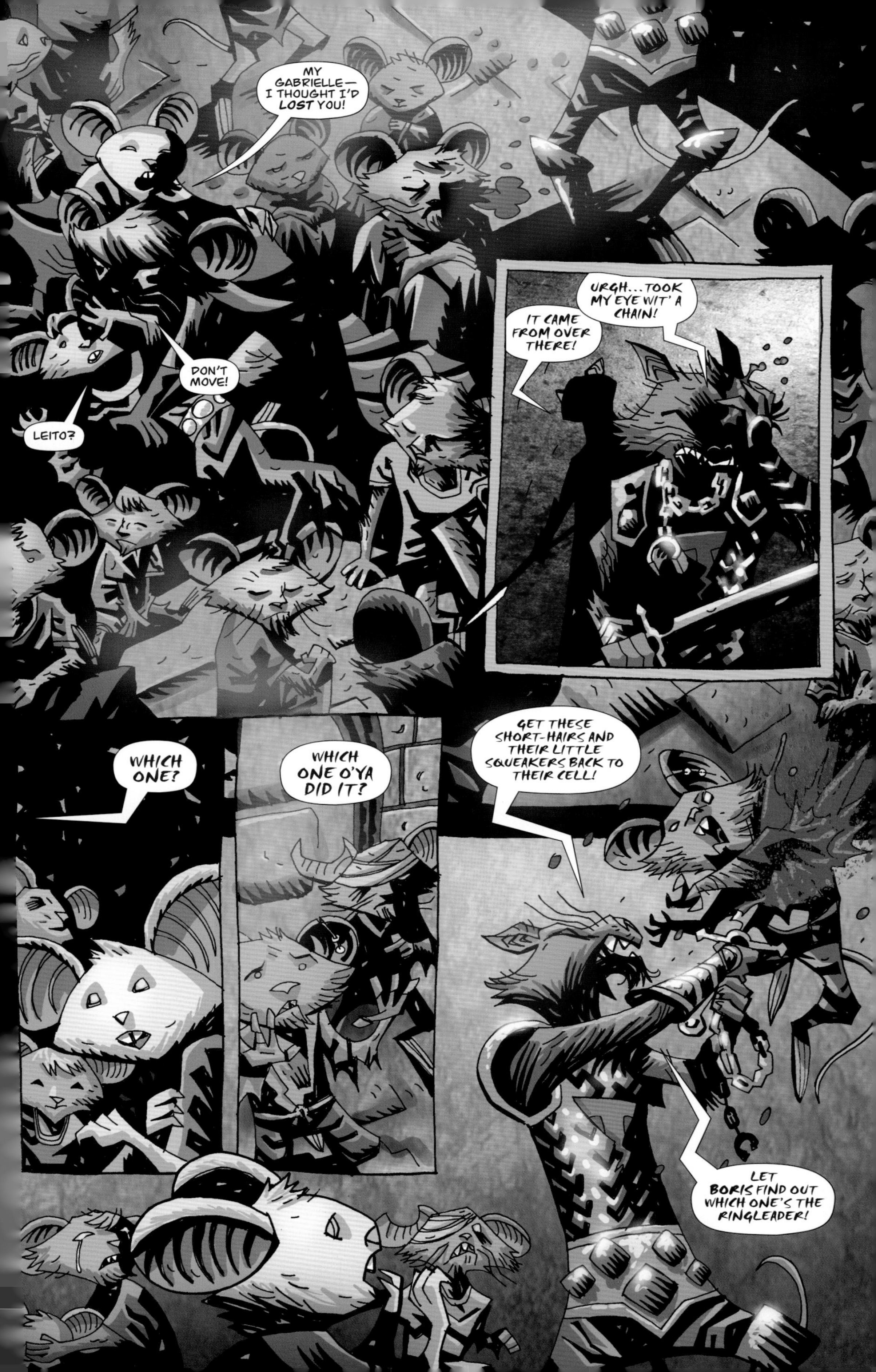
MY GABRIELLE— I THOUGHT I'D LOST YOU!
DON'T MOVE!
LEITO?
IT CAME FROM OVER THERE!
URGH... TOOK MY EYE WIT' A CHAIN!
WHICH ONE?
WHICH ONE O'YA DID IT?
GET THESE SHORT-HAIRS AND THEIR LITTLE SQUEAKERS BACK TO THEIR CELL!
LET BORIS FIND OUT WHICH ONE'S THE RINGLEADER!

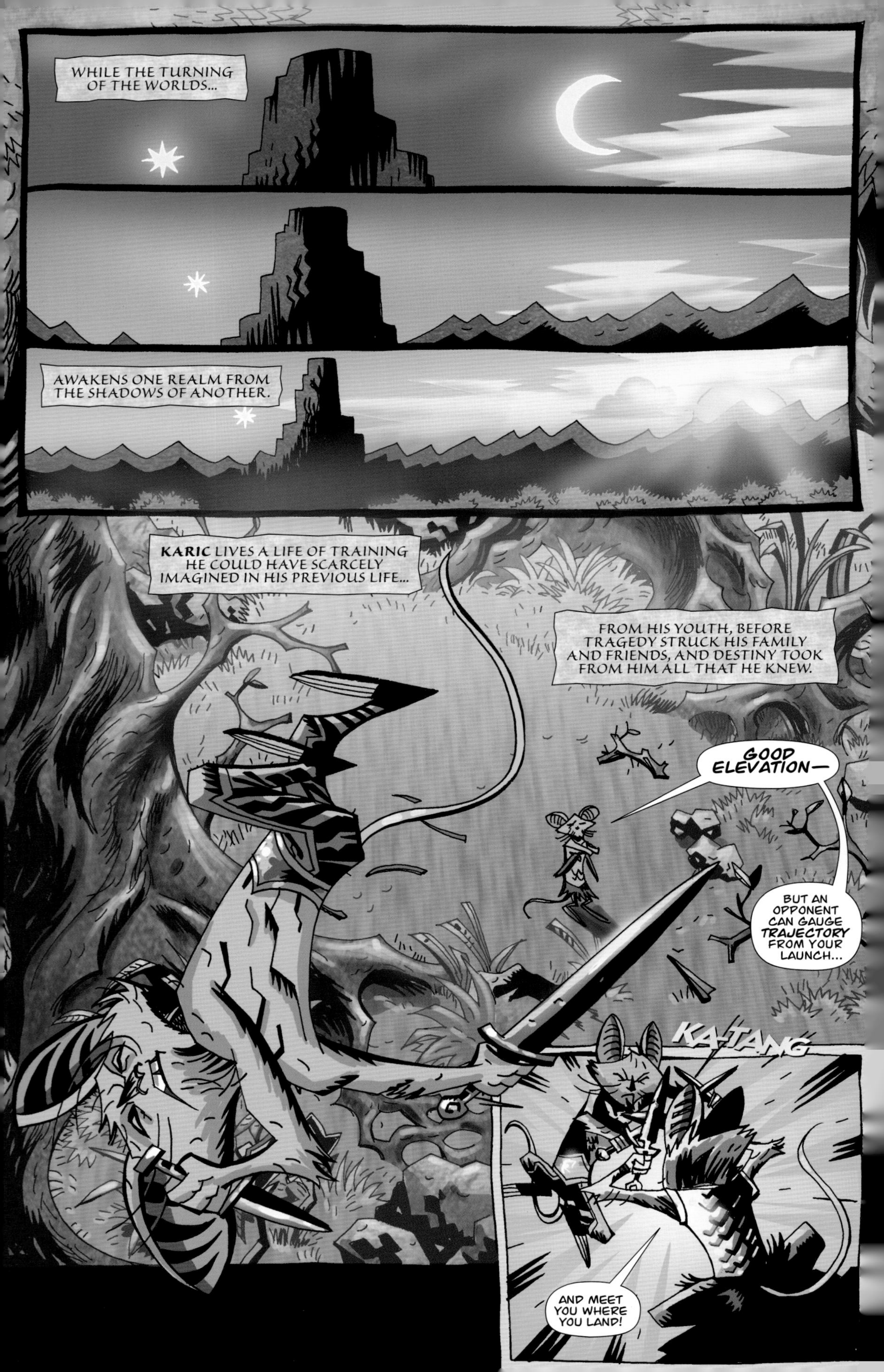

WHILE THE TURNING OF THE WORLDS...
AWAKENS ONE REALM FROM THE SHADOWS OF ANOTHER.
KARIC LIVES A LIFE OF TRAINING HE COULD HAVE SCARCELY IMAGINED IN HIS PREVIOUS LIFE...
FROM HIS YOUTH, BEFORE TRAGEDY STRUCK HIS FAMILY AND FRIENDS, AND DESTINY TOOK FROM HIM ALL THAT HE KNEW.
GOOD ELEVATION—
BUT AN OPPONENT CAN GAUGE TRAJECTORY FROM YOUR LAUNCH...
KA-TANG
AND MEET YOU WHERE YOU LAND!

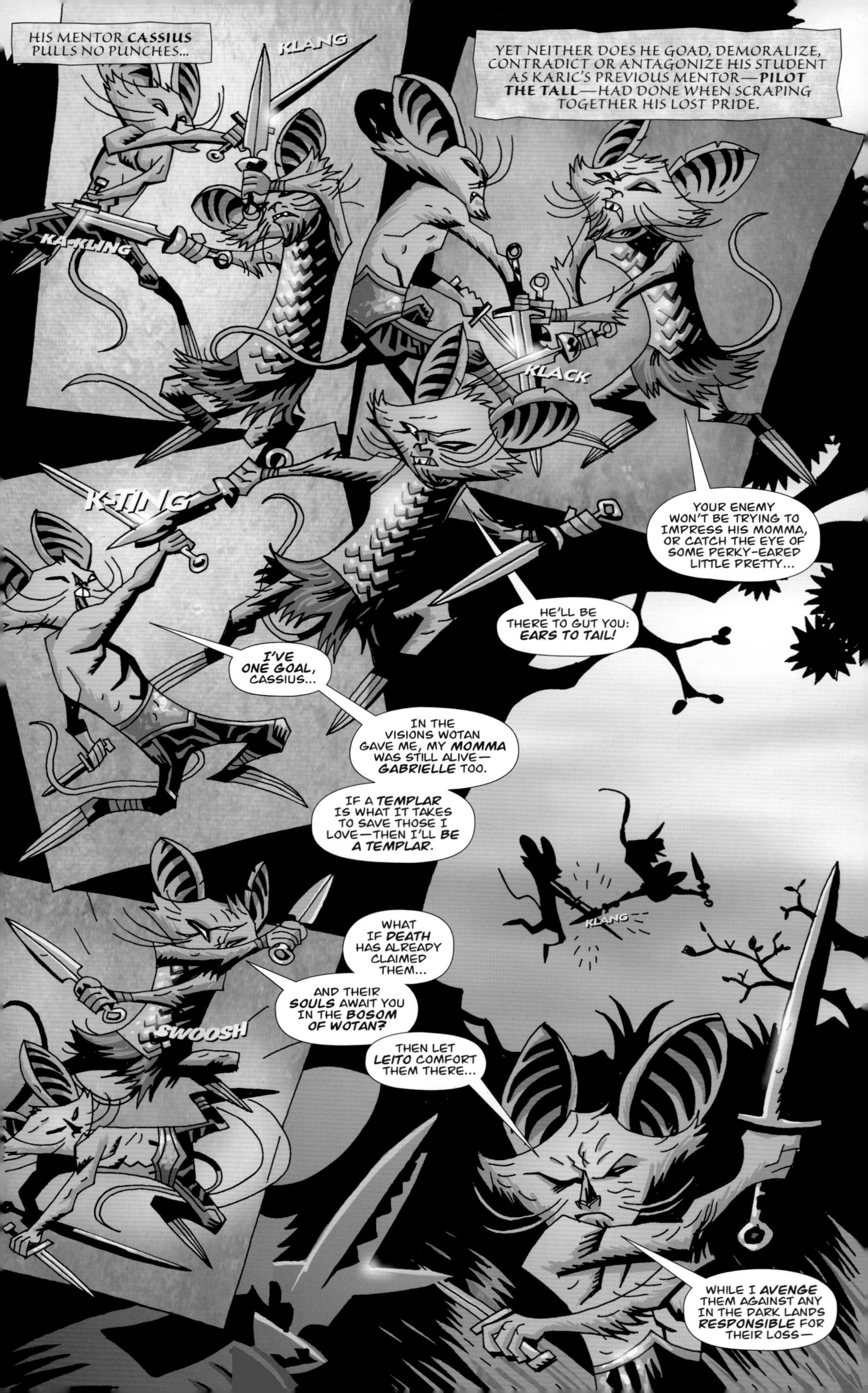
HIS MENTOR CASSIUS PULLS NO PUNCHES...
KLANG
YET NEITHER DOES HE GOAD, DEMORALIZE, CONTRADICT OR ANTAGONIZE HIS STUDENT AS KARIC'S PREVIOUS MENTOR—PILOT THE TALL—HAD DONE WHEN SCRAPING TOGETHER HIS LOST PRIDE.
KA-KLING
KLACK
K-TING
YOUR ENEMY WON'T BE TRYING TO IMPRESS HIS MOMMA, OR CATCH THE EYE OF SOME PERKY-EARED LITTLE PRETTY...
HE'LL BE THERE TO GUT YOU: EARS TO TAIL!
I'VE ONE GOAL, CASSIUS...
IN THE VISIONS WOTAN GAVE ME, MY MOMMA WAS STILL ALIVE—GABRIELLE TOO.
IF A TEMPLAR IS WHAT IT TAKES TO SAVE THOSE I LOVE—THEN I'LL BE A TEMPLAR.
KLANG
WHAT IF DEATH HAS ALREADY CLAIMED THEM...
AND THEIR SOULS AWAIT YOU IN THE BOSOM OF WOTAN?
SWOOSH
THEN LET LEITO COMFORT THEM THERE...
WHILE I AVENGE THEM AGAINST ANY IN THE DARK LANDS RESPONSIBLE FOR THEIR LOSS—

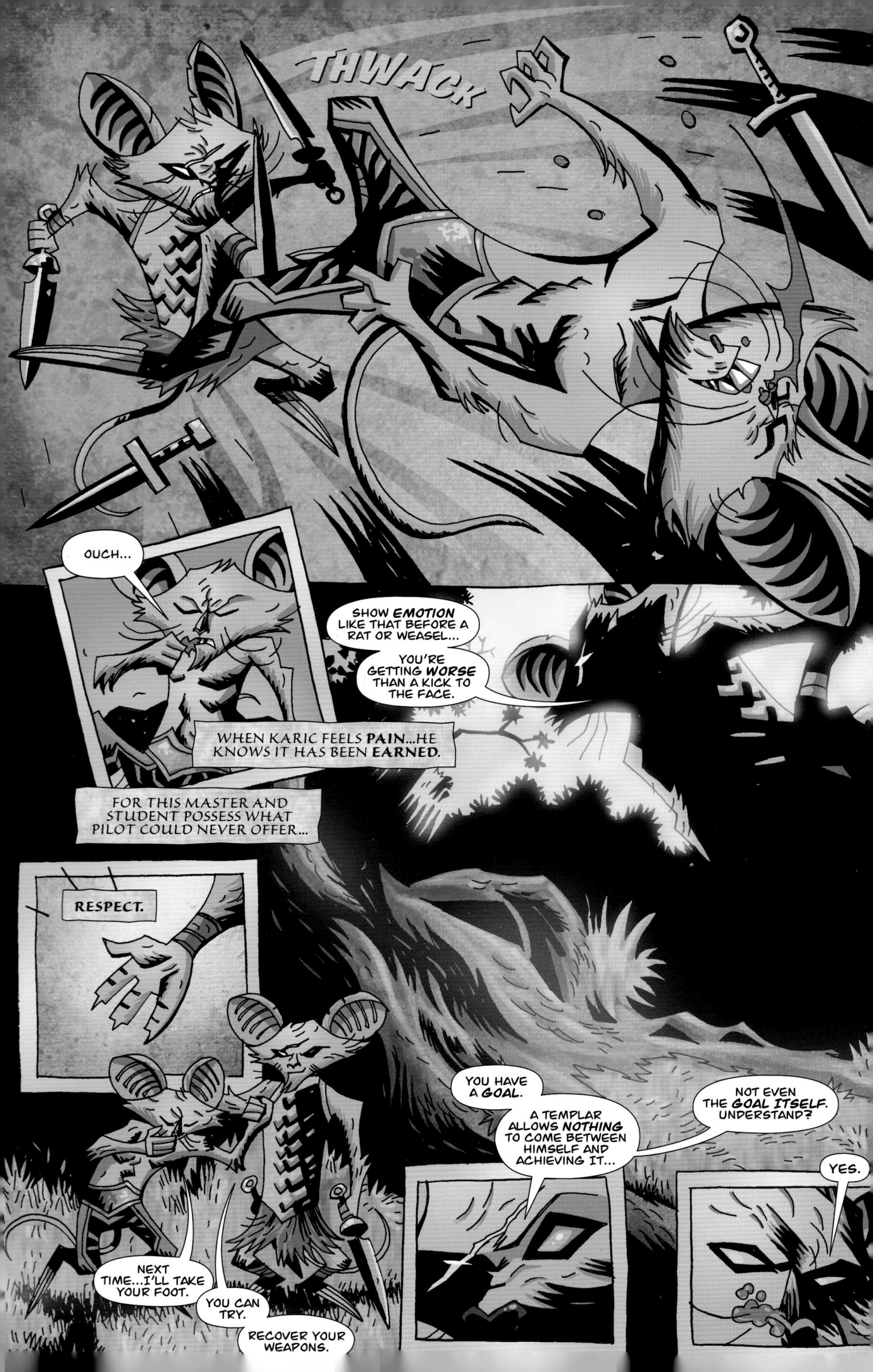
THWACK
OUCH...
SHOW EMOTION LIKE THAT BEFORE A RAT OR WEASEL...
YOU'RE GETTING WORSE THAN A KICK TO THE FACE.
WHEN KARIC FEELS PAIN...HE KNOWS IT HAS BEEN EARNED.
FOR THIS MASTER AND STUDENT POSSESS WHAT PILOT COULD NEVER OFFER...
RESPECT.
NEXT TIME...I'LL TAKE YOUR FOOT.
YOU CAN TRY.
RECOVER YOUR WEAPONS.
YOU HAVE A GOAL.
A TEMPLAR ALLOWS NOTHING TO COME BETWEEN HIMSELF AND ACHIEVING IT...
NOT EVEN THE GOAL ITSELF. UNDERSTAND?
YES.

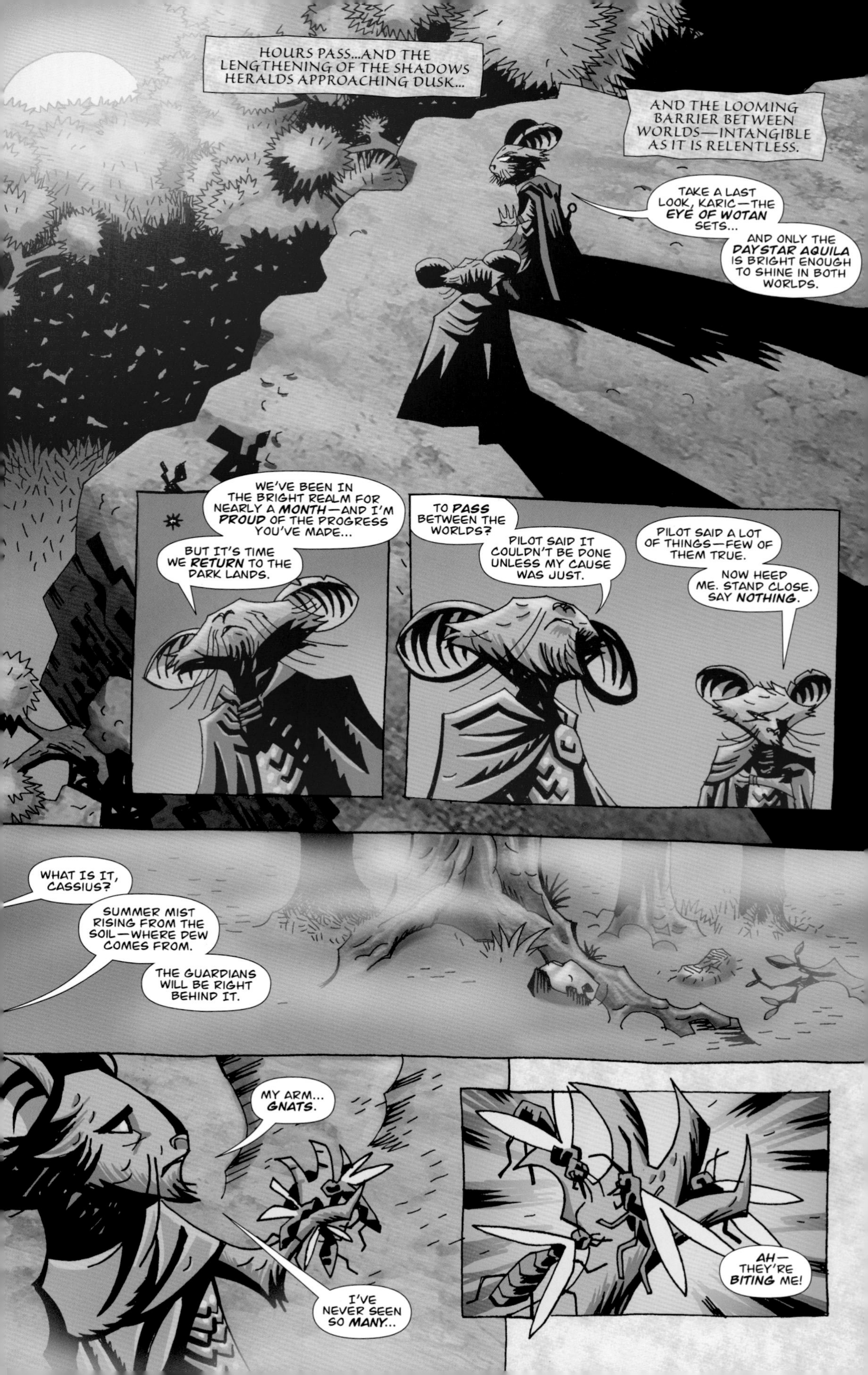
HOURS PASS...AND THE LENGTHENING OF THE SHADOWS HERALDS APPROACHING DUSK...
AND THE LOOMING BARRIER BETWEEN WORLDS—INTANGIBLE AS IT IS RELENTLESS.
TAKE A LAST LOOK, KARIC—THE EYE OF WOTAN SETS...
AND ONLY THE DAYSTAR AQUILA IS BRIGHT ENOUGH TO SHINE IN BOTH WORLDS.
WE'VE BEEN IN THE BRIGHT REALM FOR NEARLY A MONTH—AND I'M PROUD OF THE PROGRESS YOU'VE MADE...
BUT IT'S TIME WE RETURN TO THE DARK LANDS.
TO PASS BETWEEN THE WORLDS?
PILOT SAID IT COULDN'T BE DONE UNLESS MY CAUSE WAS JUST.
PILOT SAID A LOT OF THINGS—FEW OF THEM TRUE.
NOW HEED ME. STAND CLOSE. SAY NOTHING.
WHAT IS IT, CASSIUS?
SUMMER MIST RISING FROM THE SOIL—WHERE DEW COMES FROM.
THE GUARDIANS WILL BE RIGHT BEHIND IT.
MY ARM... GNATS.
I'VE NEVER SEEN SO MANY...
AH—THEY'RE BITING ME!

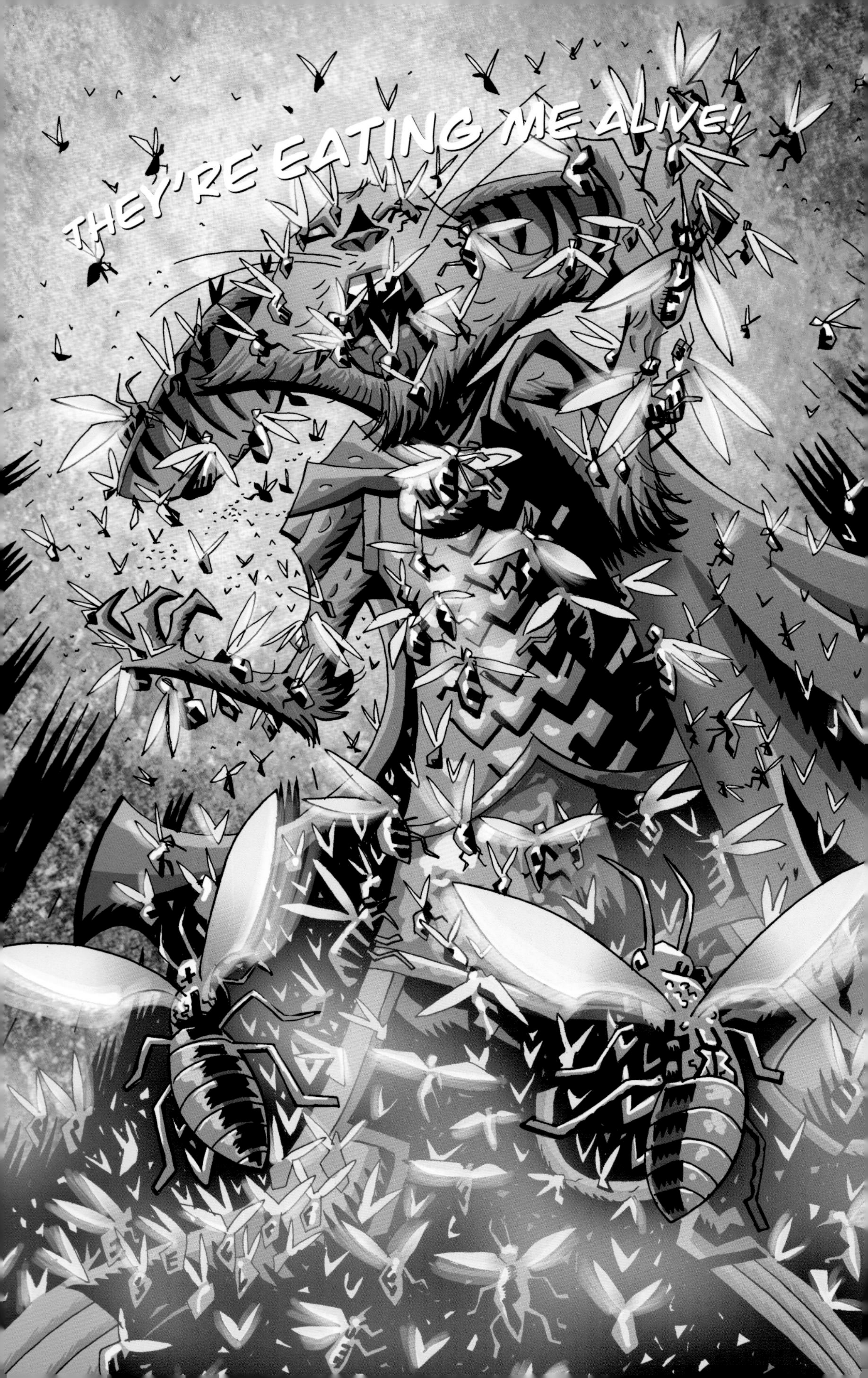
THEY'RE EATING ME ALIVE!

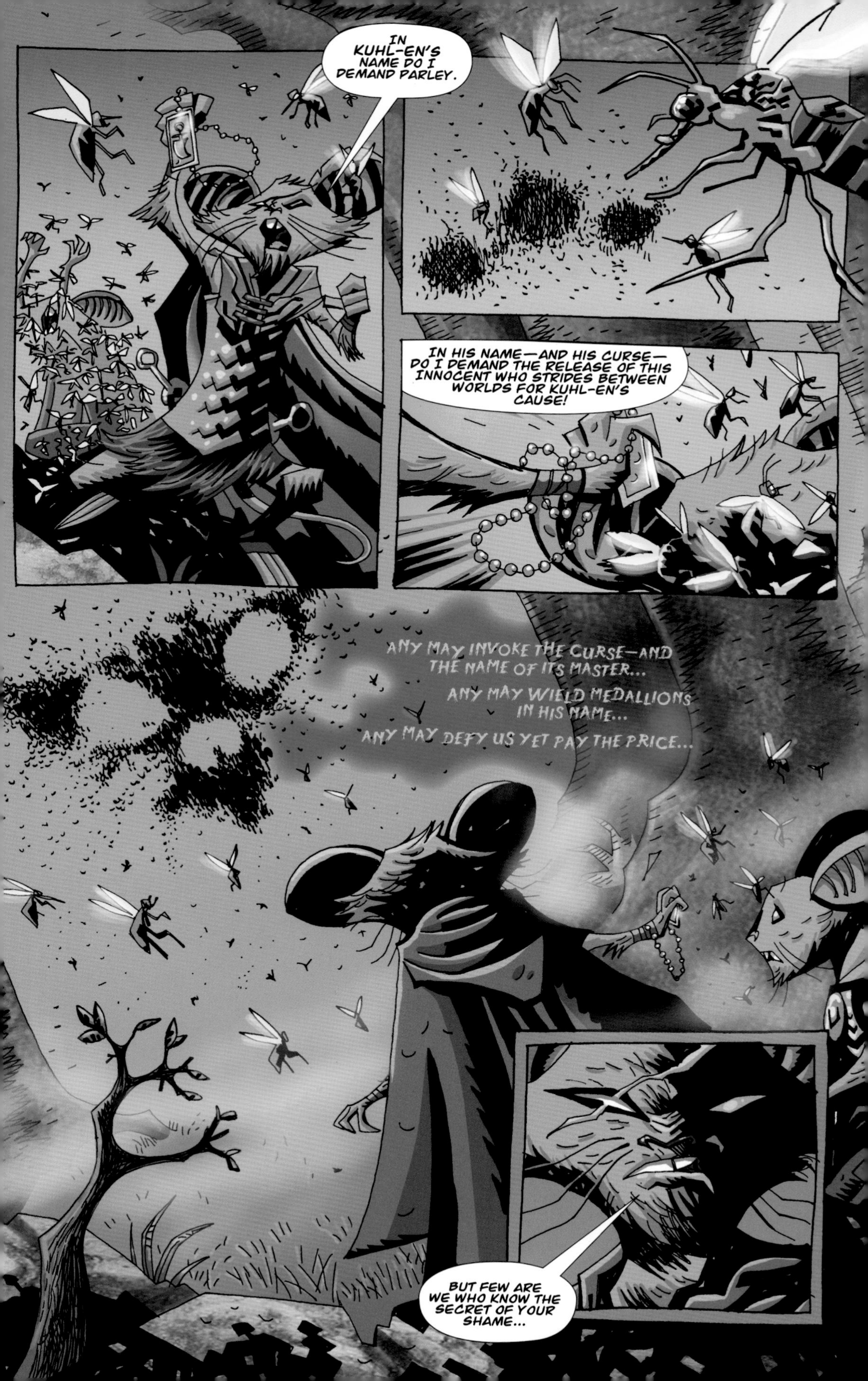
IN KUHL-EN'S NAME DO I DEMAND PARLEY.
IN HIS NAME—AND HIS CURSE—DO I DEMAND THE RELEASE OF THIS INNOCENT WHO STRIDES BETWEEN WORLDS FOR KUHL-EN'S CAUSE!
ANY MAY INVOKE THE CURSE—AND THE NAME OF ITS MASTER...
ANY MAY WIELD MEDALLIONS IN HIS NAME...
ANY MAY DEFY US YET PAY THE PRICE...
BUT FEW ARE WE WHO KNOW THE SECRET OF YOUR SHAME...

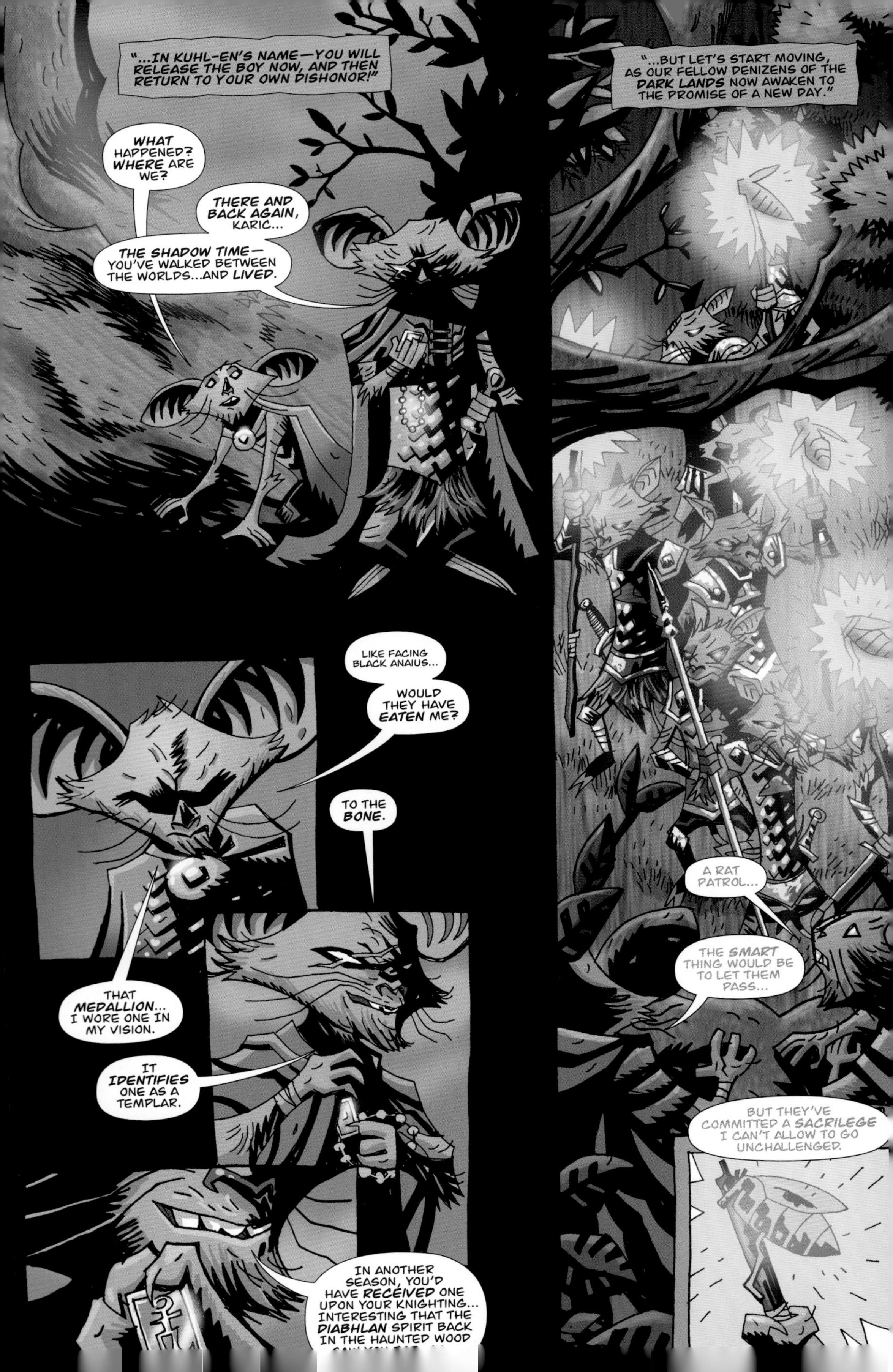
"...IN KUHL-EN'S NAME—YOU WILL RELEASE THE BOY NOW, AND THEN RETURN TO YOUR OWN DISHONOR!"
WHAT HAPPENED? WHERE ARE WE?
THERE AND BACK AGAIN, KARIC...
THE SHADOW TIME—YOU'VE WALKED BETWEEN THE WORLDS...AND LIVED.
LIKE FACING BLACK ANAIUS...
WOULD THEY HAVE EATEN ME?
TO THE BONE.
THAT MEDALLION... I WORE ONE IN MY VISION.
IT IDENTIFIES ONE AS A TEMPLAR.
IN ANOTHER SEASON, YOU'D HAVE RECEIVED ONE UPON YOUR KNIGHTING... INTERESTING THAT THE DIABHLAN SPIRIT BACK IN THE HAUNTED WOOD
"...BUT LET'S START MOVING, AS OUR FELLOW DENIZENS OF THE DARK LANDS NOW AWAKEN TO THE PROMISE OF A NEW DAY."
A RAT PATROL...
THE SMART THING WOULD BE TO LET THEM PASS...
BUT THEY'VE COMMITTED A SACRILEGE I CAN'T ALLOW TO GO UNCHALLENGED.

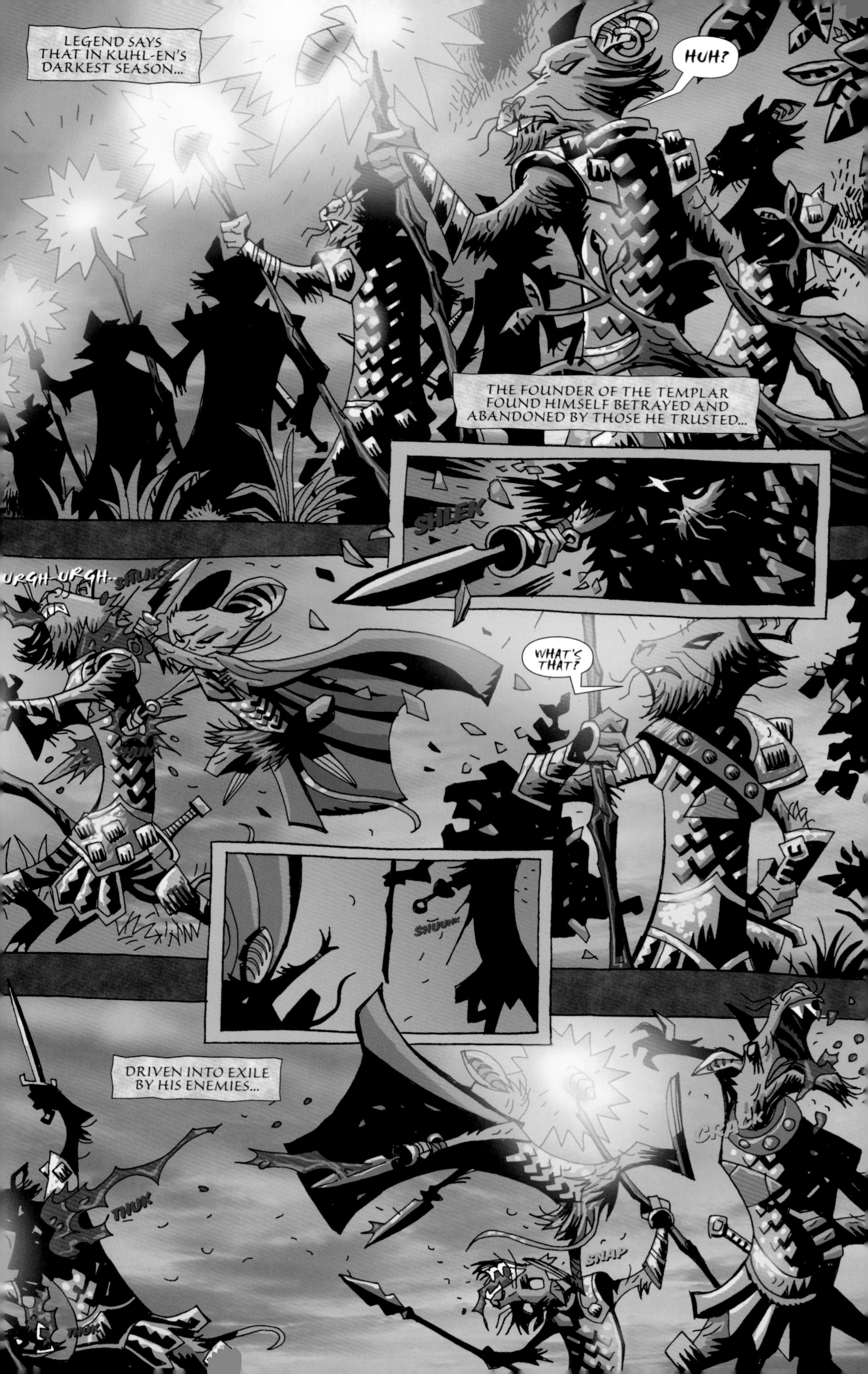
LEGEND SAYS THAT IN KUHL-EN'S DARKEST SEASON...
HUH?
THE FOUNDER OF THE TEMPLAR FOUND HIMSELF BETRAYED AND ABANDONED BY THOSE HE TRUSTED...
SHLEK
URGH-URGH...
SHLIK
THUK
WHAT'S THAT?
SHUUNK
DRIVEN INTO EXILE BY HIS ENEMIES...
THUK
SNAP
THUK

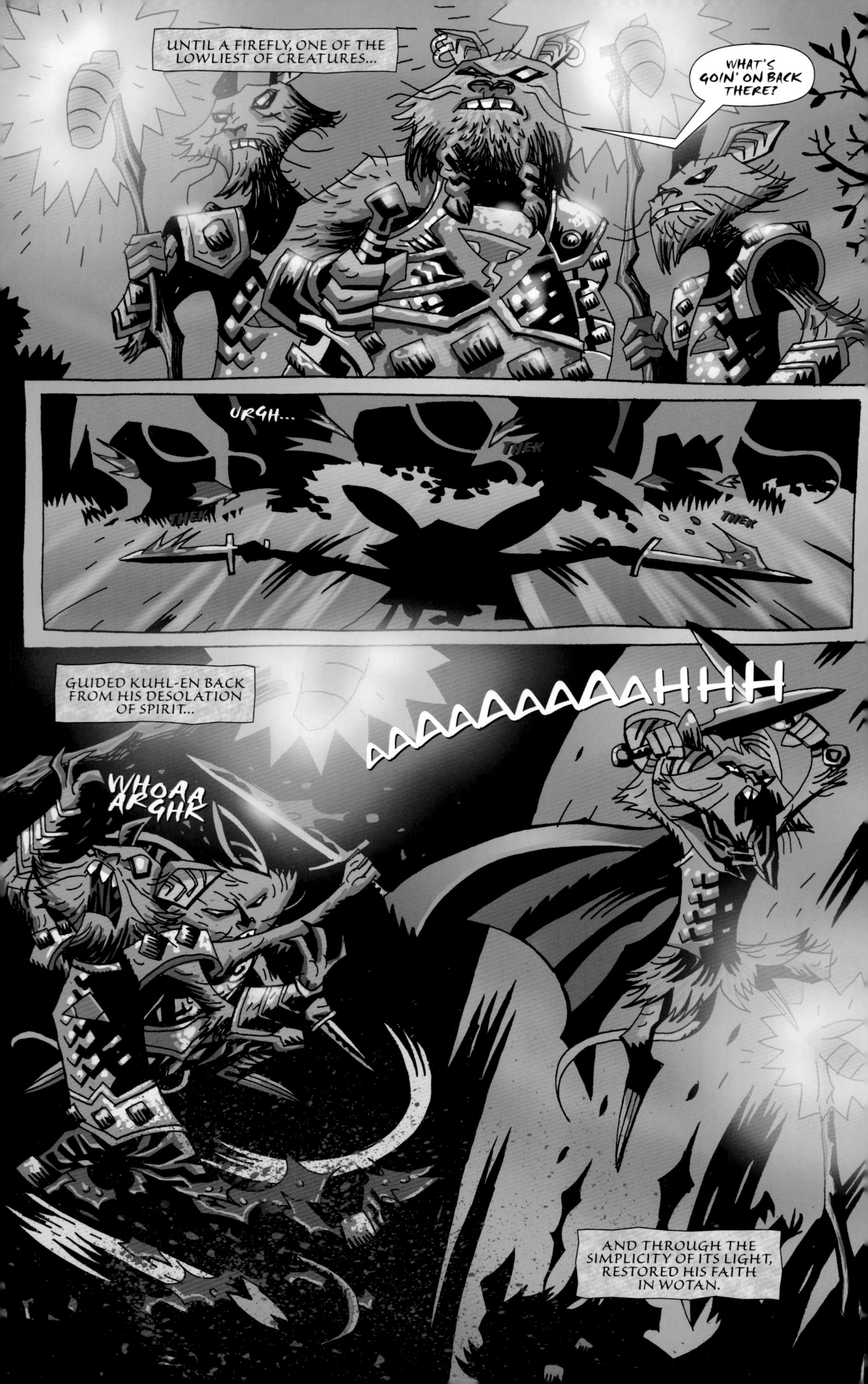
UNTIL A FIREFLY, ONE OF THE LOWLIEST OF CREATURES...
WHAT'S GOIN' ON BACK THERE?
URGH...
THEK
THEK
THEK
GUIDED KUHL-EN BACK FROM HIS DESOLATION OF SPIRIT...
AAAAAAAAAAAHHH
WHOAA ARGHR
AND THROUGH THE SIMPLICITY OF ITS LIGHT, RESTORED HIS FAITH IN WOTAN.

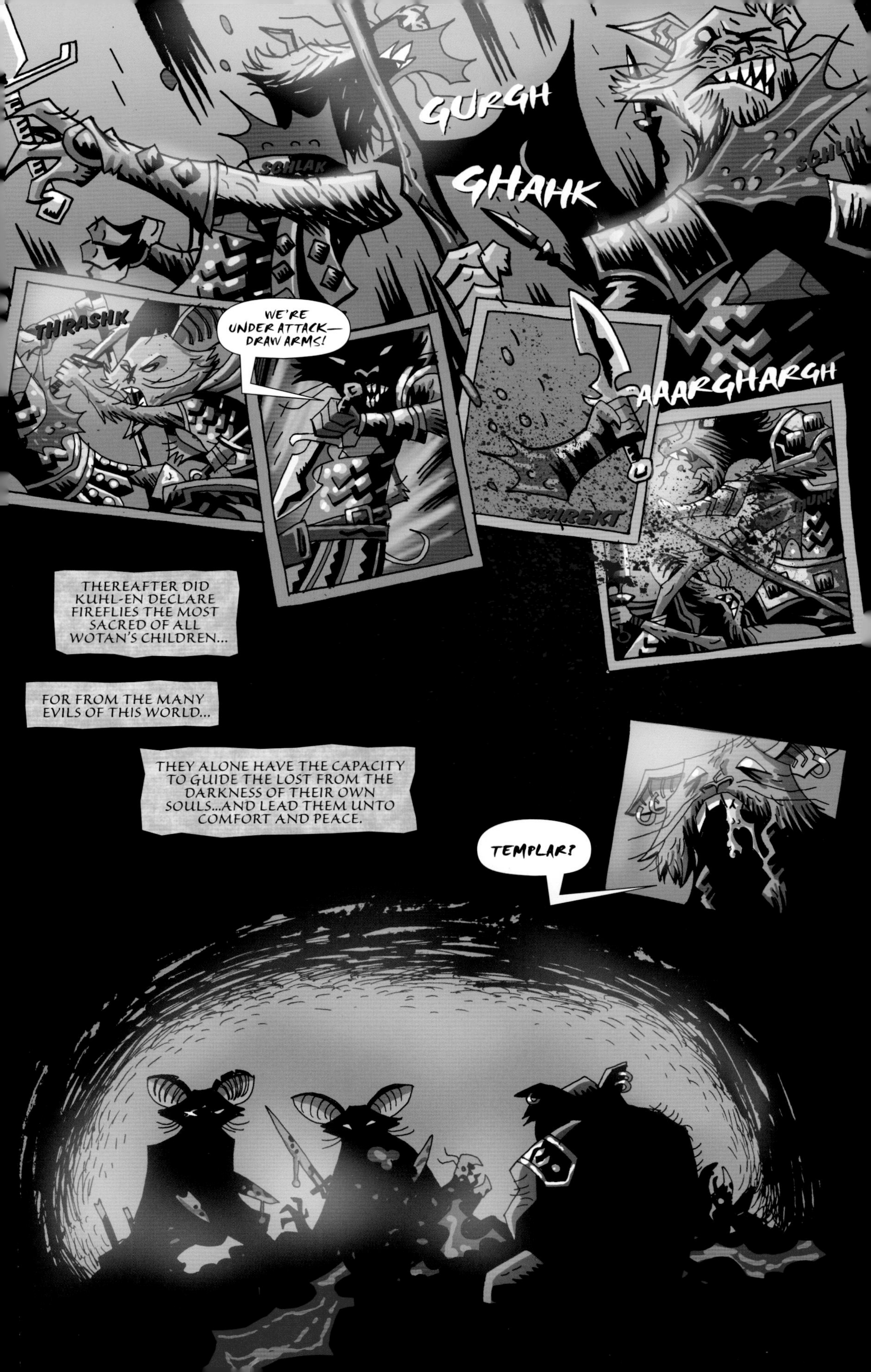
GURGH
SCHLAK
GHAHK
SCHLIK
THRASHK
WE'RE UNDER ATTACK— DRAW ARMS!
SSHREKT
AAARGHARGH
THUNK
THEREAFTER DID KUHL-EN DECLARE FIREFLIES THE MOST SACRED OF ALL WOTAN'S CHILDREN...
FOR FROM THE MANY EVILS OF THIS WORLD...
THEY ALONE HAVE THE CAPACITY TO GUIDE THE LOST FROM THE DARKNESS OF THEIR OWN SOULS...AND LEAD THEM UNTO COMFORT AND PEACE.
TEMPLAR?

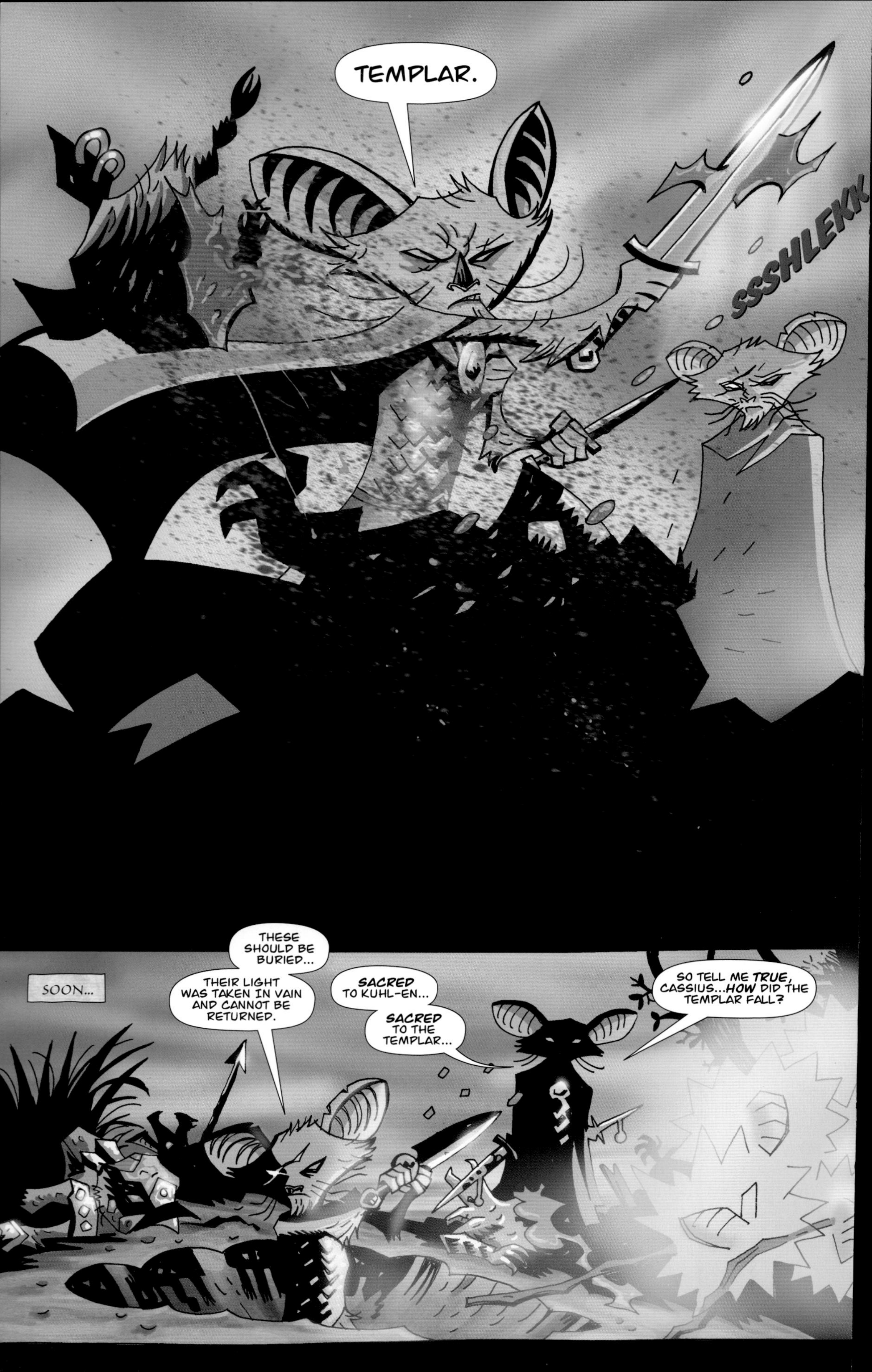
TEMPLAR.
SSSHLEKK
SOON...
THESE SHOULD BE BURIED...
THEIR LIGHT WAS TAKEN IN VAIN AND CANNOT BE RETURNED.
SACRED TO KUHL-EN...
SACRED TO THE TEMPLAR...
SO TELL ME TRUE, CASSIUS...HOW DID THE TEMPLAR FALL?

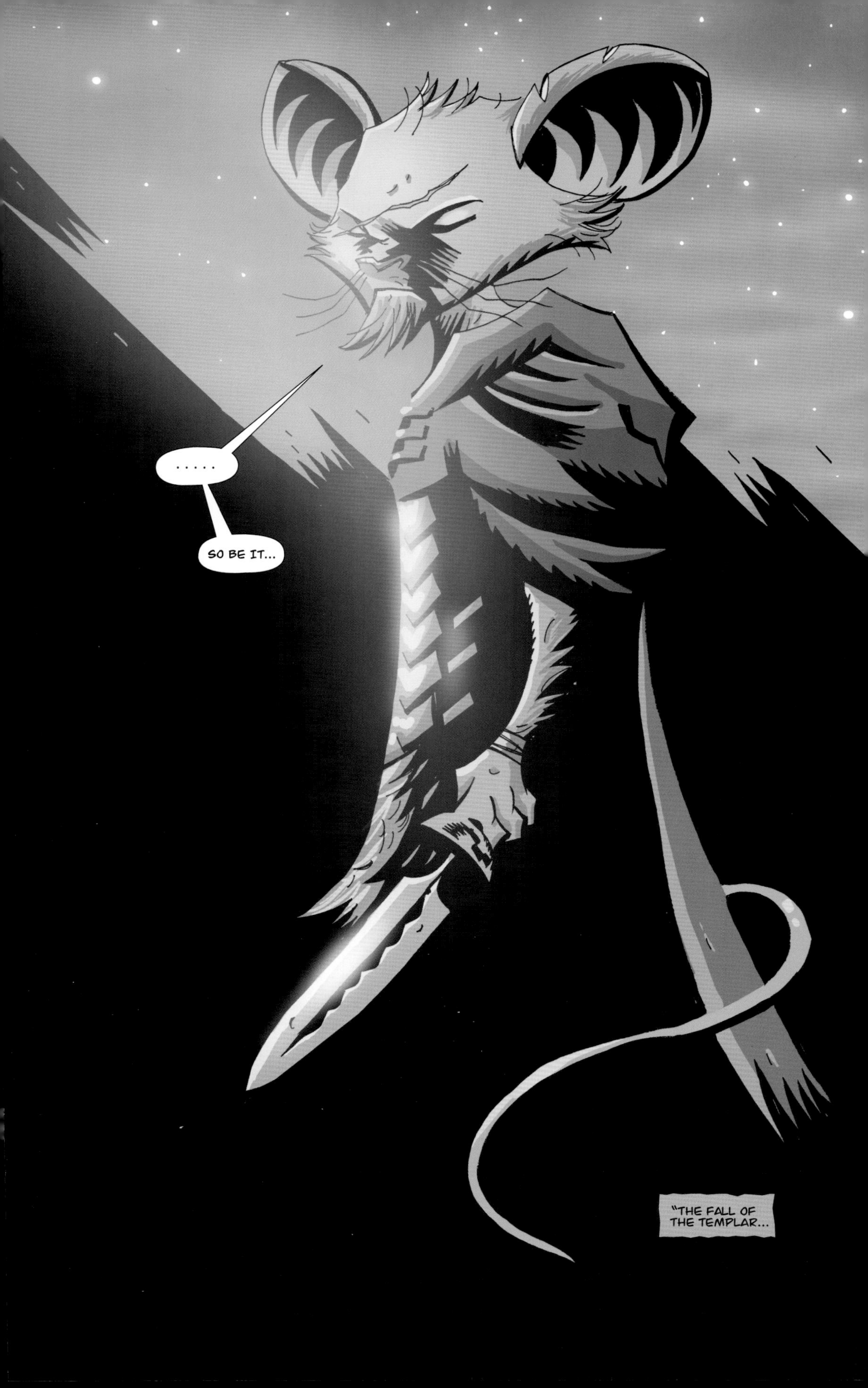
. . . . .
SO BE IT...
"THE FALL OF THE TEMPLAR...

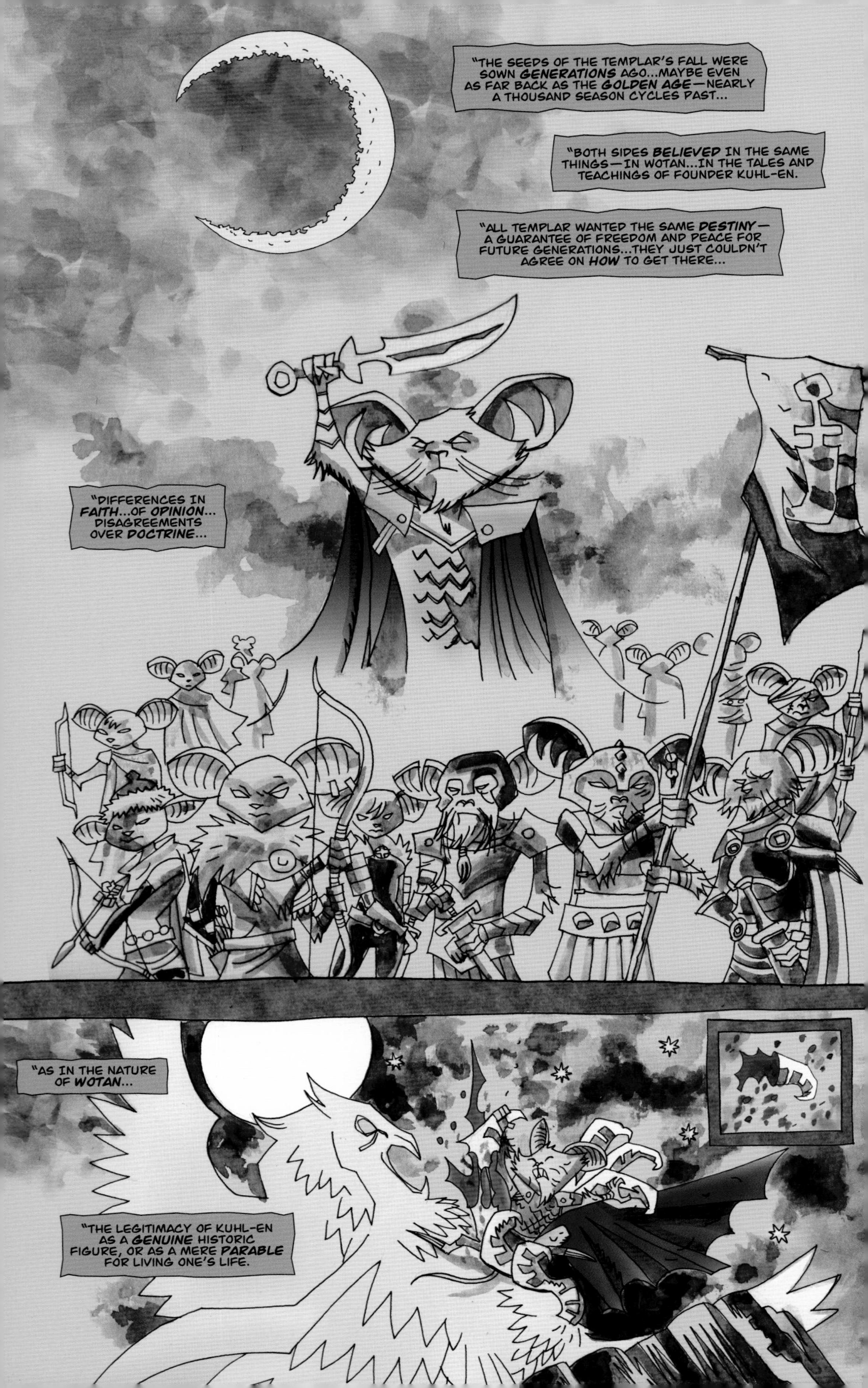
"THE SEEDS OF THE TEMPLAR'S FALL WERE SOWN GENERATIONS AGO...MAYBE EVEN AS FAR BACK AS THE GOLDEN AGE—NEARLY A THOUSAND SEASON CYCLES PAST...
"BOTH SIDES BELIEVED IN THE SAME THINGS—IN WOTAN...IN THE TALES AND TEACHINGS OF FOUNDER KUHL-EN.
"ALL TEMPLAR WANTED THE SAME DESTINY—A GUARANTEE OF FREEDOM AND PEACE FOR FUTURE GENERATIONS...THEY JUST COULDN'T AGREE ON HOW TO GET THERE...
"DIFFERENCES IN FAITH...OF OPINION... DISAGREEMENTS OVER DOCTRINE...
"AS IN THE NATURE OF WOTAN...
"THE LEGITIMACY OF KUHL-EN AS A GENUINE HISTORIC FIGURE, OR AS A MERE PARABLE FOR LIVING ONE'S LIFE.

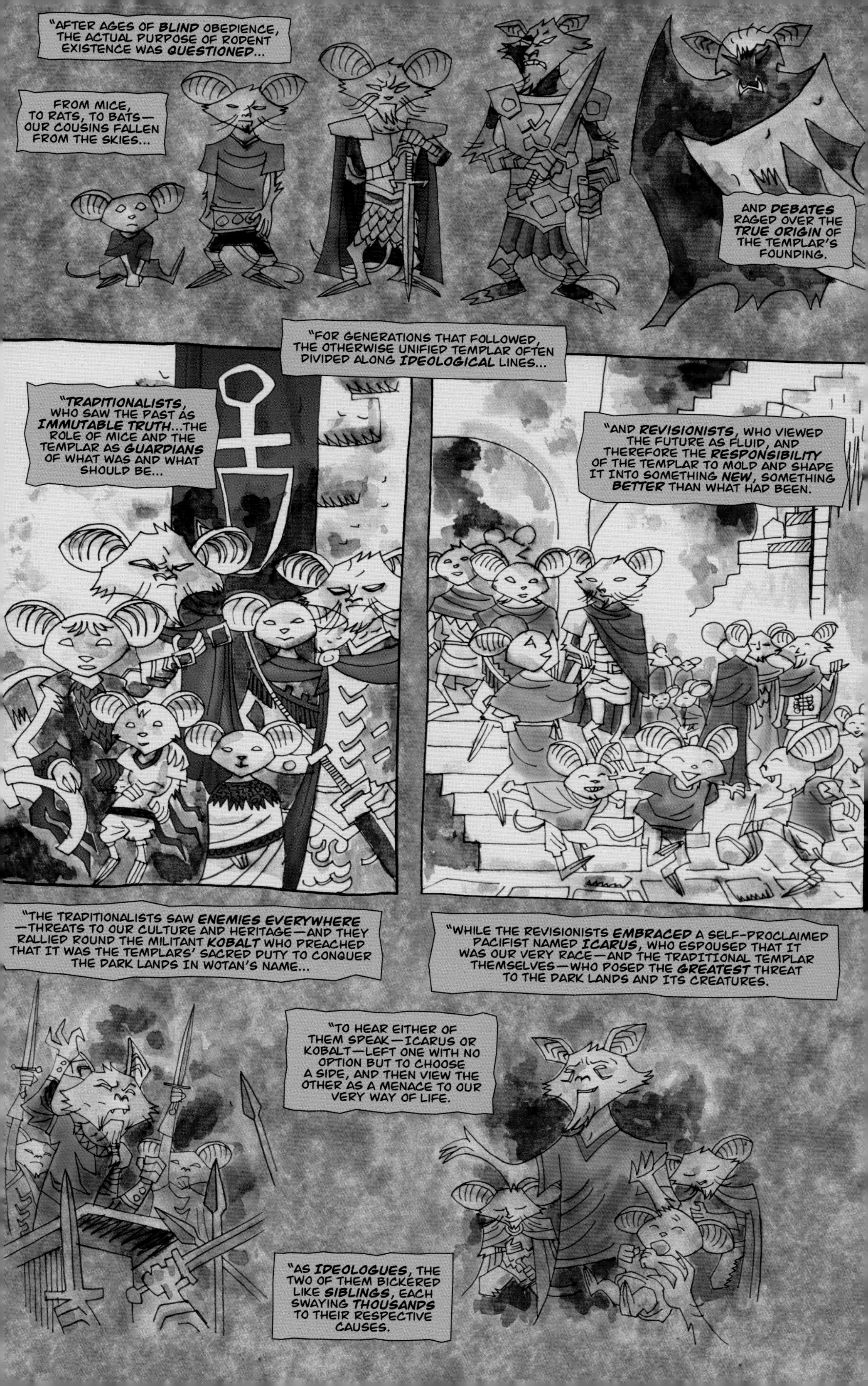
"AFTER AGES OF BLIND OBEDIENCE, THE ACTUAL PURPOSE OF RODENT EXISTENCE WAS QUESTIONED...
FROM MICE, TO RATS, TO BATS—OUR COUSINS FALLEN FROM THE SKIES...
AND DEBATES RAGED OVER THE TRUE ORIGIN OF THE TEMPLAR'S FOUNDING.
"FOR GENERATIONS THAT FOLLOWED, THE OTHERWISE UNIFIED TEMPLAR OFTEN DIVIDED ALONG IDEOLOGICAL LINES...
"TRADITIONALISTS, WHO SAW THE PAST AS IMMUTABLE TRUTH...THE ROLE OF MICE AND THE TEMPLAR AS GUARDIANS OF WHAT WAS AND WHAT SHOULD BE...
"AND REVISIONISTS, WHO VIEWED THE FUTURE AS FLUID, AND THEREFORE THE RESPONSIBILITY OF THE TEMPLAR TO MOLD AND SHAPE IT INTO SOMETHING NEW, SOMETHING BETTER THAN WHAT HAD BEEN.
"THE TRADITIONALISTS SAW ENEMIES EVERYWHERE—THREATS TO OUR CULTURE AND HERITAGE—AND THEY RALLIED ROUND THE MILITANT KOBALT WHO PREACHED THAT IT WAS THE TEMPLARS' SACRED DUTY TO CONQUER THE DARK LANDS IN WOTAN'S NAME...
"WHILE THE REVISIONISTS EMBRACED A SELF-PROCLAIMED PACIFIST NAMED ICARUS, WHO ESPOUSED THAT IT WAS OUR VERY RACE—AND THE TRADITIONAL TEMPLAR THEMSELVES—WHO POSED THE GREATEST THREAT TO THE DARK LANDS AND ITS CREATURES.
"TO HEAR EITHER OF THEM SPEAK—ICARUS OR KOBALT—LEFT ONE WITH NO OPTION BUT TO CHOOSE A SIDE, AND THEN VIEW THE OTHER AS A MENACE TO OUR VERY WAY OF LIFE.
"AS IDEOLOGUES, THE TWO OF THEM BICKERED LIKE SIBLINGS, EACH SWAYING THOUSANDS TO THEIR RESPECTIVE CAUSES.

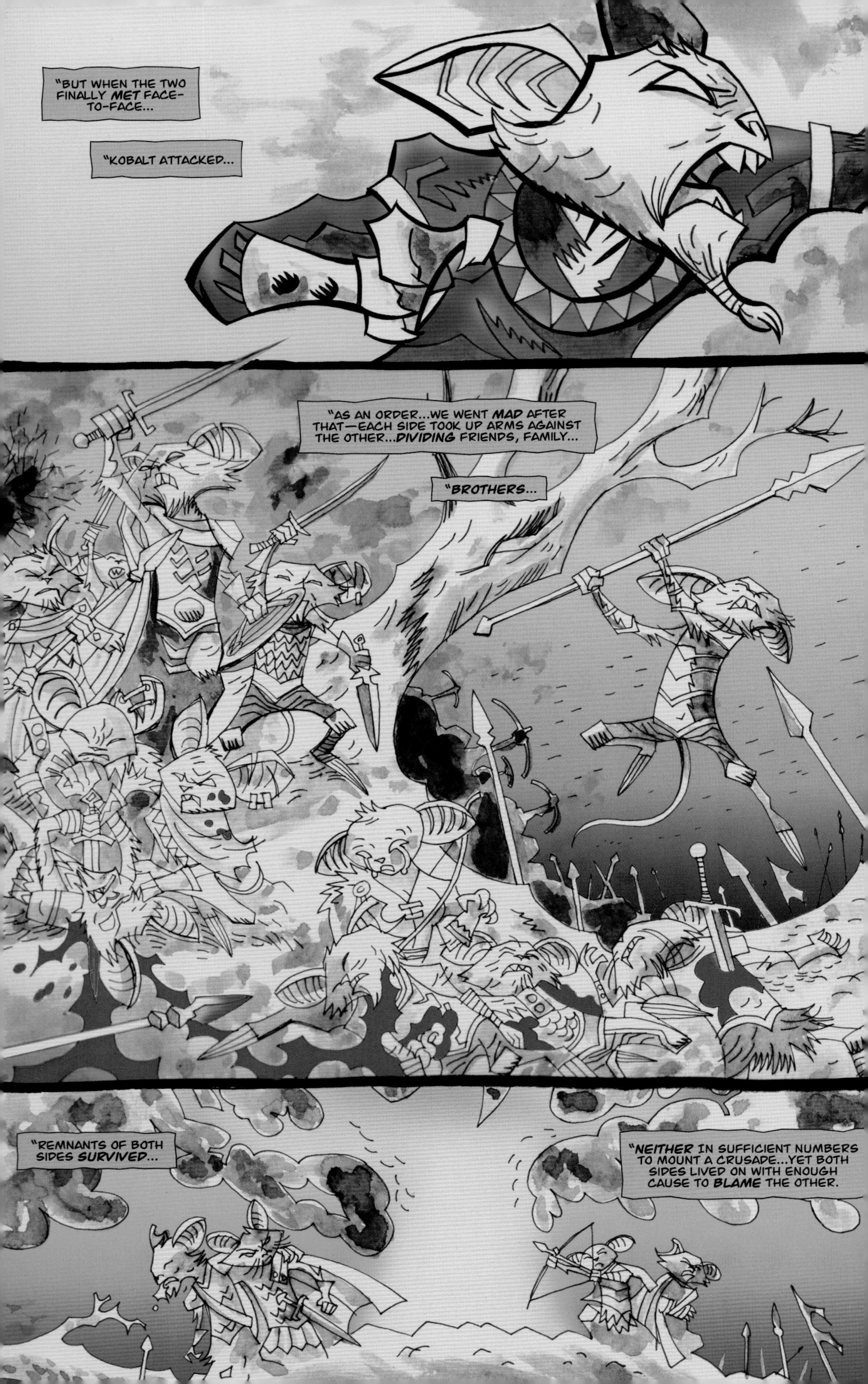
"BUT WHEN THE TWO FINALLY MET FACE-TO-FACE...
"KOBALT ATTACKED...
"AS AN ORDER...WE WENT MAD AFTER THAT—EACH SIDE TOOK UP ARMS AGAINST THE OTHER...DIVIDING FRIENDS, FAMILY...
"BROTHERS...
"REMNANTS OF BOTH SIDES SURVIVED...
"NEITHER IN SUFFICIENT NUMBERS TO MOUNT A CRUSADE...YET BOTH SIDES LIVED ON WITH ENOUGH CAUSE TO BLAME THE OTHER.

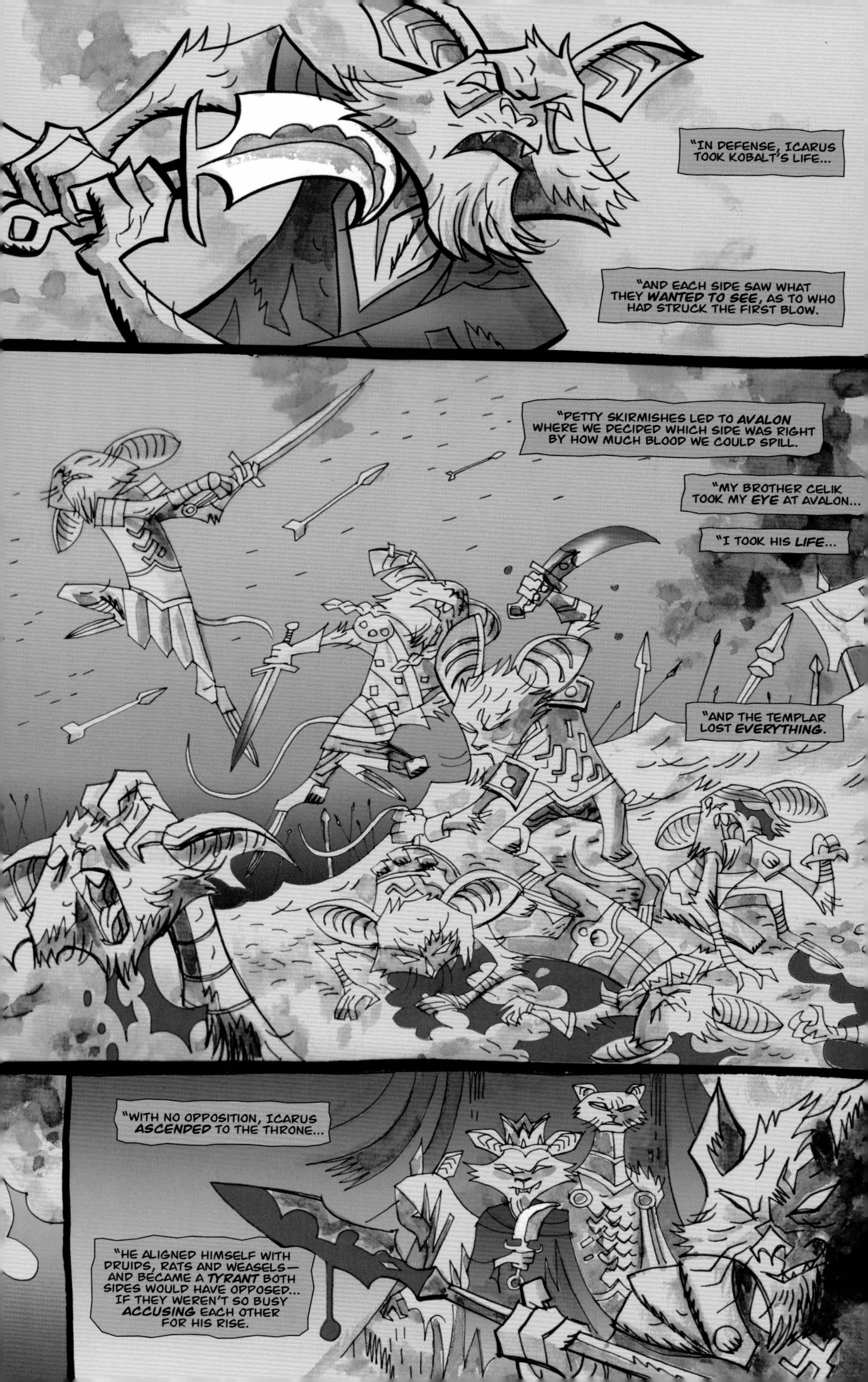
"IN DEFENSE, ICARUS TOOK KOBALT'S LIFE...
"AND EACH SIDE SAW WHAT THEY WANTED TO SEE, AS TO WHO HAD STRUCK THE FIRST BLOW.
"PETTY SKIRMISHES LED TO AVALON WHERE WE DECIDED WHICH SIDE WAS RIGHT BY HOW MUCH BLOOD WE COULD SPILL.
"MY BROTHER CELIK TOOK MY EYE AT AVALON...
"I TOOK HIS LIFE...
"AND THE TEMPLAR LOST EVERYTHING.
"WITH NO OPPOSITION, ICARUS ASCENDED TO THE THRONE...
"HE ALIGNED HIMSELF WITH DRUIDS, RATS AND WEASELS— AND BECAME A TYRANT BOTH SIDES WOULD HAVE OPPOSED... IF THEY WEREN'T SO BUSY ACCUSING EACH OTHER FOR HIS RISE.

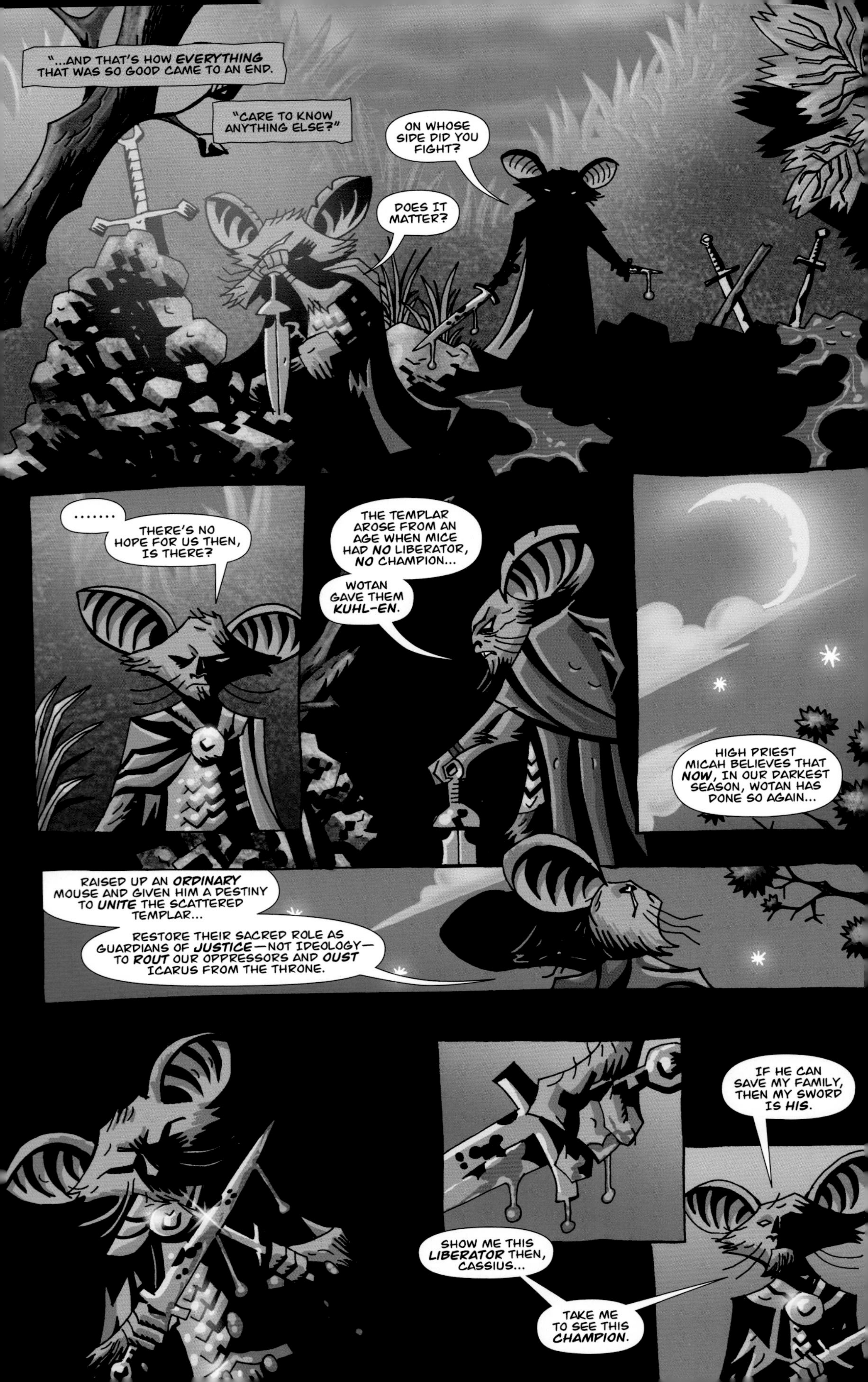
"...AND THAT'S HOW EVERYTHING THAT WAS SO GOOD CAME TO AN END.
"CARE TO KNOW ANYTHING ELSE?"
ON WHOSE SIDE DID YOU FIGHT?
DOES IT MATTER?
.... THERE'S NO HOPE FOR US THEN, IS THERE?
THE TEMPLAR AROSE FROM AN AGE WHEN MICE HAD NO LIBERATOR, NO CHAMPION...
WOTAN GAVE THEM KUHL-EN.
HIGH PRIEST MICAH BELIEVES THAT NOW, IN OUR DARKEST SEASON, WOTAN HAS DONE SO AGAIN...
RAISED UP AN ORDINARY MOUSE AND GIVEN HIM A DESTINY TO UNITE THE SCATTERED TEMPLAR...
RESTORE THEIR SACRED ROLE AS GUARDIANS OF JUSTICE—NOT IDEOLOGY—TO ROUT OUR OPPRESSORS AND OUST ICARUS FROM THE THRONE.
IF HE CAN SAVE MY FAMILY, THEN MY SWORD IS HIS.
SHOW ME THIS LIBERATOR THEN, CASSIUS...
TAKE ME TO SEE THIS CHAMPION.

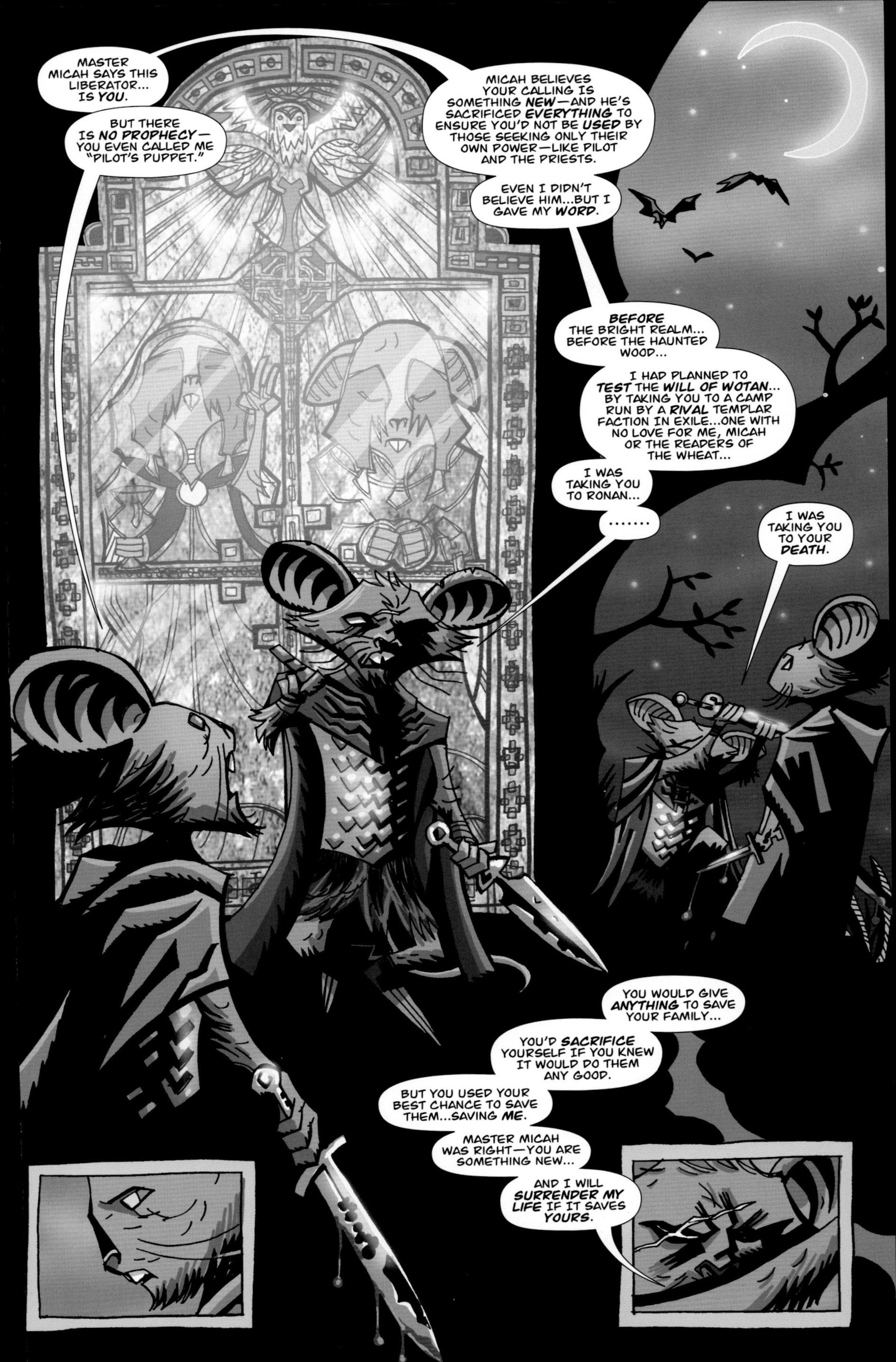
MASTER MICAH SAYS THIS LIBERATOR... IS YOU.
BUT THERE IS NO PROPHECY—YOU EVEN CALLED ME "PILOT'S PUPPET."
MICAH BELIEVES YOUR CALLING IS SOMETHING NEW—AND HE'S SACRIFICED EVERYTHING TO ENSURE YOU'D NOT BE USED BY THOSE SEEKING ONLY THEIR OWN POWER—LIKE PILOT AND THE PRIESTS.
EVEN I DIDN'T BELIEVE HIM...BUT I GAVE MY WORD.
BEFORE THE BRIGHT REALM... BEFORE THE HAUNTED WOOD...
I HAD PLANNED TO TEST THE WILL OF WOTAN... BY TAKING YOU TO A CAMP RUN BY A RIVAL TEMPLAR FACTION IN EXILE...ONE WITH NO LOVE FOR ME, MICAH OR THE READERS OF THE WHEAT...
I WAS TAKING YOU TO RONAN...
....
I WAS TAKING YOU TO YOUR DEATH.
YOU WOULD GIVE ANYTHING TO SAVE YOUR FAMILY...
YOU'D SACRIFICE YOURSELF IF YOU KNEW IT WOULD DO THEM ANY GOOD.
BUT YOU USED YOUR BEST CHANCE TO SAVE THEM...SAVING ME.
MASTER MICAH WAS RIGHT—YOU ARE SOMETHING NEW...
AND I WILL SURRENDER MY LIFE IF IT SAVES YOURS.

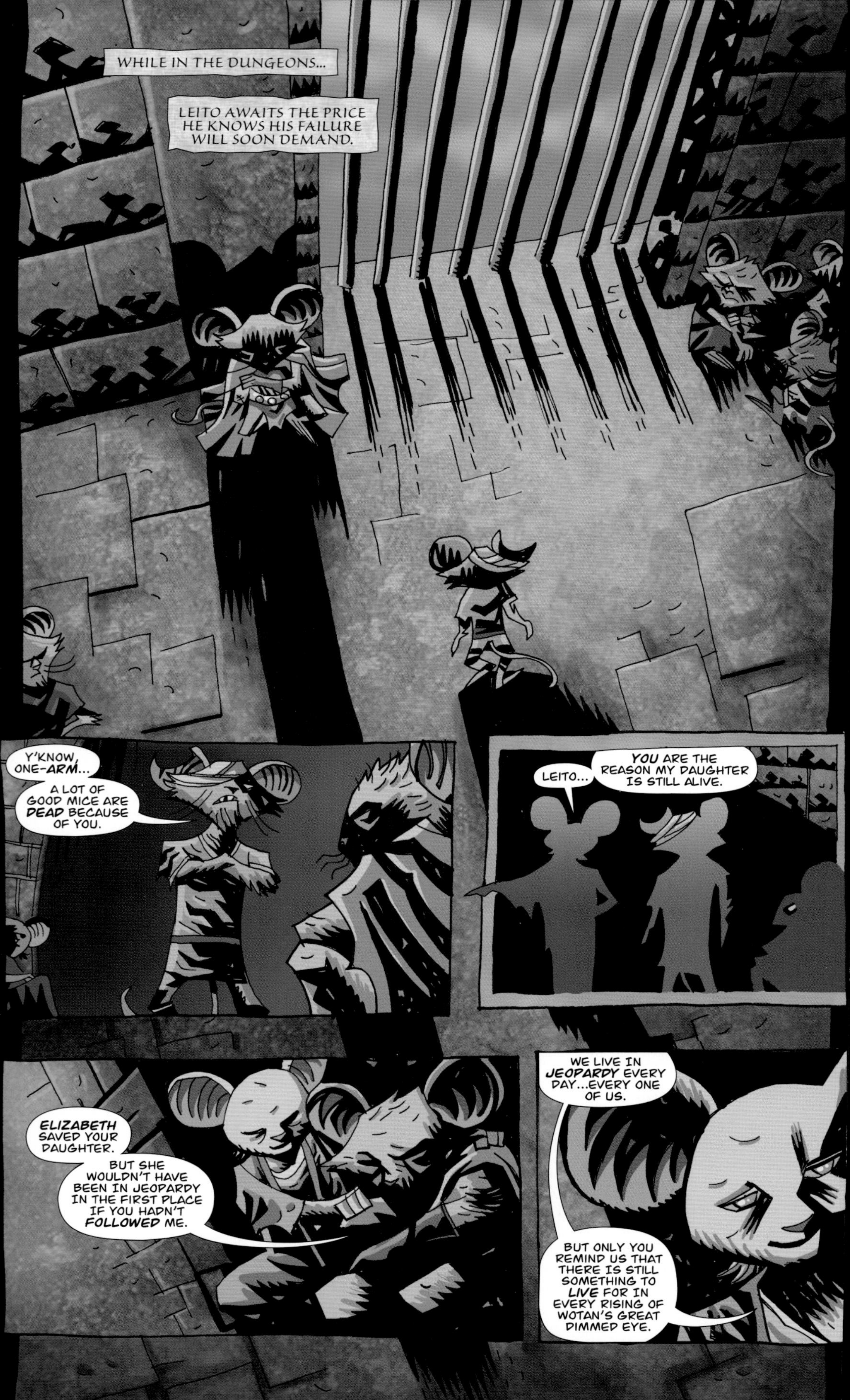
WHILE IN THE DUNGEONS...
LEITO AWAITS THE PRICE HE KNOWS HIS FAILURE WILL SOON DEMAND.
Y'KNOW, ONE-ARM...
A LOT OF GOOD MICE ARE DEAD BECAUSE OF YOU.
LEITO...
YOU ARE THE REASON MY DAUGHTER IS STILL ALIVE.
ELIZABETH SAVED YOUR DAUGHTER.
BUT SHE WOULDN'T HAVE BEEN IN JEOPARDY IN THE FIRST PLACE IF YOU HADN'T FOLLOWED ME.
WE LIVE IN JEOPARDY EVERY DAY...EVERY ONE OF US.
BUT ONLY YOU REMIND US THAT THERE IS STILL SOMETHING TO LIVE FOR IN EVERY RISING OF WOTAN'S GREAT DIMMED EYE.

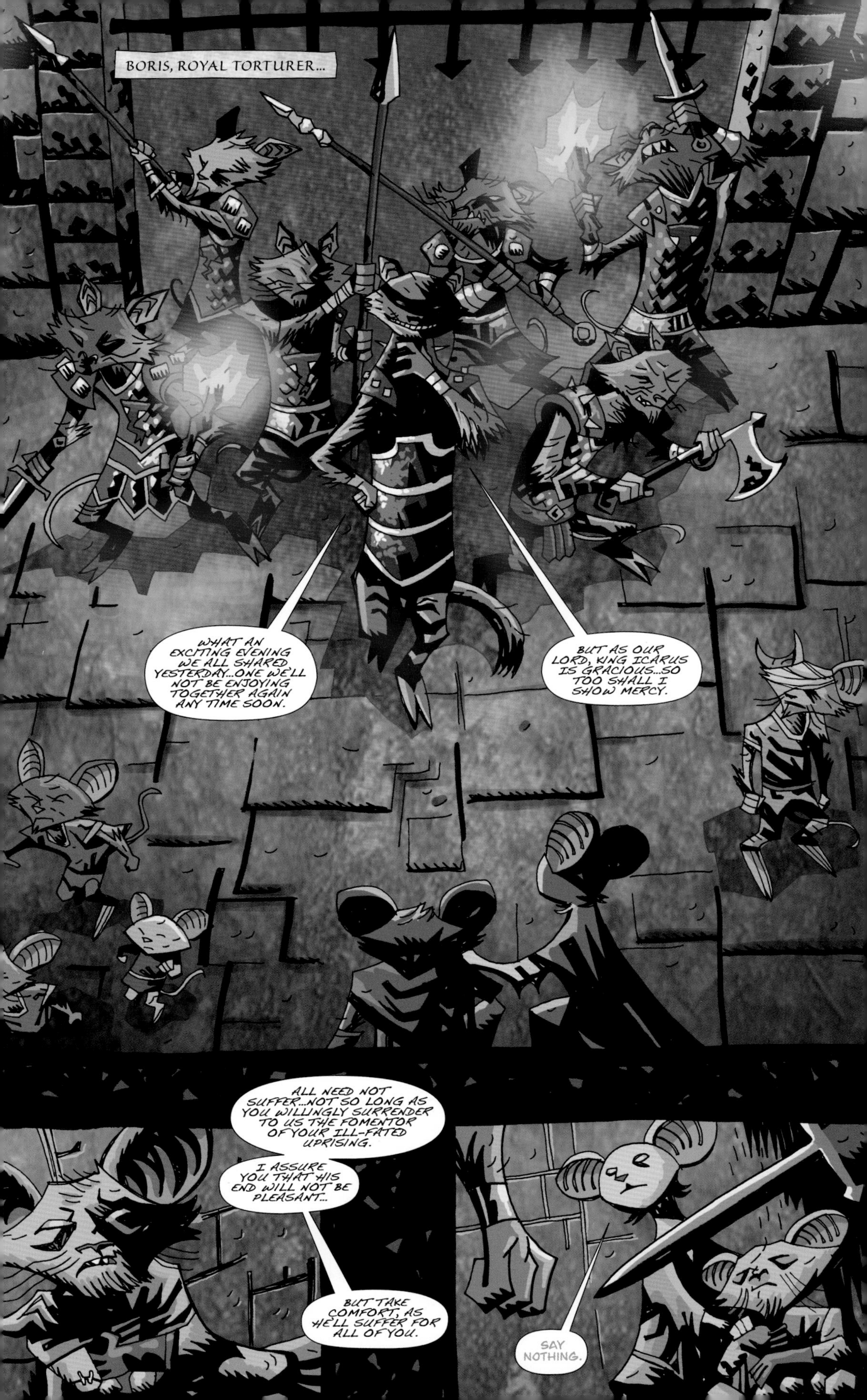
BORIS, ROYAL TORTURER...
WHAT AN EXCITING EVENING WE ALL SHARED YESTERDAY...ONE WE'LL NOT BE ENJOYING TOGETHER AGAIN ANY TIME SOON.
BUT AS OUR LORD, KING ICARUS IS GRACIOUS...SO TOO SHALL I SHOW MERCY.
ALL NEED NOT SUFFER...NOT SO LONG AS YOU WILLINGLY SURRENDER TO US THE FOMENTOR OF YOUR ILL-FATED UPRISING.
I ASSURE YOU THAT HIS END WILL NOT BE PLEASANT...
BUT TAKE COMFORT, AS HE'LL SUFFER FOR ALL OF YOU.
SAY NOTHING.

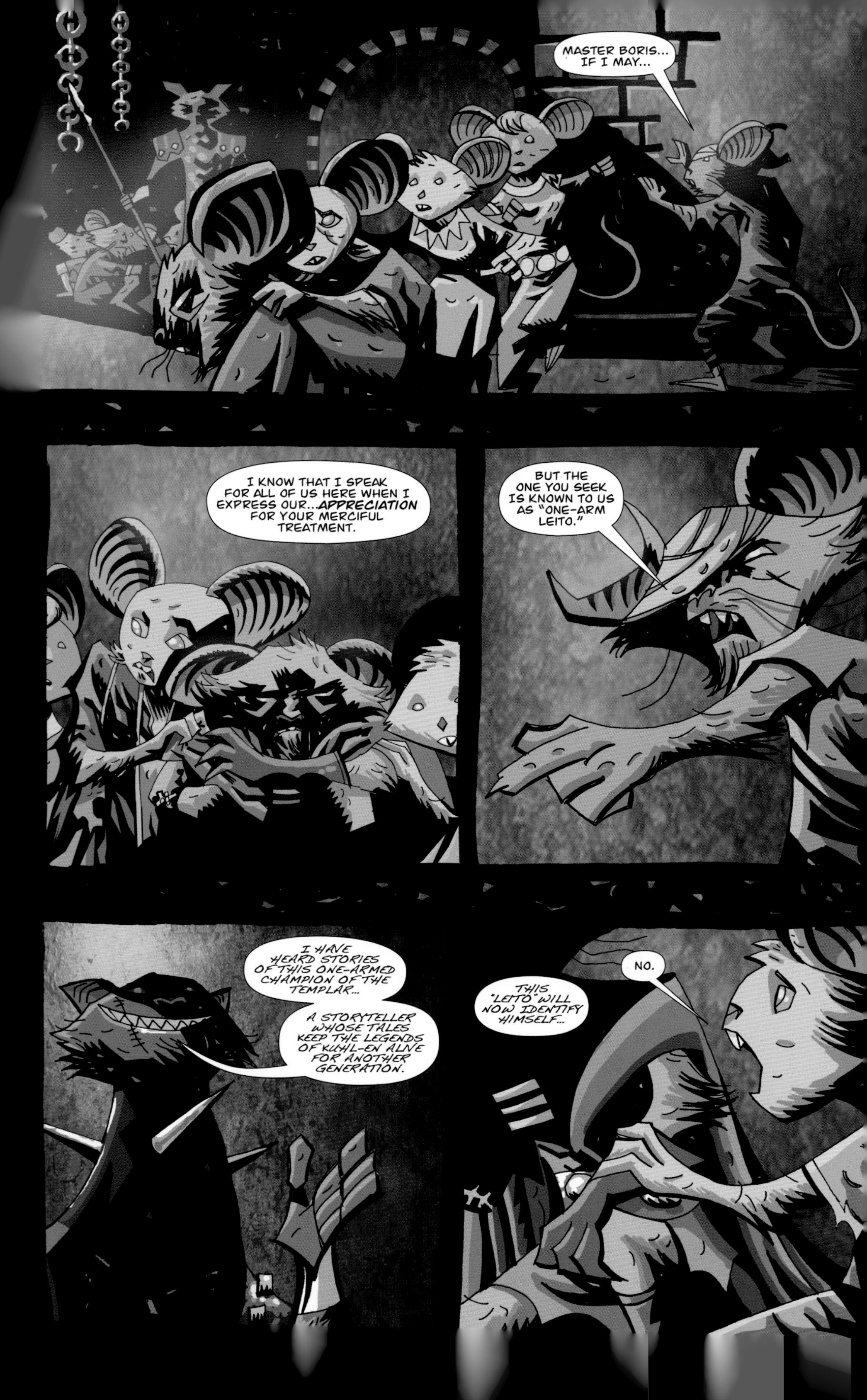
MASTER BORIS... IF I MAY...
I KNOW THAT I SPEAK FOR ALL OF US HERE WHEN I EXPRESS OUR...APPRECIATION FOR YOUR MERCIFUL TREATMENT.
BUT THE ONE YOU SEEK IS KNOWN TO US AS "ONE-ARM LEITO."
I HAVE HEARD STORIES OF THIS ONE-ARMED CHAMPION OF THE TEMPLAR...
A STORYTELLER WHOSE TALES KEEP THE LEGENDS OF KUHL-EN ALIVE FOR ANOTHER GENERATION.
NO.
THIS "LEITO" WILL NOW IDENTIFY HIMSELF...

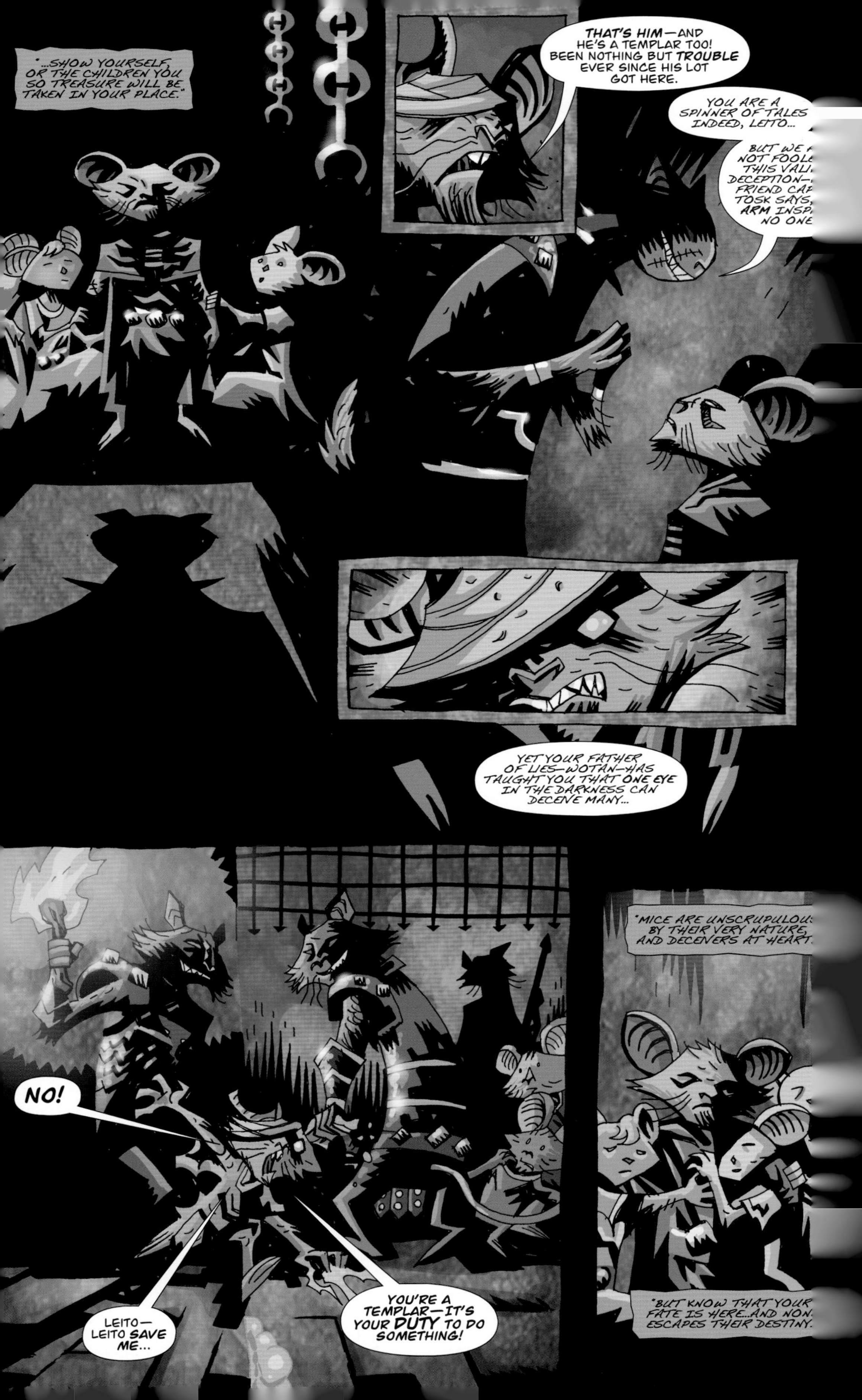
"...SHOW YOURSELF, OR THE CHILDREN YOU SO TREASURE WILL BE TAKEN IN YOUR PLACE."
THAT'S HIM—AND HE'S A TEMPLAR TOO! BEEN NOTHING BUT TROUBLE EVER SINCE HIS LOT GOT HERE.
YOU ARE A SPINNER OF TALES INDEED, LEITO...
BUT WE A NOT FOOLE THIS VALI DECEPTION— FRIEND CAP TOSK SAYS, ARM INSP NO ONE
YET YOUR FATHER OF LIES—WOTAN—HAS TAUGHT YOU THAT ONE EYE IN THE DARKNESS CAN DECEIVE MANY...
NO!
LEITO— LEITO SAVE ME...
YOU'RE A TEMPLAR—IT'S YOUR DUTY TO DO SOMETHING!
"MICE ARE UNSCRUPULOUS BY THEIR VERY NATURE, AND DECEIVERS AT HEART.
"BUT KNOW THAT YOUR FATE IS HERE...AND NONE ESCAPES THEIR DESTINY.

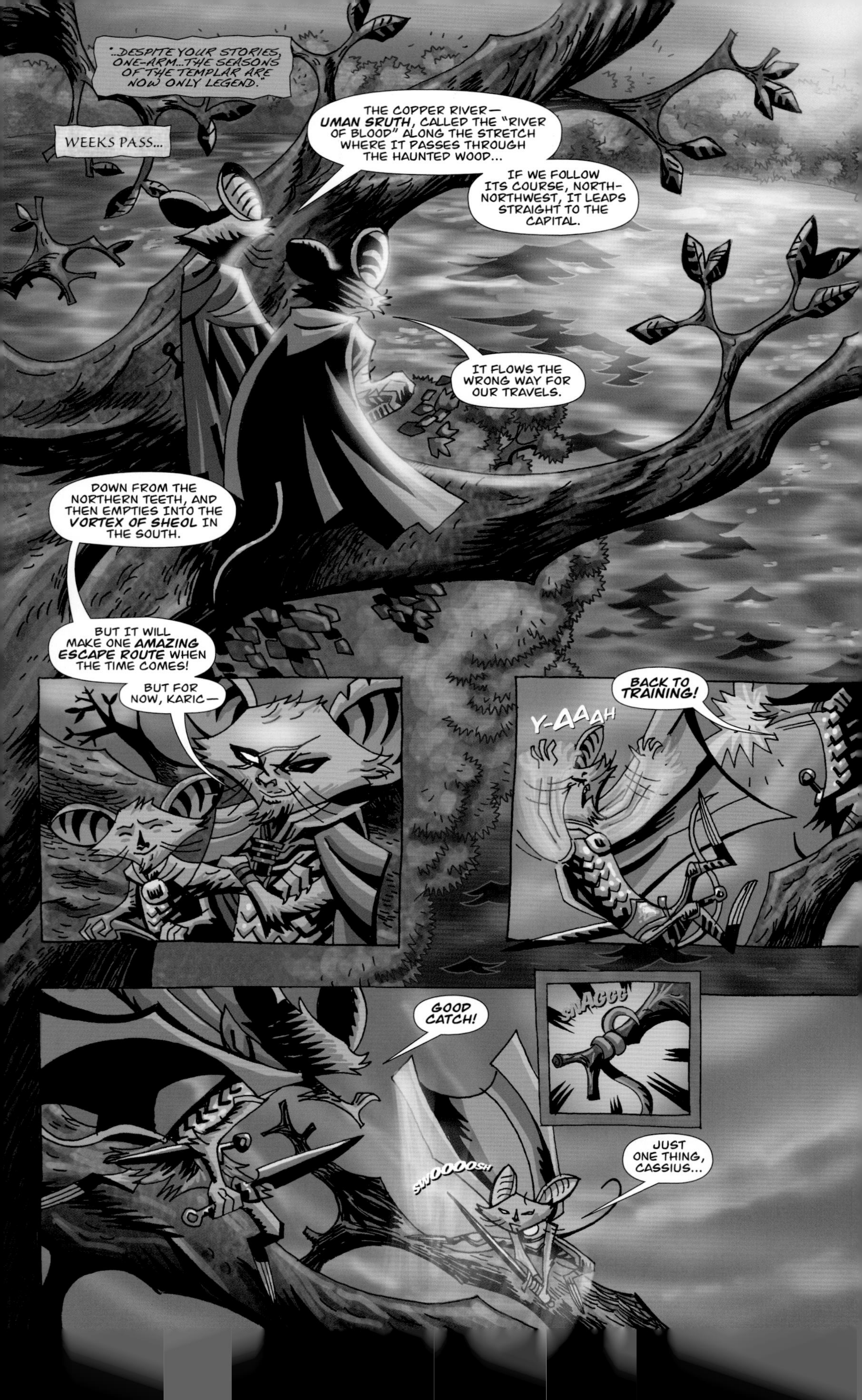
"...DESPITE YOUR STORIES, ONE-ARM...THE SEASONS OF THE TEMPLAR ARE NOW ONLY LEGEND."
WEEKS PASS...
THE COPPER RIVER— UMAN SRUTH, CALLED THE "RIVER OF BLOOD" ALONG THE STRETCH WHERE IT PASSES THROUGH THE HAUNTED WOOD...
IF WE FOLLOW ITS COURSE, NORTH-NORTHWEST, IT LEADS STRAIGHT TO THE CAPITAL.
IT FLOWS THE WRONG WAY FOR OUR TRAVELS.
DOWN FROM THE NORTHERN TEETH, AND THEN EMPTIES INTO THE VORTEX OF SHEOL IN THE SOUTH.
BUT IT WILL MAKE ONE AMAZING ESCAPE ROUTE WHEN THE TIME COMES!
BUT FOR NOW, KARIC—
BACK TO TRAINING!
Y-AAAH
GOOD CATCH!
JUST ONE THING, CASSIUS...
SWOOOOSH

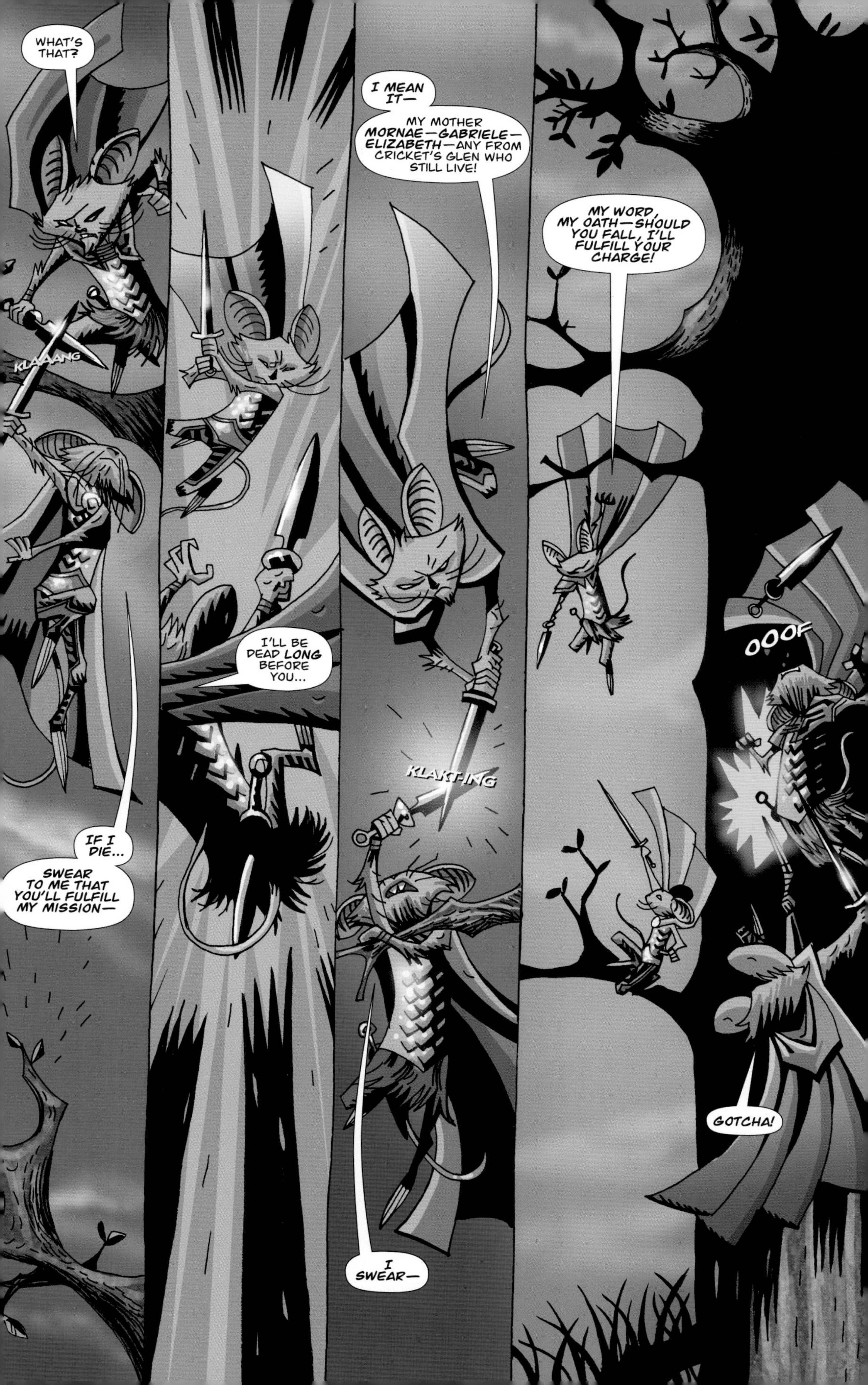
WHAT'S THAT?
KLAAANG
IF I DIE...
SWEAR TO ME THAT YOU'LL FULFILL MY MISSION—
I'LL BE DEAD LONG BEFORE YOU...
I MEAN IT—
MY MOTHER MORNAE—GABRIELE—ELIZABETH—ANY FROM CRICKET'S GLEN WHO STILL LIVE!
KLAKT-ING
I SWEAR—
MY WORD, MY OATH—SHOULD YOU FALL, I'LL FULFILL YOUR CHARGE!
OOOF
GOTCHA!

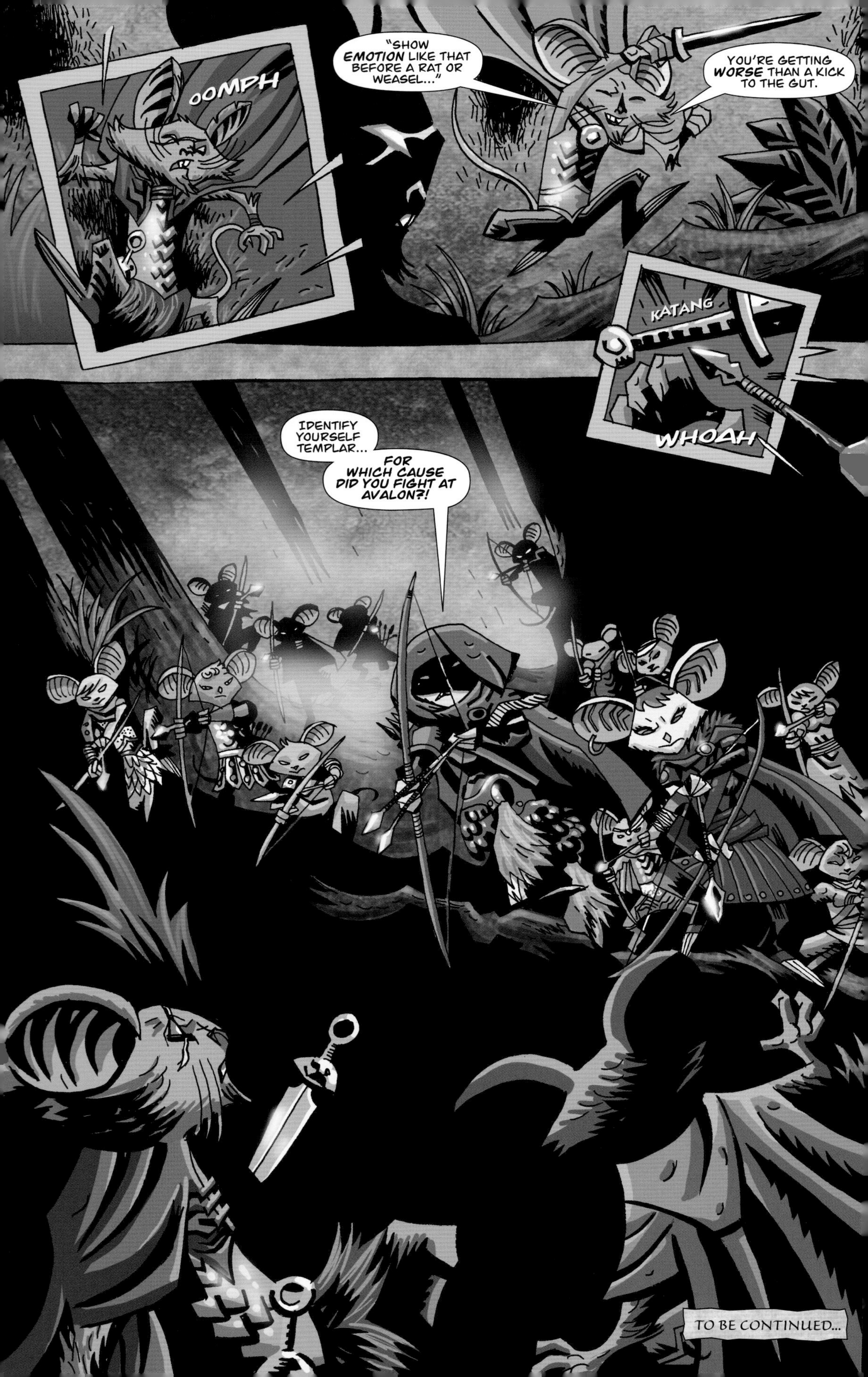
OOMPH
"SHOW EMOTION LIKE THAT BEFORE A RAT OR WEASEL..."
YOU'RE GETTING WORSE THAN A KICK TO THE GUT.
KATANG
WHOAH
IDENTIFY YOURSELF TEMPLAR...
FOR WHICH CAUSE DID YOU FIGHT AT AVALON?!
TO BE CONTINUED...

CHAPTER FIVE

AN ORDER DIVIDED

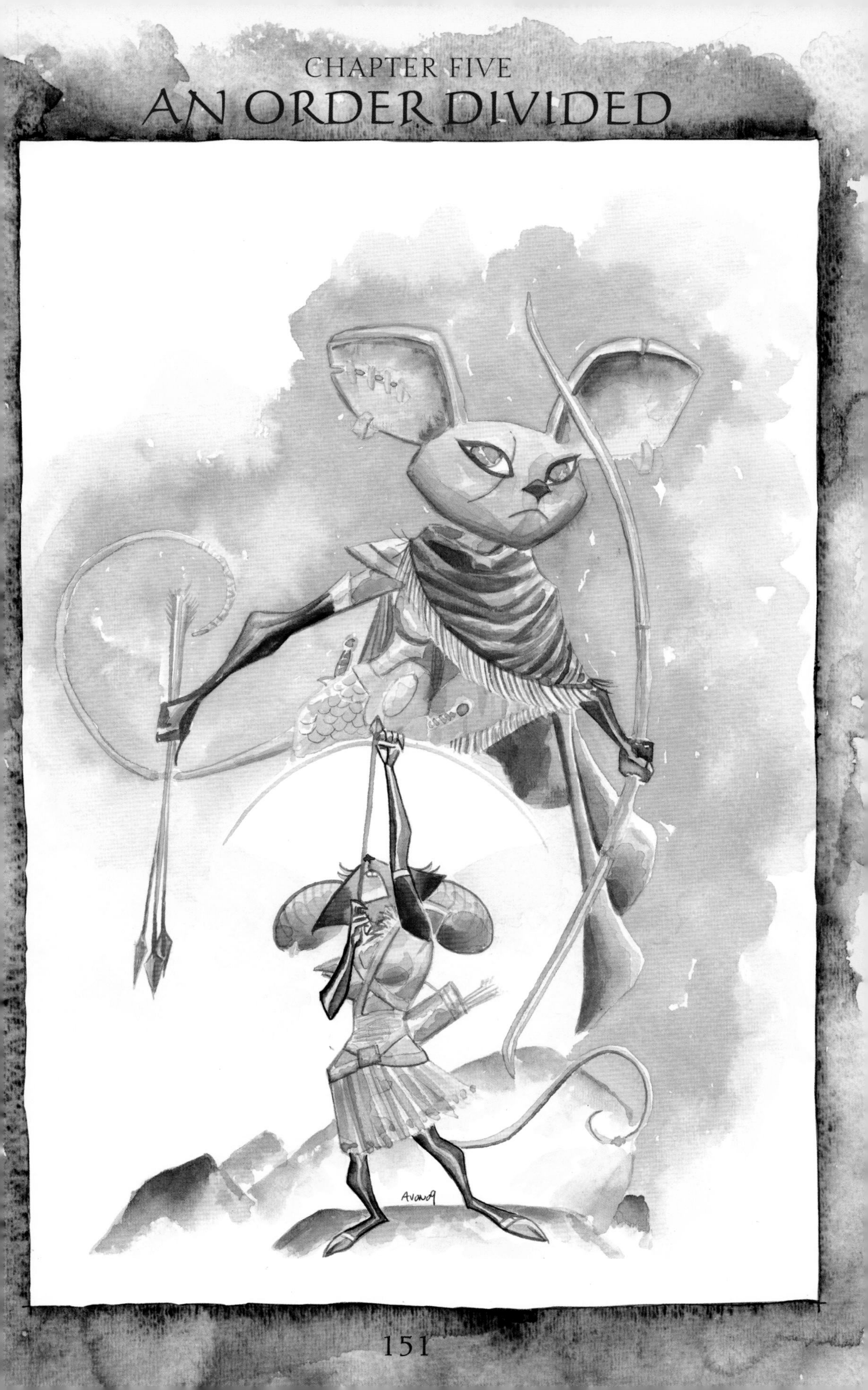

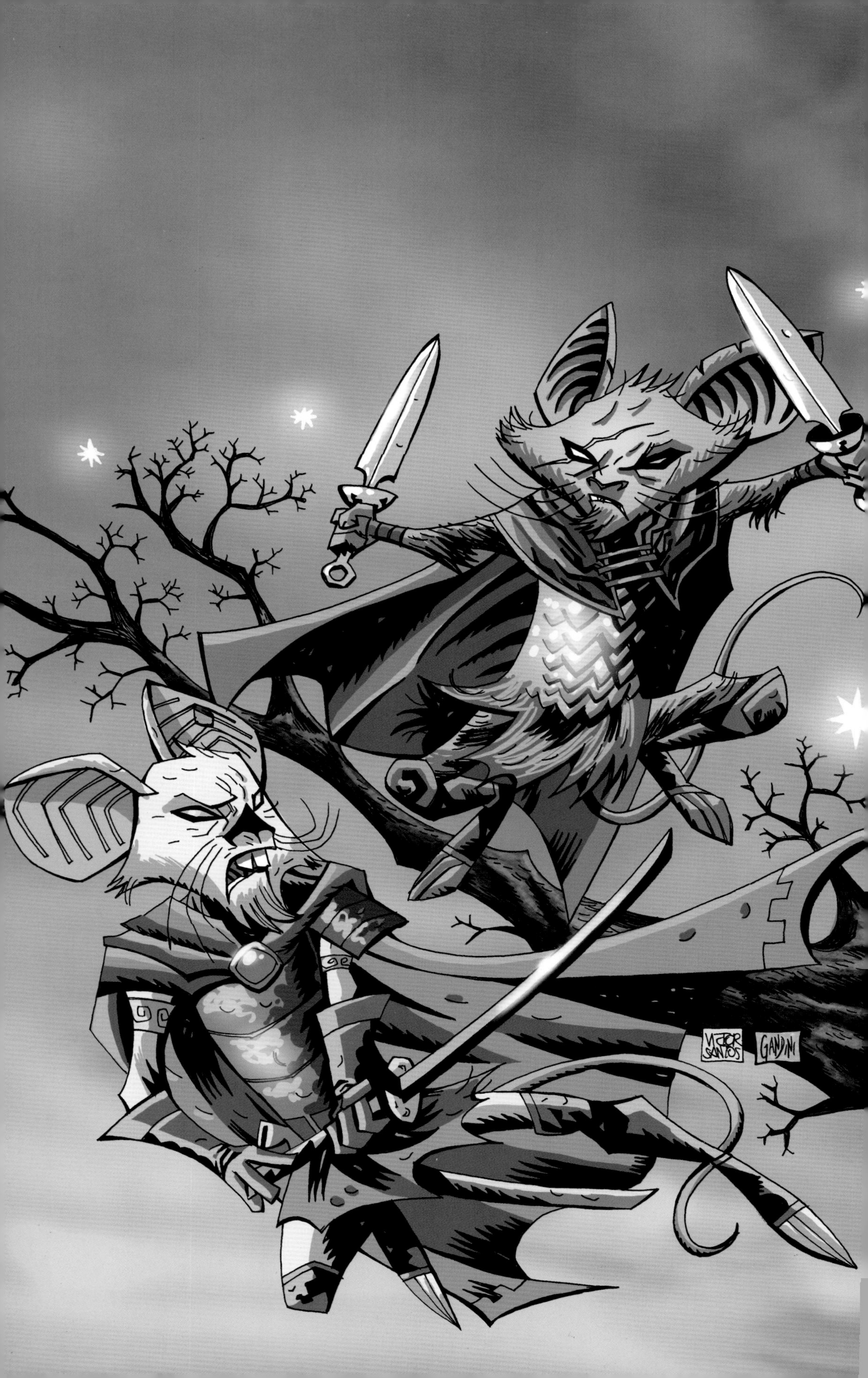
VICTOR SANTOS
GANDINI

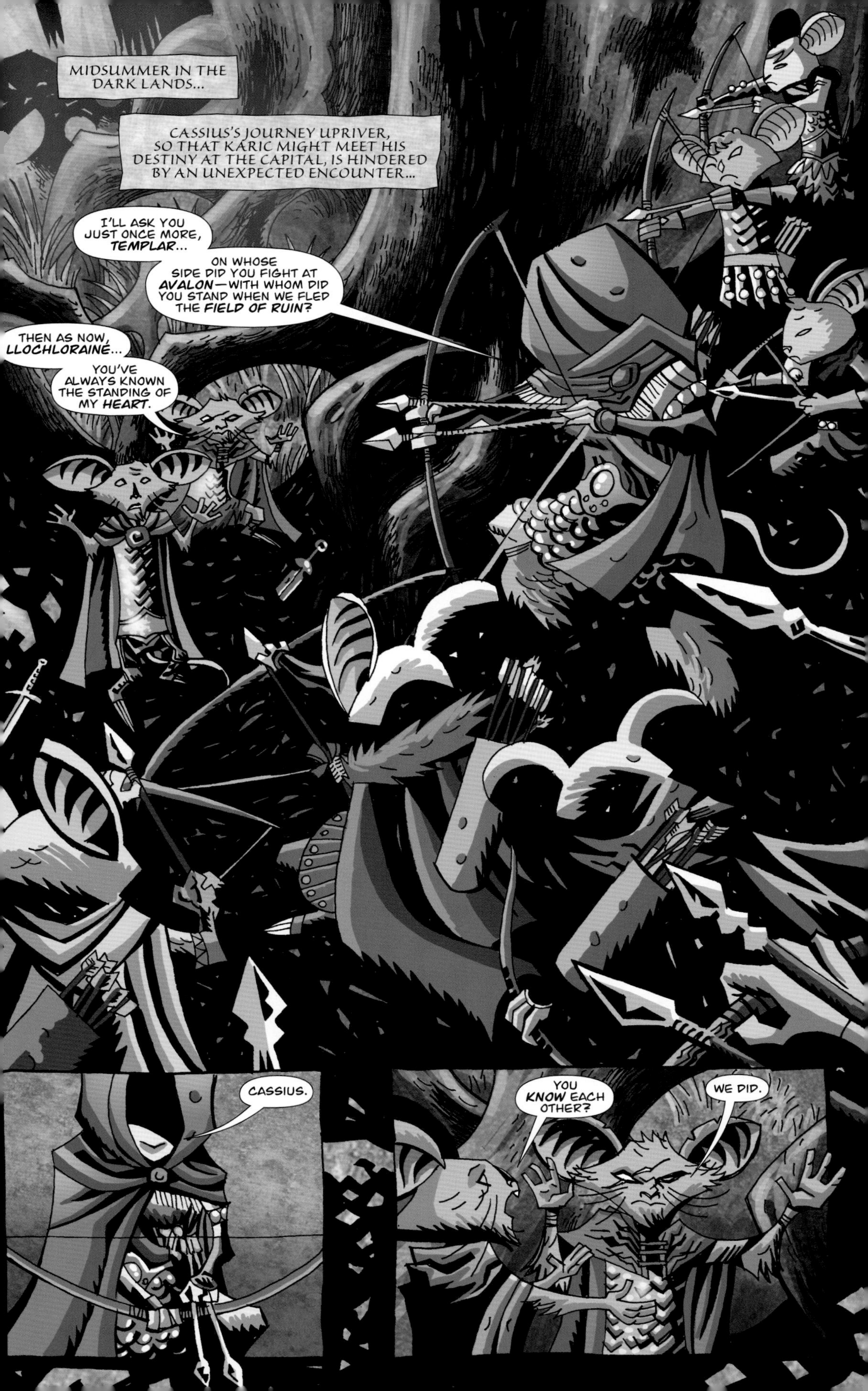

MIDSUMMER IN THE DARK LANDS...
CASSIUS'S JOURNEY UPRIVER, SO THAT KARIC MIGHT MEET HIS DESTINY AT THE CAPITAL, IS HINDERED BY AN UNEXPECTED ENCOUNTER...
I'LL ASK YOU JUST ONCE MORE, **TEMPLAR**...
ON WHOSE SIDE DID YOU FIGHT AT **AVALON**—WITH WHOM DID YOU STAND WHEN WE FLED THE **FIELD OF RUIN**?
THEN AS NOW, **LLOCHLORAINE**...
YOU'VE ALWAYS KNOWN THE STANDING OF MY **HEART**.
CASSIUS.
YOU **KNOW** EACH OTHER?
WE DID.

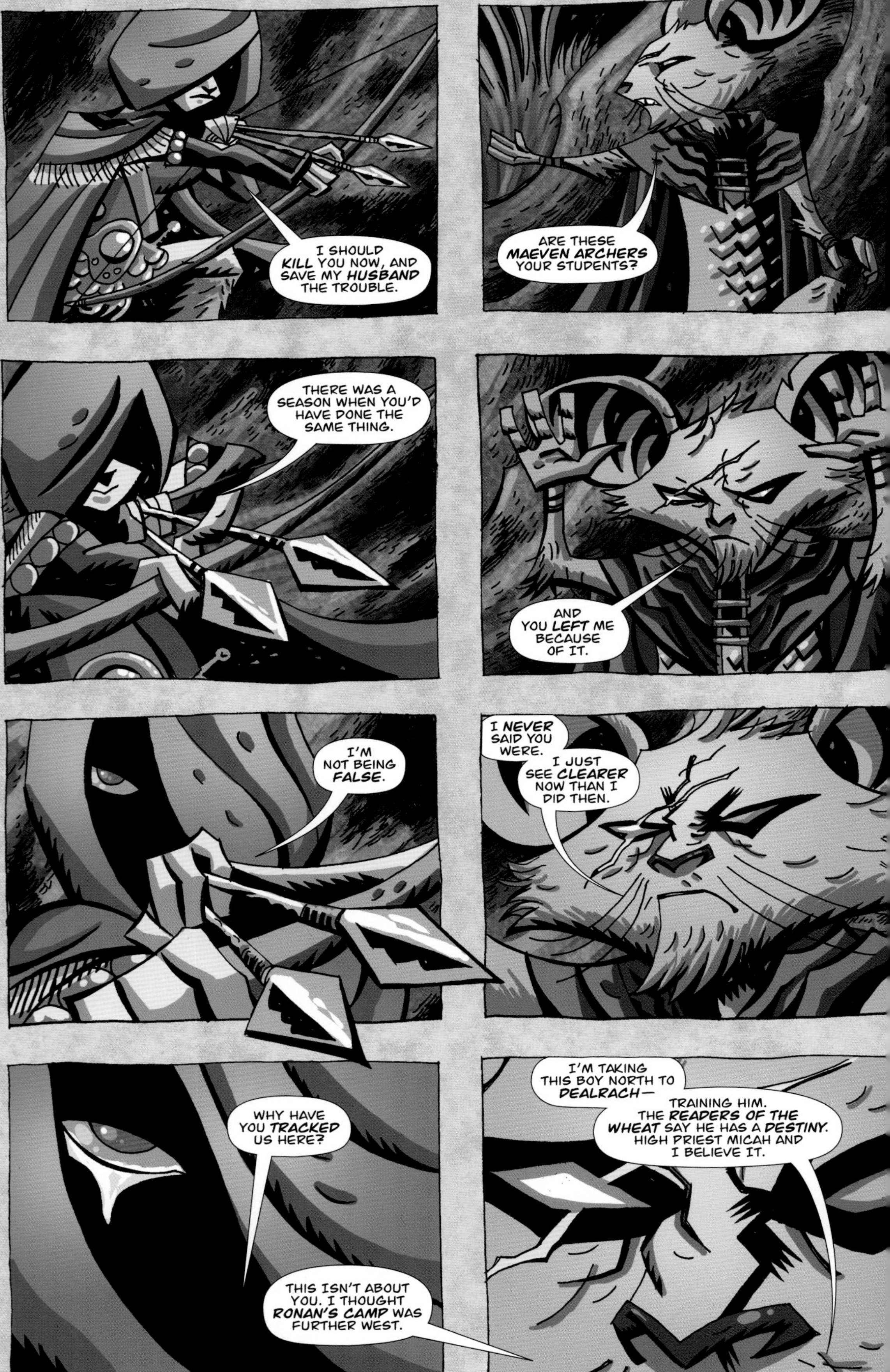
I SHOULD KILL YOU NOW, AND SAVE MY HUSBAND THE TROUBLE.
ARE THESE MAEVEN ARCHERS YOUR STUDENTS?
THERE WAS A SEASON WHEN YOU'D HAVE DONE THE SAME THING.
AND YOU LEFT ME BECAUSE OF IT.
I'M NOT BEING FALSE.
I NEVER SAID YOU WERE.
I JUST SEE CLEARER NOW THAN I DID THEN.
WHY HAVE YOU TRACKED US HERE?
THIS ISN'T ABOUT YOU. I THOUGHT RONAN'S CAMP WAS FURTHER WEST.
I'M TAKING THIS BOY NORTH TO DEALRACH—
TRAINING HIM.
THE READERS OF THE WHEAT SAY HE HAS A DESTINY. HIGH PRIEST MICAH AND I BELIEVE IT.

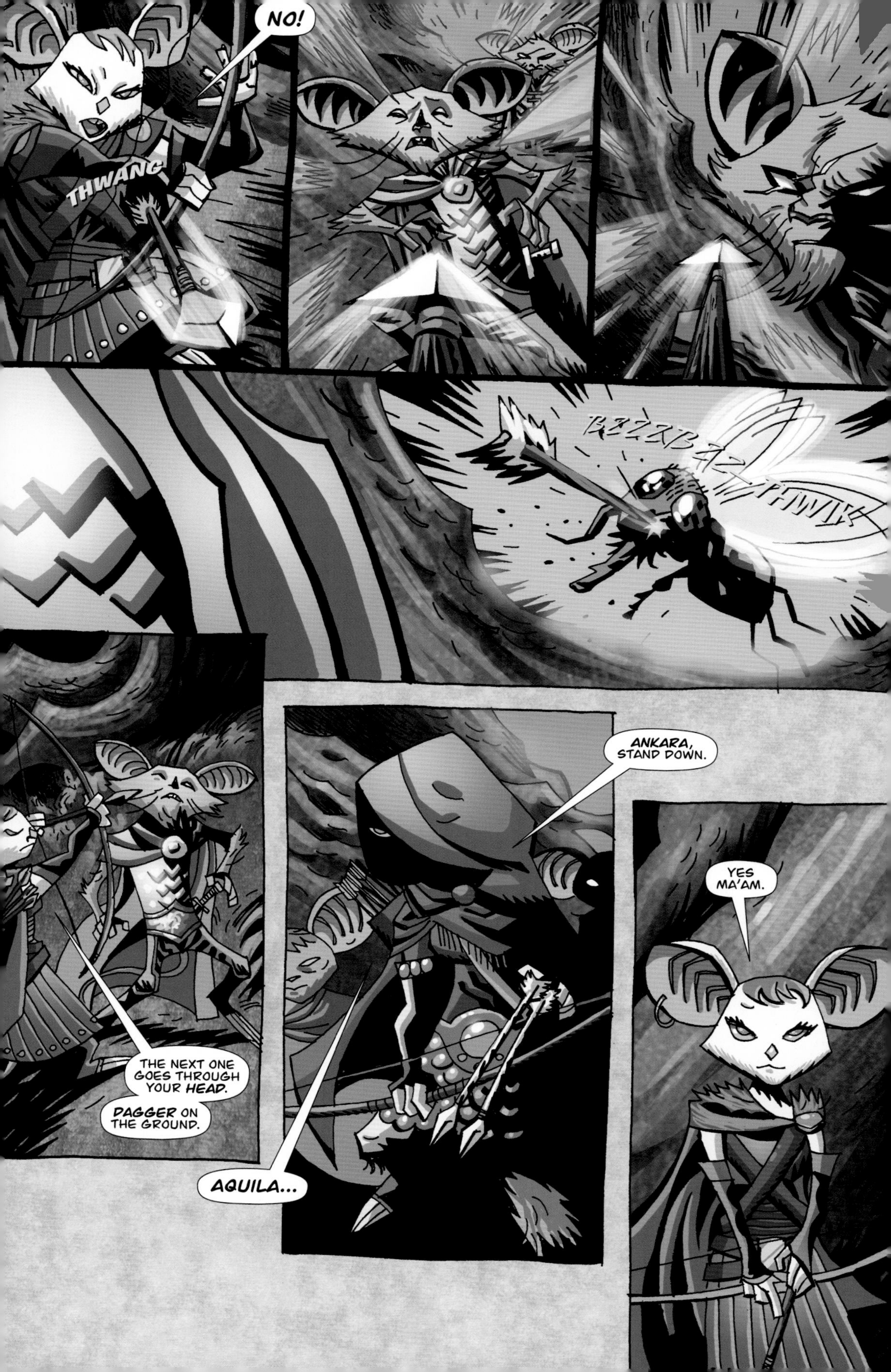
NO!
THWANG
BZZZBZZ-THWIK
THE NEXT ONE GOES THROUGH YOUR **HEAD**.
DAGGER ON THE GROUND.
AQUILA...
ANKARA, STAND DOWN.
YES MA'AM.

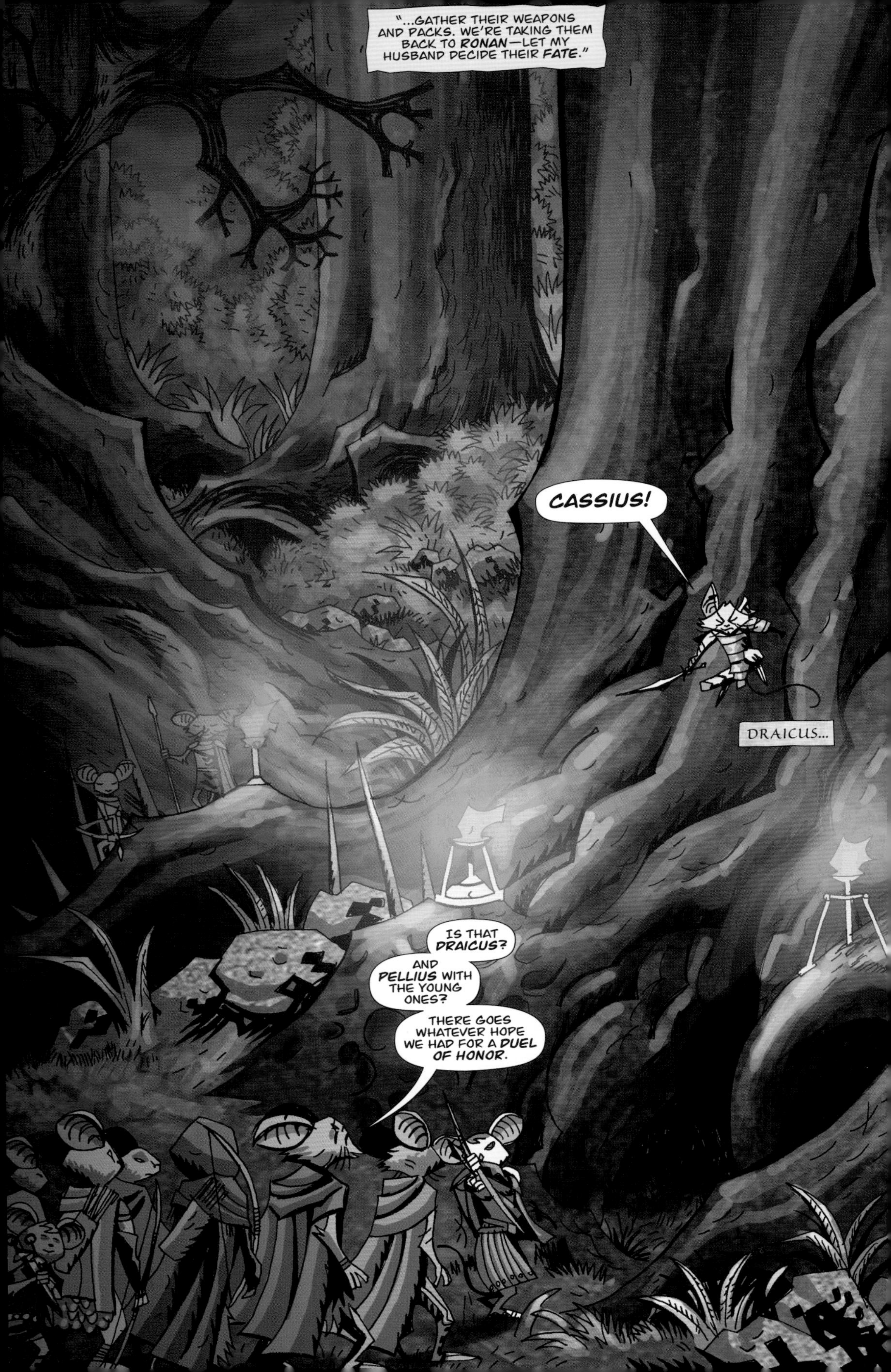
"...GATHER THEIR WEAPONS AND PACKS. WE'RE TAKING THEM BACK TO RONAN—LET MY HUSBAND DECIDE THEIR FATE."
CASSIUS!
DRAICUS...
IS THAT DRAICUS?
AND PELLIUS WITH THE YOUNG ONES?
THERE GOES WHATEVER HOPE WE HAD FOR A DUEL OF HONOR.

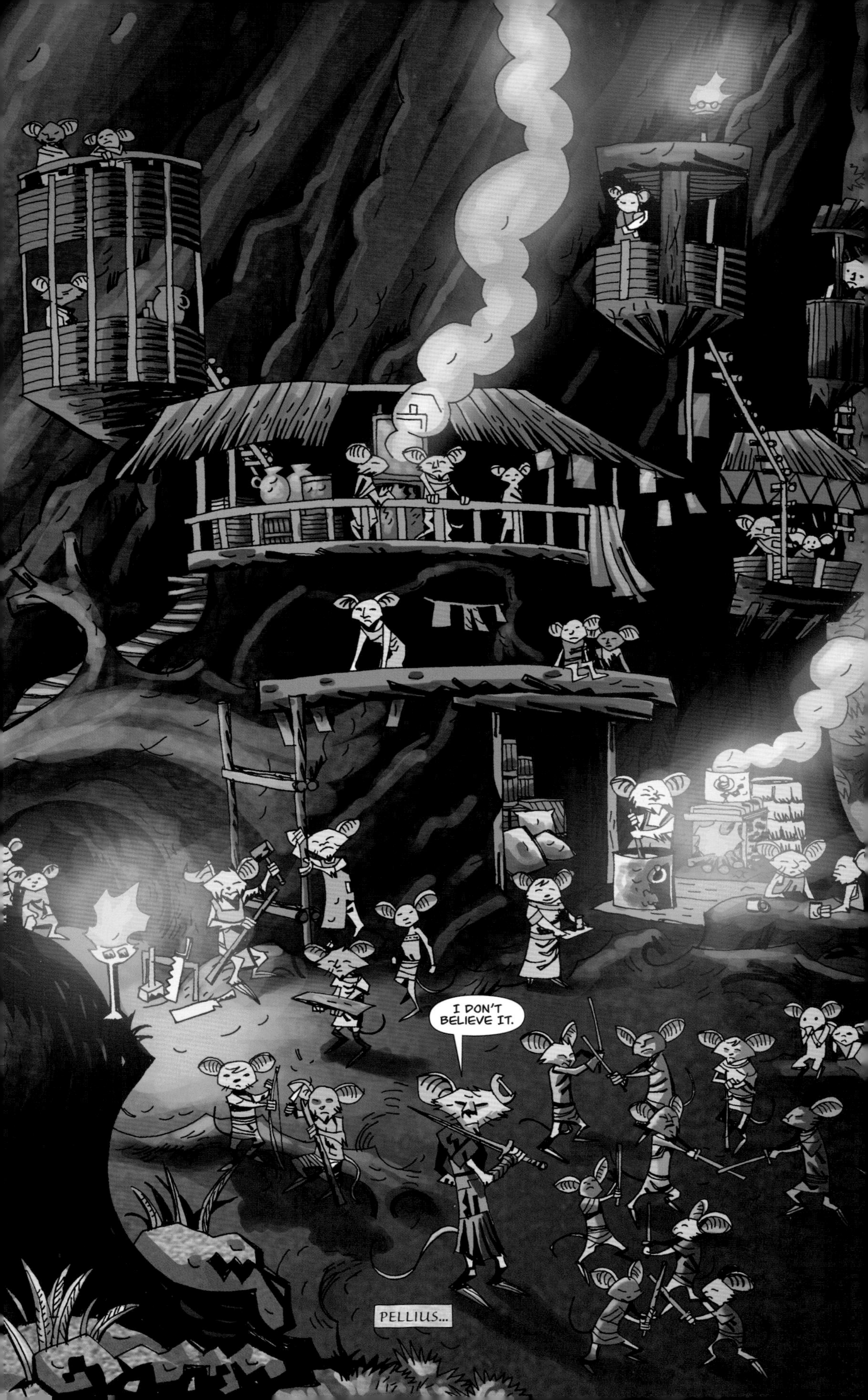
I DON'T BELIEVE IT.
PELLIUS...

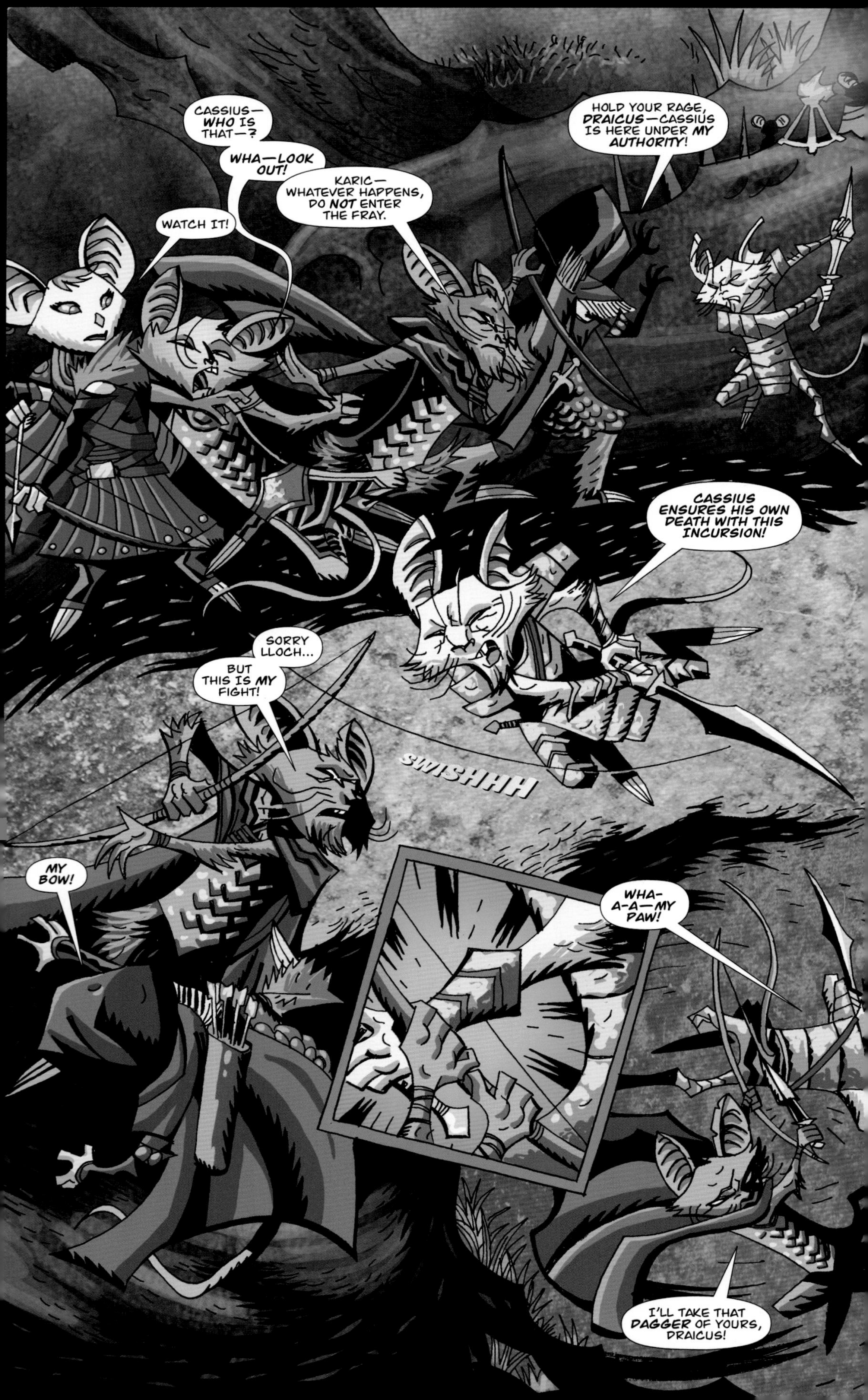

CASSIUS—WHO IS THAT—?
WHA—LOOK OUT!
WATCH IT!
KARIC—WHATEVER HAPPENS, DO NOT ENTER THE FRAY.
HOLD YOUR RAGE, DRAICUS—CASSIUS IS HERE UNDER MY AUTHORITY!
CASSIUS ENSURES HIS OWN DEATH WITH THIS INCURSION!
SORRY LLOCH...
BUT THIS IS MY FIGHT!
SWISHHH
MY BOW!
WHA-A-A—MY PAW!
I'LL TAKE THAT DAGGER OF YOURS, DRAICUS!

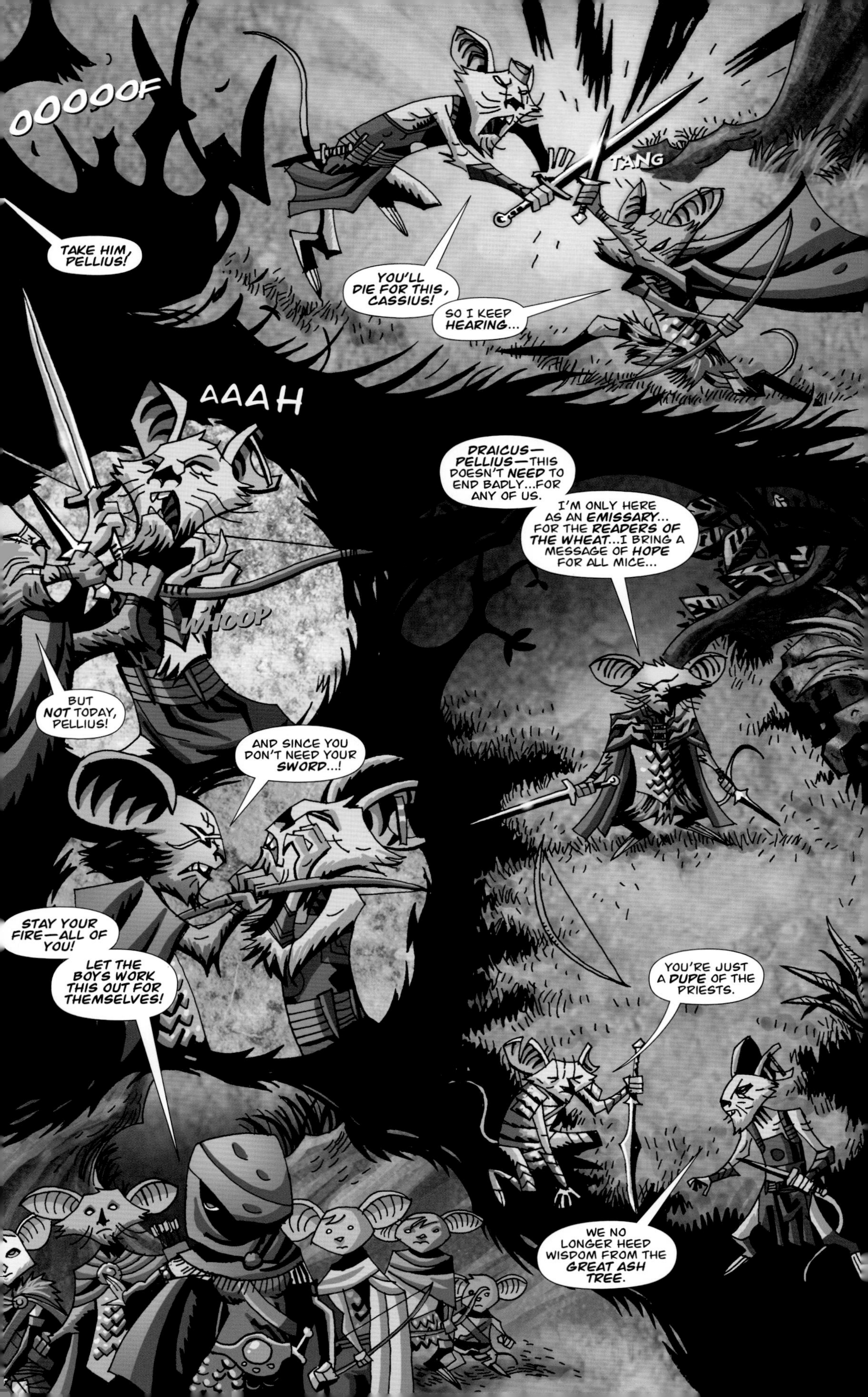
OOOOOF
TAKE HIM, PELLIUS!
TANG
YOU'LL DIE FOR THIS, CASSIUS!
SO I KEEP HEARING...
AAAH
WHOOP
BUT NOT TODAY, PELLIUS!
AND SINCE YOU DON'T NEED YOUR SWORD...!
STAY YOUR FIRE—ALL OF YOU!
LET THE BOYS WORK THIS OUT FOR THEMSELVES!
DRAICUS—PELLIUS—THIS DOESN'T NEED TO END BADLY...FOR ANY OF US.
I'M ONLY HERE AS AN EMISSARY... FOR THE READERS OF THE WHEAT...I BRING A MESSAGE OF HOPE FOR ALL MICE...
YOU'RE JUST A DUPE OF THE PRIESTS.
WE NO LONGER HEED WISDOM FROM THE GREAT ASH TREE.

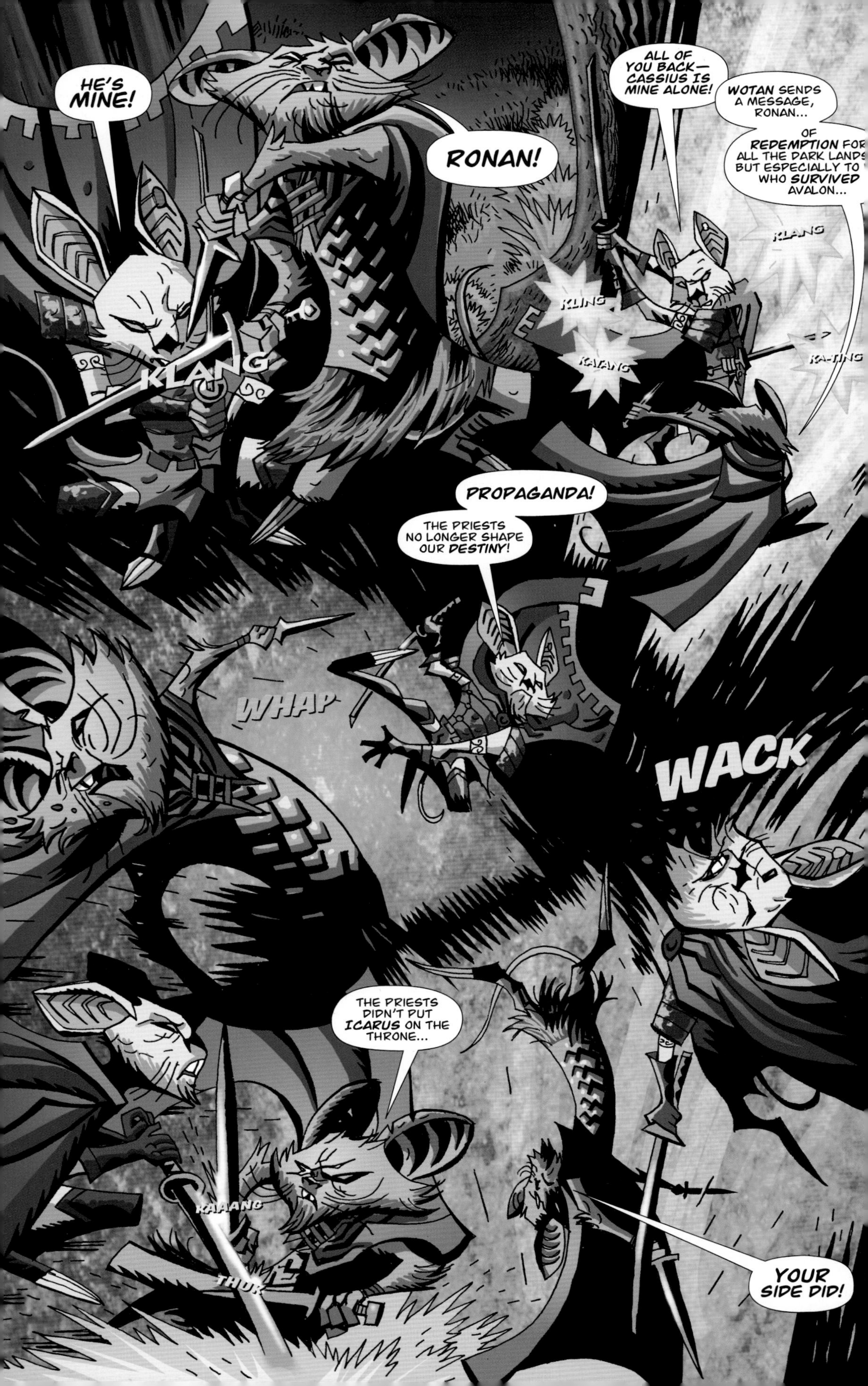
HE'S MINE!
KLANG
RONAN!
ALL OF YOU BACK— CASSIUS IS MINE ALONE!
WOTAN SENDS A MESSAGE, RONAN...
OF REDEMPTION FOR ALL THE DARK LANDS BUT ESPECIALLY TO WHO SURVIVED AVALON...
KLANG
KLING
KAYANG
KA-TING
PROPAGANDA!
THE PRIESTS NO LONGER SHAPE OUR DESTINY!
WHAP
WACK
THE PRIESTS DIDN'T PUT ICARUS ON THE THRONE...
KAAANG
THUK
YOUR SIDE DID!

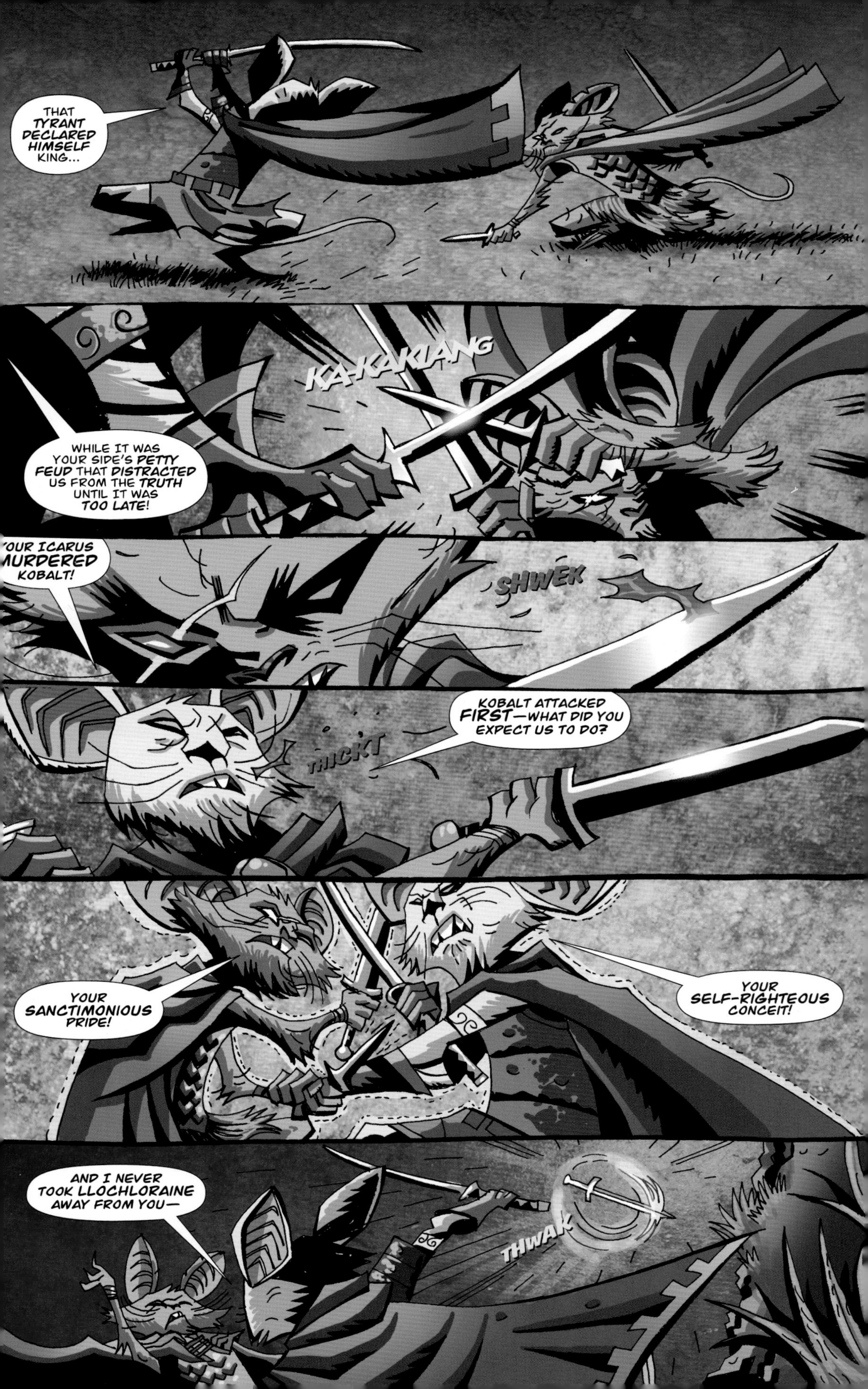
THAT TYRANT DECLARED HIMSELF KING...
KA-KAKLANG
WHILE IT WAS YOUR SIDE'S PETTY FEUD THAT DISTRACTED US FROM THE TRUTH UNTIL IT WAS TOO LATE!
YOUR ICARUS MURDERED KOBALT!
SHWEK
KOBALT ATTACKED FIRST—WHAT DID YOU EXPECT US TO DO?
THICKT
YOUR SANCTIMONIOUS PRIDE!
YOUR SELF-RIGHTEOUS CONCEIT!
AND I NEVER TOOK LLOCHLORAINE AWAY FROM YOU—
THWAK

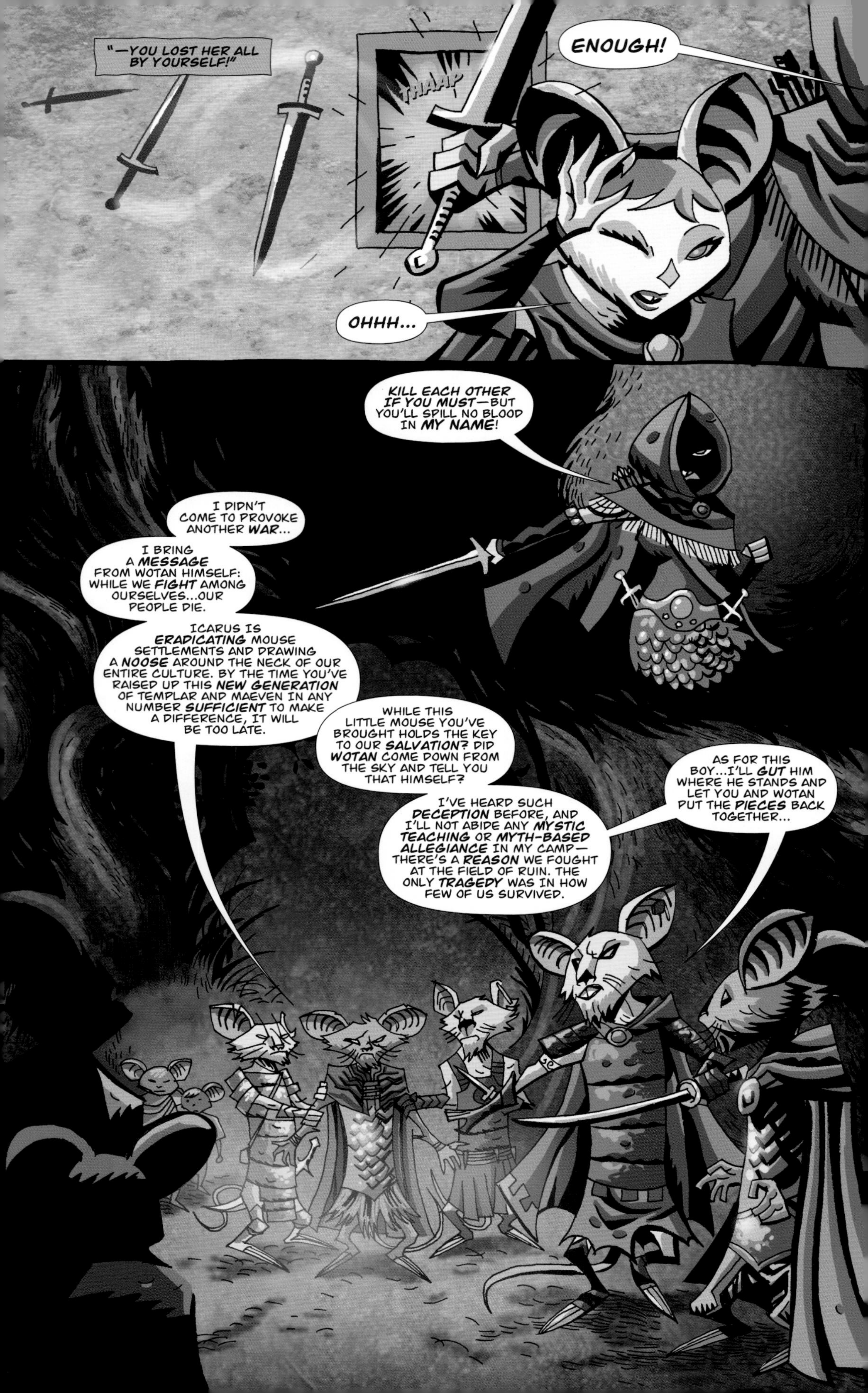
"—YOU LOST HER ALL BY YOURSELF!"
ENOUGH!
THAAP
OHHH...
KILL EACH OTHER IF YOU MUST—BUT YOU'LL SPILL NO BLOOD IN MY NAME!
I DIDN'T COME TO PROVOKE ANOTHER WAR...
I BRING A MESSAGE FROM WOTAN HIMSELF: WHILE WE FIGHT AMONG OURSELVES...OUR PEOPLE DIE.
ICARUS IS ERADICATING MOUSE SETTLEMENTS AND DRAWING A NOOSE AROUND THE NECK OF OUR ENTIRE CULTURE. BY THE TIME YOU'VE RAISED UP THIS NEW GENERATION OF TEMPLAR AND MAEVEN IN ANY NUMBER SUFFICIENT TO MAKE A DIFFERENCE, IT WILL BE TOO LATE.
WHILE THIS LITTLE MOUSE YOU'VE BROUGHT HOLDS THE KEY TO OUR SALVATION? DID WOTAN COME DOWN FROM THE SKY AND TELL YOU THAT HIMSELF?
I'VE HEARD SUCH DECEPTION BEFORE, AND I'LL NOT ABIDE ANY MYSTIC TEACHING OR MYTH-BASED ALLEGIANCE IN MY CAMP—THERE'S A REASON WE FOUGHT AT THE FIELD OF RUIN. THE ONLY TRAGEDY WAS IN HOW FEW OF US SURVIVED.
AS FOR THIS BOY...I'LL GUT HIM WHERE HE STANDS AND LET YOU AND WOTAN PUT THE PIECES BACK TOGETHER...

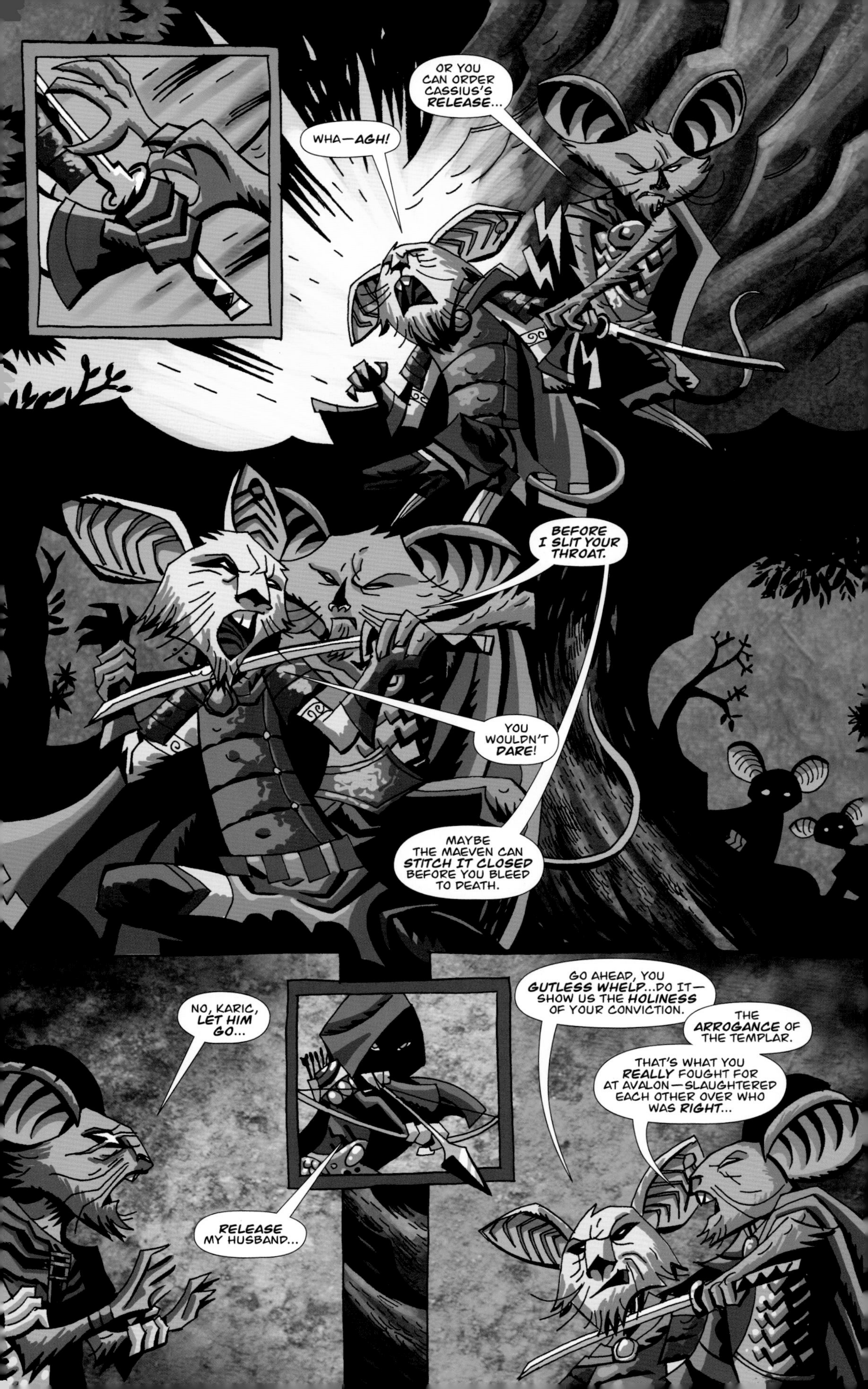
OR YOU CAN ORDER CASSIUS'S RELEASE...
WHA—AGH!
BEFORE I SLIT YOUR THROAT.
YOU WOULDN'T DARE!
MAYBE THE MAEVEN CAN STITCH IT CLOSED BEFORE YOU BLEED TO DEATH.
NO, KARIC, LET HIM GO...
RELEASE MY HUSBAND...
GO AHEAD, YOU GUTLESS WHELP...DO IT—SHOW US THE HOLINESS OF YOUR CONVICTION.
THE ARROGANCE OF THE TEMPLAR.
THAT'S WHAT YOU REALLY FOUGHT FOR AT AVALON—SLAUGHTERED EACH OTHER OVER WHO WAS RIGHT...

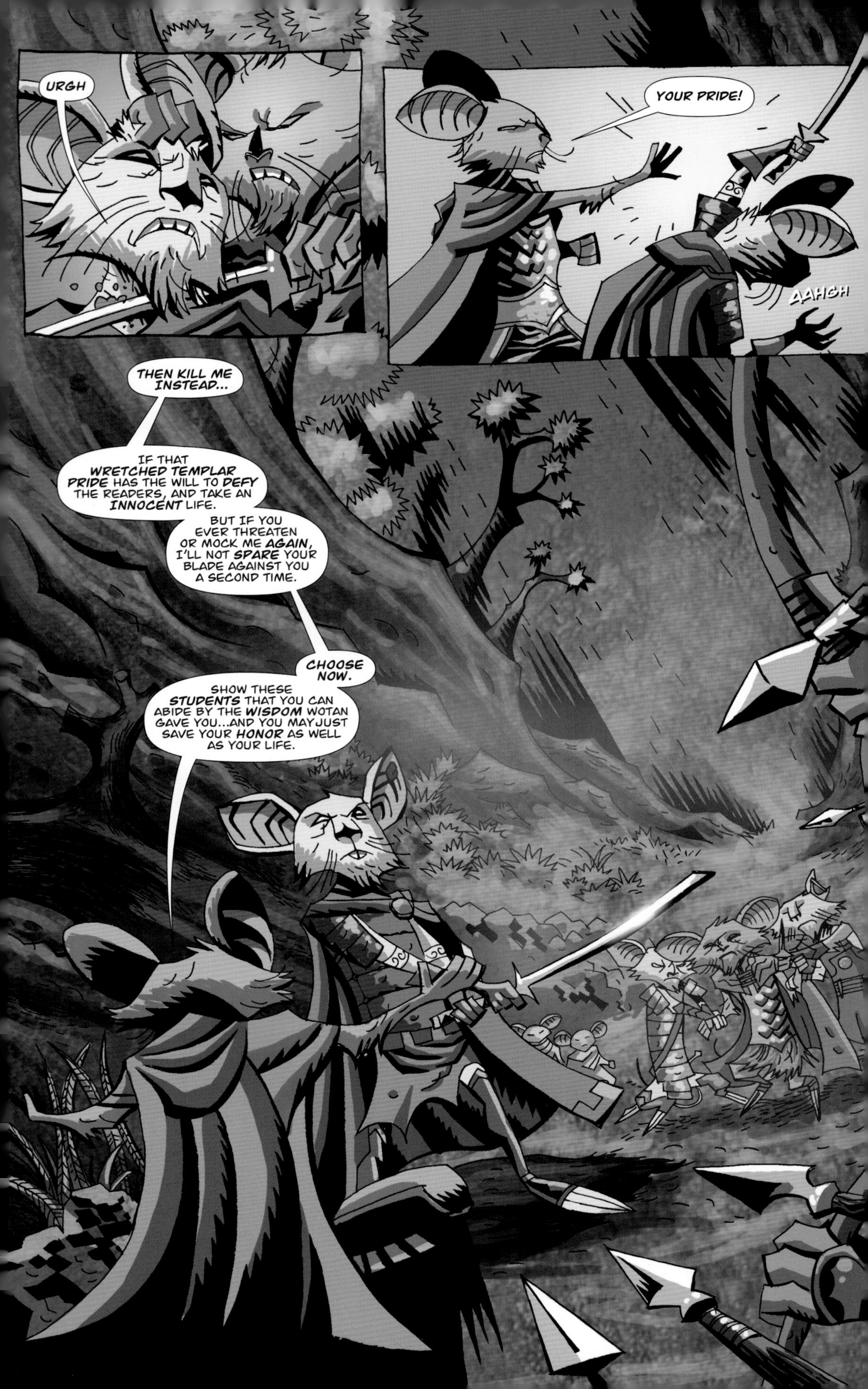
URGH
YOUR PRIDE!
AAHGH
THEN KILL ME INSTEAD...
IF THAT WRETCHED TEMPLAR PRIDE HAS THE WILL TO DEFY THE READERS, AND TAKE AN INNOCENT LIFE.
BUT IF YOU EVER THREATEN OR MOCK ME AGAIN, I'LL NOT SPARE YOUR BLADE AGAINST YOU A SECOND TIME.
CHOOSE NOW.
SHOW THESE STUDENTS THAT YOU CAN ABIDE BY THE WISDOM WOTAN GAVE YOU...AND YOU MAYJUST SAVE YOUR HONOR AS WELL AS YOUR LIFE.

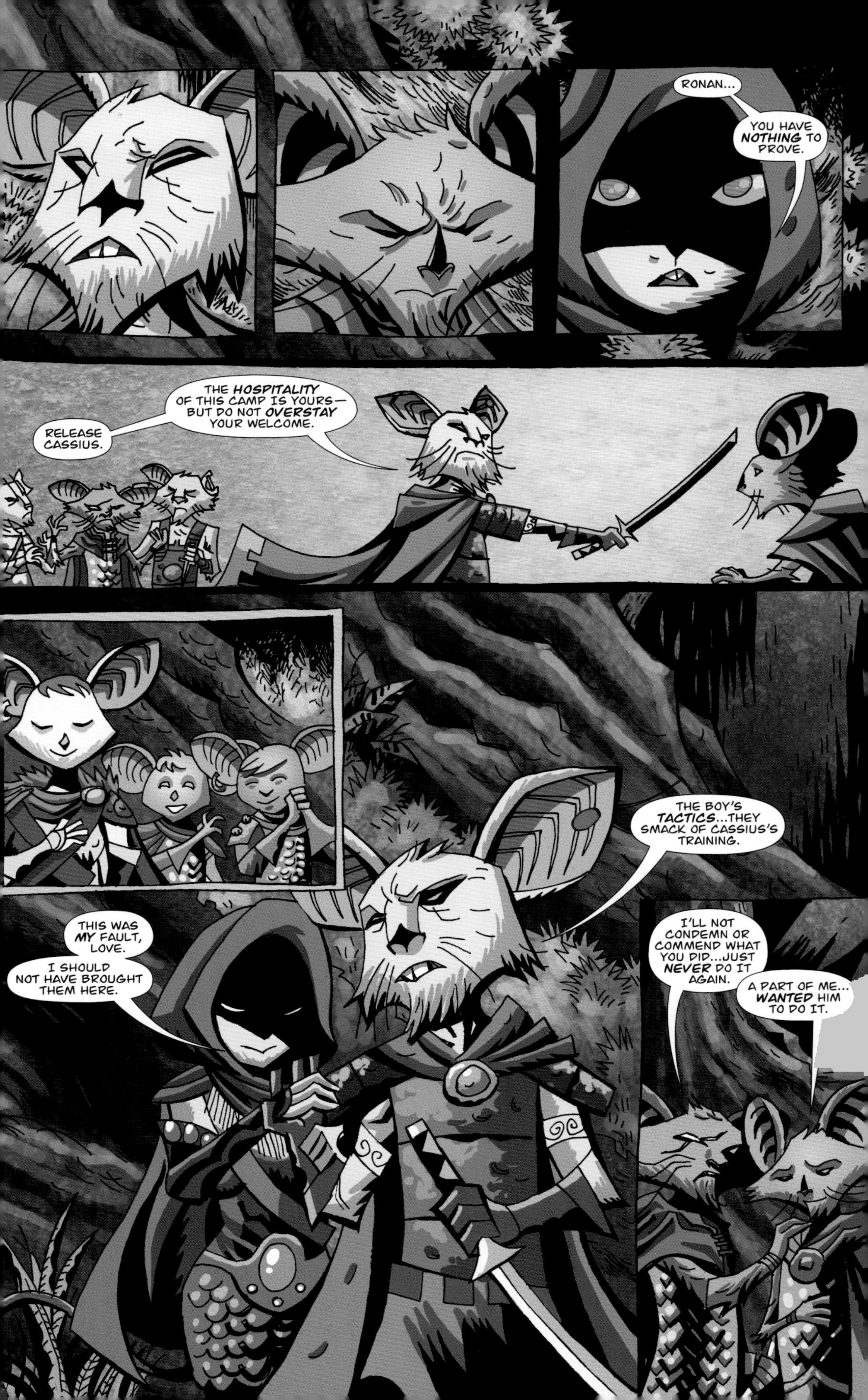
RONAN...
YOU HAVE NOTHING TO PROVE.
RELEASE CASSIUS.
THE HOSPITALITY OF THIS CAMP IS YOURS— BUT DO NOT OVERSTAY YOUR WELCOME.
THE BOY'S TACTICS...THEY SMACK OF CASSIUS'S TRAINING.
THIS WAS MY FAULT, LOVE.
I SHOULD NOT HAVE BROUGHT THEM HERE.
I'LL NOT CONDEMN OR COMMEND WHAT YOU DID...JUST NEVER DO IT AGAIN.
A PART OF ME... WANTED HIM TO DO IT.

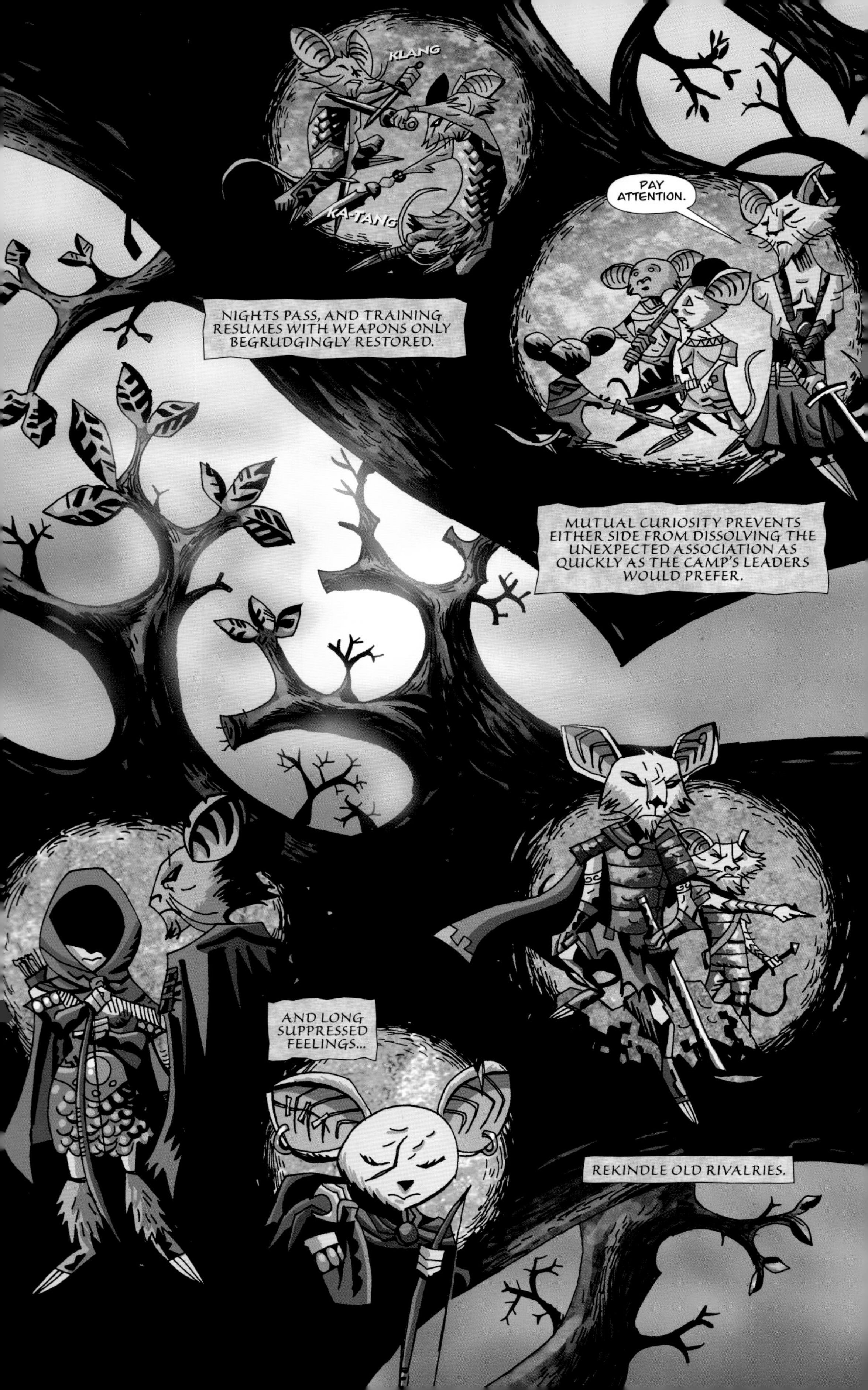
KLANG
KA-TANG
PAY ATTENTION.
NIGHTS PASS, AND TRAINING RESUMES WITH WEAPONS ONLY BEGRUDGINGLY RESTORED.
MUTUAL CURIOSITY PREVENTS EITHER SIDE FROM DISSOLVING THE UNEXPECTED ASSOCIATION AS QUICKLY AS THE CAMP'S LEADERS WOULD PREFER.
AND LONG SUPPRESSED FEELINGS...
REKINDLE OLD RIVALRIES.

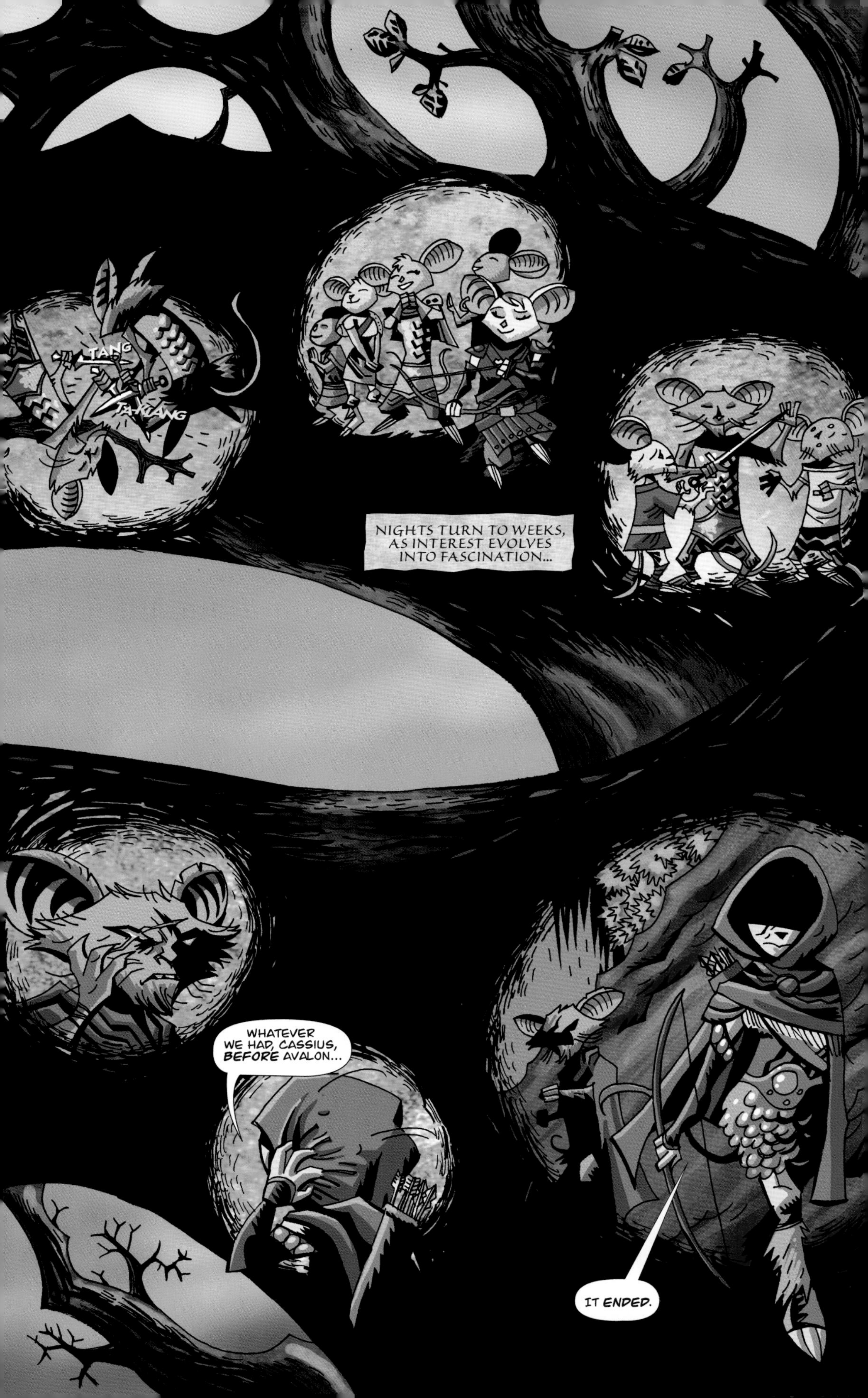
TANG
TA-KLANG
NIGHTS TURN TO WEEKS, AS INTEREST EVOLVES INTO FASCINATION...
WHATEVER WE HAD, CASSIUS, BEFORE AVALON...
IT ENDED.

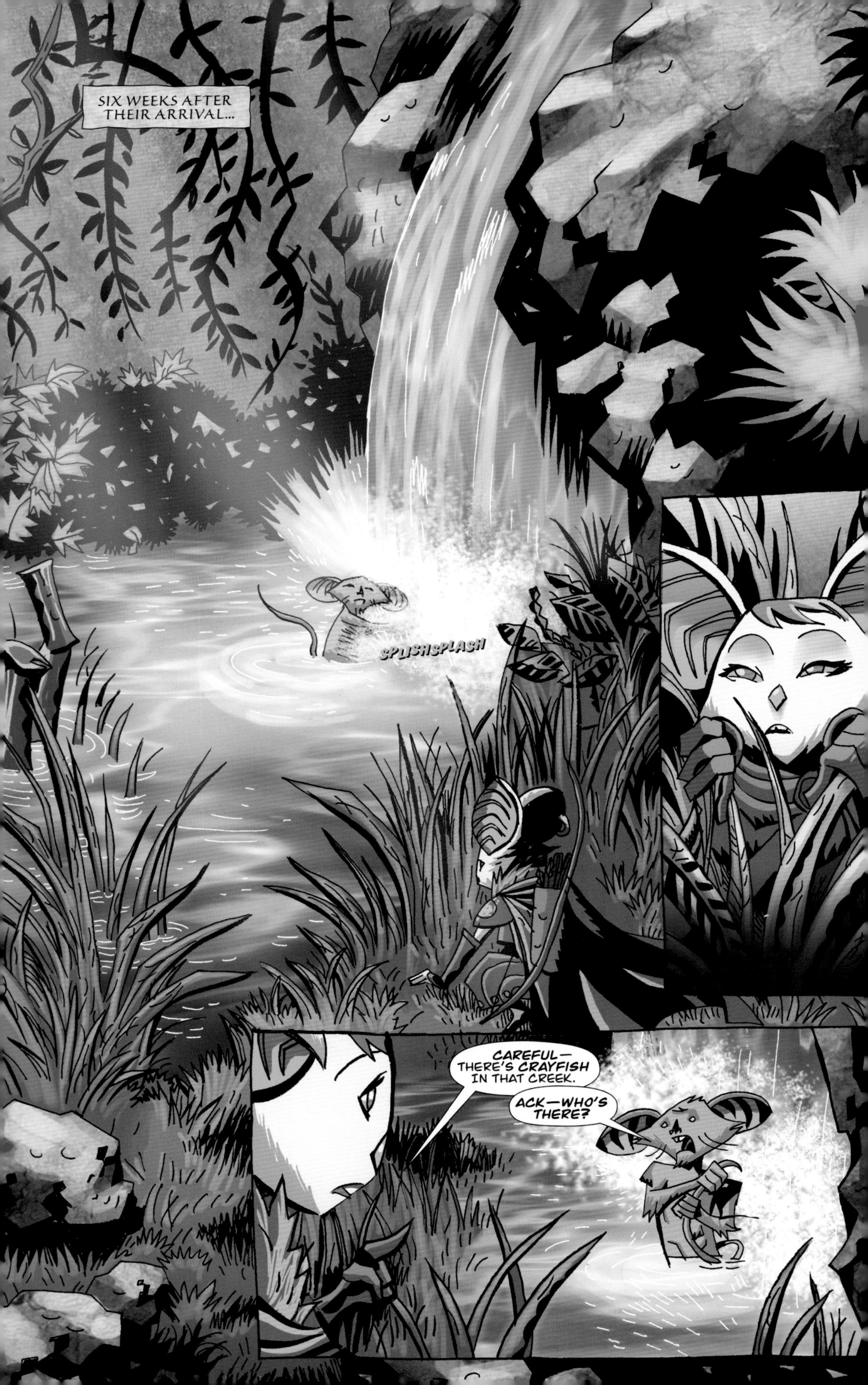
SIX WEEKS AFTER THEIR ARRIVAL...
SPLISHSPLASH
CAREFUL—THERE'S CRAYFISH IN THAT CREEK.
ACK—WHO'S THERE?

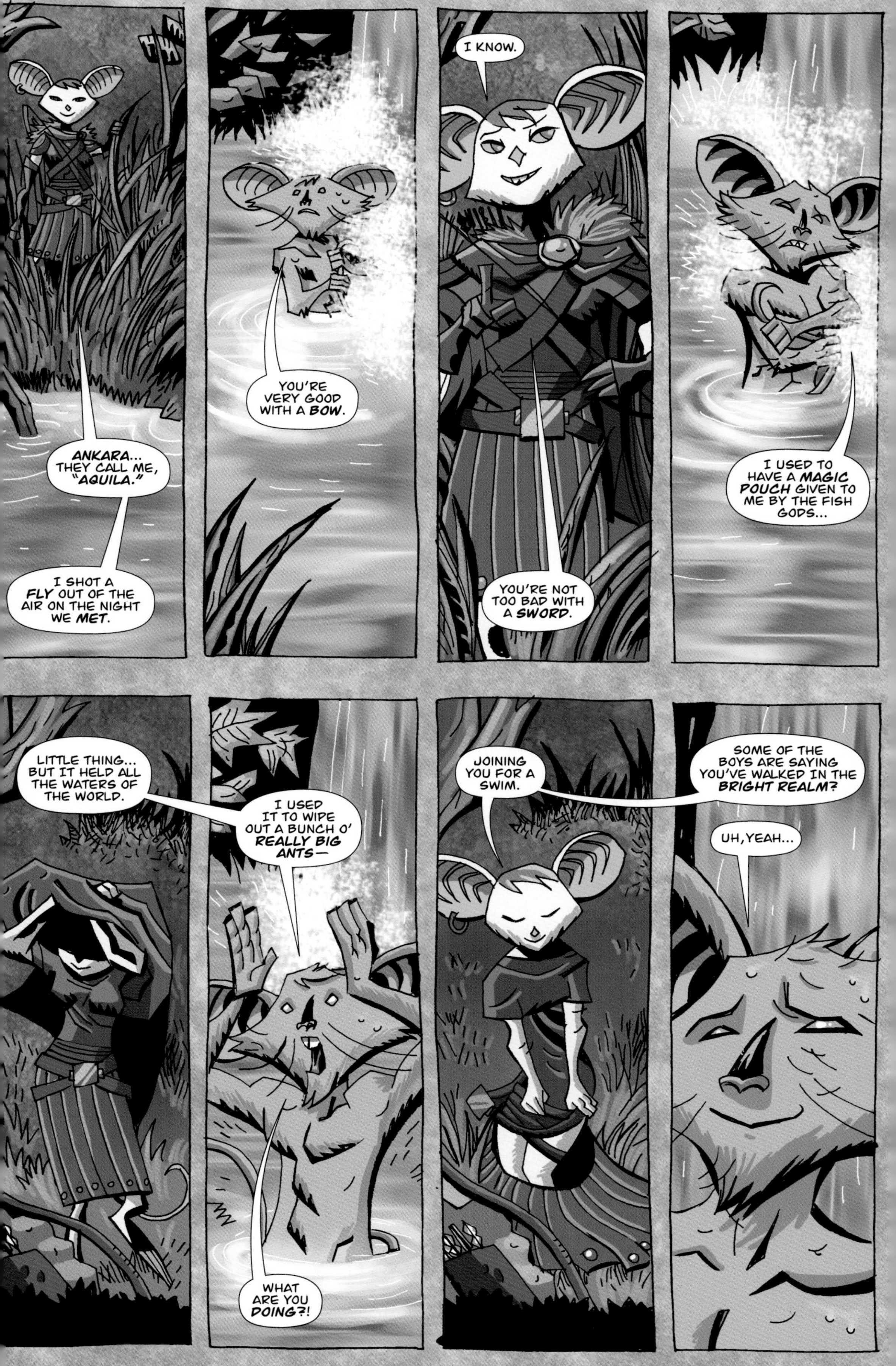
ANKARA... THEY CALL ME, "AQUILA."
I SHOT A FLY OUT OF THE AIR ON THE NIGHT WE MET.
YOU'RE VERY GOOD WITH A BOW.
I KNOW.
YOU'RE NOT TOO BAD WITH A SWORD.
I USED TO HAVE A MAGIC POUCH GIVEN TO ME BY THE FISH GODS...
LITTLE THING... BUT IT HELD ALL THE WATERS OF THE WORLD.
I USED IT TO WIPE OUT A BUNCH O' REALLY BIG ANTS—
WHAT ARE YOU DOING?!
JOINING YOU FOR A SWIM.
SOME OF THE BOYS ARE SAYING YOU'VE WALKED IN THE BRIGHT REALM?
UH, YEAH...

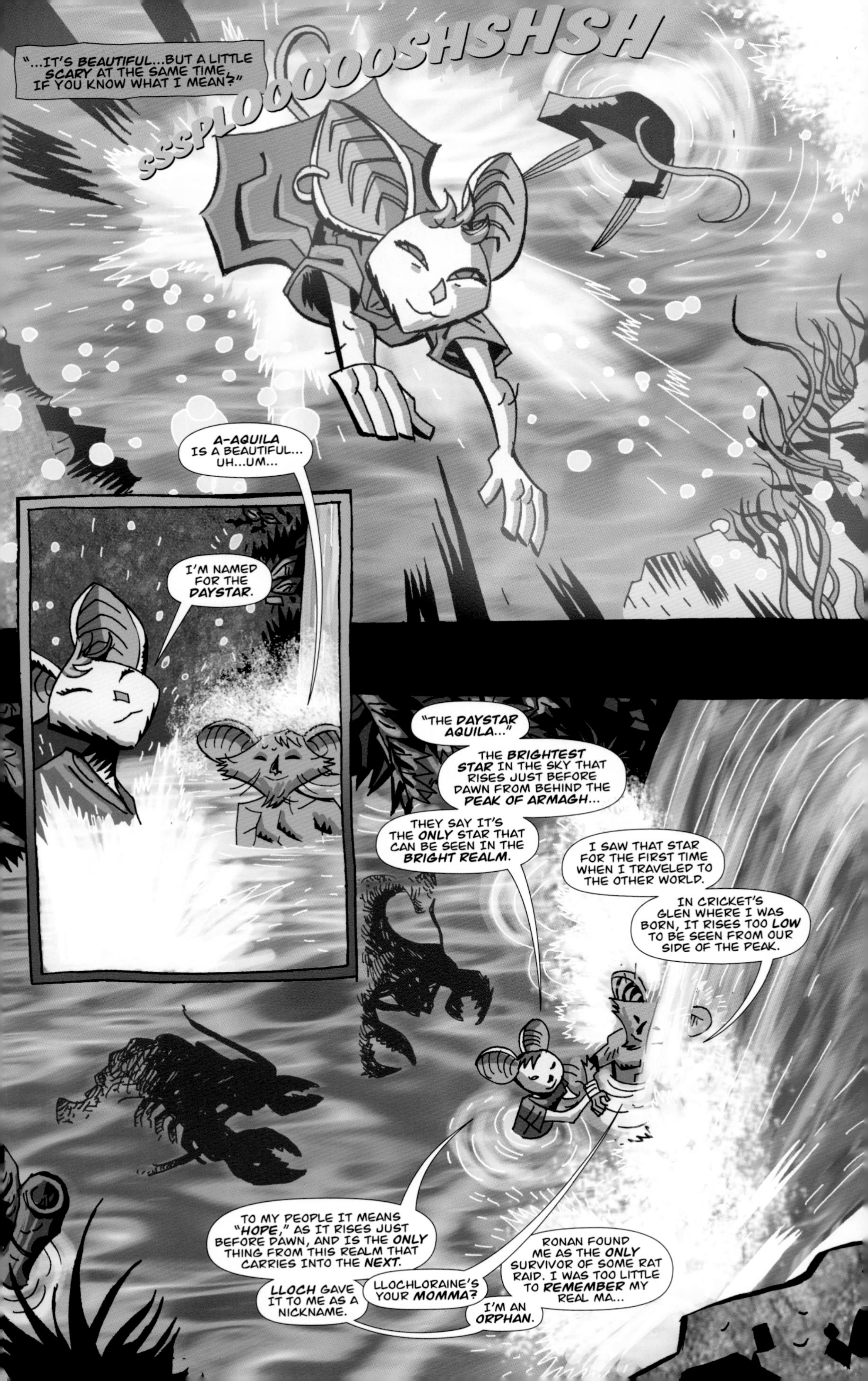
"...IT'S BEAUTIFUL...BUT A LITTLE SCARY AT THE SAME TIME, IF YOU KNOW WHAT I MEAN?"
SSSPLOOOOOOOSHSHSH
A-AQUILA IS A BEAUTIFUL... UH...UM...
I'M NAMED FOR THE DAYSTAR.
"THE DAYSTAR AQUILA..."
THE BRIGHTEST STAR IN THE SKY THAT RISES JUST BEFORE DAWN FROM BEHIND THE PEAK OF ARMAGH...
THEY SAY IT'S THE ONLY STAR THAT CAN BE SEEN IN THE BRIGHT REALM.
I SAW THAT STAR FOR THE FIRST TIME WHEN I TRAVELED TO THE OTHER WORLD.
IN CRICKET'S GLEN WHERE I WAS BORN, IT RISES TOO LOW TO BE SEEN FROM OUR SIDE OF THE PEAK.
TO MY PEOPLE IT MEANS "HOPE," AS IT RISES JUST BEFORE DAWN, AND IS THE ONLY THING FROM THIS REALM THAT CARRIES INTO THE NEXT.
LLOCH GAVE IT TO ME AS A NICKNAME.
LLOCHLORAINE'S YOUR MOMMA?
RONAN FOUND ME AS THE ONLY SURVIVOR OF SOME RAT RAID. I WAS TOO LITTLE TO REMEMBER MY REAL MA...
I'M AN ORPHAN.

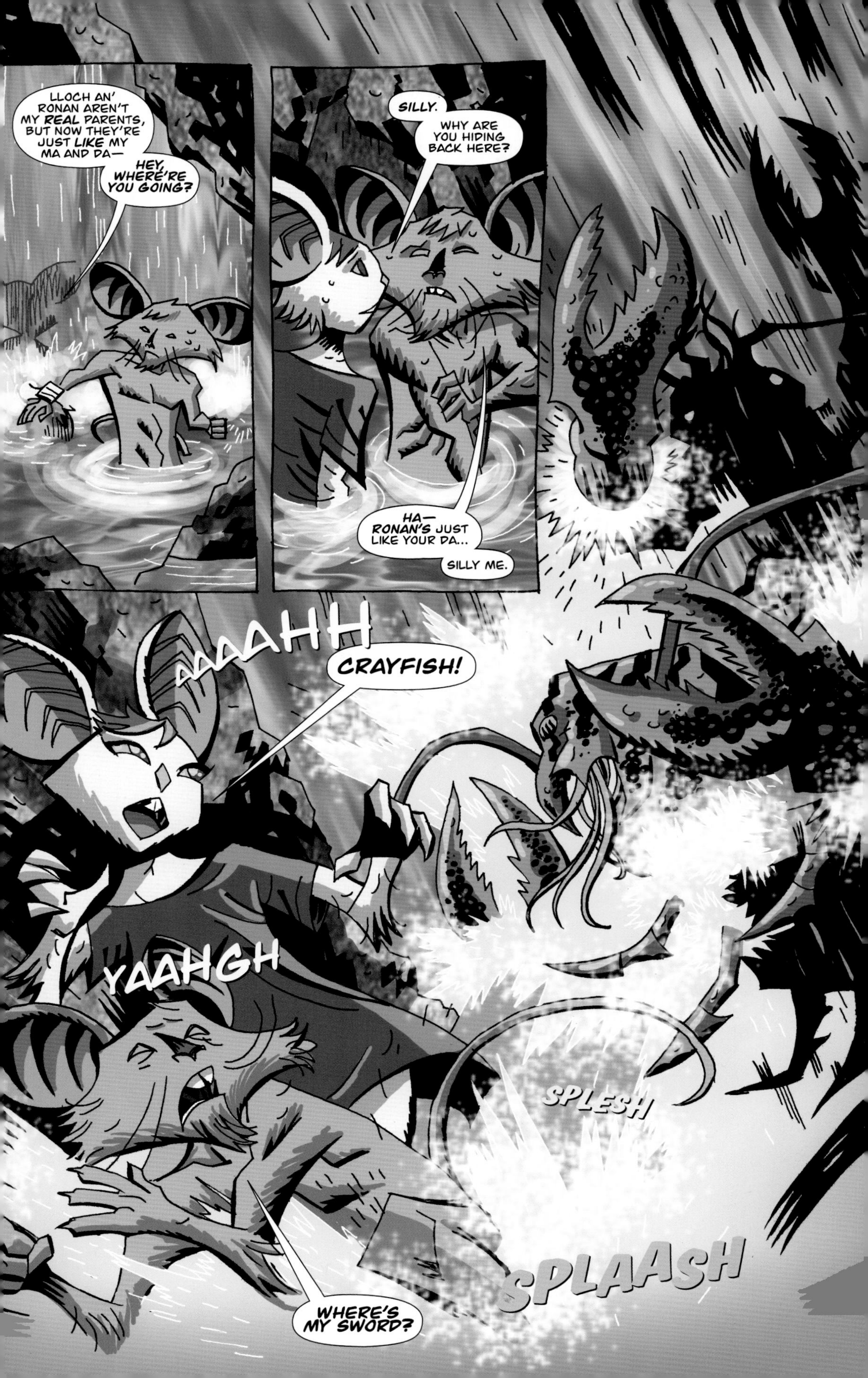
LLOCH AN' RONAN AREN'T MY REAL PARENTS, BUT NOW THEY'RE JUST LIKE MY MA AND DA—
HEY, WHERE'RE YOU GOING?
SILLY.
WHY ARE YOU HIDING BACK HERE?
HA— RONAN'S JUST LIKE YOUR DA...
SILLY ME.
AAAAHH
CRAYFISH!
YAAHGH
SPLESH
SPLAASH
WHERE'S MY SWORD?

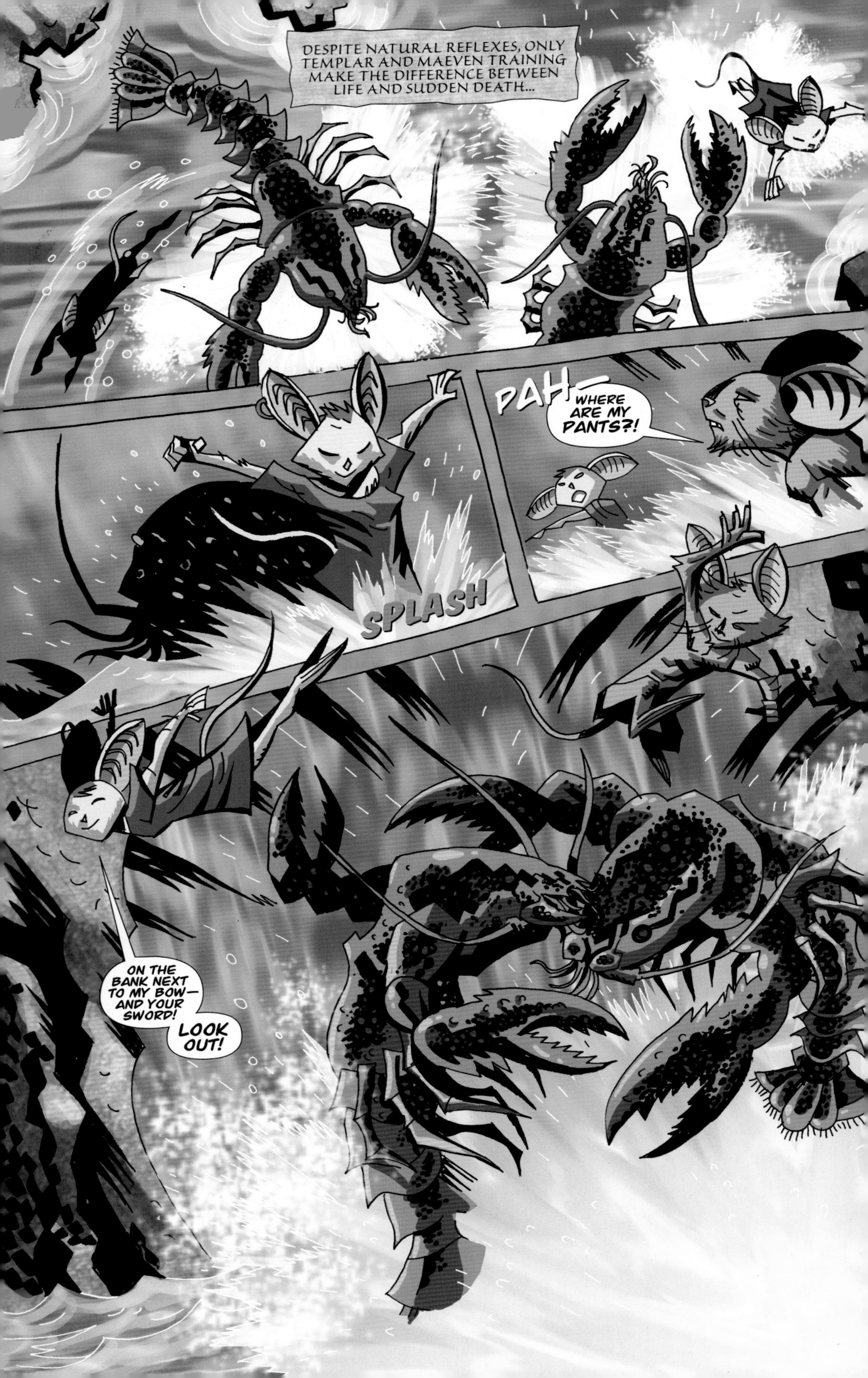

DESPITE NATURAL REFLEXES, ONLY TEMPLAR AND MAEVEN TRAINING MAKE THE DIFFERENCE BETWEEN LIFE AND SUDDEN DEATH...
SPLASH
PAH—
WHERE ARE MY PANTS?!
ON THE BANK NEXT TO MY BOW— AND YOUR SWORD!
LOOK OUT!

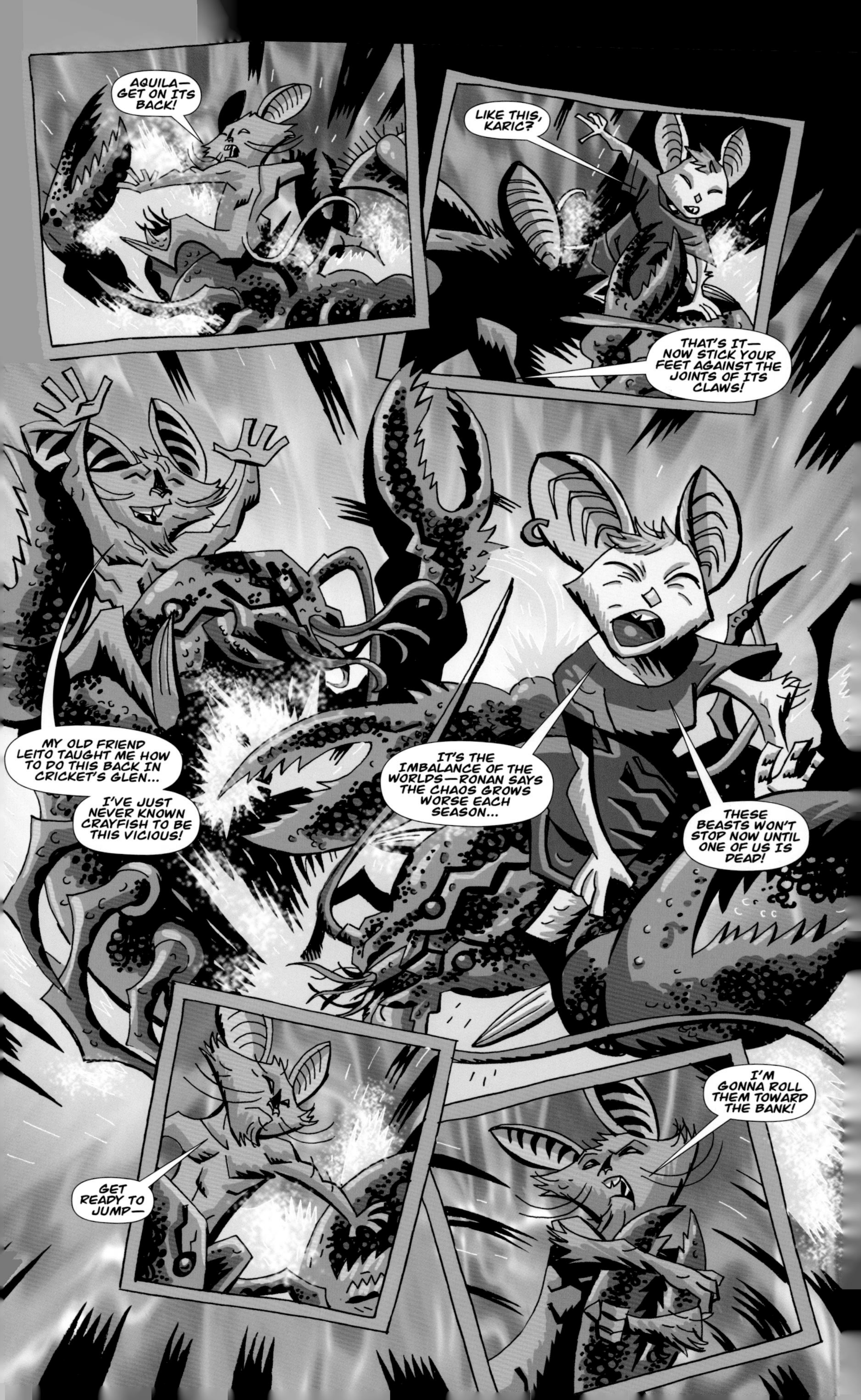
AQUILA—GET ON ITS BACK!
LIKE THIS, KARIC?
THAT'S IT—NOW STICK YOUR FEET AGAINST THE JOINTS OF ITS CLAWS!
MY OLD FRIEND LEITO TAUGHT ME HOW TO DO THIS BACK IN CRICKET'S GLEN...
I'VE JUST NEVER KNOWN CRAYFISH TO BE THIS VICIOUS!
IT'S THE IMBALANCE OF THE WORLDS—RONAN SAYS THE CHAOS GROWS WORSE EACH SEASON...
THESE BEASTS WON'T STOP NOW UNTIL ONE OF US IS DEAD!
GET READY TO JUMP—
I'M GONNA ROLL THEM TOWARD THE BANK!

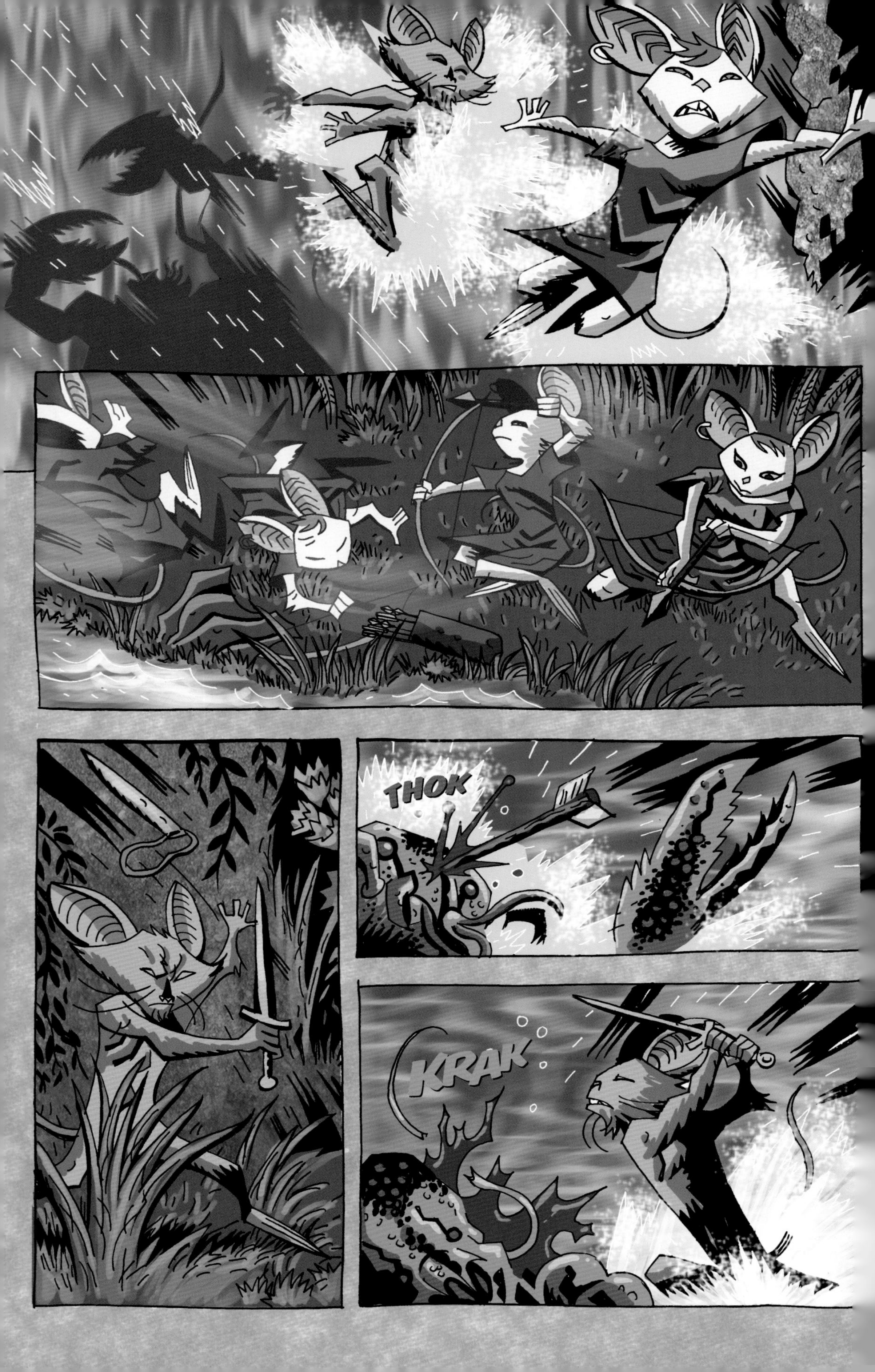
THOK
KRAK

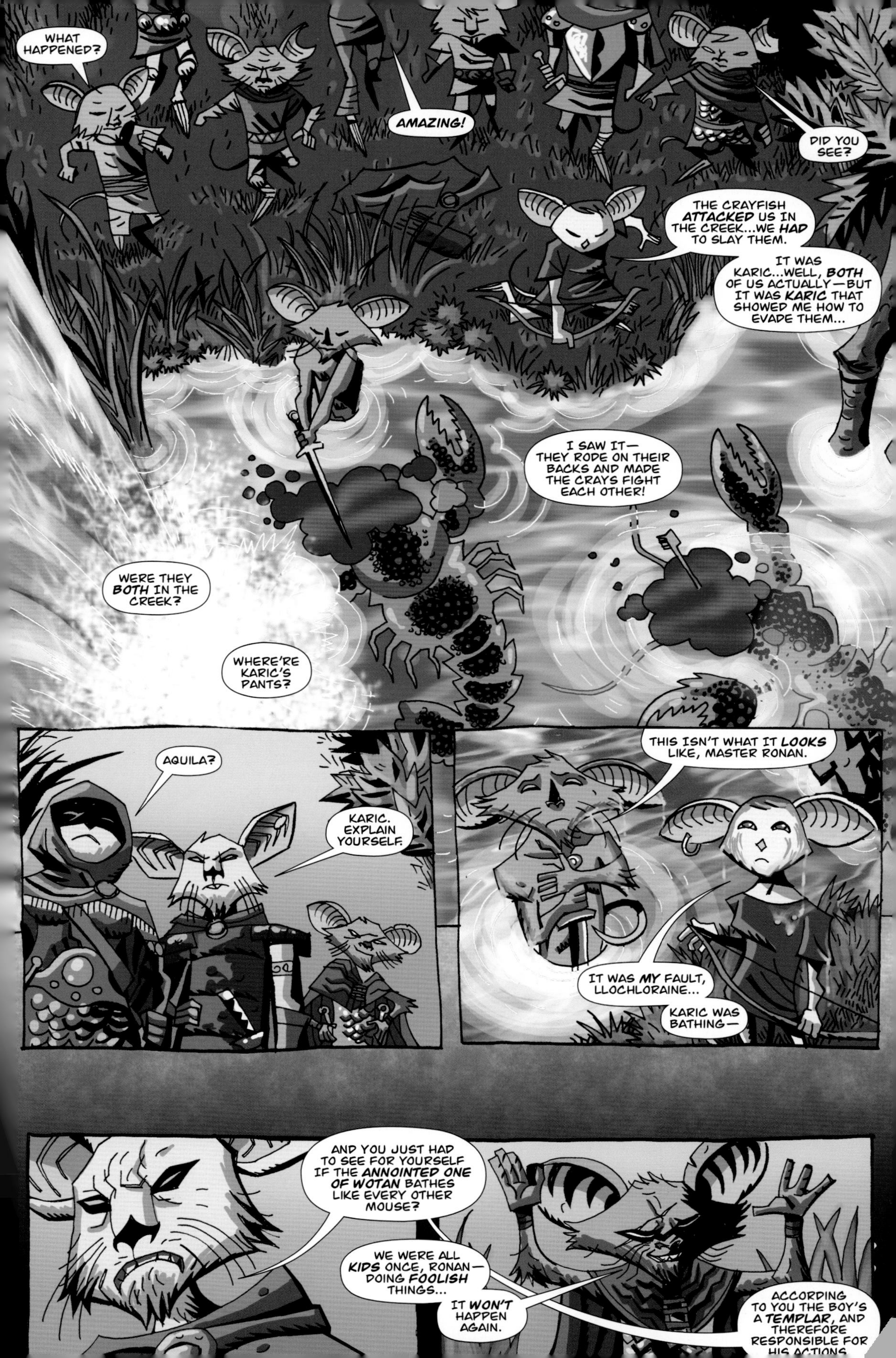
WHAT HAPPENED?
AMAZING!
DID YOU SEE?
THE CRAYFISH ATTACKED US IN THE CREEK...WE HAD TO SLAY THEM.
IT WAS KARIC...WELL, BOTH OF US ACTUALLY—BUT IT WAS KARIC THAT SHOWED ME HOW TO EVADE THEM...
I SAW IT—THEY RODE ON THEIR BACKS AND MADE THE CRAYS FIGHT EACH OTHER!
WERE THEY BOTH IN THE CREEK?
WHERE'RE KARIC'S PANTS?
AQUILA?
KARIC. EXPLAIN YOURSELF.
THIS ISN'T WHAT IT LOOKS LIKE, MASTER RONAN.
IT WAS MY FAULT, LLOCHLORAINE...
KARIC WAS BATHING—
AND YOU JUST HAD TO SEE FOR YOURSELF IF THE ANNOINTED ONE OF WOTAN BATHES LIKE EVERY OTHER MOUSE?
WE WERE ALL KIDS ONCE, RONAN—DOING FOOLISH THINGS...
IT WON'T HAPPEN AGAIN.
ACCORDING TO YOU THE BOY'S A TEMPLAR, AND THEREFORE RESPONSIBLE FOR HIS ACTIONS.

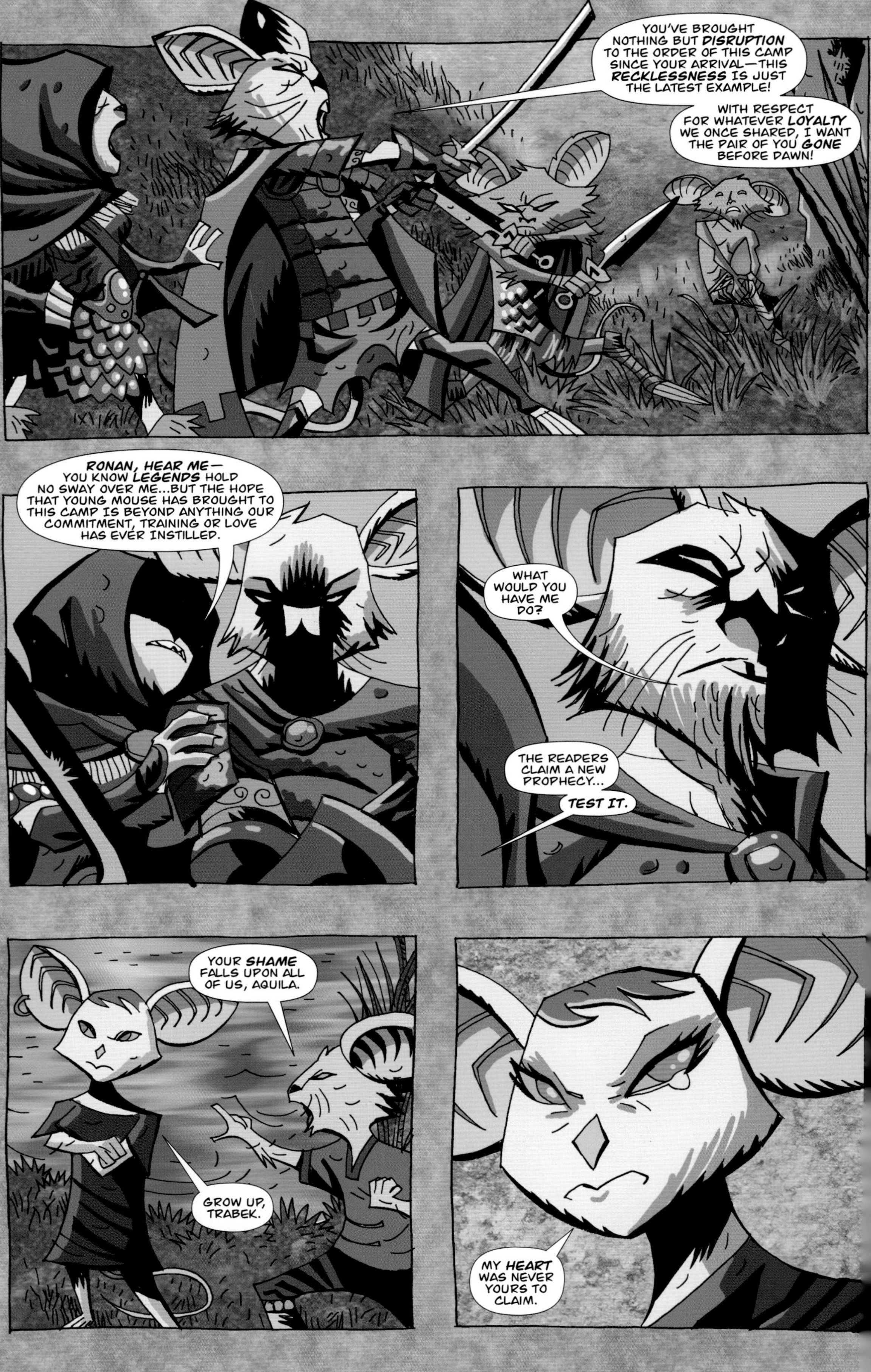
YOU'VE BROUGHT NOTHING BUT DISRUPTION TO THE ORDER OF THIS CAMP SINCE YOUR ARRIVAL—THIS RECKLESSNESS IS JUST THE LATEST EXAMPLE!
WITH RESPECT FOR WHATEVER LOYALTY WE ONCE SHARED, I WANT THE PAIR OF YOU GONE BEFORE DAWN!
RONAN, HEAR ME—YOU KNOW LEGENDS HOLD NO SWAY OVER ME...BUT THE HOPE THAT YOUNG MOUSE HAS BROUGHT TO THIS CAMP IS BEYOND ANYTHING OUR COMMITMENT, TRAINING OR LOVE HAS EVER INSTILLED.
WHAT WOULD YOU HAVE ME DO?
THE READERS CLAIM A NEW PROPHECY...
TEST IT.
YOUR SHAME FALLS UPON ALL OF US, AQUILA.
GROW UP, TRABEK.
MY HEART WAS NEVER YOURS TO CLAIM.

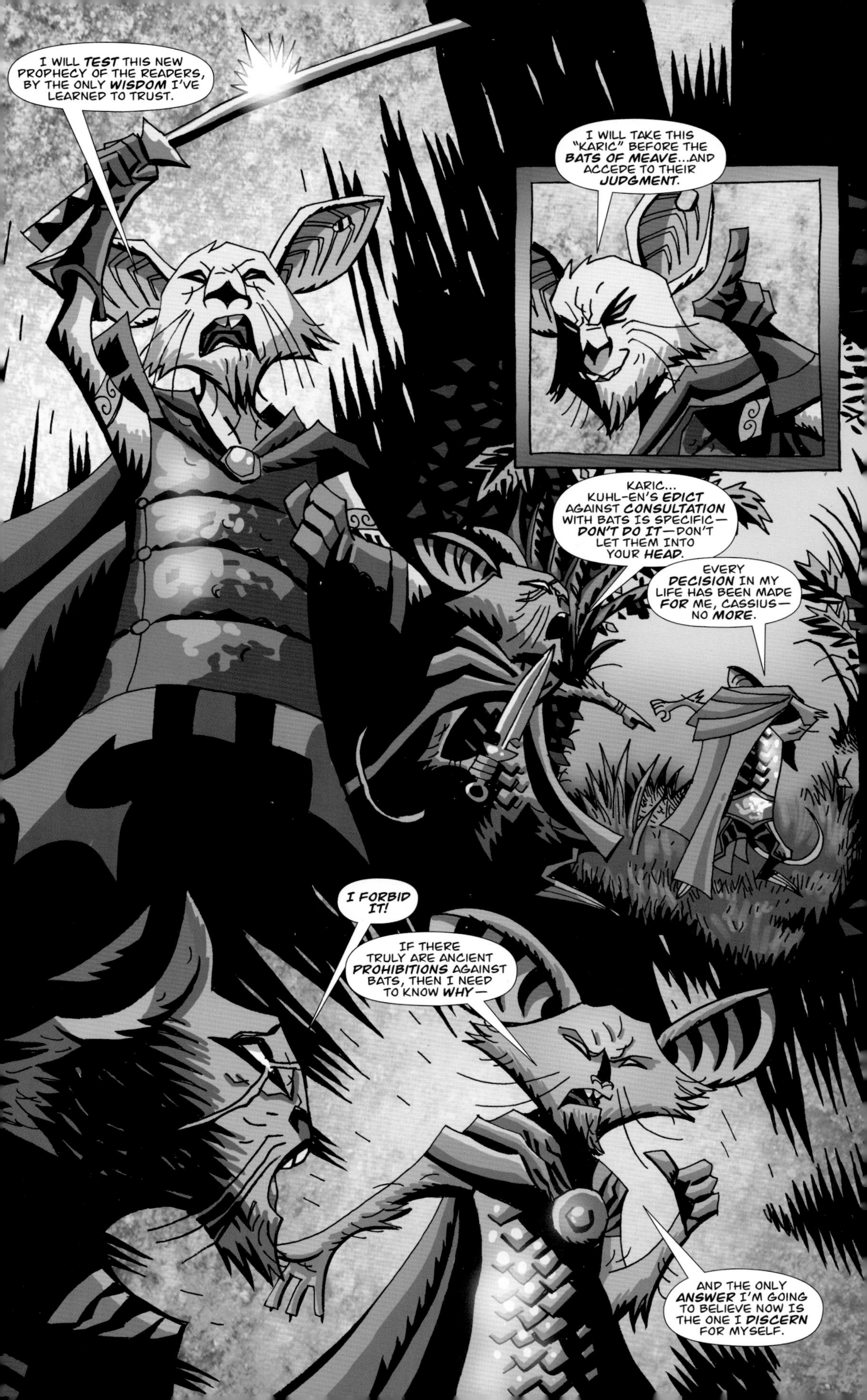

I WILL TEST THIS NEW PROPHECY OF THE READERS, BY THE ONLY WISDOM I'VE LEARNED TO TRUST.
I WILL TAKE THIS "KARIC" BEFORE THE BATS OF MEAVE...AND ACCEDE TO THEIR JUDGMENT.
KARIC... KUHL-EN'S EDICT AGAINST CONSULTATION WITH BATS IS SPECIFIC—DON'T DO IT—DON'T LET THEM INTO YOUR HEAD.
EVERY DECISION IN MY LIFE HAS BEEN MADE FOR ME, CASSIUS—NO MORE.
I FORBID IT!
IF THERE TRULY ARE ANCIENT PROHIBITIONS AGAINST BATS, THEN I NEED TO KNOW WHY—
AND THE ONLY ANSWER I'M GOING TO BELIEVE NOW IS THE ONE I DISCERN FOR MYSELF.

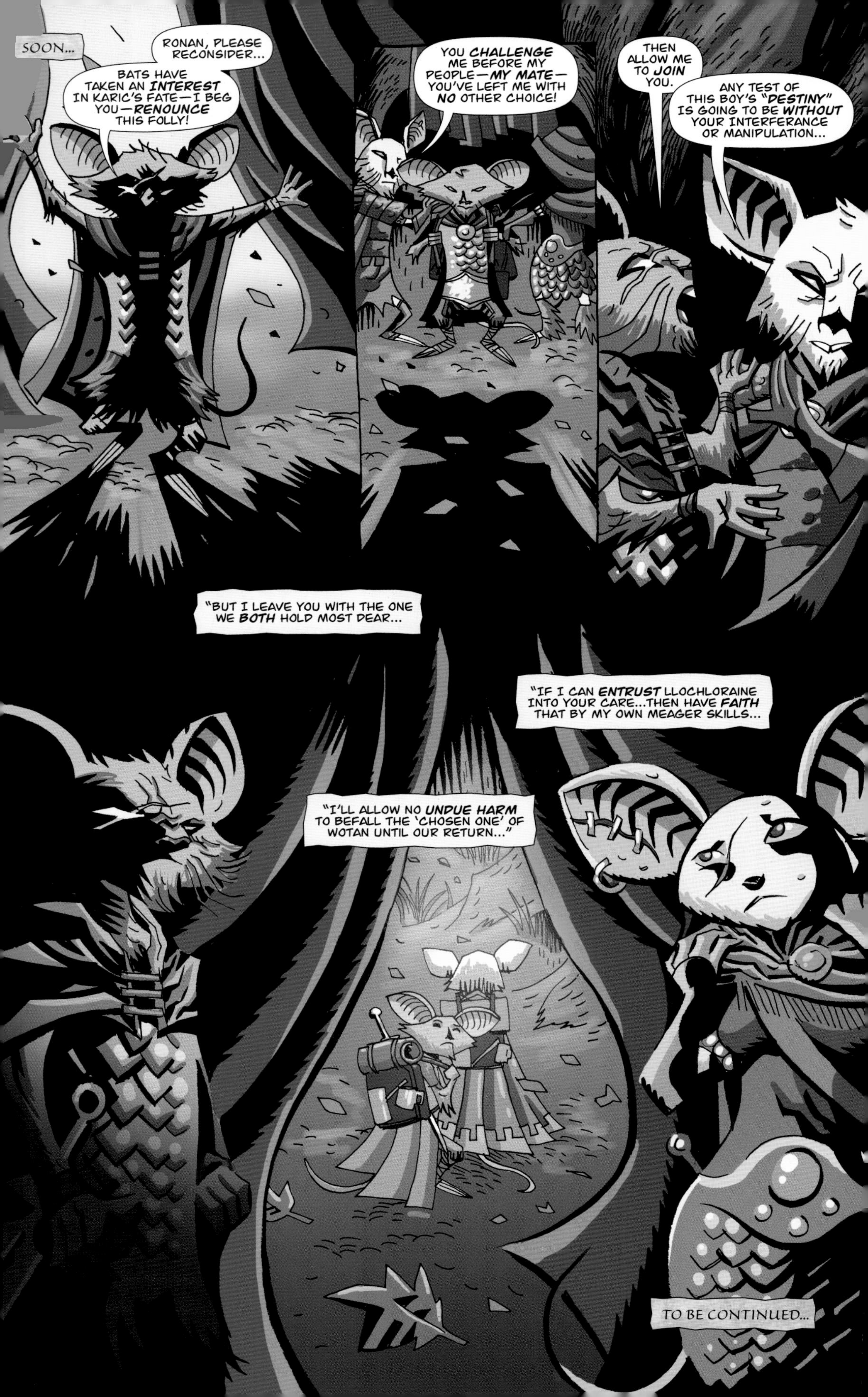
SOON...
RONAN, PLEASE RECONSIDER...
BATS HAVE TAKEN AN INTEREST IN KARIC'S FATE—I BEG YOU—RENOUNCE THIS FOLLY!
YOU CHALLENGE ME BEFORE MY PEOPLE—MY MATE—YOU'VE LEFT ME WITH NO OTHER CHOICE!
THEN ALLOW ME TO JOIN YOU.
ANY TEST OF THIS BOY'S "DESTINY" IS GOING TO BE WITHOUT YOUR INTERFERANCE OR MANIPULATION...
"BUT I LEAVE YOU WITH THE ONE WE BOTH HOLD MOST DEAR...
"IF I CAN ENTRUST LLOCHLORAINE INTO YOUR CARE...THEN HAVE FAITH THAT BY MY OWN MEAGER SKILLS...
"I'LL ALLOW NO UNDUE HARM TO BEFALL THE 'CHOSEN ONE' OF WOTAN UNTIL OUR RETURN..."
TO BE CONTINUED...

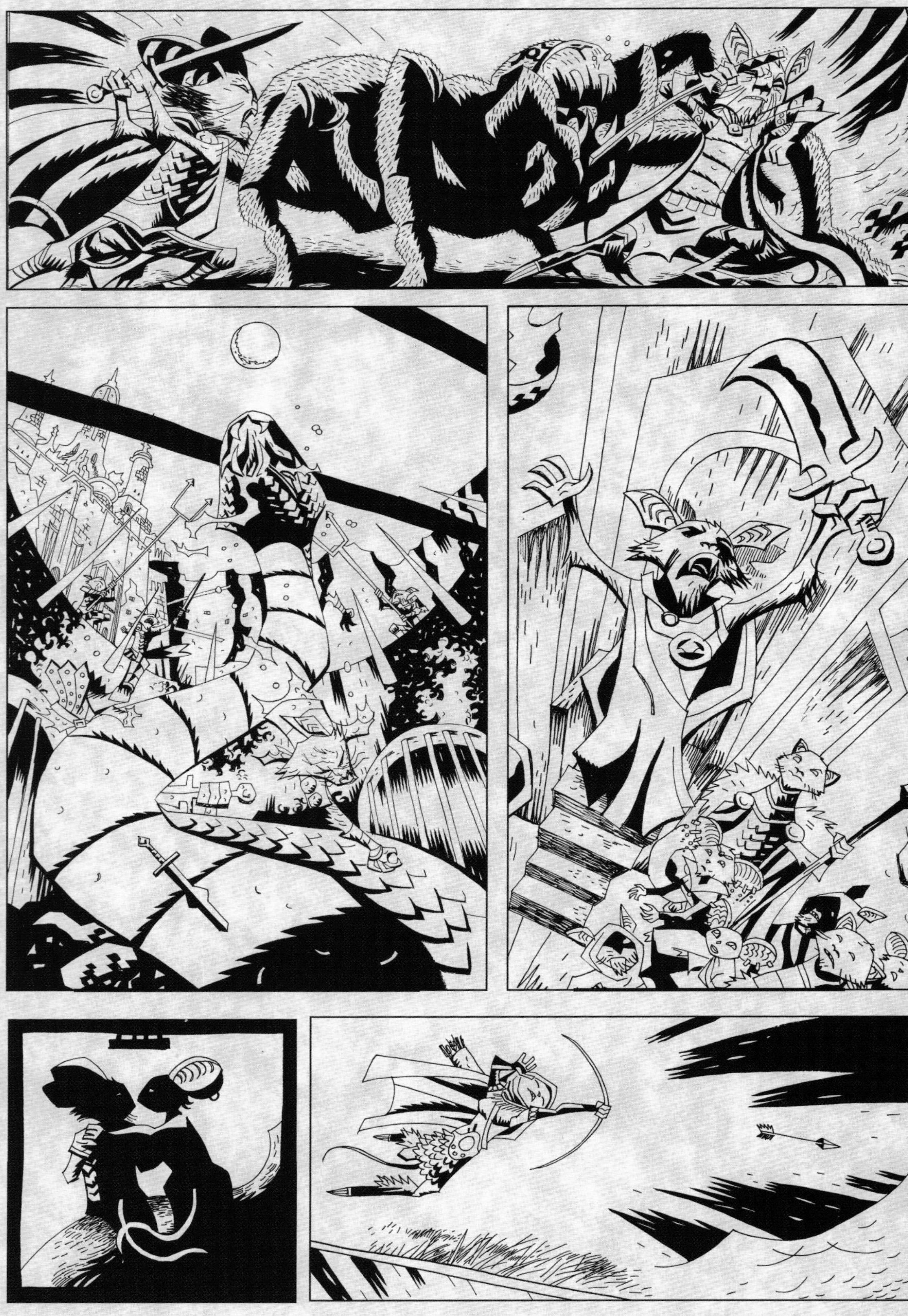

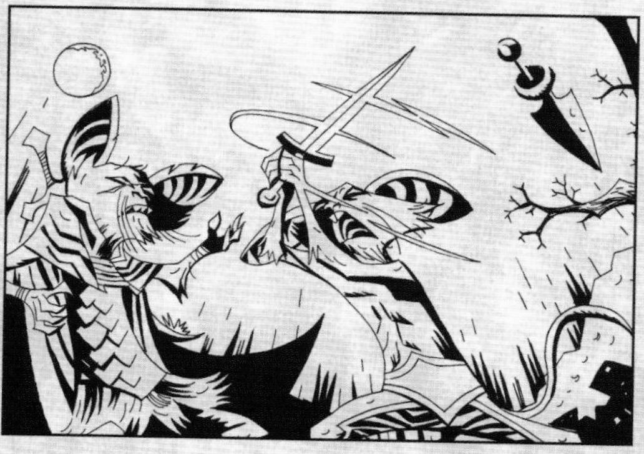

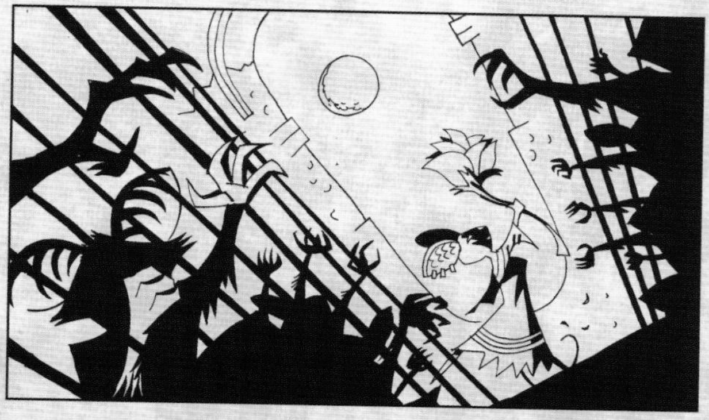

Stunning moments await
in the continuing saga of
The Mice Templar...
As Karic and Cassius,
Ronan and Llochloraine, Aquila,
Leito, Mornae, Gabrielle and
Elizabeth, Alexis, Lorelie and
mad King Icarus...
Come face to face with *Destiny!*

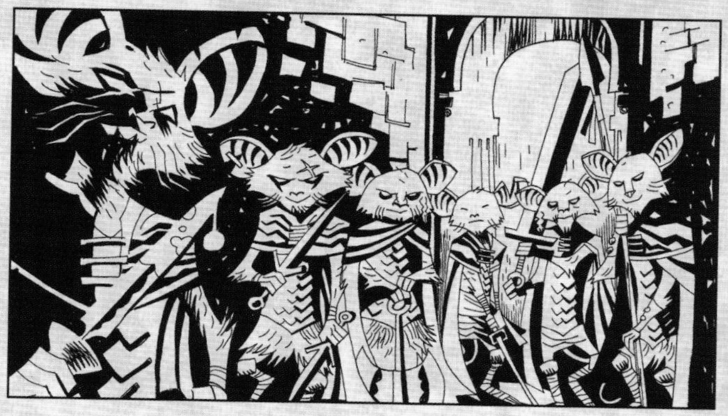

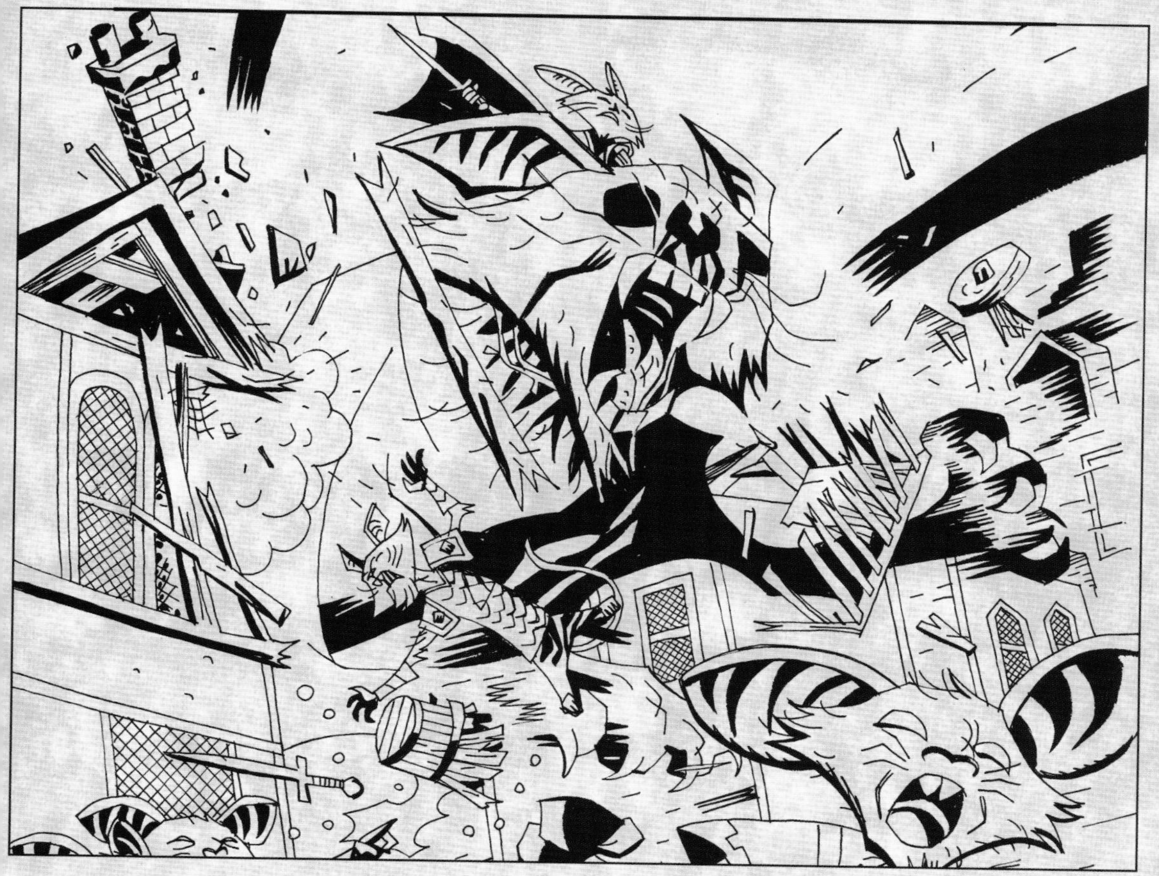

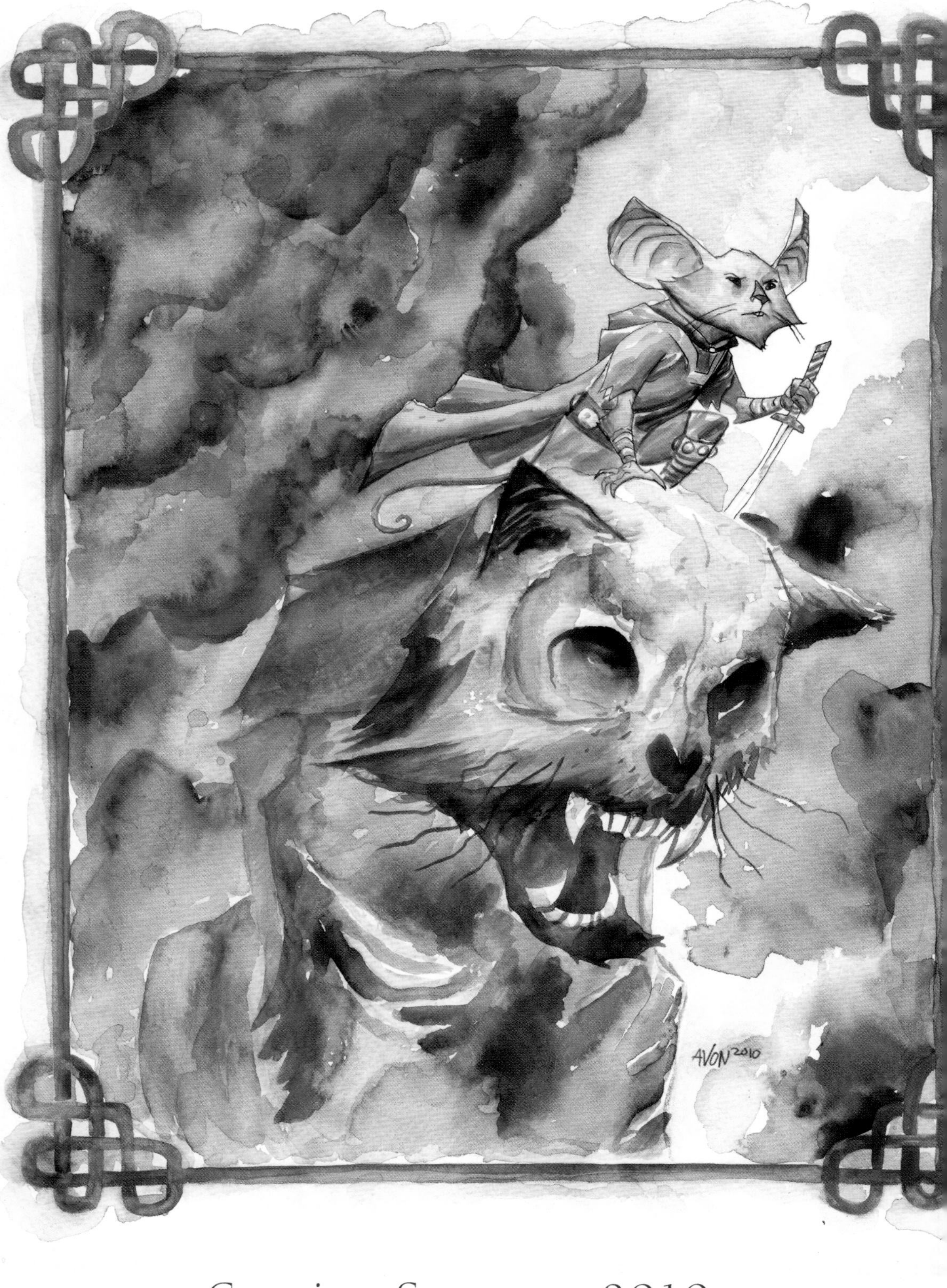
AVON 2010

Coming Summer 2010...

The Mice Templar: Volume 2.2

Destiny: Part Two

Destiny, prophecy and free will collide as the young mouse Karic prepares himself for an audacious confrontation with the fearsome Snake god of the druids, for the salvation of his family, and the fate of all mice.

Yet many forces stand in his way: the tyranny of the mad King Icarus, the twisted riddles of the Bats of Meave, the Scorpion god, the ancient Nathair, and certain doom at the claws of the Zombie Cat!

Thus continues an extraordinary adventure of magic and wonder, of faith and valor, and of one small mouse whose destiny may change the entire world. Created by Bryan J.L. Glass (*Magician Apprentice*, *Riftwar*, *Quixote*) & Michael Avon Oeming (*POWERS*, *Rapture*, *God Complex*).

Collects The Mice Templar: Destiny 6-9

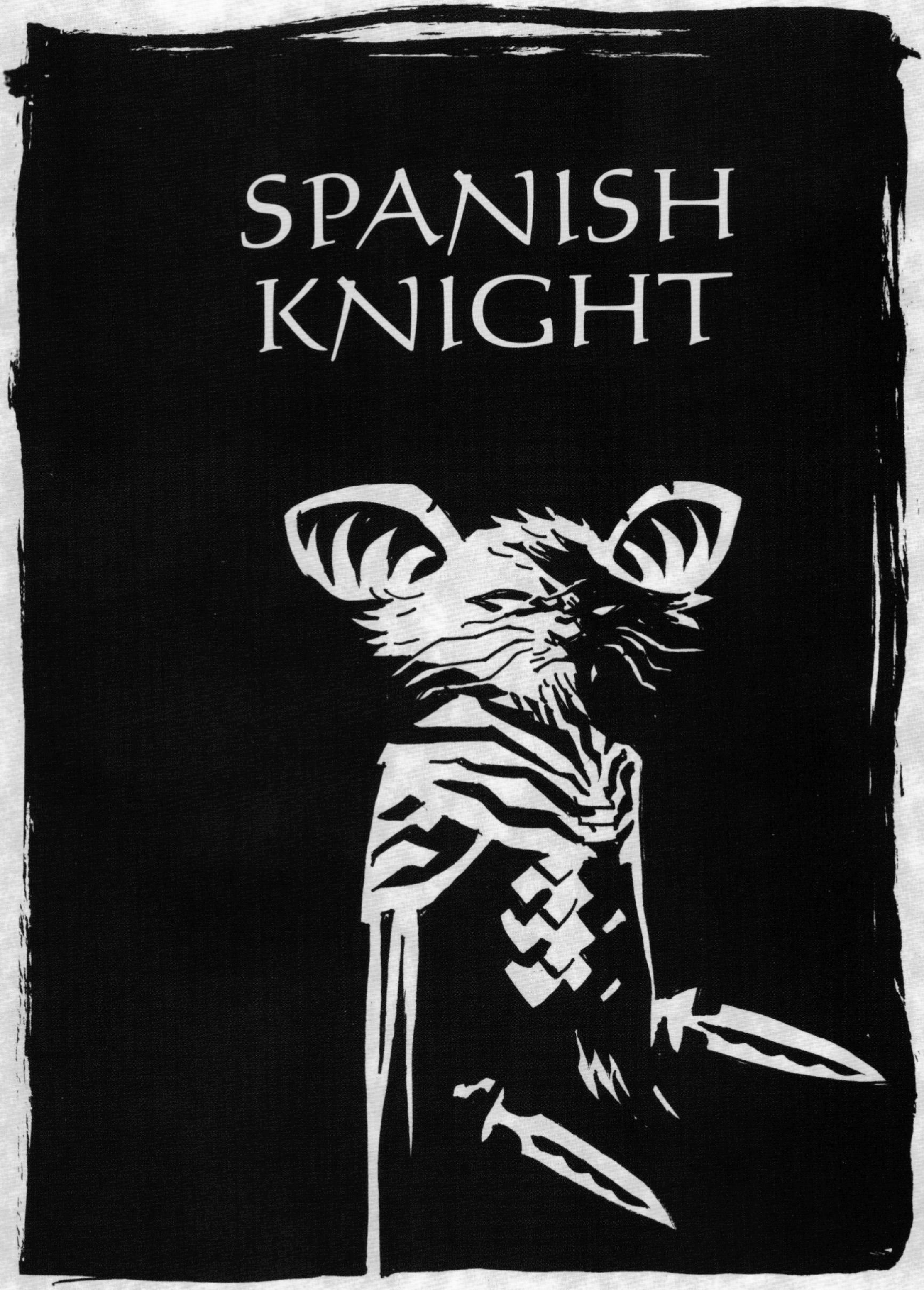
SPANISH
KNIGHT

An Afterword by Victor Santos

I was first introduced to Mike Oeming some years ago by my friends Kelsey Shannon and Miles Gunter. Then, two or three years ago, Mike wrote a short story for my Spanish series *Los Reyes Elfos* that was later published again in the ACTOR anthology. We were both very satisfied with our collaboration and wanted to work together again. And when that chance came, I couldn't refuse it!

But the really important part for me was that I had already discovered the art of Mike Oeming, back when the *POWERS* series was first published in Spain, and I became a huge fan. And when *The Mice Templar: The Prophecy* series began, I was one of the many faithful readers from the first issue, despite having to buy every chapter from the other side of the Atlantic Ocean!

To any fan, the opportunity to draw one of your favourite series can be a dream. Or a nightmare. For instance, Batman has been drawn by thousands of artists. If I screwed it up, surely there were many others who have done even worse. But *Mice Templar* was 100% Oeming, and Bryan had been collaborating with a really talented guy to bring their vivid story to life...

And as a fan, a bad replacement is something I can't forgive.

I have worked very hard to continue to give *The Mice Templar: Destiny* the same level of graphic talent and exciting storytelling that Mike gave it, and translate the epic drama of Bryan's powerful scripts into visual form. This volume is the result and I hope you enjoy it.

I want to thank Mike, Bryan, Judy, James and all the people at Image for their support and help, and Verónica for her terrific colors, improving my work beyond my own expectations. And the *Mice Templar* fans who write encouraging letters and emails, and all of you who are only now entering this wonderful world created by these two modern Templar Knights, Mike and Bryan.

Now it's your turn to judge, my friends. ✑

Victor Santos
Bilbao, Spain

185

Myth, Legend & The Mice Templar

BY ROD HANNAH

Diabhuls & Diabhlan: Celtic Demons and the Devil

Since the beginning of time, myths have been populated with supernatural beings of light and dark. Whether these spirits take the form of gods, angels, devils or demons, they represent answers to the questions of life and existence. But of all these otherworldly forces, the evil spirit stands out as the enduring antagonist of myth and legend, the preeminent metaphor for the inner struggle where the hero must prevail.

The word "Demon" derives from Greek, but the concept dates back to the dawn of mankind. In primitive cultures, the onset of sickness, for example, is usually attributed to a malevolent spirit taking possession of its victim. From a psychological perspective, the demon represents a personification of the many physical and mental infirmities that ail mankind. It has fallen on man to expel these demons through faith and thereby free the cursed from their spiritual corruption. Pre-Christian mythological races of Ireland included the magical *Fomorians* and the divine *Tuatha Dé Danann*, whom modern readers might consider to be demons, and yet to the indigenous pagan cultures, they were like the titans and gods of Greek myth. Legends say that as their days waned, the Celtic druids unsuccessfully disputed with St. Patrick over the value of the pagan traditions versus the Christian faith. Paganism gave way and the Tuatha Dé Danann retreated underground, becoming the fairies of folklore. As such, the demons were banished, seen over time metaphorically in the conspicuous absence of snakes in Irish narrative. The Celtic hero *Fion Mac Cumhail* is famed for slaying serpents in nearly every body of water in Ireland, and St. Patrick is famous for driving the snakes from the island altogether, along with many demons, including *Caoránach*, the mother of demons herself.

A Devil by Any Other Name.

In all traditions, the Devil is typically the chief spirit of the underworld, the defiant challenger of the established order. He is culpable for the temptation of man and sowing doubt, discord and defiance. The Devil has taken many shapes through the ages and throughout mythology. He is the snake that tempts Eve in the Garden of Eden, identified with Satan. In Irish mythology the Devil is also known as the Adversary; one particular manifestation is the centipedal form of the Earwig. In *The Mice Templar*, elements of both the snake and centipede are present in the physical form of the Nathair and their leader, Donas. "Nathair" is in fact the Celtic word for serpent.

The Latin "diabolus," origin of the Spanish "Diablo" as well as the English word "devil," is the etymological source for the diabhuls and diabhlan, both Celtic derivatives for demons and devils in *The Mice Templar* series. The name "Donas" also has a Celtic correlation to the Irish chthonic deity, "*Donn*," ruler of the Otherworld. Donn was the first of the Milesian invaders to land in Ireland, but he defied the goddess *Ériu*, who desired that he honor her by naming the land for her. In punishment Donn was drowned, and his spirit banished to the House of Donn, where he became god of the dead. Aspects of Donn are often associated with the Devil in Irish folklore as the ruler of the dead, with whom souls linger on their journey to hell.

The Fall of the Firstborn

The mythos of *The Mice Templar* describes Donas as the firstborn of the Nathair, who are the eldest of Wotan's creatures. Donas was the instigator, leading his brethren in the construction of the Dubhlan, the Great Catapult of Defiance. With this weapon he conspired to put out the eyes of Wotan by a mighty arrow, ushering forth a realm of darkness over which he would reign supreme. However, Donas succeeded only in dimming one of Wotan's great eyes, and together with the Nathair, was cursed, exiled from the Creation he had coveted.

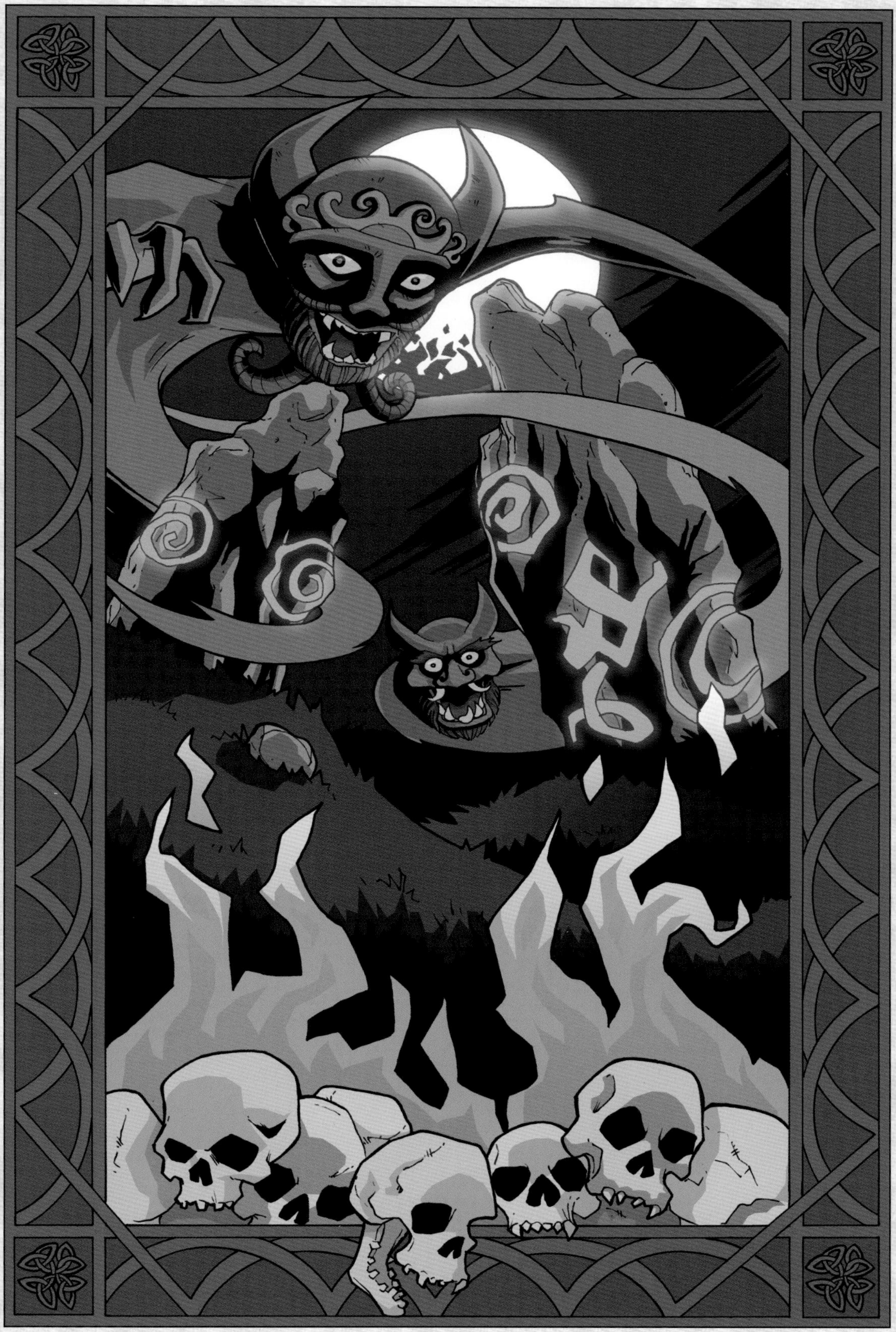
Celtic Demons by Leanne Hannah LeanneHannah.com

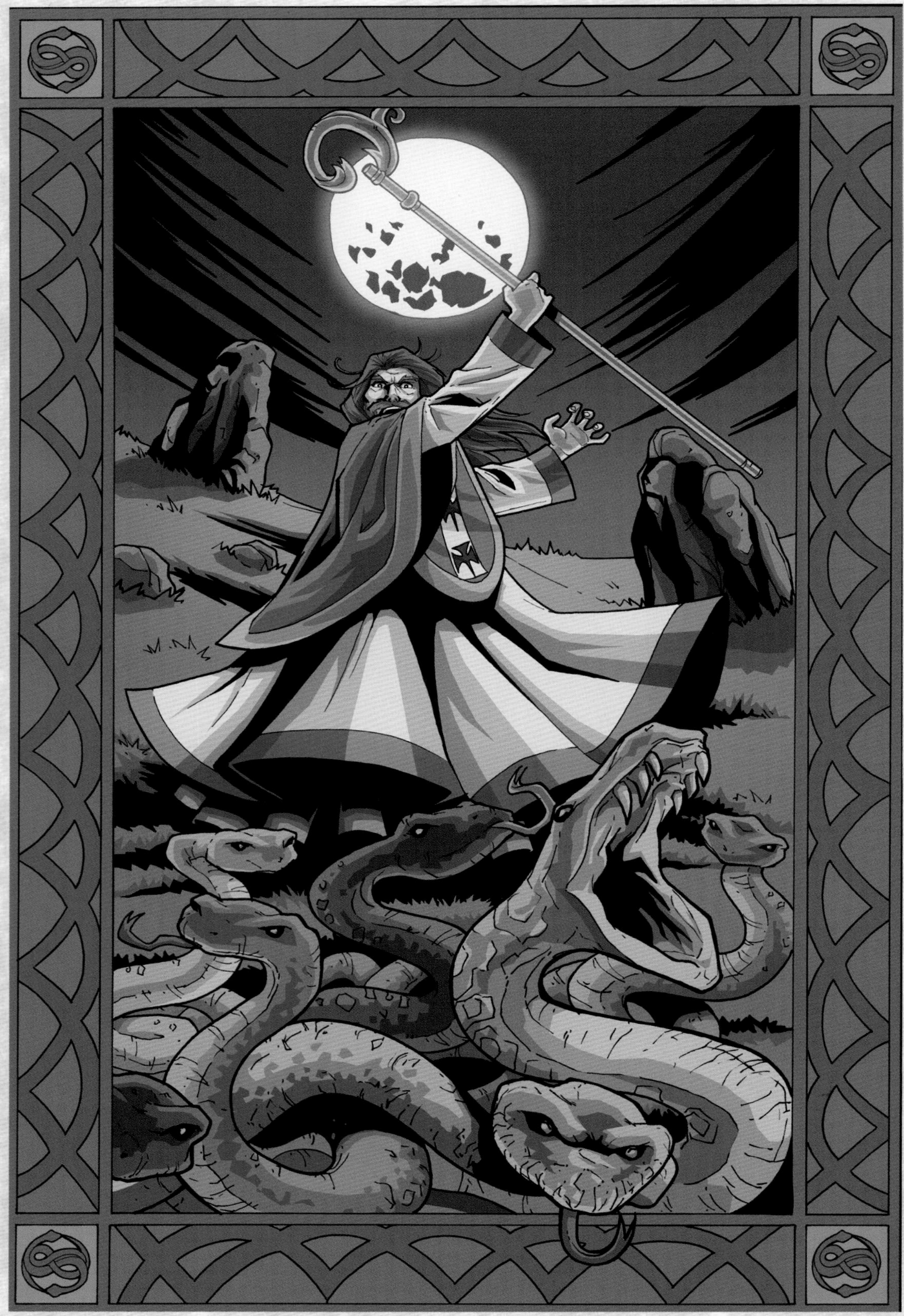

The Legend of St. Patrick by Leanne Hannah LeanneHannah.com

Like the angels cast out of heaven and the architects of Babel dispersed for their hubris, the Nathair suffered divine punishment for their defiance. Banished to the Outer Darkness, a shapeless realm of shadow, Nathair hatred seethed and grew, completing their corruption. The "Nathair-spawn" of Templar legend are the demonic diabhuls, while the surviving spirit form of the Nathair themselves are the even mightier diabhlan. Their incursions into the mortal realm are limited to the possession of lesser beings, making the Templar, the champions of Wotan, their mortal enemies.

The Haunted Wood

Karic's experience with evil spirits began during his apprenticeship under Pilot, the Deceiver. He faced evil entities conjured by the Druid-Witch Black Anaius, preparing him for the even greater test of the Haunted Wood, the site of an ancient conflict. Here desperate druids conjured ancient evil, only to have it contained by the power of the Templar priests and turned against them. Arguing and distrustful of one another, Cassius and Karic have their own inner demons at play. Unwittingly, they have reached points in their personal journeys where they must exorcise the demons that divide them, both figuratively and literally.

Cassius, the jaded Templar knight, tires of Karic's youthful impudence and hurls the young hero's sword into the dark forest. When Karic brashly enters to retrieve his sword, he is immediately struck by visions of evil demons who claim to be the spirits of the family he failed to rescue. Cassius too, in his effort to reach Karic and save him, has his sanity tested by these diabhuls. These entities prey on guilt and instill hopelessness, seeking to destroy the heroes from within.

The fallen mice and rats—now walking dead—surround the two Templar, cutting off their escape. Karic finds courage in Wotan and refuses to believe their lies. As Cassius succumbs to the spiritual assault, Karic uses his one favor from Wotan, reserved until now for the rescue of his own family, to save their lives. Calling upon Wotan's divine intervention, Karic's faith is answered by a flock of owls swooping in to deliver them from certain death.

Their respite is temporary, however, as a tangible diabhlan pursues them into the underground tunnels of the mole goblins. This demon is no mere diabhul spirit, but an ancient Nathair possessing the form of a dead and decaying cat. Two natural enemies, cat and mouse, Templar and demon, find themselves face to face.

The diabhlan, consumed with vengeance, pursues the two mice through the tunnels that run beneath the Haunted Wood, until Cassius and Karic find the light of the Bright Realm and

their escape. Into the dazzling light, they emerge to safety.

As Cassius humbly acknowledges the sacrifice Karic made in order to save their lives from the diabhuls, the nature of their confrontational relationship begins to soften with a newfound respect. Upon entering the realm of the Great Eye of Wotan, they truly see each other in a new light. Through the unity of their faith, they find a strength that far outweighs the doubts and guilt that divided them, and leads them to truly and literally conquer their personal demons. ◉

Sources:

Mythology: The Illustrated Anthology of World Myth and Storytelling, Ed., Scott Littleton, Pub., Duncan Baird, 2002
ISBN 1-904292-01-1

A Dictionary of Celtic Mythology, James MacKillop, Pub., Oxford University Press, 1998
ISBN 0-19-280120-1

The Power of Myth, Joseph Campbell with Bill Moyers, Pub., Anchor, 1991
ISBN 0385418868

Diabolic, Devil: www.etymonline.com/

Lucifer: en.wikipedia.org/wiki/Lucifer

Donas the Nathair by Michael Avon Oeming

Beowulf

Thanks to their ideal, super-human qualities, the great heroes of old have captured our imagination and endured through millennia. Heroes of myth, such as Gilgamesh, Hercules and Beowulf, are remembered mostly for the fantastic monsters they have slain, yet each hero attained greatness not only by the blood upon his sword but by his code of conduct. Whether large or small, a hero is that man or woman who is willing to go beyond the threshold and venture into a realm of the unknown for something greater than oneself.

Beowulf, the legendary sixth century champion of the *Geats* from southwestern Sweden, is a stirring example of an Anglo-Saxon mythical hero who crossed such a threshold and returned alive and triumphant. Preserved through oral tradition, Beowulf's tale was later recorded as an epic poem circa 1000 AD. Beowulf is one of the earliest heroes of western culture and has inspired heroic literature through the ages, including the works of J.R.R. Tolkien.

The Mice Templar takes some cues from the epic poem. The legendary sword made from the talon of the *Great Death Owl* came to be known as the *Mark of Kuhl-En*. Such terminology is known as a *kenning*—a compound expression that names a person or thing based upon its characteristics. Kennings are found throughout the poem of Beowulf, such as *whale-road* (ocean or sea), *word-hoard* (vocabulary) or *the sea-wind's cloak* (the ship's mast).

Furthermore, as with many heroes, the character Beowulf came to be known by many heroic epithets. One such was "lord of the rings," so named for the ring-mail shirt he wore, made by the mythical smith

Weland, and not to be confused with Tolkien's famous use of the title. Beowulf was considered the protector of nobles and of sailors, and his life was marked with the virtues of loyalty, valor, and respect, all of which built his reputation as hero. He was the living embodiment of the *comitatus*—the honor system between a lord and his thanes characteristic of Scandinavian countries in the fifth and sixth centuries. Similarly, the legendary mouse hero Kuhl-En delivered and exemplified the *Code of the Templar* and exhorted his brother mice to follow his ways and demonstrate them to others.

The Grendel and His Mother.

The hero Beowulf journeys across the sea, coming to the aid of *King Hrothgar*, whose kingdom lives under the shadow of a vicious ogre that attacks his hall each night and kills his people, the Scyldings. The ogre is called *Grendel*, and like all monsters is descended from Cain, exiled from God, and corrupted by his envy of mankind.

In off the moors, down through the mist bands
God-cursed Grendel came greedily loping.
The bane of the race of men roamed forth,

Hunting for prey in the high hall.

(*Beowulf: A New Verse Translation*, by Seamus Heaney)

Although Beowulf battles and defeats the monster in the hall of the king, he finds an even more dangerous fiend in the form of *Grendel's Mother*. Preparing to face the Mother in her dark, cavernous lair beneath a monster-infested lake, Beowulf accepts that he may not return. The hero crosses the threshold, plunging into the other realm, armed only with his faith, his courage, and a giant magical sword, with which he manages to slay the Mother. A bright heavenly light illuminates the cavern as the blade of the sword melts away, leaving only the hilt. Beowulf returns victorious and eventually becomes king of his people in a golden age of peace that would last 50 years.

The Hero's Journey

Joseph Campbell recognized the basic structure of heroic myth and named it the *hero's journey* or *monomyth*. He identified 17 typical stages of the hero's journey, although the actual number of these stages and their order can vary widely from one story to another. At their core, they comprise three basic phases, beginning with the *Departure*, followed by the

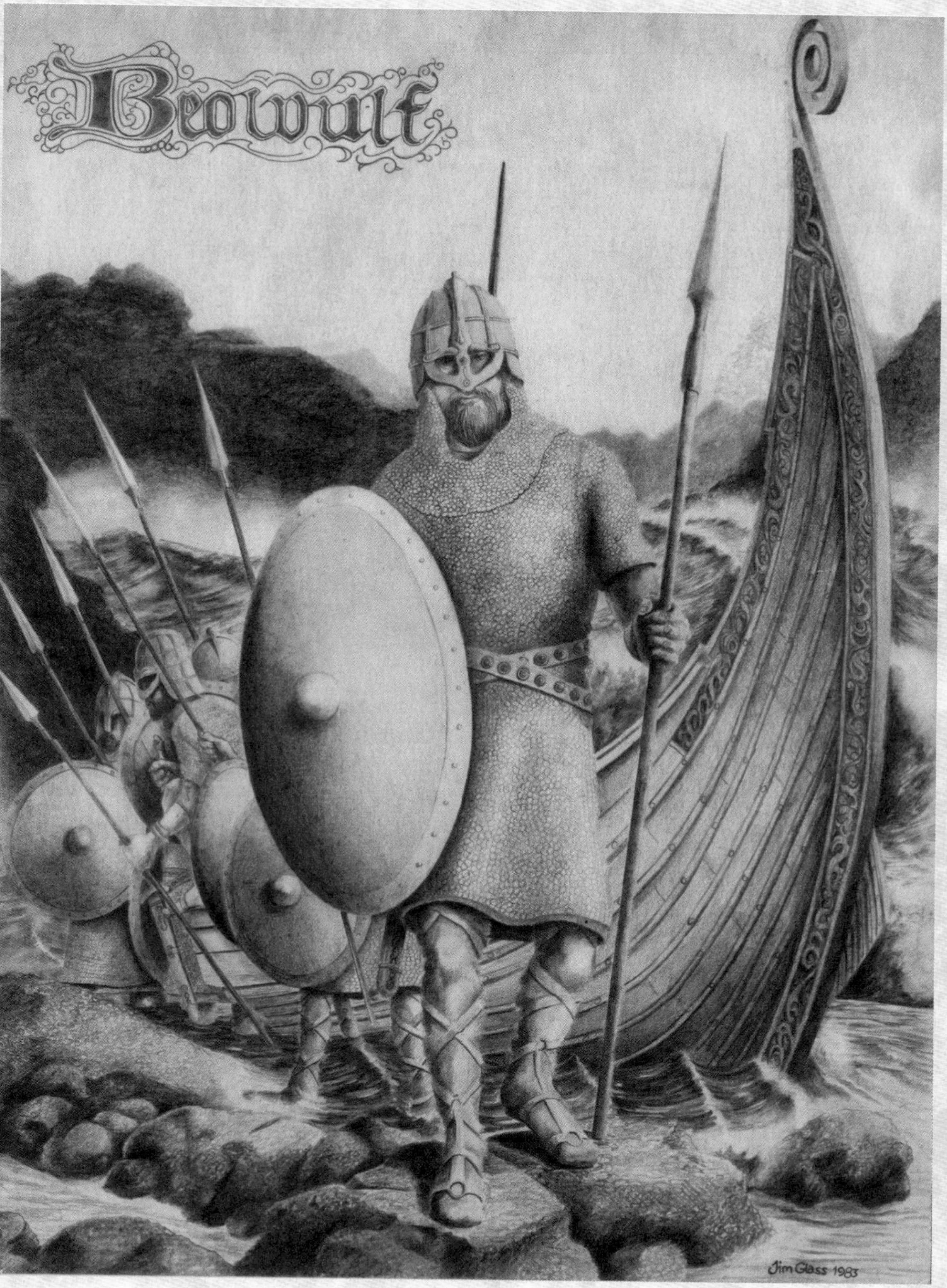
Jim Glass 1983

BEOWULF

By James H. Glass

Initiation, and ending with the *Return*. This structure is quite evident in the stories of Beowulf and in The Mice Templar.

The journeys of Karic and Beowulf are very different adventures, yet both follow Campbell's monomythic outline. On a superficial level, the spider-god that had been making incursions into Karic's village home of Cricket's Glen might be seen as a Grendel, raining upon the naïve merriment of the playful young mice. Similarly, Karic's plunge into the lake, finding himself in the otherworldly cavern of the Fish Gods, bears resemblance to Beowulf's diving adventure to reach the cavern of the Grendel's Mother.

A Mouse's Journey

Karic's *Crossing of the First Threshold* begins out of common monomyth sequence when his world is turned upside down by a rat raiding party that slaughters and enslaves his people. Heeding the prophecy of the Fish Gods, Karic is thrust into the hero's journey, answering the *Call to Adventure* by setting out into the unknown with his new mentor, Pilot. In the Barren Lands, Karic faces The Many, a swarm of killer ants that had already wiped out an entire rat raiding party. Karic calls upon the *Supernatural Aid* of the Fish Gods, unleashing "all the waters of the world" to sweep away a seemingly invincible foe.

While crossing the Fields of Gold, Karic and Pilot are attacked by Cassius, the Templar who has been shadowing them from the beginning of their travels together. With his faith mistakenly placed in Pilot, Karic leaps to the deceiver's aid, only to find himself skewered on Cassius's sword. Close to death, Karic receives a vision of Lord Wotan, to whom he promises to give himself completely in exchange for the salvation of his family.

When Karic awakens, he finds himself within the Great Ash Tree. Healed in body, he nevertheless despairs at the revelation of Pilot's deception and the apparent hopelessness of his cause. Karic's sense of defeat and his humility before Master Micah demonstrate his readiness to undergo metamorphosis. Karic accepts that more than just his family is at stake and opens himself to the greater task of lifting his people out of the darkness and back into the light of Wotan. This stage of the hero's journey, named the *Belly of the Whale*, is usually the turning point.

The Road of Trials

Karic is initiated into the order of the Templar, and it is here that we reach the *Road of Trials* in the hero's journey, where his transformation begins in earnest. Trained in combat now by Cassius, the wisdom of the young mouse begins to emerge. They contend with the evil spirits of the Haunted Wood, and together survive the mighty Diabhlan. With these trials behind them, Karic and Cassius find themselves in the Bright Realm, the wondrous world that exists on the other side of the Dawn, the Promised Land as yet denied to his people. Here Karic's spiritual awakening and his self-belief are fused.

Unlike Beowulf, Karic begins his journey as a fledgling mouse, naïve and untested in the harsh reality outside his village. For Beowulf, the largest part of his journey comes after his kinghood, where he must put aside the vain heroism of his youth in favor of the wisdom he has gleaned. His greatest test comes when his desire for revenge causes him to once again take up the sword against a dragon ravaging his land.

What lies ahead for Karic on this journey is the completion of his initiation with an *Apotheosis* to be worthy of *The Ultimate Boon*. For Arthur's knights it was the Holy Grail, the symbol of God's grace, something that only Galahad proved worthy enough to attain through his spiritual and mental purity. Just as Galahad embodies the code of chivalry and Beowulf the comitatus, Karic embodies the forgotten code of the now divided Templar. The feats performed and the creatures that lie slain are of little consequence next to the hero's moral and spiritual conduct of honor, loyalty and faith. ✺

Sources:

Beowulf: A New Verse Translation, by Seamus Heaney, W.W. Norton, 2001
ISBN 978-0-393-32097-8

The Hero With a Thousand Faces, by Joseph Campbell, Princeton University Press, 2004
ISBN 0-691-11924-4

The Power of Myth, by Joseph Campbell with Bill Moyers, Anchor, 1991
ISBN 0385418868

Alternate Dimensions

Every mythos and religious tradition describes unseen realms that coexist with our own. Within these dimensions dwell the unknown and barely fathomed, the angelic and daemonic. To the ancient Mesopotamians, the *Otherworld* lies at the edge of the known world and is that place from which the sun rises each new day. Forever hidden behind a veil just tantalizingly beyond the reach of human experience, the Otherworld might take the form of an Eden paradise, a heavenly world or a subterranean hell—the *Elysium* or Underworld of Greek myth next to our mundane Earth. In these worlds everything is heightened, with greener fields, taller hills and mountains, and thicker forests. It is the place where the greatest adventures of all lie waiting, provided, of course, that the hero returns to tell the tale...

The Celtic Otherworld

The Otherworld of northern European myth and legend was known to the Irish as the lands of *Tir na n'Og* ("Land of the Young"), *Tir na mBeo* ("Land of the Living"), and *Mag Mell* ("Delightful Plain"), and the Welsh Underworld of *Annwn* and the mystical isle of *Avalon* play heavily into the legends of the Celtic Britons. These magical kingdoms were places of magnificence where time passed quite differently from our own. In one account, the legendary *King Herla* returned after three days in the Otherworld to find, to his dismay, two hundred years had passed and the people now spoke the Saxon tongue.

From the later myths and legends of Celtic peoples came the stories of the land of Faerie, home to the *Seelie* and *Unseelie* court. It was to this magical land that newborns would be spirited away from their families, and changelings left in their place. Whether falling asleep atop a fairy mound, wandering into a sacred cavern or forest, or sailing across the western sea, entering Faerie may depend more on invitation than accident. Dwellers of the Otherworld, such as the Fairy Queen *Fand* or the Underworld King *Arawn*, would lure mortal heroes to their world to teach them a lesson or enlist their aid against their own magical enemies. In order to escape their hosts these heroes had to outwit them, although they would always return home changed in some way.

Fiction and Science

Beyond ancient and medieval tales, the Otherworld continues to add literal dimensions in modern works as it is reinterpreted by new storytellers. Alice stumbles across Wonderland by falling down a rab-

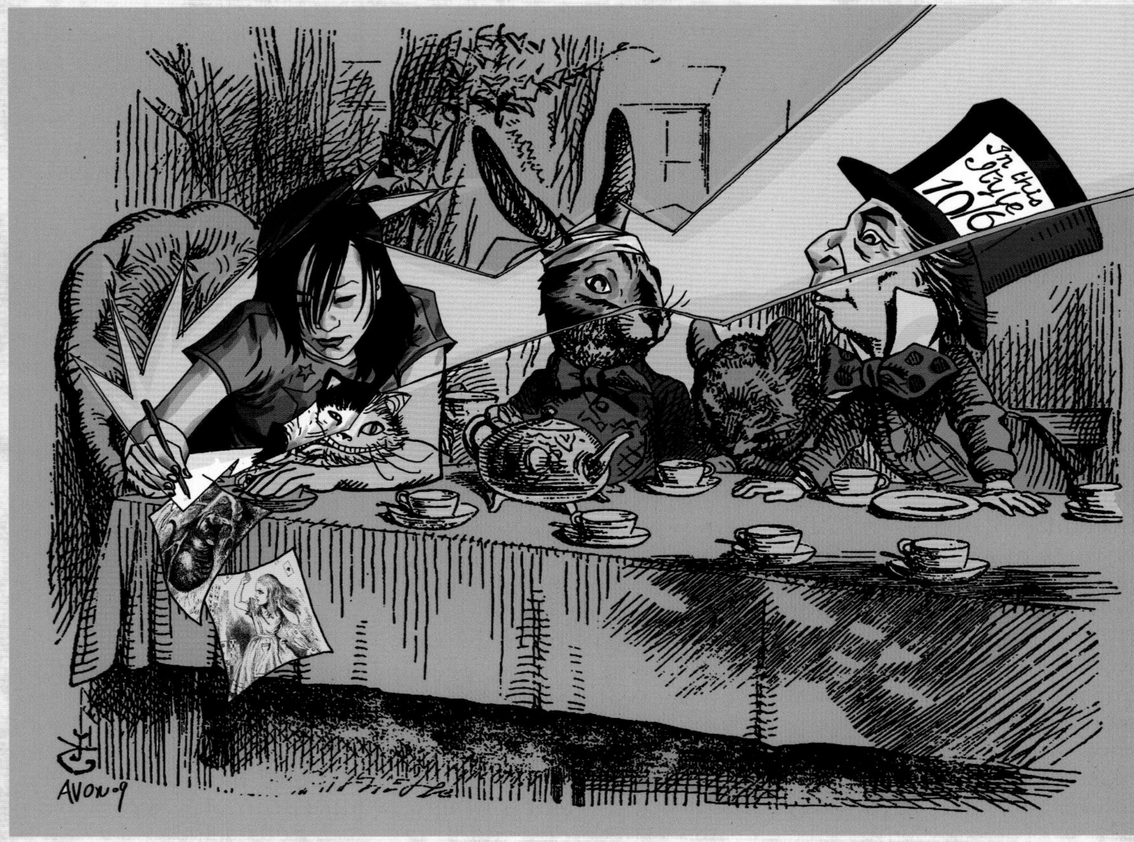
In this Style 10/6
AVON-09

Taki in Wonderland by Michael Avon Oeming

bit hole in Lewis Carroll's *Alice in Wonderland*. Similarly, Darby falls down a well into the kingdom of the leprechauns in *Darby O'Gill and the Little People*. Narnia—the land beyond the Wardrobe—welcomes the Pevensey children as its rightful kings and queens. The magical world of *Harry Potter* exists unseen alongside the world of the Muggles, visible to and accessible only by magic folk in places like the mysterious Diagon Alley and the mystical Platform 9¾ in the train station. And in *The Matrix*, a nagging suspicion leads the hero Neo to discover that his world is nothing more than a digital construct, created by sentient machines. His consciousness has now been restored to the physical world and yet both worlds, real in their own sense, operate by different rules, and to die in one means death in the other.

In the realm of nonfiction, the science of physics does allow for the possibility of alternate dimensions. The electromagnetic spectrum is comprised of countless frequencies of varying degrees of vibration up or down its length. All matter vibrates at some frequency along its length, and those beings or entities vibrating at the higher ranges of the spectrum are unseen by those vibrating at the lower degrees: multiple levels of existence can therefore, theoretically, coexist in the same space but at different frequencies of vibration that isolate them from the perception of the others.

Bright Realm / Shadow Time

In *The Mice Templar*, the Otherworld refers to the division between night and day as two separate worlds—the Bright Realm and the Shadow Time—two alternating dimensions occupying the same space yet at different times. The two worlds were once united, but after the rebellion of Donas and the Nathair, Wotan divided his world. Now his Great Dimmed Eye watches over the Shadow Time, in the form of what we recognize as the moon, while his Great Eye, watching over the Bright Realm, is what we know as the sun.

Karic and other nocturnal creatures exist within the Dark Lands of the Shadow Time, never seeing the wonders of day, nor believing them to be any more than fantasy. When dawn breaks, the world of the mice vanishes, and all traces of their world are invisible to the Bright Realm while they sleep.

Passing from the Shadow Time into the Bright Realm is impossible without incurring the wrath of the Guardians of

Dusk and Dawn. These Guardians of the Worlds are gnats and related insects that rise with daybreak and nightfall and are drawn to sentient creatures, devouring those who are not unconscious like a hunk of meat dropped into a pool of piranha.

The Guardians of the Worlds

After escaping the Mole-Goblin kingdom, Karic and Cassius emerge from the underground tunnels beneath the Haunted Wood to find the Great Eye of Wotan high in the sky. Together they enter the Bright Realm, having crossed over during their subterranean flight from the Diabhlan. Just as the Otherworld has its laws, so does this strange new land. Passage back to the Dark Realm is barred by the Guardians of the Dusk, and as darkness approaches, Cassius explains to Karic that they must abide by the same rules as the Bright Realm denizens, and they find a place to sleep for the night under a bed of flowers.

It is in the Bright Realm that Karic truly begins his Templar training, progressing to where he single-handedly overcomes one of the strange beasts of the daylight hours, and honing his skills until his mentor deems him ready to return to their world. To cross back into the Shadow Time, Cassius must parley with the Guardians of the Dusk. Partially protected by his Templar medallion, Cassius invokes the name of Kuhl-En to save Karic from being eaten alive. The Guardians concede as Cassius defiantly reminds them of the curse placed upon them by the ancient Templar Master. Cassius and Karic find themselves back in their own world, having survived the trials of the Bright Realm.

Land of Trials

The Otherworld is as much a realm of the unconscious mind as it is a fairy world of untold wonder, and it is a key part of the Hero's Journey. *"Once having traversed the threshold, the hero moves in a dream landscape of curiously fluid, ambiguous forms, where he must survive a succession of trials,"* writes mythologist Joseph Campbell. *"The original departure into the land of trials represented only the beginning. Dragons have now to be slain and surprising barriers passed—again, again, and again. Meanwhile there will be a multitude of preliminary victories, unretainable ecstasies, and momentary glimpses of the wonderful land."*

After nearly a month of training in the other world, Karic returns to the Dark Realm stronger and wiser than before. His awestruck wonder and his swelling desire that all mice should someday experience the Bright Realm for themselves are perfect examples of what Campbell describes. His independence and path to adulthood are near completion, and he is now ready for greater challenges. Cassius too returns changed. Having witnessed the self-sacrifice of his youthful charge, the fires of hope have been rekindled in him. He was sworn to protect and train the young mouse, but now he finds in himself a belief in this cause and a commitment to it with greater meaning than duty alone. And yet their greatest challenges still lie before them, back in the Dark Lands of the Shadow Time. ❧

Sources:

Mythology: The Illustrated Anthology of World Myth and Storytelling, Ed., Scott Littleton, Pub., Duncan Baird, 2002 ISBN 1-904292-01-1

Albion: A Guide to Legendary Britain, Jennifer Westwood, Pub., Salem House, 1985 ISBN 0-88162-128-5

A Dictionary of Celtic Mythology, James MacKillop, Pub., Oxford University Press, 1998 ISBN 0-19-280120-1

The Hero With a Thousand Faces, by Joseph Campbell, Princeton University Press, 2004 ISBN 0-691-11924-4

An Order Divided

From the dawn of time, mankind has known war. Whether for reasons of conquest, power, or ideology, conflict is inevitable, and diplomacy cannot solve every situation. As populations grew and primitive societies formed, it was not long before early tribes turned to organized violence as the means of one group to impose its will upon another. As history has unfolded, and war has grown more sophisticated with greater technology and more convoluted politics, the basic nature of two irreconcilable viewpoints has always been at its root.

One of the most lamentable forms of major armed conflict has always been civil war—war amongst a single people, in which the hostilities stemming from opposing ideologies are typically the result of a government's tragic failure to maintain effective balance, law, and order for its people.

Power play

Every country's history is fraught with wars, and no country has avoided some kind of civil war. In the last 50 years alone there have been over 90 civil wars around the world, with outcomes ranging from government victory, rebel victory, truce, or treaty. But in the aftermath, the cost on a more human level manifests in the large scale loss of life, the debilitation of countless wounded and maimed, and the economic collapse of entire regions. Then begins the daunting and painstaking task of rebuilding, literally and figuratively, and restoring function to society and government.

It is important to recognize the distinction between civil war and revolution. A revolution is characterized by a funda-mental change in power or organizational structures, and usually takes place in a relatively short period of time. A civil war, on the other hand, originates as a struggle between organized groups, who are already in power within a single nation state, to take power or change government policies.

The American Revolution against England (1775-1783), for example, was to establish a completely new country with its own government, in response to the Crown's failure to allow its colonial citizens the same rights and representation as its domestic population, and its disregard for the colonies' repeated attempts to appeal and rectify this miscarriage of justice. The American Civil War, nearly 100 years later (1861-1865), was the culmination of years of increasingly divergent and irreconcilable cultural and political ideologies between the Northern and Southern states. In both cases, the push for separation from the former government was a common factor. It could be argued that the Revolution began as a civil war, and the Civil War could have been deemed a revolution, had the South prevailed and thereby made permanent their secession from the Union.

English history is peppered with such clashes as the Wars of the Roses (c. 1455-1485) and the English Civil Wars occurring between 1642-1651. Similarly, throughout the history of the Roman Republic and Empire, there were numerous revolts, conspiracies and civil wars. In the final years of the Republic, political power was seized from the magistrates and the senate and split among the triumvirate of Julius Caesar, Pompey, and Marcus Licinius Crassus. However, upon the death of Crassus, the ambitions of Caesar and Pompey collided, resulting in a civil war (49-45 BC) that established Julius Caesar as the first in a long line of dictators.

In popular culture, Marvel's "Civil War" event plays out the divisive principle at the heart of such a war. Superhumans were divided on one side by a sense of responsibility as citizens, while on the other a desire to protect their own civil liberties and privacy. The fallout was far reaching as society was forced to accept the new order amidst brightly burning animosities.

"A house divided against itself cannot stand."

While these Scriptural words might describe any civil war, Abraham Lincoln made them famous two years before he became president in describing the deep divisions precipitating the devastation that was the American Civil War. Devoted as he was to the preservation of the Union, Lincoln's presidency only catalyzed the growing conflict. Within months of his inauguration, regional tensions over states' rights and slavery that had been brewing for years boiled over into the bloodiest war in American history.

As in the case of Julius Caesar's civil war, the American Civil War was in part precipitated by fears that inaction would lead to loss of power and influence. Southern states intrinsically felt threatened by Lincoln's campaign against the spread of slavery, and his sympathies with the abolitionists as well as the likelihood of federal power stripping away states' rights all threatened the South's economy in light of their already dwindling political power against an increasingly industrialized north. By early 1861, eleven of the southern states had seceded and formed the Confederate States of America, pitting federal forces against the breakaway rebels. From 1861-1865 the Union and

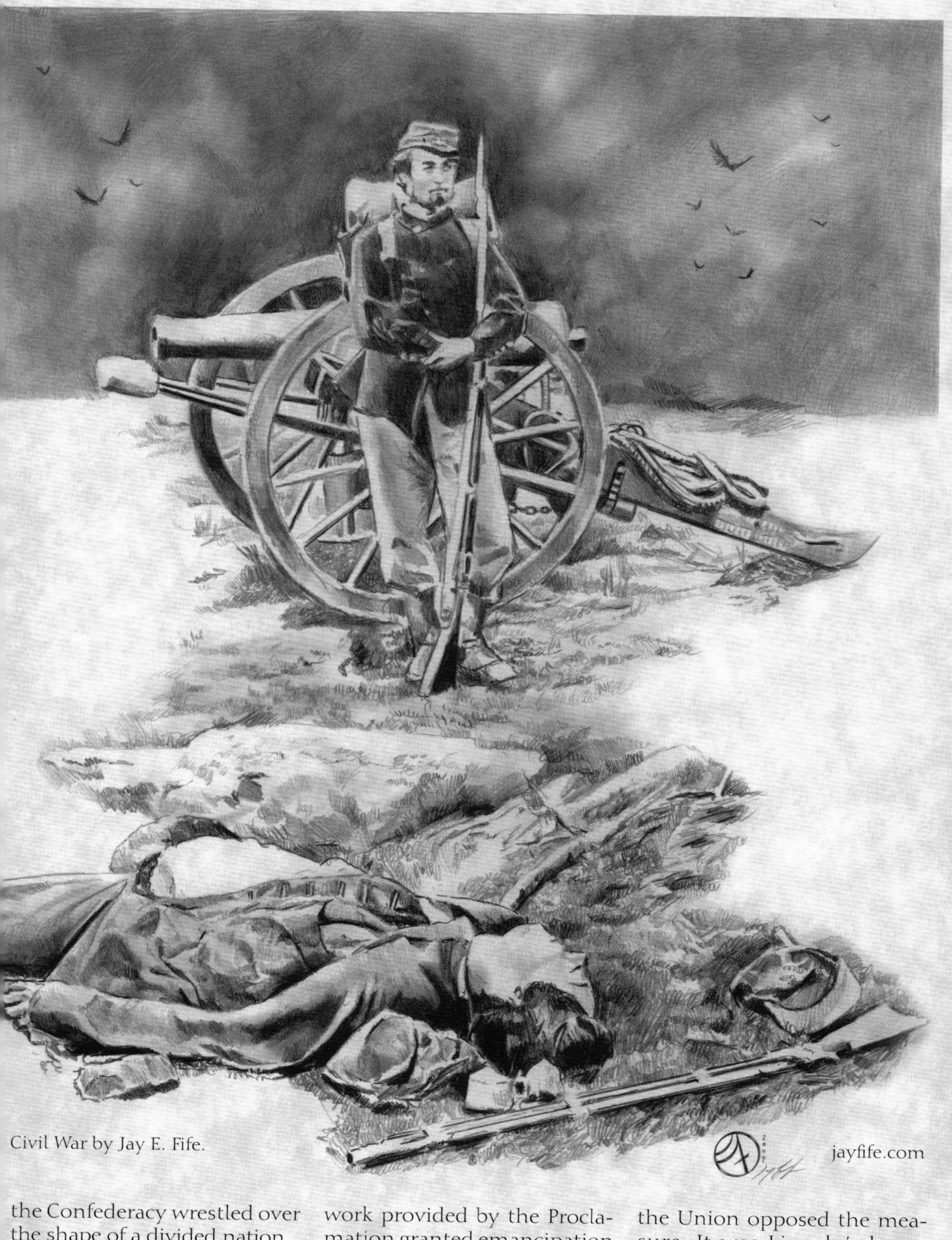

Civil War by Jay E. Fife.

jayfife.com

the Confederacy wrestled over the shape of a divided nation.

As the war got underway, Lincoln took the opportunity to issue the Emancipation Proclamation, committing the Union to ending slavery. The legal framework provided by the Proclamation granted emancipation to approximately four million slaves, a decision that was at the time controversial even in the North, and many of the war Democrats who had supported Lincoln's goal of saving the Union opposed the measure. It was Lincoln's hope, however, that he would win foreign support for the Union by adding the abolition of slavery as a war goal, placing moral pressure on Britain and France against the Confederacy.

The Union pressed its industrial and manpower advantages, leading to the surrender of General Lee on April 9, 1865. President Lincoln was assassinated just five days later. The Reconstruction era lasted 12 years, with federal troops occupying former Confederate states to ensure their gradual reintegration into the Union. The deep bitterness among the former secessionists and those economically impacted by the policies and Constitutional amendments resulting from the war lasted well into the 20th century and even up to the present day. In the South, it is still referred to by some as "The War for Southern Independence" and "The War of Northern Aggression."

Of Mice Divided

In *The Mice Templar*, the god Wotan bestowed the authority of justice into the hands of mice. Under the legendary hero Kuhl-En, the order of the Templar was established, heralding a golden age of peace and prosperity. It was at the Fields of Gold that Kuhl-En learned he was called by Wotan to share the burden of leading his people. He appointed twelve disciples, dubbing them the Readers of the Wheat. These humble priests became the leaders of the Templar order, living within the Great Ash Tree, from whence they were responsible for imparting the Will of Wotan to the people.

The legends that grew up around the Readers of the Wheat became a useful tool. The priests encouraged the belief that the Readers of the Wheat were mystical beings whom they represented. Thus they no longer had to fear the direct retribution of unpopular edicts. Corruption set in as the once genuine prophesies from the Readers were manipulated and distorted in return for political favors. Scandals within the priesthood, ongoing military service to put down revolts and secession attempts, along with an increasingly bloody conflict with the rats, led to a growing dissatisfaction among the populace and within the Templar order itself.

Perhaps most divisive of all was the declaration by some that Kuhl-En himself was mere legend, challenging the faith of many and eroding the Templar Code. The priests refused to takes sides as the ideological division grew between Kobalt, along with those loyal to the established order, and the rival faction under Icarus. When the two leaders met for public de-

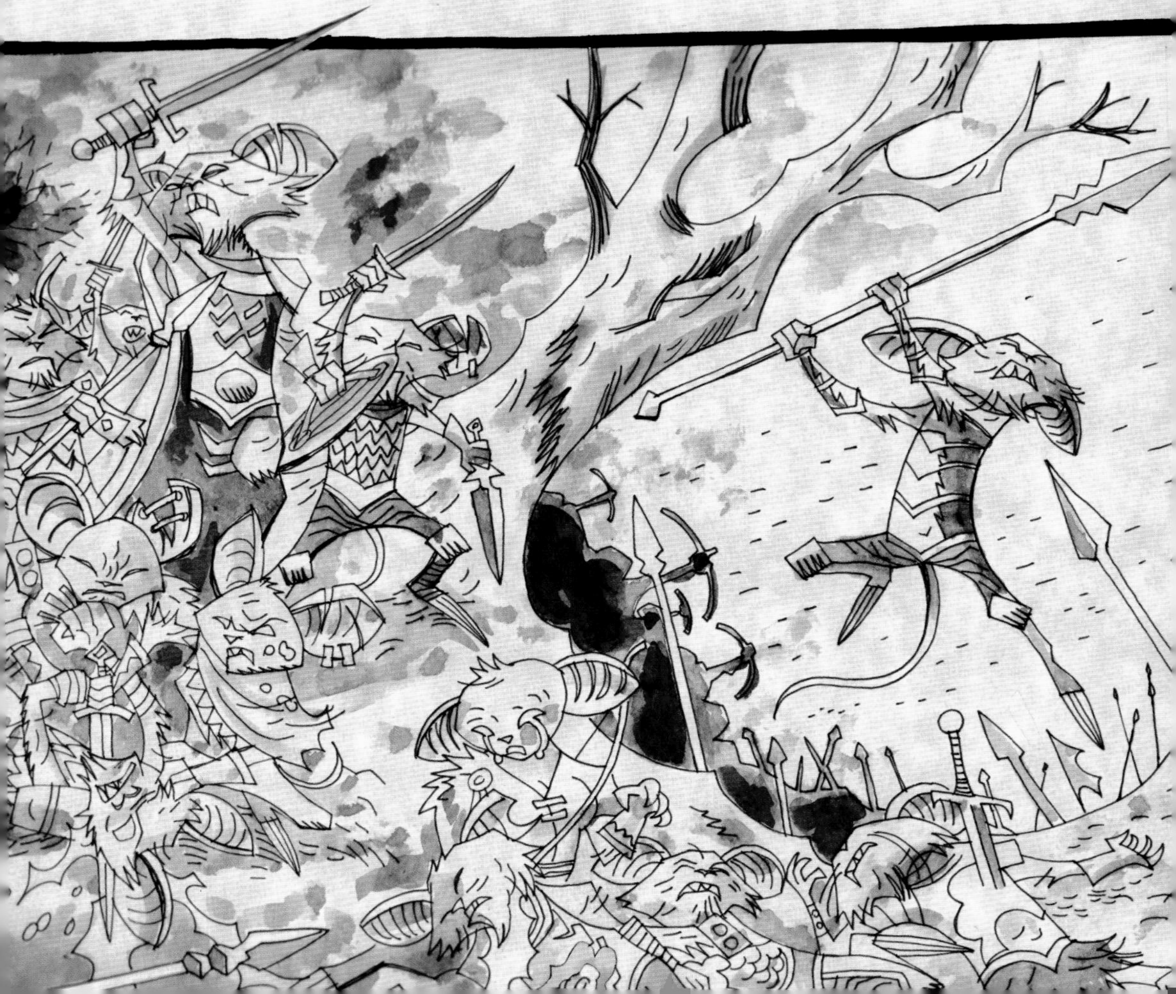

bate, Kobalt struck first, only to be killed by Icarus in apparent self-defense, an action that escalated tensions in the order to the breaking point. The two sides met at the field of Avalon, a place that was once a symbol of unity for their people, in a savage battle. The deep animosity split families, as we have seen in the tragic outcome between the brothers Cassius and Celik. At Avalon, these two Templar brothers embodied the irreconcilable views that had swept the order. Neither side was willing to compromise or give any quarter. Locked in single combat, there could be only one resolution.

Aftermath

The war ended with the Templar removed from the political sphere, their ranks decimated, as Icarus took the throne and began an oppressive reign, supported by the rats and weasels who eagerly exploited the vacuum of a divided and disgraced order. The priests and the Templar were exiled and isolated. Remnants of the Templar order hid away in the wilderness, unwilling to admit defeat or surrender their animosities. Under Ronan, a new generation of Templar banned mystic teaching and myth-based allegiance in their camps, whilst the old guard viewed them as responsible for Icarus's seizing of the throne—threatening unity itself to become a thing of legend.

In the end, the lesson of the Templar civil war demonstrates the tragic devastation that comes from wars of ideology. In issue #4, Karic asks Cassius on which side had he fought. The war had cost him his eye, his brother, his friends, and the woman he loved. Hearkening to the grander scheme of life, Cassius answers, "Does it matter?"

Sources:

James M. McPherson, *Battle Cry of Freedom: The Civil War Era*, Oxford University Press, 2003
ISBN 019516895X

War: Stanford Encyclopedia of Philosophy
http://plato.stanford.edu/entries/war/

Civil War
http://en.wikipedia.org/wiki/Civil_war

Revolution
http://en.wikipedia.org/wiki/Revolution

Civil War (comics)
http://en.wikipedia.org/wiki/Marvel_civil_war

Lincoln's "House Divided" Speech
http://en.wikipedia.org/wiki/Lincoln%27s_House_Divided_Speech

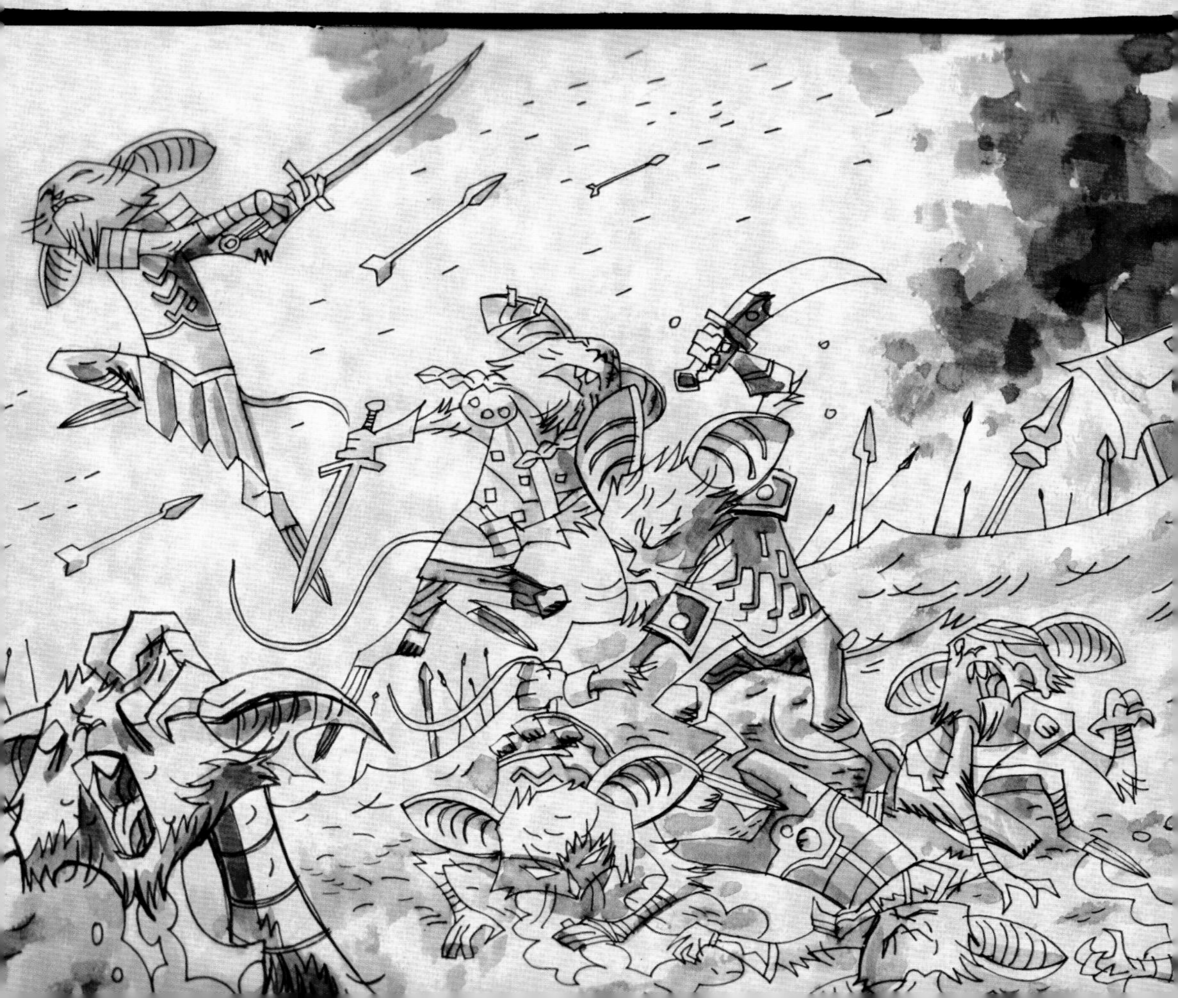

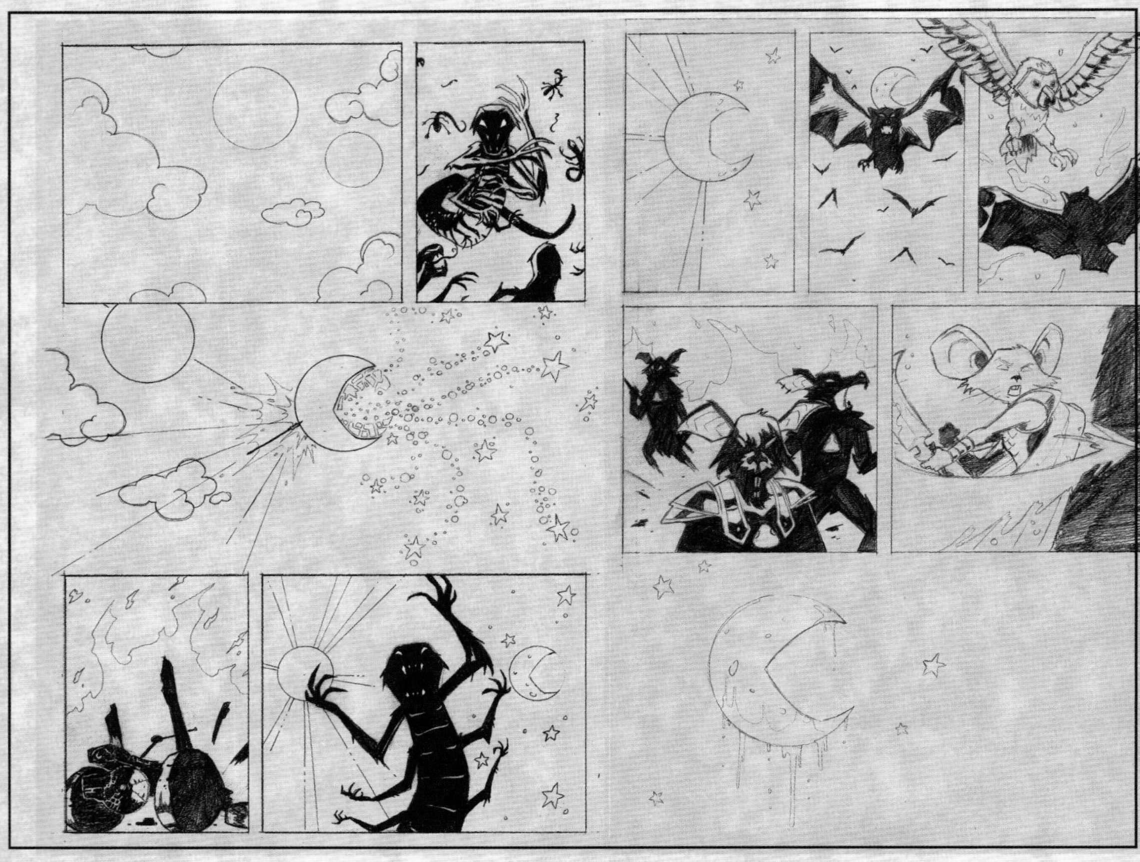

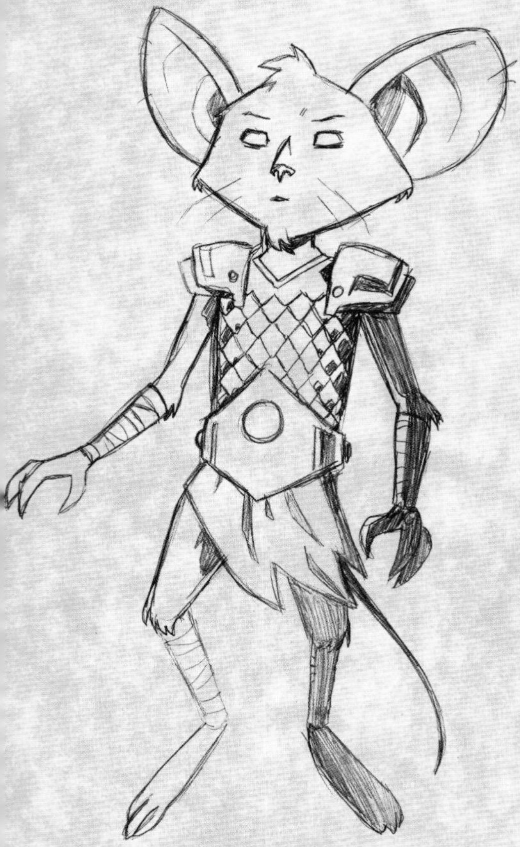

As Mike Oeming passed the art torch to Victor Santos for the continuation of the *Mice Templar* series, he realized he would also need to find someone to reproduce his lush watercolors used in the many sequences of history, mythology and sacred dreams that abound throughout this story.

These sketches and layouts by Jamie Fay reveal a vision of *The Mice Templar* that almost was... and we're honored to reproduce them here.

More of Jamie's work can be found on his DeviantArt page, and in the upcoming *Neverminds* graphic novel from Drumfish Productions.

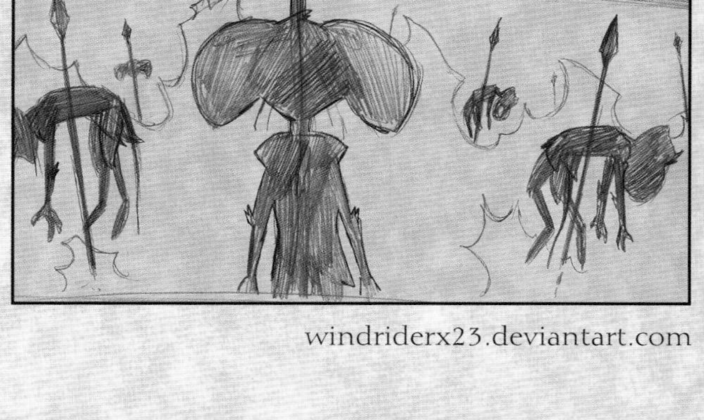

windriderx23.deviantart.com

CREDITS & ACKNOWLEDGMENTS

THE MICE TEMPLAR
Created by Michael Avon Oeming & Bryan J.L. Glass

PRODUCTION TEAM
Victor Santos • Veronica Gandini • James H. Glass • Judy Glass • Harry Lee

FOREWORD
Gail Simone
Illustration: Adam Withers • uniquescomic.com

MAP OF THE DARK LANDS
Brian Quinn • bcqillustrator.blogspot.com

MYTH, LEGENDS & THE MICE TEMPLAR
Rod Hannah • rodhannah.com
    Celtic Demons: Leanne Hannah • LeanneHannah.com
    The Legend of St. Patrick: Leanne Hannah • LeanneHannah.com
    Beowulf: James H. Glass
    Taki in Wonderland: Michael Avon Oeming • michaeloeming.com
    Civil War: Jay E. Fife • jayfife.com

WEBMASTER
Tim Daniel • hiddenrobot.com

SPECIAL THANKS
Allen Hui • M. Sean McManus
Marc Nathan • Will Swyer

Image Comics: Branwyn Bigglestone,
Drew Gill, Monica Howard,
Joe Keatinge, Tyler Shainline,
Eric Stephenson

For as long as he can remember, Bryan has told stories. Expressing himself in a variety of media, all of his efforts inevitably returned him to the craft of storytelling. While originally pursuing a career in filmmaking, his first work in the comics industry was providing a photo-cover to Bill Willingham's *The Elementals* in 1983. That led to shooting another photo-cover for Matt Wagner's *Mage*, followed by a series of interior photos for Eliot R. Brown's *Punisher Armory* for Marvel Comics.

Exchanging his pursuit of film in the early '90s for the pursuit of writing, Bryan collaborated with his good friend Mike Oeming and created the indie comic series *Spandex Tights*, a humorous take on the superhero genre. When Mike's career soon took him away to work at the "Big Two," Bryan continued his series with artists P. Sky Owens, Bob Dix, Paul Bonanno and G.W. Fisher. Later, Bryan collaborated again with Mike Oeming on their dark humored sci-fi series *Ship of Fools*.

Mike's success on *POWERS* enabled him to reunite with Bryan again for the prose novel *Quixote*, for which he provided hundreds of spot illustrations. Their collaborations continued with *86 Voltz: The Dead Girl*, the comic adaptation of the Raymond E. Feist fantasy classic *Magician Apprentice*, and *The Mice Templar*.

Bryan won the 2009 Harvey Award for "Best New Talent" for his work on *The Mice Templar* (which had been nominated in four categories).

Outside of his comic work, Bryan founded the touring theatre troupe *mere*Breath Drama (mereBreathDrama.blogspot.com), alongside John J. McGready and Elliot Silver, where he served as producer, writer, director, and sometimes actor, in the original stage productions *Asylum*, *Perfect Justice*, *Edifice*, *Skit*, *The Eschaton*, and *The Inner Room*. Here is where he met Judy Hummel, his amazing wife—as well as his first and best editor.

Bryan appeared as the face of Eastern State Penitentiary's annual event, *Terror Behind the Walls*, as featured on the Travel Channel's *America's Scariest Halloween Attractions*. He also achieved anonymous notoriety in 1997 as the infamous "Area 51 Caller" on the *Coast-to-Coast A.M.* radio program—a call that can now be heard on the Tool album *Lateralus*: "Faaip de Oiad."

Bryan's three primary interests are books, movies, and music. J.R.R. Tolkien's *The Lord of the Rings*, Richard Adams's *Watership Down*, Stephen King's *The Shining*, Dan Simmons's *Hyperion*, and F. Paul Wilson's *The Keep* were all major influences in his work. *Casblanca* and *The Fisher King* are his favorite films. The film scores of John Williams, Jerry Goldsmith, Hans Zimmer, and Howard Shore typically accompany him as he writes. And he sings along to Kerry Livgren in each of his musical incarnations: Kansas, A.D., solo, and his original band Proto-Kaw.

Bryan is currently developing several new comic series in multiple genres. 🔗

micetemplar@gmail.com
bryanjlglass.blogspot.com

Bryan with his father Harry on Bryan's wedding day,

Mike began his comics career at the age of 14, breaking in as an inker. From inker to penciling/inking to writing, Mike has spread his creative wings in both indie and mainstream comics. Growing up in a small town, Mike found tutelage under Neil Vokes and Adam Hughes, while corresponding with *Nexus* creators Steve Rude and Mike Baron. Dedicated to his craft, Mike was eventually kicked out of high school for skipping class—to stay home and draw—and from his teens into his twenties, he languished in the indie field.

His first big break was as an inker on *Daredevil*, and shortly after as penciler/inker on DC's version of *Judge Dredd*, then *Foot Soldiers* at Dark Horse Comics. During the mid-'90s comics crash, Mike moved back into indie comics, starting on his path of creator-owned comics with *Ship of Fools*, co-created with Bryan J.L. Glass. While drawing *Ship of Fools*, Mike continued with other paying work, such as inking Neil Vokes on *Ninjack* and drawing *Bulletproof Monk*, which later became a John Woo film. Business was slow, so when Mike's first child was born, he got a "real job" working as a security guard—where he drew on the job, of course. This was when Mike experimented with a new, simpler style of drawing, and began developing several projects, including *The Mice Templar*, *Hammer of the Gods*, *Quixote*, and what would become *POWERS* with Brian Michael Bendis, whom Mike had met several years earlier.

POWERS became the dream project Mike and Brian had worked so hard for—a creator-owned project they could live on. *POWERS* has been nominated for a Harvey Award and won an Eisner Award, and Mike himself was nominated for an Eisner for his work on the book. With *POWERS* ongoing, Mike has since tackled several other projects, including *Hammer of the Gods*, *Bastard Samurai*, *Bluntman and Chronic*, *Parliament of Justice*, *Hellboy*, *Catwoman*, *86 Voltz: The Dead Girl*, *The Goon*, *Quixote*, *Blood River*, *Six*, *What If?*, *Magician Apprentice* (with Bryan J.L. Glass) *The Cross Bronx*, *The Darkness*, *The Spirit* and *Red Sonja*. His writing stint on the final run of the original *Thor* as well as on *Thor: Blood Oath* has been widely acclaimed. *Beta Ray Bill* and *Ares* are amongst his other Marvel Comics writing credits.

Currently he is busy with *POWERS*, *The Mice Templar*, *God Complex* and the upcoming *Rapture* trade paperback collection with creator Taki Soma...even as you read this. ◉

michaeloeming.com

VICTOR SANTOS

Born in Valencia in 1977, Victor has written and illustrated a variety of comics in Spain and France, including *Los Reyes Elfos*, *Pulp Heroes* and *Young Ronins*. In recent years he has begun his American adventures with *Demon Cleaner* and *Zombee*, written by Miles Gunter, and *Filthy Rich*, written by Brian Azzarello, one of the first titles of DC Vertigo's new crime line. He lives in Bilbao, Spain.
victorsantoscomics.blogspot.com.

VERONICA GANDINI

A native of Buenos Aires, Argentina, Vero first started coloring when her boyfriend, Leo Freites, a penciller, inker and sculptor, asked her to try coloring one of his drawings. She had been studying architecture for two years by then, but loved this experience of coloring so much that she changed her major to Graphic Design. In 2005, she and Freites self-published Ñorairo, their first comic, in Argentina. She subsequently worked for Ape Entertainment, Atlantis Studios, Silent Devil Productions and BOOM! Studios on several comic series and graphic albums. Following her work on Image's *The Mice Templar*, she is now also working for Marvel Comics. Vero loves her work and looks forward to continuing to meet more amazing people like everyone she has had the pleasure of working with so far, including those on the *Mice Templar* team.
verogandini.blogspot.com.

JAMES H. GLASS

Despite his relationship to the author, there is absolutely no nepotism whatsoever responsible for securing Jim's distinguished position as *The Mice Templar* letterer. He has crafted a distinct voice for each race represented through his discerning use of font styles. Jim shares his love of great stories—fantasy, sci-fi, and sweeping historic narrative—with his brother Bryan, and is proud to be associated with the outstanding creative team responsible for this book.

JUDY GLASS

Judy has always loved good stories, and from an early age aspired to write her own. While that hasn't yet materialized formally, she has nevertheless had a lifelong enjoyment and profound appreciation for the craft of writing and the art of a well-turned phrase, and has tended to gravitate to jobs and other venues that enable her to use these skills. As luck would have it, she met and married Bryan Glass, who has no lack of stories to tell and who proved a quick study on a few grammatical basics to better communicate the brilliant creative universes in his mind. When not exercising her editing skills, Judy enjoys yoga and Pilates, as well as healthy but yummy cooking. Judy is privileged to be part of the team producing *The Mice Templar.*

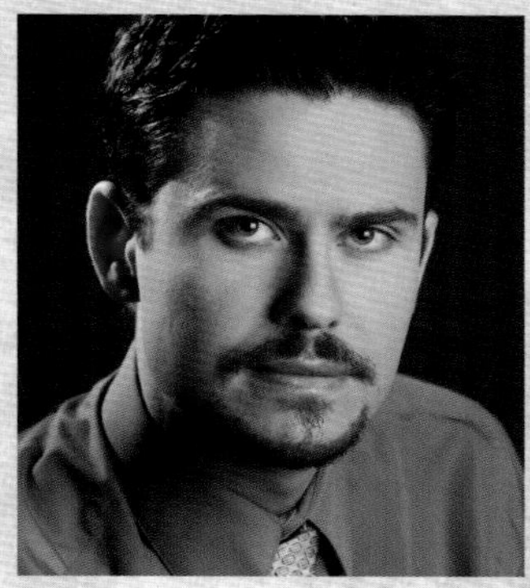

ROD HANNAH

Born in the UK and raised in New Zealand, Rod now writes articles for UK-based animation magazine *Cereal:Geek* from his home in Maryland, U.S.A. He has written his own comic, *Sovena Red*, and is the co-creator of the *Star Wars* parody webcomic Blue Milk Special (bluemilkspecial.com) with his illustrator wife Leanne Hannah. In between working on new writing projects, including children's books, Rod holds down a day job in marketing and design to pay the bills, supporting his hobby and first love of storytelling.
rodhannah.com

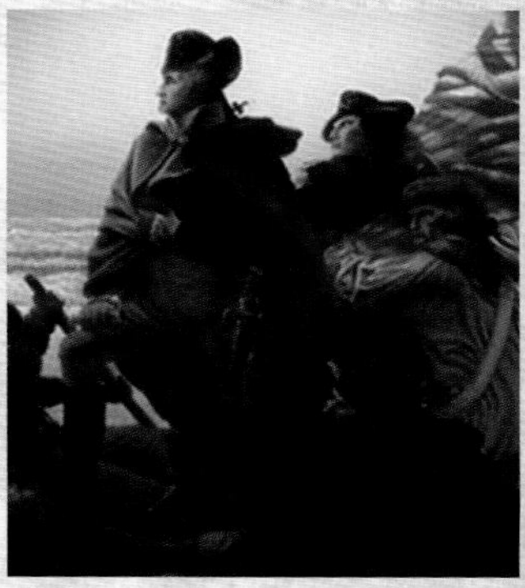

HARRY LEE

Upon receiving word that Hessians were running amuck through Trenton, NJ, Harry Lee put his production responsibilities temporarily aside to lead a rag-tag band of volunteers on a daring Christmas Eve raid to run the miscreants to ground.

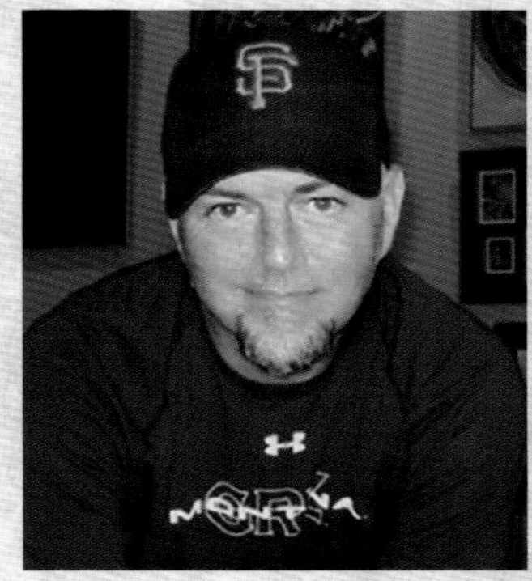

TIM DANIEL

Born in Philly, raised in Northern California, Tim discovered comics at about the time Jean Grey was sacrificing herself on a hidden moon base and saving humanity. In the process, she saved Tim too, opening the door to a lifelong love affair with comics. After earning a BA in English from Southern Oregon University in 1997, Tim fell in love with Erin, now his wife of 11 years, had a daughter (Elle), and has since gotten older but has never grown up. Tim has written for Image Comics' *Popgun Anthology* Vol. 2, the *POWERS Encyclopedia*, and his design work can be seen on covers of books such as *Sky Pirates of Neo Terra, Existence 2.0, Forgetless, God Complex, Shuddertown* and more!
hiddenrobot.com

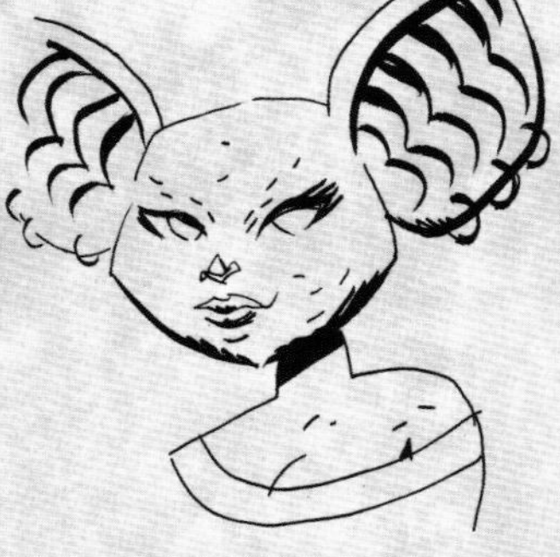

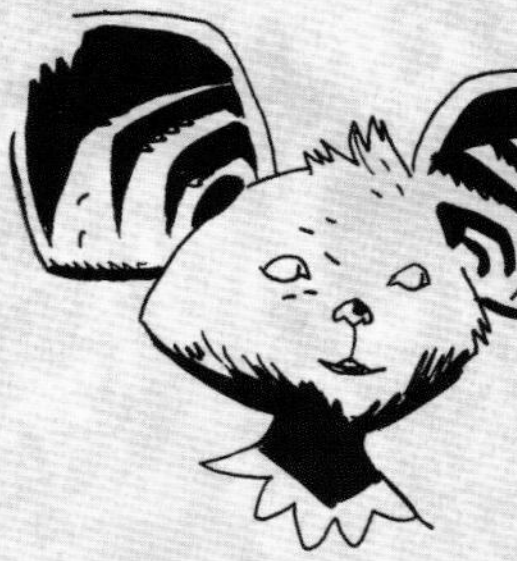

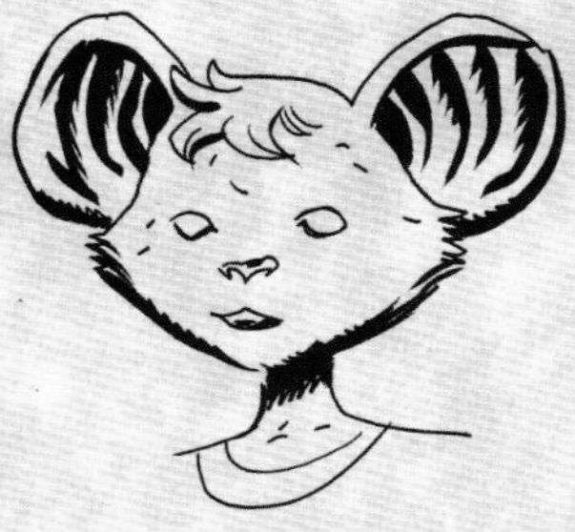

BY BRYAN J.L. GLASS

The Mice Templar
    The Prophecy
Magician Apprentice
    Volumes 1 & 2
Riftwar
    Comic adaptation of the
    Raymond E. Feist novel

86 Volts: The Dead Girl
Quixote: A Novel
Ship of Fools
    Dante's Compass
    Death & Taxes

BY MICHAEL AVON OEMING

Powers
    Who Killed Retro Girl
    Roleplay
    Little Deaths
    Supergroup
    Anarchy
    Sellouts
    Forever
    Legends
    Psychotic
    Cosmic
    Secret Identity
    The 25 Coolest Dead Superheroes
    of All Time
    Definitive Hardcover Collection
    Volumes 1-3
Rapture
The Mice Templar
    The Prophecy
Spider-Man/Red Sonja
Highlander Volume 1
Red Sonja: She-Devil with a Sword
    Volumes 1-5
Omega Flight: Alpha to Omega

Magician Apprentice
Volume 1 Comic Adaptation
The Cross Bronx
Thor: Blood Oath
Ares: God of War
Blood River
Wings of Anansi
Stormbreaker: The Saga of Beta Ray Bill
Doctor Cyborg
86 Voltz: The Dead Girl
Quixote: A Novel
Avengers: Disassembled—Thor
SIX
Parliament of Justice
Bastard Samurai
Hammer of the Gods
    Mortal Enemy
    Hammer Hits China
    Back From the Dead
Bluntman & Chronic
Bulletproof Monk
Ship of Fools
    Dante's Compass
    Death & Taxes
The Foot Soldiers

BY VICTOR SANTOS

SPAIN

Los Reyes Elfos (The Elf Kings)
   El Señor de Alfheim
   (The Lord of Alfheim)
   La Emperatriz del Hielo
   (The Empress of the Ice)
   La Espada de los Inocentes
   (The Sword of the Innocents)
   Hasta los Dioses mueren
   (Until Gods Die)
   La Doncella y los Lobos
   (The Maiden and the Wolves)
   Historias de Faerie
   (Tales from Faerie) Vol. 1-3
   Glirenn, Reina de los Elfos Negros
   (Glirenn, Queen of the Dark Elfs)
Pulp Heroes
   Pulp Heroes
   Bushido
Faeric Gangs
Protector
Lone in Heaven
Aventuras en el Mundo Jung
(Adventures in Jung World)
Al mejor postor y otros relatos

violentos (To the highest gigger and other violent tales)
Black Kaiser
La Sangre de las Valkirias
(The Blood of the Valkyries)
Silhouette

FRANCE

Young Ronins
   Rentrée des classes
   (The beginning of the class)
   Lóffensive Osaki
   (Osaki attacks)

USA

Zombee
Demon Cleaner
Filthy Rich

BY VERONICA GANDINI

Fiction Clemons
Minions of Ka
Toy Story: Mysterious Stranger
Finding Nemo: Reef Rescue
Warhammer 40k:
   Defenders of Ultramar
   Fire and Honor

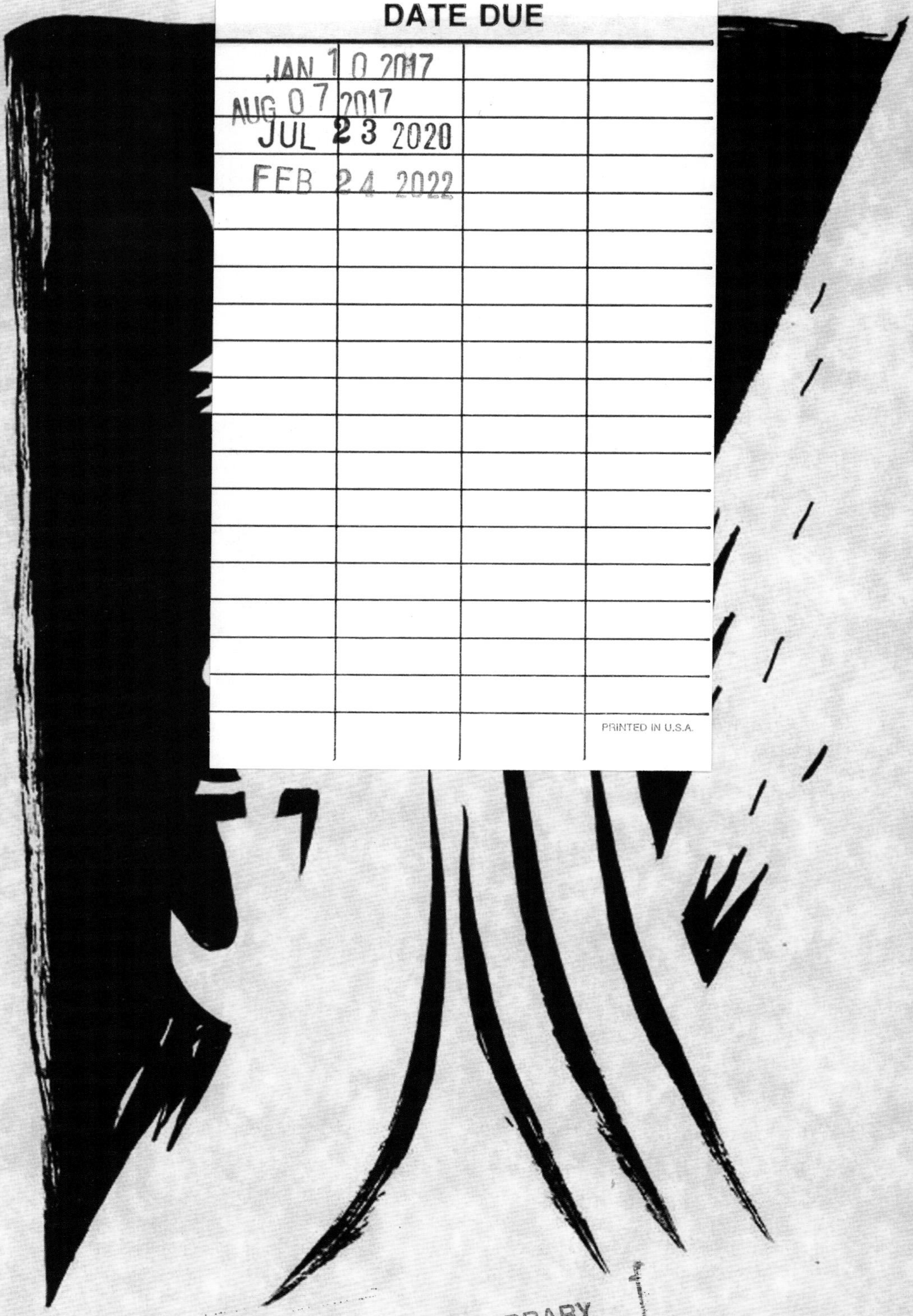